Trends in Romance Linguistics and Philology
Volume 1

Trends in Linguistics
Studies and Monographs 12

Editor

Werner Winter

Mouton Publishers
The Hague · Paris · New York

Trends in Romance Linguistics and Philology

Volume 1: Romance Comparative and Historical Linguistics

edited by

Rebecca Posner
John N. Green

Mouton Publishers
The Hague · Paris · New York

ISBN 90 279 7886 7
Typesetting: Georg Appl, Wemding. – Printing: Karl Gerike, Berlin. – Binding: Lüderitz & Bauer Buchgewerbe GmbH, Berlin.
Printed in Germany

Foreword

It is with great relief that I preface these brief remarks to the first volume of Trends in Romance Linguistics and Philology. For a collection of essays on this theme was first suggested in 1972 by Thomas Sebeok; and since then I have lived with the project which at one time was apparently moribund, but then, happily, was revived through the intervention of Werner Winter, general editor of *Trends in Linguistics*. Contributors to the volume have loyally born with the vicissitudes, including changes in format and style: some of the original contributors, alas, have had to withdraw, in many cases for reasons of health. In these cases other scholars have sometimes nobly stepped into the breach, but otherwise John Green and myself have attempted to plug the gaps by extending our introductory chapters. Some of those contributors who completed their original essays as early as 1974 have chosen to supplement them with additional bibliographical references; others have preferred to leave them in the original state. Sad to say, two contributors, Knud Togeby and Gerard Moignet, did not live to see the publication of their essays: we have made the minimum of editorial amendments, respecting their own wishes as much as we could. Professor Moignet's article appears in French, as he himself was unsure about the viability of translation into English. One other essay – that of Michel Arrivé – has been left in the original French: its form, that of a *bibliographie commentée,* made translation unnecessary. Otherwise articles appear in English, in some cases translated by myself. Where the author is not a native speaker of English, we have suggested stylistic changes, but have refrained from imposing our own tastes on native speakers; hence the reader will discern a certain lack of uniformity in style as well as of format, of content and of length. Authors were encouraged to select for discussion those features of their topics that appeared particularly important: some authors thought that a more comprehensive view was more valuable; others found that they could concentrate on highlights. The original suggestion that essays should be little more than 6000 words long was accepted by some, but others demonstrated that their topics could not be covered in so short a space. The bibliographies, concerned mainly with works published after 1945, and especially after 1960, are not meant to be exhaustive, their coverage varying according to the availability of other bibliographical resources. The volume on historical Romance linguistics has a single amalgamated bibliography, but in the other volumes, where the subject matter has less cohesion, each essay is followed by its own bibliography.

I owe heartfelt thanks to John Green who has been associated with the editorship since almost the beginning and who took charge of volume 2 (synchronic linguistics) and of much of volume 3 at a rather later stage. I alone, however, am to be held responsible for faults in design and content in the whole work. To Professor Winter, and to his successive assistants, Sally Allendorff and Susan Daugherty, we are greatly indebted. The typists who have ably assisted us, both in York and at Oxford, are too numerous to mention, but I know that John Green would like to single out his wife Kaye, for especial thanks, for her editorial and secretarial help as well as more general encouragement. We should also like to thank Susan van der Werff and Asta Wonneberger at Mouton for their patience and assistance.

Rebecca Posner
1 August 1980

Contents

Contributors

Prof. Jerry R. Craddock

Dept. of Spanish and Portuguese, University of California at Berkeley

Prof. Peter F. Dembowski

Dept. of Romance languages and literatures, University of Chicago

Prof. Steven N. Dworkin

University of Ottawa

Prof. Thomas E. Hope

Dept. of French, University of Leeds

Prof. Clifford S. Leonard

University of Michigan

Prof. Dr. Giovanni B. Pellegrini

Università di Padova

Prof. Cicerone Poghirc

Institutul de lingvistică, Bucureşti

Prof. Rebecca Posner

University of Oxford

Prof. Julius Purczinsky

Hunter College, CUNY

†Prof. Knud Togeby

formerly Københavns Universitet

1.1 Comparative linguistics

REBECCA POSNER

Introduction

The very title of this set of volumes within the Trends in Linguistics series presupposes that the field 'Romance linguistics and philology' has some identity of its own. Yet, apart from geographical accident, what can constitute the identity of such a field? This is a question that exercises the minds of Romanists whenever they gather together, but, in spite of such penetrating studies as Malkiel 1961-2, 1964, no truly agreed answer has been found. Nevertheless, Romanists do gather together in greater and greater numbers, triennally for an International Congress held in different Romance-speaking cultural centres, annually in North America and in Britain, and regularly in Scandinavia (cf. *Cong. RSc* 1973). Some centres – like Strasbourg, Bucharest, Berkeley, Heidelberg or Tübingen – can be regarded as permanent gathering places for Romanists. It is true that there are less such centres today than half-a-century ago and that once-unitary Romance Studies have tended to be split prismatically into regionally-oriented or subject-differentiated bands of interest – with, say, local dialect studies at one end of the spectrum and literary theory at the other end. Yet, in spite of links, often institutionalized, with colleagues in other literary or linguistic fields, Romanists seem glad enough to meet together, almost with a sort of family feeling, and to exchange information and views.

In the area of historical and comparative linguistics, the family feeling is perfectly comprehensible – for the metaphor of the language family here seems a reality. The common cultural and linguistic heritage of the Romance languages cannot fail to make itself felt, not only in the distant past but throughout the history of the languages. Whatever the theoretical status of the Romance proto-language, it would be absurd not to recognize its relationship to the Latin we know from texts – but that is not the only way in which the languages are related; inter-influence between the languages, as well as direct influence from Latin itself, has always been evident, and, indeed, it might be suggested that the 'language bounds' placed between the languages are more the artefacts of nationalist pride than natural consequences of language evolution. For the historical linguist, then, the Romance languages may sometimes be viewed as one 'super-language' in which evidence from one variety may well cast light on the development of another (cf. Posner 1976). Historical and comparative linguistics might then be considered the proper domain of Romanists as such: that it is the least disputed domain is marked by our launching these *Trends in Romance linguistics and philology* volumes with the historically-oriented sections.

Yet it is far from true that Romanists are primarily historical linguists and that the field is merely a testing-ground for historical linguistic theory. The last three International Congresses held by the Société de Linguistique Romane (at Bucharest in 1968, Quebec in 1971 and Naples in 1974, cf. *Cong.* 12, 13, 14) boasted substantially more papers on synchronic topics than historical – even then many 'historical' papers, while dealing with material drawn from the past, treated it from a synchronic point of view. Of the North American conferences of Romance linguistics so far (cf. Casagrande – Saciuk, 1972, Campbell et al. 1974, Saltarelli – Wanner 1975, Luján – Hensey 1976, Hagiwara 1977) only that held in 1972 (Saltarelli – Wanner 1975) has been specifically devoted to diachronic linguistics – and even then several of the papers could be described as atemporal in their approach.

Perhaps, however, it is true that Romanists are among those who resist most the drawing of a rigid line between diachronic and synchronic linguistics, such as characterized dominant schools of linguistic thought in the first half of the twentieth century. Romance Linguistics early began to opt out of the orthodoxy of neo-grammarian regularism in historical studies, and of its corollary in synchronic studies, the treatment of language as an object-in-itself, to be studied in isolation. The vitality of Romance dialectology, the awareness among Romanists of the creative, artistic aspects of language and the never-failing attention to social factors tended to insulate Romance Linguistics against some of the prevailing fashions in General Linguistics. Now, in the seventies, the wheel has come full circle and once out-moded Romanist prejudices are in fashion again: the similarity, nay often identity, of synchronic and diachronic processes is generally rec-ognized, and study of geographical or social variation in language is closely linked with the investigation of language change (cf. especially Vàrvaro 1972-3).

Even if Romanists are not necessarily primarily historicists, one might expect them to be first and foremost comparatists. Yet, here again, this is not wholly true: at the international congresses more papers are concerned with individual languages than with the Romance field as a whole. In some cases, comparison is made between two or more languages, but apart from the few investigations of the very early ('Vulgar Latin') period, it is comparatively rare for the whole family to be taken into consideration. As might be expected, given the composi-tion of membership in the Société de Linguistique Romane, more attention is paid to French than to other languages; the second place is usually taken by the language spoken in the country where the Con-gress is held (a laudable point of policy on the part of the organizers). But it is important to realize that the Congresses provide a forum for the discussion of non-national languages and non-standard dialects, the study of which forms an essential part of the Romanist field (here we should mention the bibliography (Blass et al. 1969) which includes in its scope some 'neglected' Romance languages and creoles). Apart from the intrinsic interest of such studies, the information they provide adds new dimensions to our knowledge of the better-known languages and of the links between language on the one hand and culture and society on the other. Of recent years, too, much attention has been paid to non-European Romance, including Romance creoles: the 1971 Quebec Congress was followed by one in Rio de Janeiro in 1977, establishing, we hope, a tradition of alternating Congresses between Europe and America, in recognition of the immense interest of con-tact-language and transplanted-culture studies. Because we believe these areas to be among the growing-points of Romance Linguistics and Philology we include, in our *Trends in Romance linguistics and philology* volumes, articles concerned with them, to the exclusion of individual studies on the 'major' European languages. This is not because we regard these latter as less important (how could we?) but rather because their study forms sub-disciplines of their own, and (here a purely practical reason) because developments within these sub-disciplines are fully covered elsewhere (cf. especially *Current Trends in Linguistics* 4, 9, 10, 11, 12).

For similar reasons, we have not included individual articles on Romance studies in separate Romance-speaking European nations. Understandably enough, each of these nations is particularly concerned with its own language. A comparative approach is often preferred in non-Romance-speaking countries, and we have included articles which attempt to capture the scholarly atmosphere of Romanist work in such countries, and which describe the preoccupations and aspirations of those engaged in such work.

Apart from articles on out-of-the-way languages and faraway places, we have tried to concentrate on work that is not specific to one language and that uses insights from the Romance field as whole to elucidate problems that arise. We seek to define what constitutes a 'problem' for the Romanist (who often refuses to accept that there are 'mysteries', and to play with mere 'riddles'), and to show the methods with which he attempts to solve them. Though, in the main, topic classifications are used, with our subject-matter subdivided according to rather traditional criteria, we have also chosen to approach it from another angle, that of the application of theory within the Romance field.

It is our conviction that Romance studies are in need of a survey of this type at the present time. Although young scholars are still entering the discipline they may be discouraged by the plethora of disparate works in the field, with little to give them a sense of direction. If Romance Linguistics and Philology is to survive as an undivided, identifiable discipline, its practitioners must present a coherent account of its scope and prospects. This we aim to do in these volumes: we do not seek to sketch out the whole history of the discipline, but to concentrate on the more recent periods and on the future, showing new recruits that there still remain exciting things to be done, building on the impressive achievements of the past.

I hope I may be excused in referring here to my supplement (Posner 1970) to Iordan – Orr (1937) in which I outline the theoretical changes in linguistics that occurred between 1937 and 1969 and the effects they had on Romance. At that time, it looked as though Romance Linguistics might decline and be swallowed up in the more dynamic General Linguistics with its newly-won popular appeal, and its promise to provide answers to fundamental human questions. That Romanists were slow to be caught up in the giddy ascent of transformational grammar may turn out to be their salvation; the steady progress of the Romanist tortoise may outpace eventually the frantic dash of the TG hare.

In 1969, the apparent decline of Romance Linguistics could be illustrated by listing those venerable scholars who had died in preceding years. Needless to say, the list today is even longer and sadder; not only have some of the most honoured older scholars left us since 1970 – like Bull, Devoto, Ernout, Gamillscheg, Gardette, Griera, Hasselrot, Migliorini, Rheinfelder, Séguy, Söll, Tilander, Ullmann, Wartburg – but we lost also Togeby in his prime (his last article appears in these volumes) and a young promising scholar, Jonathan Butler (who was to have contributed to these volumes), both alas in motor accidents. However, leaving the legacy not only of their written works, but also of the students they have inspired, such scholars cannot be said to be dead for Romance Linguistics which they will continue to vitalise for generations to come.

The number of presentation volumes to distinguished scholars over the last few years is revelatory of both the activity of younger Romanists and of the esteem in which their elders are held: recent Festschriften and memorial volumes worthy of note include: Buyssens 1970, Parlangèli 1970, Straka 1970, Harmer 1970; Boutière 1971, Meier 1971, S. Pellegrini 1971, Wandruszka 1971, Wartburg 1971; Budagov 1972, Delattre 1972, Giese 1972, Haudricourt 1972b, Reid 1972, Tovar 1972; Flasche 1973, Høybe 1973, Imbs 1973, Iordan 1973, Kahane 1973, Mohrmann 1973, Pei 1973; Bolelli 1974, Brummer 1974, Gardette 1974, Godel 1974, Lapesa 1974; Benveniste 1975, Butler 1975, Devoto 1975, Diez 1975, Togeby 1975; Bonfante 1976, Frappier 1976; Hall 1977.

Bibliographies of Romance Linguistics are also abundant; apart from those included in the presentation volumes, we can mention the following in recent years: Bach – Price 1977, Grossmann – Mazzoni 1974, Hall 1973, Mourin – Pohl 1971, Hamlin 1970-76, Ineichen 1972, 1975, forthcoming, Kröll 1969, Littlefield 1974; (individual bibliographies) Alarcos Llorach 1975, Badía Margarit 1971, Baldinger 1969, 1975, Deanović 1971, Iordan 1974, Richter 1973, Tilander 1973, Viscardi 1970, Wagner 1970, Wartburg 1974. The *Year's Work in Modern Language Studies* continues to include annual bibliographic survey articles on Romance Linguistics, as well as on the individual languages (Green 1971-1979) and an annual cyclostyled 'Comparative Romance Linguistics Newletter', circulated to subscribers and originating in the USA, provides exhaustive up-to-date bibliographies including references to unpublished dissertations. The *Revue de Linguistique Romane* and the *Zeitschrift für romanische Philologie* always include an extensive and wide-ranging review section, which cover periodicals as well as books.

Introductory and survey works in comparative Romance also continue to appear in abundance: since 1970 noteworthy additions include translations of Iordan 1962, Iordan – Manoliu 1965, Lausberg 1956-62, Tagliavini 1949, and of Wartburg 1951; a revised edition of Elcock 1960; and new works: Bec 1970-71, Canfield – Cary Davis 1975, Camproux 1974, Cremona 1973, Deutschmann 1971, Gadzaru 1970, Hall 1974, 1976, Pei 1976, Renzi 1977. We might also note Malkiel's survey of the field on the occasion of *Romance Philology's* silver jubilee and his review of work by European scholars (Malkiel 1972a and d), and my own article in the most recent edition of the Encyclopedia Britannica (1974). Collections of mainly previously published articles are to be found in D. Alonso 1972-3, Anderson – Creore 1972, Boléo 1974-5, Elwert 1973, Gadzaru 1969, Hallig 1970, Hatzfeld 1971, 1975a and b, Haudricourt 1972a, Jud 1973, Malkiel 1970a, Malmberg 1971, 1973, Sandmann 1973, Schürr 1971, Terracini 1976, Ullmann 1972a, Viscardi 1970; classic articles are reprinted in Kontzi 1978a, b. The most important recently-published collection of texts is Iordan 1962-74; Bec (1970-1) also takes texts as his starting point for wider comment.

The place of philological studies within our field is difficult to define and I leave more detailed discussion to Karl Uitti in Volume 3 of this sub-series (cf. also Contini 1970). Investigations into medieval texts and into language history are, of course, indissolubly intertwined; the literary styles of the different Romance languages may have much in common, stemming from similar linguistic structures and common cultural heritage. The similarities may be more evident in folk-literature (cf. Karlinger's article in a later volume and Karlinger 1974) especially in more recent times when it may be more profitable to encompass all

European literatures in one's comparison rather than limit oneself to one language family. Within the bounds of each language, philological and linguistic studies are frequently closely linked, but modern linguistics and literary criticism both overspill the confines of the more traditional philological domain. Concerned primarily as we are with language, we have not trespassed far into literary criticism, a vast field which overlaps with ours insofar as it treats of linguistic stylistics, semiology, regional cultures and so on, but which is also concerned with universal human values and aesthetics. We have therefore limited the strictly philological part of our collection to topics in which language study plays a major role. Nevertheless we should emphasise that a Romance Linguistics without the philological element would be little more than a subsection of Linguistics, with scant methodological or topical differentiation from other subsections of Linguistics. Romanists' special contribution to the world of knowledge, is, I repeat, an awareness of the interaction of language with culture and society, paying attention to peculiarities of the languages and not only to universals of language.

Among the topics not separately discussed in the articles that follow, the interface between 'Latin' and 'Romance' is one which poses many problems for both philologists and linguists, not only because Latinists and Romanists are often separated institutionally – though in Italy, where the term 'neo-Latin' is commonly used, the division is less sharp. It is, however, fair to say that self-styled Romanists (those, for instance, who attend international congresses) comparatively rarely concentrate on Latin, though most would accept that the Romance languages are, in some sense, continuators of a form of Latin and that a philological approach is fruitful. Clifford S. Leonard, on 'Comparative grammar' in this volume, argues strongly that this is not so; the reconstructed proto-language is *not* Latin, from which it differs in important ways, though undoubtedly there must have been considerable influence from Latin on Romance, at every period. He develops this suggestion in a more lengthy work (1978) in which he follows another reconstructionist of note, Robert Hall Jr., who maintains that Proto-Romance is a 'sister' of Classical Latin, which split 'seriously' into popular and literary varieties from about 100 B.C. For Hall, as for Pulgram (1964), a Proto-language is a 'diasystem' abstracted from the shared features of spoken dialects. In this view the language of Classical texts provides little material of direct relevance to Romance, though evidence can be gleaned from texts which contain non-standard features. Ferguson (1976) shares this point of view; W. Mańczak (1974, 1977), on the other hand, maintains that Proto-Romance can be derived from Classical Latin (of which it is logically, if not chronologically, an outcome) and that there is no need to postulate a 'Vulgar Latin' intermediate stage.

The 'Vulgar Latin' label for the postulated common ancestor of the Romance languages is so consecrated by usage, since Schuchardt 1866, that it is hard to throw off, even though most Romanists protest that it is ambiguous and misleading. Latinists have no scruples in using it to designate a popular spoken variety of Latin, sometimes distinct from 'Late Latin' or 'Christian Latin' (cf. Palmer 1954 and, for a survey of European work on Latin, Devoto 1972). That there should be direct continuity between Romance and spoken Latin is rarely doubted by them – for instance Allen (1965) uses evidence from modern Romance to extrapolate to the pronunciation of Classical times (cf. also Serbat 1975). Among Romanists, specialist writers on 'Vulgar Latin' usually are more cautious. Some postulate an extreme form of diglossia in the Roman Empire with the living speech of the populace growing further and further away from the standard written language; others assume normal register and regional variation without loss of intercomprehension, with the written language lagging behind. For all, the evidence of texts, either of popular character or of late date, of inscriptions and of grammarians' comments are to be matched against reconstructions of comparative Romance grammar, in the belief that shared features of the Romance languages must actually have been in common use by speakers during the Imperial period. Among noteworthy recent works that take this point of view, we should especially mention Herman 1970, 1976, and Väänänen 1963/1967.

Other basic works on Vulgar Latin include: – Avalle 1965, 1968, Battisti 1949, Campanile 1967, Coseriu 1954, Grandgent 1962, Haadsma – Nuchelmans 1963, Löfstedt 1959, Maurer 1959, 1962, Rohlfs 1951, Silva Neto 1957, Sofer 1963, Vossler 1954. Studies of late texts and inscriptions include: – Adams 1977, Baehrens 1922, Carlton 1973, Gaeng 1968, Klein – Labhardt 1968, Löfstedt 1911, Mihăescu 1960, Pei 1932, Politzer 1949, Stati 1961, Stefenelli 1962, Taylor 1932, Väänänen 1966. On Late Latin prosodies Kiss 1972 and Pulgram 1975 are important new contributions. Önnersfors 1975 is a collection of articles originally published between 1959 and 1965, with a bibliography. Other recent articles include: – Campanile 1971, Coseriu 1972, Engels 1970, Graur 1970, Itkonen 1969, Rosetti 1970, Safarewicz 1969, Sofer 1970, Tovar 1964, Väänänen 1963b, 1969.

If the Romance languages are not modern versions of the Latin we know from our schooldays, the question 'When did Latin die?' is not very meaningful: possibly the final death-blow came in 1965, when the Roman Catholic Mass abandoned Latin (*pace* Monseigneur Lefèvre), but the language has never ceased to be written, and even spoken by, admittedly diminishing, sections of European society. Behind the stable façade of Latin, however, vernacular Romance has taken over. The appearance of indisputably Romance texts from the ninth century onwards marks the first important stage, with the Renaissance and Reformation almost completing the process.

Yet we are still left asking 'When did Romance split up into several languages?' – merely a variant of the former question. For both are concerned with the formation of 'language bounds' (Dyen 1975) between hitherto mutually intelligible dialect variants. At what stage the various Romance dialects became mutually incomprehensible is not known – indeed it is not wholly clear that they are so. Armed with a set of rules, mainly phonological, a competent speaker of one language can usually, with practice, make some sense of another. With the written language the task is, of course, easier, as etymological spelling is common. Curiously enough, French, which for cultural reasons serves as a lingua franca among Romanists, is possibly the least Romance of the languages, in that it is not easily intelligible to naïve speakers of other Romance tongues.

Mutual intelligibility as such is however rarely considered diagnostic by Romanists: indeed participants in a 1971 colloquium (Straka 1973) specifically distinguish between objective linguistic criteria and the socially determined criterion of mutual intelligibility in the early history of Romance. Once clearly localised and differentiated texts begin to appear, we can be sure that speakers are aware of their 'language' as distinct from that of their neighbours even though intercommunication may have remained possible. By the ninth century some Northern French speakers had certainly become so aware, though some other parts of the Romance area took longer. Whether, however, the appearance of vernacular texts long postdates the actual differentiation of the languages is debatable.

Those who seek the origin of Romance in the speech of the uneducated will quite logically argue that quite extensive regional variation must have existed within the vast area covered by the Roman Empire, and that, given the socio-cultural set-up, we should not be surprised that there is little evidence of this in writing. Basing their arguments mainly on phonological (Wartburg 1950, Straka 1953, 1956) or lexical (Rohlfs 1954, B. Muller 1971 a, b, 1974, Schmitt 1974) evidence from later periods, they reconstruct early dialect differentiation, which can be connected with language contact (substratum cf. Pellegrini's article in this volume) or with social strata differences. Further differentiation is believed to have been caused by the adoption by barbarian tribes of Romance (superstratum). Often a distressing picture of disintegration, chaos and disaster is drawn, consequent on the dissolution of the Western Roman Empire (474 A. D.) – social conditions which favoured extremely rapid linguistic change.

On the other hand, it is pointed out (expecially by H.-F. Muller 1929, 1945) that the political collapse did not necessarily bring about social catastrophe, and that there is evidence that life went on much as usual (though less comfortable and secure), with the language, supported by religion, remaining fairly unified throughout the West, at least. Differentiation between the languages may then be more a positive consequence of the Carolingian renaissance or of the growth of feudalism than a negative result of disintegrating society.

Many of the attempts at classification of Romance languages have had as their avowed aim the solution of the problem of the chronology of differentiation of the languages. In the classic 'family-tree' model, a 'shared innovation' (usually phonological) will group together languages under a 'proto'-node, as a sub-family. Among Romanists grouping has rarely been attempted without reference to geographical distribution, and most often a 'standard' form has been regarded as the archetype of a language group (even though the choice of standard is known to be determined largely by historical accident). The phenomena of convergence, with neighbouring languages adopting each other's speech habits, and of 'rayonnement', with features spreading out from prestigious speech communities, are familiar to Romanists, and seen to preclude neat classification of the languages. Some linguists attempt to overcome the difficulty by using the earliest attested forms of the languages for classification purposes – perhaps feeling that the differences are shown there in a more pristine state (Hall 1976 confesses that for him the procedure is a *pis aller* adopted because of the practical difficulty of using dialectal material). But it can be legitimately questioned whether the early Romance texts are truly representative of speech and whether they may not reflect conscious attempts at conventional literary usage smoothing out the 'irregularities' of everyday speech, inspired by the model of written Latin.

One central question posed by Romanists has always been 'How many Romance languages are there?' One answer might be – As many as there are Romance speakers, or, at any rate, Romance speaking communities. Yet this answer does not satisfy Romanists who, like the man in the street, usually distinguish between 'language' and 'dialects'. When the former is used as the equivalent of 'national language', the candidates for the title are, of course, French, Italian, Spanish, Portuguese and Rumanian (the Romance character of 'Wallachian' had been recognized at least since 1580 (Coseriu 1976, also 1975 a, b) and, indeed, Rumanian was claimed as the 'purest' neo-Latin tongue by 18th century nationalists – Close 1974).

The earliest Romance linguists also granted to Provençal language status, in view of its rich medieval literary heritage: today the name Occitan (cf. Bec's article in Volume 3) is favoured to cover the fairly homogeneous group of languages (dialects?) spoken in the South of France, bilingually with Standard French, which has undoubtedly exercised great influence on Occitan usage (cf. Muljačić 1971 a, for the classification of Occitan). Catalan, on similar cultural grounds, is also regarded as a 'language', (cf. Gulsoy's article in Volume 3), though whether it fits in better with the other peninsular languages, or with Southern French was long a matter of dispute (cf. recently Kuen 1973, Colón 1976).

The other two 'languages' recognized by most Romance linguists have quite different status. 'Ladino' was the name given by Ascoli (1873) to a reconstruction based on the so-called 'Rhaetian' languages of Switzerland (e. g. 'Churwälsch' which had been singled out since 1671) and of North Italy, which are neither mutually intelligible nor geographically contiguous. Francescato, in a later volume, discusses their position within the Romance world, proposing the designation

'Rhaeto-Friulian' and casting doubt on the hypothesis of one-time unity. These languages can scarcely be called vehicles of culture (though there are texts dating as far back as the 16th century, and dialect literature has flourished in Friulian for the last hundred years or so), nor national languages (though Switzerland recognises the use of Romantsch in cantonal affairs).

'Sardinian' (cf. Contini and Tuttle in Volume 3) is the other modern 'language' recognized by Romanists, on linguistic and historical grounds. Although the languages of the island are heterogeneous (so much so that speakers find inter-communication in Italian much easier than in dialect) it is usually assumed that true Sardinian has persisted in the East-Central region of Barbagia where there has been less foreign influence than elsewhere and where the language is closer to that of the earliest texts. However, some doubt has been expressed (Sanna 1957) about whether in fact this region was ever thoroughly Romanized during the classical era; the language may be a result of 'secondary Romanization' accompanying the advent of Christianity. Besides the 'conservative' Logudorian dialects, languages in Sardinia are classified as Campidanian, thought to be profoundly influenced by mainland Italian dialects, and as Gallurian and Sassarese, more closely related to Corsican dialects (which Rohlfs 1941 views as originally Sardinian but penetrated by Tuscan).

If we grant 'language' status to Sardinian and Rhaeto-Friulian on the grounds of their linguistic distinctiveness – then we can count nine separate Romance languages. Some Romanists also discern a 'Franco-Provençal' language behind the fast disappearing dialects spoken in East France and neighbouring Italy and Switzerland (cf. Ascoli 1878 and, more recently, Jochnowitz 1973 and Fisher 1976; for a bibliography cf. Sala – Reinheimer 1967-8 and Šabršula 1974). Although heterogeneous and penetrated by French influence, the dialects share features that set them off from French and Occitan, suggesting that they may once have formed a more homogeneous group.

To these ten is usually added the now-extinct Dalmatian Romance, attested in texts supplemented by more direct evidence collected from the last surviving speaker of Vegliote (cf. Bartoli 1906), suggesting that linguistically Dalmatian stood apart from other Romance tongues, though doubtless greatly influenced by Venetian (cf. Muljačić 1969 for a bibliography). That other Romance languages were once spoken is sometimes deduced from the long-standing existence of Latin words in Albanian, Berber and Welsh, suggesting that these languages were in contact for some time with a spoken form of Latin.

If Albanian, for instance, can be called 'semi-Romance' how much more so can the Romance creoles, spoken in America, and in Indian Ocean and Pacific Ocean islands and seaports. The genesis of these 'contact-languages' and their classification within Romance is well worth study, for the light that may be shed on the early development of European Romance languages, as well as for their intrinsic interest. In Volume 2 of this series John Green examines creoles in the framework of a discussion of dialectology, while in Volume 3 Auguste Viatte discusses French creoles in the context of non-European French.

But even if we can, on some basis or other, enumerate the Romance 'languages', drawing a dividing line between 'fully' and 'partly' Romance tongues, and estimating the distance between each language, we are not necessarily any nearer to a classification of Romance 'dialects'.

Classification has been one of the principal preoccupations of Romance Linguistics throughout its history: Yakov Malkiel's (1978) wide-ranging historical survey learnedly and perceptively surveys the numerous different approaches and solutions to the question. Most classificatory essays are, I repeat, frankly geared towards clarifying historical evolution and seek to unravel the tangle of more recent events to arrive at an intuitively selected set of features that will demarcate one group of dialects from another, at some given point in history. No such clear demarcation emerges from the quantitative studies that utilise synchronic or diachronic data: at best the languages can be ranked but not grouped; at worst, lines drawn by each criterion criss-cross inextricably. Such classificatory exercises include: Muljačić 1967, who uses forty parameters from different linguistic levels chosen as diagnostic; Contreras 1963 and Iliescu 1969, who use morphosyntactical criteria; Grimes – Agard 1959 and Pei 1949, who try to quantify phonological distances; lexicostatistic studies such as Mańczak 1959, Makarov 1971, Rea 1958, 1973 and Séguy 1971. At the thirteenth Congress of Romance Linguistics (Quebec 1971) a section was devoted to typological questions: noteworthy published papers include Katagochtina 1976 and Saltarelli 1976.

In nearly all cases the data used are taken from standard literary languages – though for Sardinian and Rhaeto-Friulian, for example, 'representative dialects' are chosen. The comparison of data from highly focussed language stereotypes, like the French used by educated monolinguals, with those from diffused and uncertain non-standard uses, like a mountain village dialect spoken only by a handful of bilingual septuagenarians, must surely be unsound. That the standard Romance languages are in some sense distinct from each other needs no demonstration – greater or less similarities can be linked with contacts and influences in historical times, or perhaps with still-mysterious Sapirian 'drift', as well as with common ancestry. But that there has been 'collusion', in Bloomfield's term, even between the standard languages since the Imperial era is also in little doubt (on vocabulary – cf. T. E. Hope's essay in this volume; on other types of convergence cf. Posner forthcoming).

How far spoken usage, except insofar as it is polarized towards a standard, has ever been so clearly differentiated, is not certain. It is a commonplace to claim that there are no dialect boundaries within European Romance (or at least within 'Romania continua' – Alonso 1943a), that there is catenate mutual intelligibility across the geographical area covered by the languages and that thus, in some sense, there is only one Romance language (Dyen 1975). This was a position strongly maintained especially by the French dialectologists at the beginning of this century (e. g. Gaston Paris – cf. Millardet 1923) although opposed by some Italian experts (e. g. Ascoli – cf. Maccarone 1929).

The difference in opinion may stem from the dialect scene in the two countries. In France, the prestige of the standard is such as to have virtually eliminated dialect in most of the North, so that where it survives at all, it is as an unprestigious, unfocussed form of speech that is at the mercy of penetration by French. In the South, dialects have survived, mainly because of resistance to French and by dint of focussing dialect usage towards a semi-mythical Occitan, which symbolizes local pride and community identity (cf. Bec in Volume 3). Recent work among French dialectologists (cf. Straka 1973) has tended to confirm the existence of dialect boundaries, with bands of interference between them (cf. Bec 1968). Séguy (in Straka 1973) speaks of 'functional dialects' which both differentiate themselves from their neighbours and allow comprehension with them. In his dialect atlas (cf. Séguy 1973) he shows the way in which dialects merge into each other within the Gascon area. But though Gascon shades into Languedocian without seriously hindering mutual comprehension it meets with a barrier when it comes up against Catalan or Saintongeais – just as against Basque. This is because the languages are focussed towards a different stereotype, so no attempt is made by speakers to communicate *in their own dialects* (in fact, very few speakers today could effectively use Saintongeais in any case – cf. Doussinet 1971). A similar communication barrier is found between Picard and Walloon within Belgium (cf. Deparis in Straka 1973): here French, not dialect, is used for intercommunication. Historical factors account for a focussing of the Picard dialect towards French, whereas Walloon has maintained more of a sense of identity.

In Italy, where 'dialects' are still widely used, they are consciously differentiated from the standard as stereotypes, though in actual usage they are strongly influenced by the standard, so it is mainly by virtue of its prestige that living dialect usage differs from the popular language of 'Italia mediana' – Tuscany, Umbria and Latium – which is regarded as 'imperfect' Italian, rather than as dialect. Nevertheless dialect speakers in different parts of Italy claim not to understand each other and prefer to use the standard for intercommunication: Pellegrini (1970) has shown, using Muljačić's parameters, that a stereotyped Southern Italian dialect differs more from a Northern one than so-called Romance 'languages' differ between themselves. Grouping usually reflects earlier political divisions with rural dialects focussing towards urban koinai (Pellegrini 1960); *'italianità'* of the koinai is socio-cultural, in that they turn towards the standard as their 'guide language' (Parlangèli 1969). How far the geographical unit stretching from the Alps out into the Mediterranean is a linguistic unit, any more than it is an economic or cultural unit, is doubtful. Indeed the best-known account of the split up of Romance (Wartburg 1950) draws the most fundamental demarcation line (between East and West Romania) right across Italy, from Spezia to Rimini. Possibly in modern times the unifying factor is indeed the literary language, which Ascoli regarded as 'truly Italian' and which nearly all adult Italians now know.

The comparative linguistic unity of the Iberian Peninsula is undoubtedly connected with its history, with the three major languages, Portuguese, Castilian and Catalan, advancing southwards with the Reconquista. Rumania on the other hand is something of a puzzle: the relative lack of dialectal diversity (Dumistrăcel 1971) north of the Danube may be due to the feeling of solidarity among the speakers in face of Magyar and Turkish persecution. The language was slow to emerge as a literary vehicle, but focussed towards other Romance languages, especially French and Italian (Niculescu 1971, Poalelungi 1973, Close 1974), favouring a fairly homogeneous set of linguistic habits.

Sardinia never achieved any such degree of homogeneity, although some attempts have been made since the 16th century to create a *sardo illustre;* there are few features of modern dialects that would allow dialects of the island to be grouped together linguistically, though there is some evidence that at one time they may have been less heterogeneous. Even this is not true of the Rhaeto-Friulian dialects, which may by some criteria be better grouped with neighbouring Italian dialects than with each other (cf. Kramer 1976). That they have remained distinct from the Italian dialects may be due to historical accident, in that at some time during the course of their history the areas in which they are spoken have been under the domination of German speakers. Friulian, which has developed a literary stereotype more than the others, has moved closer to the Venetan dialects with which it has been in close contact during much of its history.

Classification may therefore be more a socio-cultural question than a linguistic one, and articles in this series that concern the 'minor' and the non-European Romance languages discuss their cultural status, as well as their linguistic features. Moreover one section is devoted particularly to Romance questions of a sociolinguistic character with Lavandera discussing dialects and non-standard languages, and Rogers the question of language nationalism (cf. also Price 1976 for a bibliographical survey of works on standardization).

In other volumes some articles are more technically linguistic whereas others pay more attention to socio-cultural factors, as their subject-matter demands. Among the historically oriented articles of the first volume we might place Giovanni Pellegrini's on substratum, and those concerned with lexical and semantic studies in the second category.

Phonology and morphology are topics that fall more within technical linguistics and so may appear less open to 'philological' or socio-cultural approaches, though, needless to say, textual and sociological evidence is always used in dating changes. In Romance historical phonology, moreover, as Julius Purczinsky points out, scholars are as concerned to discover the causes of change as to describe the changes – most often external factors (language contact, socio-cultural conditions) are adduced as determiners of change. In Knud Togeby's contribution to Romance historical morphology, on the other hand, causation is viewed in a traditional light: sound-change and analogy are the factors at work. In keeping with his expressed views of the futility of seeking direct internal 'structural' or external (social or psychological) causes for linguistic change, he concentrates more on description of events. At an era in which the status of morphology within linguistic description is in dispute (with derivational morphology assigned to the lexicon, and inflectional morphology to the transformational or phonological components in TG grammar) it is as well to remember that the Romance languages can satisfactorily be described in Word-and-Paradigm terms, and that a good deal of Romanist work has been devoted to historical morphology (precisely because the differences, and similarities, between Latin and Romance are so obvious at this level). Togeby's present article is a mini-version of a historico-comparative Romance morphology, a topic to which he has made major contributions in the past. His modesty was such that he was unwilling to refer to his own work: I was able to persuade him that it was desirable he should do so, but what remains unacknowledged is the fact that this, his last lengthy article, represents his own synthesis, rather than simply a survey of work in the field. His prediction, at the end of his article, that generative grammar will one day have a fruitful impact on Romance historical morphology, may perhaps be in process of realization (for a bibliography with a few items of Romance topics cf. Gazdar et al. 1978). For instance the topic treated in Togeby 1972 was taken up again by generativist James Harris (in Saltarelli – Wanner 1975) using historical documentation presented by Malkiel (1966); Penny 1972, Montgomery 1976 and Posner 1977 have since discussed the same problem – that of stem-vowel alternation within the Spanish verb paradigm which Harris sees as determined by an abstract conjugation marker. Harris (in Campbell et al. 1974), considering data from non-standard New Mexican Spanish, seems to be coming round to more traditional ideas, in that he recognizes a tendency towards levelling of the surface paradigm ('analogy') even though it leads to complication of phonological rules. Saltarelli further develops the theme in Milán et al. 1975. The rules governing stress-placement in the Romance verb are also discussed in terms of generative grammar, by Saltarelli (in Casagrande – Saciuk 1972), by J. W. Harris (in Milán et al. 1975), by Posner (1976), and by Pullum (1976).

Other recent generativist works concerned with problems of historical morphology include the papers presented by S. A. Schane ("Some diachronic deletion processes and their synchronic consequences in French") and R. Skousen ("The verbal system of French") at the 1972 American Romanists Conference (Saltarelli – Wanner 1975): Skousen (1975) develops the case in favour of old-fashioned analogy further. Also noteworthy are Vincent 1974, and Wanner 1975, but as yet, no great breakthrough in historical morphology has been made by generativists (though in post-*Aspects* synchronic grammar, inflectional morphology is being reinstated – Kiefer 1973 is one example of interest to generativists). So far, indeed, it seems that generativists are discovering again old truths, of the sort Togeby expounds so well. On derivational morphology Togeby says little: more extensive discussion is to be found under the head of lexicology.

As Peter Dembowski points out in his article, Romanists rarely consistently distinguish syntax from morphology: indeed at the International Congresses the designation 'morpho-syntax' is habitual. Some of the problems traditionally treated as syntactic are moreover nowadays considered as semantic – like conditions for use of verbal tense (cf. most recently Wunderli 1976). So, narrowly-defined syntactic history is not well represented in Romance studies. Indeed it may even be questioned whether the study of syntax is possible in the absence of native speakers. This doubt was expressed at the 1972 American Romanist Conference by Robin Lakoff, the only representative of generativist historical syntax discussed by Dembowski. It is to be noted that his article, like that of Purczinsky, was in completed form by 1974; but since that date no spectacular developments have occurred in the field of historical syntax. One should mention the generativist papers in Saltarelli – Wanner 1975, by J. Casagrande ("Diachronic fossilization in French syntax: a propos of *voici* and *voilà*"), by D. Gulstad ("Syntactico-semantic reconstruction in Romance") and by C. Otero ("The development of the clitics in Hispano-Romance"); in Campbell et al. 1974 by D. Wanner ("The evolution of Romance clitic order"); and in Luján – Hensey 1976 by M. Saltarelli ("Theoretical implications in the development of the accusativus cum infinitivo constructions") as well as M. B. Harris 1971, 1972, 1974, 1976, 1978 and Green 1972 b. A welcome newcomer to comparative Romance syntax is A. Radford, a generativist who leans towards relational grammar (cf. Radford 1977, 1978).

It remains true, however, that generativist historical syntax is almost non-existent, and that, for Romanists, syntactic research is philological as well as linguistic in its orientation.

In historical phonology, generativists have more to offer and since Purczinsky wrote his article, the American Romanist Conferences and the 1974 International Congress in Naples have thrown up numerous new contributions. Otero 1971 is a longer work that deserves mention in this context. One "live" issue in generative phonology – the status of rule ordering – is considered in relation to pan-Romance history in Posner 1974.

The section concerned with historical lexical studies in Romance – etymology, borrowing, semantics and lexicology – covers the area in which Romanists have perhaps made the greatest contribution, for it is here that the relationship between language and society is most evident. It needs very little introduction from me; indeed as a contributor myself, I found it hard to see what was left for me to say that would not overlap with the contributions of my distinguished collaborators. I should mention that it was necessary for me to consider lexicological studies that are not, properly speaking, historical in orientation, as no space is allotted specifically to such studies in the synchronic part of our enterprise. Besides, in this domain, perhaps even more than in others, it is hard to draw the line between synchrony and diachrony – a line, I repeat, that Romanists are loath to draw.

There is no need either for me to introduce in detail the articles which will appear in subsequent volumes of this series, as each of these will be preceded by its own introduction – on synchronic linguistic studies by John Green, on philological and stylistic studies by Karl Uitti and on the trends within Romanist studies in different parts of the world, by myself. It remains only for me to say that, in the hope that this new work will take a place in the history of Romance studies alongside Gröber's *Grundriss*, now almost a century old, it is, I think, fitting to dedicate it to the memory of Knud Togeby (1918-1974).

CLIFFORD S. LEONARD, JR.

Comparative grammar

Again and again it has been urged (Bloomfield 1933: 300, Hall 1950: 311, Hall 1964a: 309) that the Romance family of languages offers a unique opportunity to comparative linguists to prove and perfect their method, on the grounds that here, unlike most other language families, there is copious documentation of the parent language, Latin. Therefore, it is ironic that the majority of comparativists work exclusively outside Romance and appear to be quite ignorant of, and indifferent to, the debates and crises of our diachronic scene. The fault in this lies not with them but with us, for the comparative method does not dominate in Romance diachronic studies as it does in Germanic, Slavic, or Semitic. Hence, the situations are not commensurable. Far from it, it is safe to say that little of the Romance linguistics of the past thirty years that purports to be comparative in scope is actually comparative in method. It is instead historical. As new tools and insights have become available to the diachronic investigator – and most have originated outside Romance linguistics – they have been applied within our discipline to the historical frame of reference, for which they were not intended. The effects have been a stubborn reinforcement of the claim of Latin as the parent language and a proliferation of detailed circular explanations of Romance linguistic developments. The same years have seen other proto-languages enormously advanced: consider the revisions that laryngeal theory and the analogical explanation of tense development have made in Indo-European since Meillet's day. Small wonder that the outsiders are not listening!

The comparative linguist begins a priori from the principle that, other factors permitting, sound change is regular; and regularism furnishes the theoretical basis for linguistic reconstruction. The first task is to isolate the cognate linguistic structures in a set of related languages by applying the criterion of regularly recurrent correspondences of sounds occupying the same relative position in words of similar meaning. The attempt to state these correspondences transformationally then projects a uniform proto-language, subject, within rather narrow limits, to intuitive structural interpretation. A proto-language is thus a synchronic description that embraces the qualifying parts of two or more languages at once and is by that very fact diachronic in implication. Inasmuch as it is inductive and antichronological, comparative reconstruction is not an historical discipline. A proto-language need not be equatable with, or assignable as a dialect to, any historically attested language. The Romance comparativist owes no special allegiance to Latin.

For instance, in reconstructing the Proto-Romance medial cluster in Fr. *nuit,* It. *notte,* Rum. *noapte* 'night' or Fr. *cuit,* It. *cotto,* Rum. *copt* 'cooked', there is no inexorable need to posit /kt/ because of Lat. *ct* in *noctem, coctum.* The indicated reconstruction is /kʷt/. When we examine Fr. *quatre,* It. *quattro,* Rum. *patru* 'four' or Sp. *agua,* It. *acqua,* Rum. *apă* 'water', we see, first, that It. *qu* is the *lectio difficilior* linking the French or Spanish and the Rumanian developments and, second, that Proto-Romance obviously retained the IE *kʷ* of **kʷₑtwor-*'four' (Buck 1933: 230) and that it became /p/ in Rumanian. With this Rumanian development in mind we return to the cluster in 'cooked' and 'night'. A labiovelar is implied here, too, for both Occam's Razor and regularism apply. If the Romance starting point is assumed to be /kt/, Rumanian has treated this /k/ differently from all others (cf. *cantāre* > *cînta* 'to sing'). But if it was /kʷt/, then Rumanian behavior is consistent, treating this /kʷ/ like that of *patru* 'four'. Hence, PRom. /kʷt/. Now, the antecedents of Lat. *noctem* and *coctum* were not the same. The former reflects IE *kt,* cf. Gk. *nuktós,* Goth. *nahts* 'night'; but the latter reflects IE *kʷt,* cf. the intervocalic form of the stem in Lat. *coquō, coquere* 'to cook' (Buck 1933: 128). The two clusters evidently merged as /kt/ in Latin, but there is no theoretical objection to their having merged as /kʷt/ in a language that did not share the final evolution of Latin. Thus the best transformational description is confirmed as realistic by Indo-European criteria and is obviously the reconstruction to retain. Note, however, that it interposes an isogloss between

Latin and Romance; in Indo-European terms Latin and Romance are separate Italic dialects.

While the comparative method cannot provide an exact date in the preliterary period when the pre-Latin linguistic stock split into conservative Latin and innovating Romance branches, nor yet a date for their reunion in close social juxtaposition within a single commonwealth, it nevertheless urges us to be extremely leery of the Vulgar Latin model. Thus, the orthodoxy of the period under review is a kind of monism briefly to be summarized thus: Classical Latin begat Vulgar Latin, which in turn begat the Romance languages. In the discourse of specialists various nuances creep in; 'Classical Latin' is replaced by 'Plautine Latin' (Weinrich 1958: 18, "Altlatein") or 'Gracchan Latin' (Hall 1974: 16); 'Vulgar Latin' is replaced by 'Proto-Romance', and so on. But essentially the same diachronic model is used by historical linguists from Diez to Hall[1]. All accept without demur the statement that French, Italian, or Rumanian is Latin transformed by the passage of time (cf. Tagliavini 1949, "lingua neolatina"). Only how the latter became the former is open to debate.

If we ask how the Vulgar Latin model imposed itself and why it has not been discarded as unworkable, the fault lies partly with the comparative method itself. If we adopt the dualistic model suggested by the reconstruction of PRom. /k^{w}t/ and many other specifically non-Latin features, then it follows that, in the formative early period of the Romance dialects, Latin was a hitherto unacknowledged superstrate language. Superstrate features betray themselves readily enough when the source language was not a cognate. When the latter was not only a cognate but typologically more primitive, however, they are extremely hard to detect; but not impossible, as we shall point out. The effect of features coincidentally borrowed by several dialects in a set under comparison is to muddy the interrelationships of the correspondences.

After a compensated change in which an increase in contrastiveness (a phonemic split) has taken place at one point in the word as a result of a reduction in contrastiveness (a phonemic merger) at another point, a superstrate influence may entail the hypercorrect reestablishment of the contrasts in the reduced position while leaving those in the increased position unaffected. Later the comparativist comes along and finds correspondences reflecting both the compensating split and the hypercorrectly reestablished contrast system, and behold! they are in

Table 1.   The umlaut split im *mortuum/mortuam* (notation phonemic)

1. Standard Portuguese	*mórtu*	*mɔ́rtə*
2. Asturias (Lena)	*mwírtu*	*mwérta*
3. Surselva (Trun)	*míart*	*mɔ́rta*
4. Ticino (*AIS* pt. 109)	*mö̆rt*	*mɔ́rta*
5. Marche (Servigliano)	*mórtu*	*mɔ́rta*
6. Naples Bay (*AIS* pt. 720)	*mwórtə*	*mɔ́rtə*
7. East Lucania (*AIS* pt. 736)	*múrtə*	*méərtə*
8. Puglia (*AIS* pt. 718)	*múrtə*	*məórtə*
9. Central Lucania (*AIS* pt. 733)	*múərtə*	*mɔ́rtə*
10. South Lucania (*AIS* pt. 744)	*mwértu*	*mórta*
11. North Calabria (*AIS* pt. 762)	*múortu*	*mórta*
12. Sicily (*AIS* pt. 844)	*múartu*	*mórta*
13. Sicily (*AIS* pt. 826)	*mwórtu*	*mórta*
14. Standard Rumanian	*mórt*	*moártə*
15. Campidano (*AIS* pt. 967)	*mórtu*	*mɔ́rta*

complementation. At a snick of Occam's Razor an essential feature of Proto-Romance structure, one which perhaps defines a crucial classificatory isogloss between Romance and Latin, disappears under the mat, and a conservative Latinate feature appears in our reconstruction in its place. If this is done consistently, the proto-language ends up stripped of its indigenous structure and becomes a detailed portrait of the superstrate language.

As an illustration, consider stressed-vowel umlaut. Umlaut is the presence of two complementary stressed vocalisms, one with a phonetically higher set of outcomes than the other, each with its own grammatical incidence, in representative marginal dialects from every part of the Romania. Observe in Table 1 the reflexes of the adjective meaning 'dead' and note the phonemic split of the stressed vowels. Any development with this wide a distribution deserves consideration as a feature of Proto-Romance.

When we collect the posttonic-vowel correspondences, we find the situation shown in Table 2. About half the dialects present evidence of more than three posttonic vowels, while most of the rest show evidence for fewer then three; but Portuguese, Castilian, Campidanese, and Sicilian agree in showing three and only three. In comparative linguistics it is normal to assume that the most complex of a set of rival situations is the most primitive and hence to reconstruct at least six posttonic vowels

Table 2. Romance final-vowel correspondences

Latin	Asturian	Marchigiano	Logudorese	Standard Italian	Standard Rumanian	Standard French	Lucanian	Portuguese	Castilian	Campidanese	Sicilian
1 ī	i	i	i	i	j	–	ə	i	e	i	i
2 ĭ	e	e	i	e	e	–	ə	i	e	i	i
3 ĕ	e	e	e	e	e	–	ə	i	e	i	i
4 ă	a	a	a	a	ə	–	ə	ə	a	a	a
5 ō	o	o	o	o	–	–	ə	u	o	u	u
6 um	u	u	u	o	–	–	ə	u	o	u	u

here. If this is done, it is then evident that the higher, or 'umlauted', of the two stressed-vowel sets is redundant with posttonic correspondences 1 and 6 of Table 2. Anything redundant is structurally irrelevant and is forthwith removed from the reconstruction. Proto-Romance emerges with stable stressed vowels (i. e. no umlaut) – like Latin – and with a complex set of posttonics, each with a definite morphological role – again, like Latin. In the past the comparative method has stuck at this point.

But we still have the phonemic split of Table 1; how are we to explain it? The classical structural understanding of all phonemic splits is, first, that allophones develop in certain environments and, second, that the allophones are promoted to rival phonemes when the older environments collapse. But the older environments here never collapsed, as witness the 'conservative' posttonic systems at the left of Table 2. In Asturian or (Servigliano) Marchigiano, for example, we find phonemically split umlaut still largely redundant with the reflexes of correspondences 1 and 6. Only in a system with three posttonic vowels, distributed as in Portuguese, Castilian, Campidanese, and Sicilian, can we motivate the split; and we must motivate it. We cannot borrow umlaut from Etruscan or some such substrate language, nor can we pretend to discern in the input structure of orthodox Latinate Proto-Romance some gross imbalance, some irresistible propensity to umlaut after dialectalization. But we have the right to borrow from adstrate Latin and to conclude that pre-Romance final posttonic vowels did indeed dwindle to three through the merger of the mid and high timbres, thus splitting formerly anticipatory allophones of the stressed vowels and yielding Proto-Romance morphophonemic umlaut. This was the ruin of Indo-European suffixation; gone were many categories of inflexion that could not be expressed with umlaut and three post-tonic vowels. After the earliest dialectalization speakers of some local varieties of Romance, acknowledging that the suffixing morphology of Latin was a more efficient morphological process than their own, borrowed some vocalic suffixes or calqued some vocalic distinctions in the final syllable. And thereby some Romance dialects came to be more like Latin than they should be.

The chief weakness of the comparative method is its dependence upon the regular phonological correspondence. What is regular passes muster; yet what is cognate and borrowed is bound to appear regular. Before the concepts of descriptivism, structuralism, and the economy of sound changes became available, the comparativist was at an impasse. Now, to the extent that the eclectic proto-language assembled out of everything shared and regular is implausible as a 'système où tout se tient', and to the extent that Latinate and non-Latinate shared features impinge on one another, the comparativist can proceed by policy to reject the Latinate features. But this has scarcely been attempted yet.

What has been attempted all too often in our period is diachronic phonemics, the unholy marriage of an appeal to structural plausibility and the historical method[2]. The concepts of diachronic structuralism were first elaborated outside Romance linguistics by descriptivists of the Prague School: Jakobson, Haudricourt, Martinet, and so on, who rationalized and codified the empirical procedures of comparativists extrapolating backwards towards a proto-language. In the Romance field, however, these concepts were put to work chronologically and appeared to hold great promise of revealing the internal causes of otherwise unmotivated structural convergences (such as umlaut). If Latin were indeed the parent language, these essentially deductive findings might be of some validity. As it is, they express as simple A > B transformations falsely perceived relationships between distantly cognate linguistic systems. Too often they trace fictional trajectories. If, on the other hand, those skilled in structuralism and the whole-system perspective took the trouble to reconstruct a realistic Proto-Romance before seeking to state its chronological development, they would find that their ingenuity had been wholly invested in their preliminary anti-chronological extrapolations. Deduction would bring them back out of the reconstructed past at the same point from which induction carried them in. In other words, the best that can be expected from their method is perfect circularity.

The redeeming grace of the diachronic phonemicists has been that, while conveniently grouping certain related phenomena for us, they have fooled no one (Corbett 1970/71: 273)[3]. The efforts of this group have subjected the Vulgar Latin model to a strain from which it can hardly be expected to recover. The attention of diachronic linguists is riveted on certain patterns of non-Latinate features that have not yet been satisfactorily motivated as convergences from a putative Latinate starting point. Just as few will accept the specific diachronic trajectories proposed by the historical structuralists, so also few are prepared to return to a verdict of coincidence.

Perhaps all of the following points will qualify as revisions in the structure of Proto-Romance.

1. The *b-v* merger. Not only do two well separated centers in the Romania not distinguish Lat. *b* and consonantal *u*, for which we reserve the symbol *v* in any position, but Portuguese and Rumanian fail to distinguish them after liquids, and no Romance dialect keeps them distinct in intervocalic position. Furthermore, even among the dialects that present a /b/-/v/ contrast in initial position in general agreement with the Latin incidence, irregular developments of /b/ for expected /v/ appear to characterize every one (Politzer 1952: 212). Hypercorrection alone can satisfactorily explain such irregularity. Proto-Romance should be reconstructed with only /b/, merging Lat. *b* and *v*, but allowance should be made for two allophones, a [b] and a [β], [w], or [v].

2. The loss of voiced stops after nasals. The paired simplifications of Lat. *mb* > *mm* and *nd* > *nn* are found in insular and peninsular Italy up to the Rome-Ancona line and in the Ticino, Trentine, and Dolomite dialects; they occurred in Vegliote; and hypercorrections point to their earlier occurrence in the area of Lucca also. They are further found, regularly or irregularly, in Catalan, Aragonese, Castilian, and Gascon. The simplification of these clusters must have been a feature of Proto-Romance and their replacement in a wide variety of dialects, the effect of superstrate Latin influence.

The preceding items entail consonantal simplifications in Romance as against a conservative situation in Latin. To them we must continue to add the loss of *h-* and *-m*. The next item reconstructs phonetic differences having phonemic repercussions.

3. The retraction of *l*. A number of putative convergences concern the allophones of PRom. /l/. If the marginally distributed structures are cast back to the proto-language, PRom. /l/ will be found to have been made up of a group of phonetically disparate sounds which neverthe-less consistently share a distinctive feature, that of retraction from the dental articulation. While Lat. /l/ was apparently more consistently a dental lateral continuant – or became this in the Classical period – PRom. /l/ was initially and intervocalically an occlusive cacuminal [ḍ], postconsonantally a palatal [λ], preconsonantally a *u*-colored or dark [ł], and in the sequence /lj/ a palatalized occlusive [ḍ']. A clear dental [l] found today in the first three of these environments and a clear palatal [λ] found in the last result from borrowings from superstrate Latin. On the other hand a /d/ (Sp. *dejar* < *laxāre* 'to let go', etc.) reflects an early Romance lapse entailing the substitution of [d] for [ḍ], while [l] for IE *d* may represent a Latin mishearing of Rom. /d/ as /ḍ/ and a facetious hypercorrection (Lat. *lingua* 'tongue' for earlier *dingua*, etc.)[4]. Note that in an early Romance dialect a borrowed clear dental [l] in any of the environments would fail to show the retraction, would by that very fact be a new phomene, and would be likely to cause the remaining retracted allophones to split apart into separate phonemes of restricted distribution.

The next three items entail the reconstruction of Proto-Romance morphophonemic alternations.

4. Initial alternation and the nature of 'gemination'. Latin orthogra-phy implies that geminate consonants were a special medial cluster of a consonant with itself or with some feature of extra strength, length, or ambisyllabicity, while single medial consonants were allophonically aligned with the neutralized phones of other environments. The Romance evidence points to the opposite assignment, however: the fortis medial as the normal allophone between vowels of the neu-tralized phones in other positions, and the intervocalic so-called single as a two-phoneme segment combining the consonant with a feature of reduced articulatory energy, clear syllable-initial status, and shorter

prolation. The sum of these features may be termed 'lenition'. Three observations within the Romance evidence support this reconstruction: the merger of the 'geminates' with the neutralized phones whenever there has been loss of the contrast of two strengths, while the 'singles' – more systematically in the West than the East, but here also – promote their weakness to segmental status and split away from the neutralized phones; second, the fact that in the insular and peninsular Italian dialects below Spezia-Rimini which preserve the contrast of the two strengths, the strong is phonetically uniform in all regions while the weak can have dozens of local articulations (Weinrich 1958: 43-81); and, finally, the fact that in Italian three consonants occur intervocalically only as strongs, implying that this is the unmarked pole of the contrast.

The need to reject gemination and to reconstruct lenition in Proto-Romance is confirmed by observation of the pattern of initial 'doubling' (rafforzamento iniziale) in Italian dialects. Depending on syntactic factors all initial consonants may be either strong or weak. When weak, they are phonetically identical with the word-medial so-called singles; when strong, with the so-called geminates[5]. Proto-Celtic had just such an alternation, and it is reasonable to connect the two; but the fortis medials in the two proto-languages are usually not cognate. Therefore, they must be the unmarked pole of both the strength contrast and the initial alternation. What is cognate in Celtic and Romance is the phoneme of lenition and its incidence both in medial position and syntactically as a feature of the end of a word that combines with the initial consonant of a following word (Leonard 1968).

5. Unstable final *s* and *t*. At the beginning of our period it was claimed that the Eastern Romance change of -*s* to -*i* was phonological and that as such it had great significance as a classificatory criterion (Wartburg 1950: 20). It has since been argued (Rohlfs 1949-54: II, 52; Hall 1962) that what is at issue here is actually the phonetic loss of -*s* and its subsequent analogical replacement by -*i* in Italy and the Balkans independently. The fact remains, however, that the morphologically significant -*s* underwent this development in the two areas at an apparently very remote period, since the new incidence of -*i* plays a role in the rise of umlaut (next item). The problem is whether to reconstruct /-s/ for Proto-Romance, whether, that is, we can attain uniformity in the proto-language.

Pressing the lenition analysis discussed in the preceding item into use, we observe that -s in the environment before a vowel, because it has voiced in French and Portuguese, must reflect the lenited Proto-Romance cluster /ls/, in which /l/ symbolizes the phoneme of lenition. This phonemic structure would have been impossible in the complementary environments before a consonant and before pause, because a lenited consonant is marked as syllable-initial. There must have been, therefore, other allomorphs, positional variants containing in part other phonemes. We can perhaps never recover these allomorphs from the available evidence; but it is not unreasonable to speculate that the preconsonantal one entailed loss of [s], and the prepausal entailed generation of an inorganic high front vowel reminiscent of the prothetic /i/ generated before /sC-/ in some environments. If we postulate such a structurally necessitated morphophonemic alternation for Proto-Romance, we can achieve uniformity in the proto-language and also reconcile the ideas of regular phonetic change and analogical replacement. The genesis of /-i/ would thus be regular, but its generalization into the complementary environments at the expense of [s] would be analogical, culminating independently in the Italian and the Rumanian dialects. Implied, of course, is that Sard and western Romance also leveled the alternation, but with different results. Old Latin shows morphophonemically unstable final s, followed just before Cicero's day (*Orat.* 48, 161) by the generalization of -s even before consonants. This suggests that a stable -s is another superstrate influence on Romance.

What has been said for -s applies mutatis mutandis to -t.

6. Umlaut. The development of the Romance stressed-vowel system has been much debated in our period. It was once often argued that the diphthongs reflecting Lat. ĕ and ŏ are so widely distributed in the Romania that they should be reconstructed in some form for Proto-Romance (Wartburg 1950: 76). It proves to be impossible to reconcile the conditions of all the diphthongs in a single prototype, however; and the absence of the diphthongs in Portuguese raises a further obstacle. Later it became fashionable to frame structurally motivated trajectories (see Corbett 1970/71, for bibliography) from a starting point which must now be impugned. Yet it seems that the attempt to motivate convergence in the diphthongs should not be abandoned, for in an

umlauting Proto-Romance vocalism there would be more crowding, more inherent instability, and more pressure to change than in the nine-vowel system of orthodox Proto-Romance.

Of the ten pre-Latin accented vowels, two – ī and ū – are unaffected by the umlaut split in any Romance dialect, and there is no reason to think they ever were. Of the remainder, two – ā and ă – merged and resplit, while six – ĭ, ē, ĕ, ŏ, ō, ŭ – made uncomplicated splits. There are thus sixteen distinctive stressed-vowel entities to be set up in Proto-Romance umlaut. Certain of them have behaved historically in ways that will suggest a firm reconstruction. Others may remain conjectural; but this much may be said: One has to start from a system of two phonemic lengths in a seven-vowel four-level triangle, plus diphthongs, or there will not be enough vowels to go around.

The issue is further complicated by the revised chronology. The Old Latin diphthongs enter the picture, as do many details of primitive structure no longer present in Classical Latin. For example, when the umlaut split was described in Vulgar Latin terms, one could say that it was conditioned by -ī and by -ŭm, -ŭnt and feel sure that it was a simple raising of the stressed vowels before these suffixes. We must now think etymologically of -ei and -ŏm, -ŏnt and wonder which of their phonetic features were anticipated in the accented vowels. These considerations will affect the outcome of the vocalic reconstruction, which is not likely to be worked out quickly.

The next item arises from the issue of umlaut and illustrates one of the many morphological revisions likely to accrue to Proto-Romance.

7. The 'mass-neuter' and the case system. What case system must we reconstruct for Proto-Romance? Historical linguists, duly cataloguing survivals, point to a scattering of genitives and locative ablatives in Romance onomastics, plus the datives of the pronominal system and the vocatives of Rumanian, and claim that the latest common source of the Romance languages retained all the cases[6].

Medieval Gallo-Romance case inflection and the modern Romansh predicative adjective (Leonard 1972: 64f.) attest that early Romance retained a primary dichotomy between nominative and oblique. The Western and Sard plurals in -as, -os implicate the accusative, and the Rumanian dialects contribute the vocative and the inflected feminine singulars *(unei capre* 'of or to a goat'). The last-named implicate either the genitive or the dative. Nowhere is there evidence that ablative forms were ever used outside idioms borrowed from Latin[7].

Attention has recently been focused on the 'neutro de materia' or 'mass neuter', a phenomenon linking the Asturian dialects with those of the Rome-Ancona corridor (Rohlfs 1949-54: I, 241; Lausberg 1951, D. Alonso 1958, Blaylock 1964a, Lüdtke 1965, Hall 1968a). In both areas masculine nouns normally show umlaut of the stressed vowel and end in -*u*, but nonfeminines construed as mass-nouns fail to show umlaut and end in -*o*; and since the adjectives agreeing with each type display the same characteristics, the term 'neuter' has found favor. It has been demonstrated, however, that in each area doublets were inherited and usually leveled out in favor of one or the other form or a compromise between the two (D. Alonso 1958). Thus, beside masc. *pilu* 'a hair' in each area there is the rival so-called neut. *pelo* 'hair in the mass, hair the substance'. This is evidence for the contrast, not of rival nonfeminine genders, but of rival oblique cases farther west than the Balkans.

How are we to reconstruct the second oblique case? Rum. *capre* is formally indeterminate and has the meanings of both the genitive and the dative; but the Asturian and central Italian *pelo,* while it has a meaning akin to the Latin partitive genitive, can only reflect the dative in form. Putting this evidence together, we have reason to reconstruct in Proto-Romance a three-case system (leaving aside the vocative): a nominative, an accusative characterized in the singular of the second declension by umlaut, and a 'second oblique' without umlaut, reflecting the dative in form[8], but preserving both the dative and the genitive meanings.

The most attractive repercussion of this reconstruction is that modern western Romance and Italian second declension masculine singulars that fail to show umlaut need not be cognate with those that do: the former reflect second oblique case forms and the latter, accusatives. This observation greatly enhances the regular incidence of Proto-Romance umlaut.

Even this brief discussion will suffice to show the kinds of changes that can be effected in the latest common source of the Romance languages if the techniques and assumptions of comparative linguistics as currently practiced outside the Romance field are allowed to take precedence over the circularity of the historical method.

Let us now turn to the subject of the availability of data in our field as against that of other areas of diachronic linguistics. How well off are we? It was recently my experience to attend a seminar in comparative Germanic and to be impressed by the enormous amount of systematic dialect fieldwork that has been carried out in each of the Germanic-speaking countries. The findings, even if not published, are catalogued, archived, and available to the serious scholar. Furthermore, as a result of their dependence on the comparative method, Germanists have an impressive number of journals devoted to it. The journals in the Romance field, by contrast, are dominated by the historical method, and articles on dialect X or some strangely similar phenomenon in dialects Y and Z tend to be buried between others on philological or literary themes. Romance comparativism should have at least one forum of its own. Finally, I was impressed by the Germanists' respect for, and awareness of, developments in Indo-European. I have tried to indicate how a little more of that would do us no harm.

Our period has seen noteworthy advances in the availability of data, nonetheless. Rohlfs' (1949-54) compendium, while it is atomistic rather than structural in approach, is invaluable for Italo-Romance. When dialects have been studied as phonemic systems, intriguing points have emerged; Heilman (1955), Martinet (1956), and Bjerrome (1957) have been particularly useful to me. Parrino's (1967) study of the blatantly hypercorrect final vowels of a village close under the Rome-Ancona line casts much doubt on the validity of posttonic systems with five contrasts in nearby dialects. Mazzola's (1967) treatment of Sicilian includes an enlightening systematic statement of the syntactic variations of initial consonants. It is to be hoped that this will become a standard feature of descriptions of Italo-Romance dialects undertaken hereafter. Asturian dialect studies have enjoyed a praiseworthy proliferation since the Second World War (Neira Martínez 1955, Diaz Castañon 1966, Penny 1970, etc.), but other areas of Spain and Portugal are still poorly served, especially inasmuch as most of the projected linguistic atlas, the *ALPI*, remains stubbornly forthcoming. On the other hand, the new series of regional atlases for France and Rumania are proceeding apace (for listings, see Hall 1974: 248, n. 64). Tagliavini's (1949) manual is excellent both for its bibliography and for its refusal to treat the standard languages exclusively. Lausberg's (1956-62) compendium packs much valuable information but is unfortunately imbued with the historical method. Hall's projected *Comparative Romance Grammar* (of which Hall 1974 is the first volume and Hall 1976 the second) promises to be of immense value. There is nothing like the codification of an outworn orthodoxy to stimulate innovation.

If we have left the discussion of the classification of the Romance dialects until last, it is because the issue of shared Latinate structure must logically precede it. We classify dialects genetically according to their common innovations, and we attach greater weight to regular phonological evidence than to the less rigorously patterned evidence of morphology and syntax. These criteria have too often been masked by the historical model, which has induced us to mistake common superstrate borrowings for conservative traits, widely distributed 'convergences' for linguistic innovations, and even morphological developments for phonemic ones[9]. If marginal dialects share something that for this reason we decide to project back to Proto-Romance (e. g. umlaut), then the survival of this feature tells us nothing about the degree of closeness between the dialects that show it. On the other hand, if marginal dialects share a borrowed Latinate feature (like -*s* in Spanish and Sard), this tells us nothing of taxonomic value either. For these reasons the only criteria that stand up through a revolutionary change of proto-language are the phonemic mergers the results of which are themselves non-Latinate.

The old East-West division of the Romania – still actively advocated after the end of World War II by some who wished to stress the primacy of the Spezia-Rimini line – was thus based on shaky assumptions. Wartburg (1950: 20-34) used the survival of -*s*, although admitting it as a restoration in many of its Imperial Latin contexts, and the voicing of medial weak (single) *p, t, k,* while conceding its collapse in the Pyrenees, to delimit a dialectal province, bounded at Spezia-Rimini, which, with his predecessors back to Diez, he called the West, as opposed to an East assembled from the dialects of the Balkans and the Italian Boot. Sardinia emerged as a third province, sharing -*s* with the West, but retaining medial voicelessness with the East. What one was to do with Béarnais and Upper Aragonese, which lack voicing, or western Sicilian and Logudorese Sard, which have it, or whether one was to see any essential differences at all between Rumanian and Central Italian, were issues grandly ignored. A classification can be either generic or genetic; it may, that is, connect actual similarities in form without explaining how they arose, or it may connect shared developments even when they do not everywhere yield the same final form. Wartburg's scheme is generic only, though he attempted to justify it as genetic. To put this another way, the linguistic changes he set up as defining provinces were not the earliest to have occurred.

The discoveries on which the most promising scheme of classification we have today is based, the existence in southern Italy of 'archaic' zones with Sardinian and with Rumanian vocalisms, were made and documented before the war, but not publicized until afterwards (Rohlfs 1949-54: I, 43-51; Lausberg 1956-62: I, 144-9). The implications of these discoveries for genetic, as opposed to generic, classification were first noted by Hall (1950), whose well-known proposed stammbaum began by presenting the new three-way division into Southern, Balkan, and Italo-Western Romance based on the Rohlfs-Lausberg fieldwork, but then continued, after the separation of Italo-Romance, with the attempt to retain Wartburg's shaky concept of the monolithic West. The viable early part of Hall's stammbaum is determined by the mergers of the reflexes of pre-Lat. *ĭ, ŭ* with other vowels. This stammbaum sets up three vocalic provinces in the Romania, one (the Southern) in which *ĭ, ŭ* merge with *ī, ū*; one (the Italo-Western) in which they merge with *ē, ō*; and one (the Rumanian) in which *ĭ* merges with *ē*, but *ŭ* merges with *ū*. These vocalic developments are clearly earlier than any of the consonantal developments proposed as criteria for a rival classification.

In 1965 Hadlich attacked Hall's classification of Vegliote: on the evidence of its vocalism it is clearly (Italo-)Western, not Balkan, as Hall had had it, even though its consonants fail to show the medial voicing hitherto deemed essential in an Italo-Western dialect which has lost the single-geminate contrast. Hall (1974: 14) has since redrawn the stammbaum accordingly.

In 1956 Lausberg challenged Hall over the classification of Sicilian. In a diagram (Lausberg 1956-62: I, 149, retained in subsequent reprintings) he shows the vocalism of that dialect as having passed through an intermediate stage identical with that of Italo-Western Romance (his "Vulgärlatein", p. 145), while Hall derived it from Southern Romance[10]. Hall has not changed his stammbaum here, and two of his pupils have attempted to defend the Southern pedigree.

Mazzola (1967, 1976), assuming that the intermediate stage by which Sicilian vocalism came about is unrecoverable, argued that the dialect presents a continuity of consonantal developments with Sardinia and the southern Boot. This attempt to clarify the classification fails because it appeals to consonantal criteria, thus implicating dialects up to Campania that obviously violate the basic vocalic province division. Mazzola is thus not defending Hall's Southern Romance, but setting up a rival. Leonard (1977, 1978b) points this out, and tries to show that, in an appeal to comparative morphophonemics, the Sicilian vocalism is not so mute on its antecedents as Mazzola assumed: the reconstructed vocalic system needed to explain both Southern Lucanian and insular Sard also yields Sicilian.

Thus it appears that every Romance dialect fits into one of the three vocalically defined proto-dialects. Each dialect zone embraces a corner of peninsular Italy, from which we know the Romance linguistic stock originally spread; and, since each dialect (as defined by these mergers) appears to have spread centrifugally without interfering with the others – the Southern into Magna Graecia, Sicily, Sardinia, Corsica, and perhaps North Africa; the Italo-Western into northern Italy, France, and Spain; and the Rumanian into (apparently Illyricum, then Moesia, and) Rumania proper – this configuration of isoglosses, alone of all that have been proposed previously, lets us look at the first dispersion of Italian peoples overseas in the conquests of the Punic and the Macedonian Wars. Reflexes of the three proto-dialects are least unlike each other in what must be a part of their original range, Lucania. Here the consensus is for umlaut, reduction of *mb* and *nd* to *mm* and *nn*, Lat. *-ll-* > *-ḍḍ-*, palatalization of postconsonantal *l*, the *b-v* merger, and unstable *-s* and *-t*, and even the labiovelar plus dental type of cluster discussed above apropos of /k^{w}t/ (Leonard 1969). Thus this scheme of classification seems to be truly genetic.

What happens in the much-debated stammbaum after the intermediate stage of Italo-Western Romance, however, is by no means so clear. There are no obvious patterns of vocalic mergers to guide us, and we are obliged to change criteria. I have argued elsewhere (Leonard 1970) that Hall's selection of consonantal criteria that first delimit a Western Romance and then subdivide it into an Ibero-Romance and a Gallo-Romance is too drastic a change; we want a criterion that continues to be vocalic. A common split of free and checked stressed-vowel allophones links the North French dialects with those of Rhaeto-Romance, Franco-Provençal, Gallo-Italian, Abruzzese, and northern Pugliese, in all of which it is in at least some contexts phonemic. Even the dialects of the west coast of peninsular Italy show this split as a subphonemic difference in length. But there is no evidence that present or earlier stages of Portuguese, Spanish, Catalan, South French, or Venetian were ever characterized by this difference of length. One may set up a Vowel-Length group among Italo-Western dialects, with an intermediate stage implied, but this should be done with caution, for we are grouping here on the basis of a common split which may simply have been healed in the excluded dialects and may actually have characterized Proto-Italo-Western. Certainly, no choice of criteria yet proposed accounts satisfactorily for the geographical distribution of the defining features as expansions from historically realistic centers of linguistic prestige. While this consideration in itself may not be crucial, to ignore social groupings in our attempts to explain western Romance developments is to ignore the lesson of dialect geography. Much further research will have to be devoted to this problem before a completely convincing later stammbaum emerges.

But the earlier part of the stammbaum is hardly to be denied. Obviously, pari passu with our reconstruction of an umlauting Proto-Romance, we will need to reconstruct Proto-Southern-Romance, Proto-Rumeno-Romance, and Proto-Italo-Western-Romance in conformity with our revised overall proto-language. Each appears to require a seven-vowel system and remnants of Indo-European phonemic length to make up the number of stressed vowels needed in umlaut.

Romance comparativists, I venture to predict, will proceed to acknowledge greater and greater typological divergences between Proto-Romance and even the oldest known Latin, an earlier date for the split of the common parent language, and the existence of two competing adstrate languages in the Roman state, Latin and Romance. These positions will necessitate various reinterpretations of all the evidence in an effort to determine and assess the influence of spoken Latin on early Romance, the reciprocal impact of early Romance on Latin, and the varying roles of language mixture in the development of the Romance dialects. The two stocks may be so thoroughly scrambled that in some segments the puzzle can never be read. But the attempt will be made, for a theory of language mixture appears to hold out a great hope of explaining the origin of not only the Romance standards, but the dialects as well; and a better theory must prevail.

But prevail with whom? The long and the short of the matter is that the history of the Romance languages, which for a long time has been taken as given, resumes the status of a problem. Those equipped to face the issues will welcome the opportunity to try their steel; but those so equipped are few, and most others who think of themselves as diachronic Romance linguists will react with bewilderment, if not with hostility, to the removal of their orthodoxy. If it is one's purpose to explain the development of only one literary language, appeal to an unlimited number of other dialects may strike one as perverse; and appeal to anything avowedly rustic and nonstandard, overly anthropological. If one is not a phonologist, and nowadays it is quite unfashionable to be one, he will be impatient to reconstruct higher levels of structure despite the fact that the comparative method, grounded in phonetic regularism, must proceed methodically from the phonological level on up. The ranks of the many may close – indeed, have long been closed – against the few. Long live Vulgar Latin!

Nevertheless, once the role of Latin as a red herring in comparative Romance linguistics has been recognized, our future progress will have implications outside the field that will make scholars in other areas look on our diachronic studies with quickened interest.

Notes

1 The latter is a crypto-historical linguist who has long proclaimed the virtues of the comparative method (Hall 1950, 1960), though he views it as an ancillary to historical orthodoxy and not as a heuristic tool. He guides the reconstruction past points of uncertainty by referring to "the back of the book [i. e. Latin]" (Hall 1964: 308) and speaks with pride of the high marks due to his proto-language for its structural proximity to Latin as known from other sources. This is logical circularity.

2 As Weinrich (1958: 12) puts it: "The history of the Romance languages begins with the language of Rome. Latin and Romance linguistics thus form a unitary historical discipline. If we wish to interpret the historical development in structural terms, the sound system of Latin is our natural starting point." [Translation mine.]

3 Works of the diachronic phonemics school include Lausberg 1947 a, c, Haudricourt – Juilland 1949, Martinet 1951/52, 1952, 1955, Politzer 1952, 1954 a, Jungemann 1955, Lüdtke 1956, Weinrich 1958, Romeo 1968, Purczinsky 1970, and Ferguson 1976.

4 Hall (1974: 59), following recent Italian opinion, attributes Latin forms with *l-* for *d-* to Sabine loans; Palmer (1954: 38), in discussing this issue, says: "We can achieve no more than 'a presumption of Sabine origin'," adding: "In fact the few remnants

preserved of this dialect show that it was so strongly influenced by Latin at a very early date that its classification with the Osco-Umbrian group itself is a matter of doubt".

5 Martinet ([1952] 1955: 281-4) and Sala (1963) speculate as to why the Romance initial "merged with the geminate" both in Rumanian and in western Romance. It emerges from our reconstruction, however, that, in their terms, there always was a geminate initial. What these dialects have lost is the weak initial variant, for evidence of the sporadic survival of which cf. Figge (1966).

6 Hall (1960: 204) claims the nominative, accusative, genitive, dative, and vocative; in Hall (1968) he triumphantly adds the ablative.

7 We observe that the medieval Gallo-Romance 'cas régime', while it could on occasion express dative and genitive notions as well as the basic accusative idea, never functioned as an ablative.

8 At least in the singular – we know nothing about the plural in nouns and adjectives, but recall dat. *leur, loro, llur* < gen. *illōrum* among pronouns.

9 For example, 'North Italian' versus 'South Italian' umlaut, consequent on point 7, above. In the former, masc. sg. 2nd decl. substantives are not umlauted, while in the latter they are.

10 In this Lausberg may be following Rohlfs, who has uncovered much in Sicilian that looks like it came in with the Normans, but who correctly points out an older linguistic layer preserved in the phonology: "Invece di trovare in questa più antica colonia latina un baluardo di un'antica latinità con fisionomia individuale al pari della Sardegna, notiamo dei dialetti che sembrano appartenere ad una più recente romanità, se lasciamo fuori considerazione alcune particolarità fonetiche … che la Sicilia ha in commune con la Sardegna e con molti altri dialetti del Mezzogiorno" (Rohlfs 1972: 30f.).

GIOVANNI BATTISTA PELLEGRINI

Substrata

Translated from Italian by Rebecca Posner

1. Latin has a truly unique history in the ancient world: it was a language originally spoken in a small area (circumscribed by the Tiber, the Aniene, the Tivoli, Praeneste and Alban hills and the sea) which became, with Roman conquests, the most widely spoken language of the orbis antiquus, then developing (in the sixth to eighth centuries A. D.) into a group of languages that spread over a good part of Europe and into the New World.

Archaic Latin – formed in 'Latium vetus' – recalls the threefold origins of Rome, with alongside the original tribes of the Tities, the Ramnes and the Luceres, the Proto-Latins, Etruscans and Proto-Sabines. Latin at the time of the monarchy – 'Numan Latin' – has rather special features that are only partly known through scant inscriptions (seventh to fifth centuries B. C.). From the fifth century on, it underwent radical and rapid transformation and spread as far as the river Po within three centuries: with the *Lex Julia* of 90 B. C. Roman citizenship spread to Cisalpine regions and with the *Lex Pompeia* of 89 Latin citizenship spread to the Alps (transformed in 49 B. C. by Caesar to Roman citizenship).

Colonies within the scope of Latin law were vehicles and centres of diffusion of the conquerors' language – even though their citizens kept their linguistic privileges, they were desirous of integration with the Latin linguistic community (Devoto 1974a: 133) – especially in those colonies that rapidly developed on the South East of Rome, inhabited by Aequi and Volsci.

The Latin colony of Velitrae (Velletri) dates from 494 B. C., that of Ardea in the Rutuli territory from 442; the first Roman colony in

Volscian territory was Antium (338). But Roman culture soon took root in the most viable regions, and roads ran from Rome in all directions: the via Appia to Brindisi, with the Popilia branching off it at Capua towards the Straits of Messina, the Aurelia to the borders of Transalpine Gaul, the Flaminia to Spoleto and Rimini, the Aemilia from Piacenza to the Alps. From Rimini the Popilia branched off, with sections built from the second century B. C. onwards running to the Alpine passes and to the Danube (e. g. by way of the Claudia Augusta Altinate). For a rapid survey of the Roman conquest of Italy with a map, cf. Pulgram 1958: 282-7. The chapter on Latin in Italy in Devoto 1944: 183-211 remains fundamental; he shows that Romanisation went through two stages: a) colonialisation and b) assimilation, during which non-Latins learned Latin with more or less interference from their native tongues (hence 'substratum influence'). Devoto insists that Latin did not expand gradually from one centre but from a network of centres: for instance, at the most ancient period Latin was spoken at Sutrium but not at Caere, and, in the Pontine region, at Setia but not Velitrae.

2. Thus Latin was taking over sporadically from other languages in the sixth and fifth centuries, – first displacing Sabelline, Etruscan and Faliscan (this latter having particular affinity with Latin) – and then with increasing speed in the fourth century. Roman policy was astute enough not to impose the conquerors' language, but gradually official usage spontaneously adopted Latin, which was becoming more and more prestigious and was recognized as useful and essential to learn (cf. Budinsky 1881, Pulgram 1958: 264-81, Monteverdi 1952: 7-15). Rome's conquests spread far and wide and with them the Latin language, which did not however completely supplant indigenous languages; it was however resisted by only one language of high cultural prestige: Greek. Latin became the official language of administration, of commerce, of the army, of education and of culture, ousting the numerous languages of subject peoples even in everyday speech (though often much later than in the written language). To unified Italy – divided by Augustus into ten regions – were added the provinciae, considered as subject territories, of which the first was Sicily (241) followed by Sardinia and Corsica (238), Spain (197), Illyrium (167), Africa (146), southern Gaul (120), northern Gaul (50), Rhaetia (15)

and, last of all, Dacia conquered by Trajan in 107 A. D. (For the diffusion of Latin through the Empire cf. Budinsky 1881, Pulgram 1958: 264-81 (for Italy only) and Monteverdi 1952: 7-15.)

3. In learning Latin, the peoples of Italy and the Empire must have passed through various stages of more or less prolonged bilingualism in which the two languages influenced each other, followed by the victory of the conqueror's language except in the case of Greek. Articulatory habits, characteristic phonemes, constructions and especially words of the ousted language were often kept by the new Latin-speakers and became from the beginning special characteristics of Latin (here we are not concerned with ancient Latin dialectal elements).

In the peripheral areas of the orbis romanus where Latin did not succeed in becoming established (spoken only in the big towns and by the higher social strata, but not in the less densely populated country-side) it is easy to find, even now, traces of transparent Latinisms in place names, in the lexicon of individual languages, (e. g. in the Rhine valley, in Britain, in many Balkan and Danubian areas, in North Africa and in the Alps). Tagliavini (1949/1972: 173-193) gives precise infor-mation on this score, citing Latin elements in Berber, Basque, Celtic languages, Old English, Germanic languages and Albanian.

What is most interesting about 'substratum' concerns those traits of regional Latin that have been ascribed by Romanists, especially Italian Romanists, to so-called 'ethnic pressures'. Ascoli was one of the princi-pal proponents of this point of view (cf. Ascoli 1881, 1886: 1-17). As Timpanaro (1969, 1972) has shown, Ascoli drew much of his inspira-tion from Cattaneo (1801-69), who had discerned Celtic influence in some phenomena. Terracini (1938) points out that Ascoli's model was opposed to the abstraction of the neogrammarians: phonetic change was related to concrete historical events and languages were seen to be enriched by innovations from the substrata. The model assumes a phase of language mixture with the subordinate language fading away, but leaving traces in the dominant language (for an interpretation of comparable data in South America cf. Amado Alonso 1951a: 315-330 and for a general survey cf. Vàrvaro 1968: 167-197).

The most consistent proponent of the Ascolian model has been that great Italian dialectologist Clemente Merlo who states (Merlo 1933: 4): "A language which for any reason succumbs to another, does not disappear without having exerted a not inconsiderable pressure on it, and without having imprinted itself on it. In the case of the Romance languages, in spite of the marvellous assimilatory power of Rome, the indigenous peoples exerted pressure on the Latin language and left on it their indelible imprint". Brøndal (1917) prefers to talk more abstractly of a "general tendency of the basis of articulation". Among the most authoritative opponents of substratum explanations of important phonetic evolutions in Romance we should mention Meyer-Lübke and, more recently, Gerhard Rohlfs, who adduce historical evidence to show that some too hastily accepted substratum explanations are inconsistent and dubious. But traditional explanations are challenged especially by structural-functionalists like Martinet (1955). In fact, the older hypotheses about ethnic pressure are not rejected, but they are incorporated into a more general diachronic phonological framework. Nevertheless there are some who vociferously condemn nineteenth-century substratum ideas: to Jungemann (1955) must go the credit of having aired the substratum problems of the Iberian peninsula and Gascony (his lengthy study is a methodological model for the whole of the Romance area) in the light of structural linguistics. He does not reject substratum theory but confines it to its rightful place. He maintains (1955: 418) that to identify substratum influence (in phonology) four conditions should be fulfilled:

1. that in the substratum language there should exist characteristics that have a direct or indirect relationship with the phenomenon studied;
2. that the phenomenon cannot be explained by means of internal factors alone;
3. that in the community in question, there should have been a long period of bilingualism;
4. that during this period the community was isolated from the influence of other centres of prestige and that the community itself enjoyed a certain prestige.

In the absence of such circumstances recourse cannot be made to substratum for an explanation of linguistic change.

4. Of particular interest is the study of a type of Latin influenced by the pre-Roman languages of Italy, a region which forms a sort of Romania all to itself, by virtue of the variety of its dialects which owe their often

profound diversity to the substrata among other things (it is well known that it is impossible to construct a 'proto-Italian' or an 'Italian diasystem'; cf. Pellegrini 1973 a on this point and for information on the Italian substrata). Here we should emphasise what may seem obvious: two languages intermingle more easily, giving rise to substratum phenomena, the more structurally and lexically alike they are, as bilinguals have difficulty in keeping them apart. Parlangèli (1969: 137) formulates the so-called 'Merlo law' thus: "The pressure exerted by the substratum is directly proportional to the degree of affinity between the substratum and the dominant language". Interpenetration is less common when bilinguals use clearly differentiated means of expression (as can be seen in present-day situations). It is no accident that the Latin of ancient Etruria was of particular purity, where the local language, highly prestigious Etruscan, profoundly different structurally from Latin (indeed almost surely non-Indo-European) made hardly any inroads (save for very few loan-words) on the language of the conquerors. And it was the closeness of Tuscan to Latin, the language of scholars and scribes, the *grammatica* of Dante, that in part led to its adoption throughout Italy. The degree of divergence of Italian dialects from Latin, related to the substratum influence they have undergone, is discussed by Devoto (1970). And perhaps Provençal is closer to Latin than is French partly because the Ligurian substratum had not been completely overlaid in Southern France by Gaulish, which was the dominant language of Northern France.

5. One problem that has not been resolved is to establish how far and up to what time substratum languages retained their vitality within Romania, in town or countryside and among the different social strata. As Pulgram (1958: 274) points out we have no means of finding out "because the ancients were not in the habit of keeping statistics". We can be certain only that for example Italy, unlike other parts of the Empire, was eventually completely Romanized. However Quintilian's affirmation (cf. Elcock 1960: 171) is not convincing, when he writes in the first century A. D. that all indigenous languages had been eliminated and only Latin was spoken. In fact there are indications that the older languages were not completely extinct at that time; and in any case we should distinguish between the official use of Latin in monuments, and the survival, perhaps for centuries, of spoken languages,

especially in isolated areas far from urban centres (cf. Pellegrini 1964). It is however notable that the ancient languages of Italy abandoned the official use of the local alphabets of Etruscan origin (or, more rarely, of Greek origin) for the Latin alphabet, in the second and first centuries B. C. This is clearly seen e. g. for Oscan, in the *Tabula Bantina* which dates from the first century B. C. Some of the *Tabulae Iguvinae* could not have been written before the first century B. C., but for Paelignian and Marrucinian and other 'minor Italic' inscriptions, the Latin alphabet was already used at the end of the third century (Pisani 1964: 45-51). In Northern Italy, too, the Latin alphabet replaced local graphies in the second and first centuries B. C., as can be seen from the Lepontine and especially the Venetic inscriptions, (Pellegrini – Prosdocimi 1967: 1: 221-35). Alongside various compromises in graphy, particularly interesting are some bilingual texts like the Etrusco-Latin inscriptions from Pesaro (TLE 697) and the Gaulish-Latin texts from Todi (PID 339) which date from the second half of the second century B. C. The gradual process of Romanisation is clearly discernible in the Venetic or Venetic-Latin inscriptions on funeral urns from Este and Treviso and in votive texts from Làgole di Calalzo (Pellegrini – Prosodicimi 1967: 1. 788-283, 404-426, and 485-568), which show, between the fourth and first centuries B. C., a gradual passage from Venetic, through a mixture of Venetic and Latin, to Latin with traces of Venetic names and formulae (Pellegrini – Prosodicimi 1967: 1. 188-283).

6. It is likely that the first languages to die out were those nearest the small region from which Latin spread (a Latin that was already in Praeneste different from that of Rome, because of Sabine influences), though not without leaving some traces, especially rustic words – like *bos* and *lupus*. Perhaps at the time of the Social War the lesser Italic languages and Faliscan were extinct, but Umbrian was still living in the first century B. C., and Oscan lasted longer, as first century A. D. inscriptions attest. It is probable that Messapian and especially Etruscan survived even later (Etruscan was spoken in the second century A. D., as attested by Gellius N. A. XI, 7). This is not to mention Greek which was current in the colonies of Magna Graecia and Sicily – the language of a superior civilisation, on which Romans drew in every cultural sphere.

Some scholars believe that Gaulish survived among the populace until the fifth century A. D. – the evidence, of doubtful authenticity, is to be found in the Dialogues (1.27.1) of Sulpicius Severus (c. 350-425).

Outside Italy, it is easy to pick out regions where Latin did not completely triumph. Thus in Africa proconsularis, where Roman political and cultural penetration was massive (after the destruction of Carthage in 146 B. C.), Latin did not manage to supplant Carthaginian for several centuries, as St. Augustine attests for Hippo Regius (Numidia Proc. Inf.), especially in the surrounding countryside (Sermo XXV, *De verbo apost.* and *De haer.* 87) where the peasants continued to use the Semitic language (Reichenkron 1965: 294-6). Moreover, neo-Carthaginian inscriptions continued to be used alongside Latin, and Greek (and Libyan Berber). It seems obvious that where Latin has not been continued as Romance it was used only as an administrative language and a lingua franca among subject peoples. Among the provinces, apart from the above-mentioned islands, Latin soon took root in the Narboniensis (first century), while in Celtic Gaul and Belgica it triumphed only a century later. The Iberian regions too were not completely Romanised, as witnessed by the survival of Basque, which was at one time more widely spoken. The Balkan-Danubian provinces were Romanised in a discontinuous way, with more profound and lasting penetration in Dacia (most Rumanian linguists favour a so-called 'continuity' theory for this region: cf. Tagliavini 1949/1972: 373-4).

7. Let us survey the various languages in Italy and the Empire which were replaced by Latin and which may have left substratum influences on the Latin spoken.

We are not so concerned with the Italic and Etruscan features found in the earliest attested Latin, nor with the 'Proto-Sabine' cultural elements discussed by Peruzzi 1970a, 1973; for instance, the postposition of the patronymic to the family name in the primitive onomastic formulae, or other juridicial elements that cast light on the origins of Rome, or the formation of the Latin alphabet (which Peruzzi believes comes directly from Greek, without Etruscan intervention), part of a very ancient Greek influence on Early Latin; cf. his Greek etymologies *diphtéra* > *littera,* or *elementum* from *elóphas* 'ivory tablet engraved with the alphabet'. The contact of Latin with Proto-Sabine is attested in the *fhefhaked* of the Praenestine fibula (7th c. B. C.?). Giacomelli

(1962) has recently assembled Faliscan inscriptions: as already stated, these show particular affinity with Latin, with obvious Italic influence and some surprising features, like the *o*-stem genitive in -*osio,* compared with Latin -*ī.* Pisani (1964: 334-55) presents a brief sketch of Faliscan as close to Latin, but rather more archaic: his suggestion that -*ī* derives from -*osio* (> -*oio* > *oi* > *ei* > *ī*) has not met with agreement among scholars. Ribezzo (1932) and Devoto (1944: 54-8) pick out a 'Proto-Latin' lineage in an ancient Southern Italian substratum – without written attestation – due to the Enotri and the Opici: this is by all accounts characterized e. g. by the -*t*- of *Rutulus* < IE **reudh*- 'red', to which we can link the -*t*- of *Aitna,* Mount Etna in Sicily, from **aidh*- 'to burn'. To the North of the Opici were located the Ausoni, known later as the Aurunci; *Rutuli* was an Ausonian name, well known at the time of Virgil. A similar Opican phonological development can be seen in *Liternum* (Gk. *Leuterno*-) < IE **leudh*- (the Oscan development would have **Louferno*-).

But Romanists are more concerned with emphasising the importance of Italic or Osco-Umbrian substratum influence, which was exerted over a fairly wide area. 'Italic' is here understood in its narrow sense used especially by the Italian school (Devoto, Pisani), opposing Osco-Umbrian to Latin: this view is shared by many other scholars, including Beeler (1952). Devoto (1967b) presents an original picture of the 'Italic' people before they merged with the Romans, harmonizing data from various disciplines (archaeology, religious history) by means of linguistic analysis of documents. He also tries to pick out the original linguistic differences between Latin-Faliscan and Osco-Umbrian.

There are in fact several linguistic traits that differentiate Italic and Latin and it is probable that many of the convergences are due to contact, in Italy rather than in a prehistoric homeland. The Osco-Umbrian texts are without doubt the most important of ancient Italy (leaving aside Latin), both because of their relative richness but also because they are intelligible enough for us to be able, thanks especially to the lengthy Gubbio Tables, to reconstruct a grammar and to assemble a good-sized lexicon. They have been published in recent years in reliable anthologies by Vetter (1953), Pisani (1964), Bottiglioni (1954), Poultney (1959) and, especially (for Umbrian texts), Devoto (1948, 1962b). Untermann (1960) gives us a survey of studies on the *Tabulae Iguvinae:* cf. also Prosdocimi 1969b and 1972b. Lejeune

(1971, 1972) has edited, with his usual competence, Oscan inscriptions.

8. The area covered by the Italic inscriptions is fairly vast since it covers almost all of Southern Italy, with offshoots in Sicily, and much of Central Italy; the linguistic consequences and the influence of such a stratum on Latin and neo-Latin, (which grew from it) are very important. The Oscan inscriptions are concentrated in Campania (Pompei, Capua, Cuma, Nola, Abella), in the territory of the Frentani (Vasto in Abruzzo), in Samnium (Agnone, Pietrabbondante) in Apulia and Lucania (Bantia-Banzi) added to recently by epigraphs from Rossano del Vaglio – in Bruttium (Vibo Valentia) and at Messina (inscriptions of the Mamertini), to which we can now add a new Sicilian 'italicizing' text studied by Parlangèli (1964-5) – an inscription on stone inserted in the town wall of Mendolito, containing Italic elements like *touto* = 'civitas'.

Coins have numerous inscriptions with place-names and, alongside Oscan, there are 'Sabelline' or 'Minor Italic' inscriptions, of which the most important is the bronze from Rapino (on the edge of Frentani country) already using the Latin alphabet. The language of the Volsci (e. g. in the Tabula Veliterna, from Velletri) who lived South of Rome, seems closer to Umbrian. According to Devoto (1974: 59), the inscriptions called 'Southern Picenian' (Pisani 1964: 225-32, 1959: 75-92) are in a sort of archaic Umbrian, that is nothing like the Northern Picenian, found on the Stele of Novilara, which remains largely enigmatic (cf. Camporeale-Giacomelli 1959); Durante (1963) tried to pick out Greek elements in a prevalently pre-Indo-European context; Ribezzo's (1938) interpretation of what he calls this 'Etruscan-Picenian' text is not very successful.

Our knowledge of Umbrian, we repeat, is based on the *Tabulae Iguvinae* at first in a local alphabet, and later in the Latin alphabet.

9. Among the Italic phonetic traits that affect the Romance dialects, via substratum influence, the ones that have most plausibly been put forward are.
   1. assimilation *nd* > *nn* and *mb* > *mm* (cf. Oscan *upsannam* = Latin *operandam* or Umbrian *umen* < **omben, *ongwen* = Latin *unguen*);

2. the frequent appearance of intervocalic -*f*- (usually continuing IE -*dh*-, -*bh*-, where Latin has -*d*- or -*b*-);
3. the tendency to close *o* to *u* and *e* to *i*;
4. rhotacism of *d* to *r*, with a special pronunciation (in local graphies a symbol corresponding to Latin *rs* is used).
5. the voicing of voiceless consonants after continuants (e.g. Umbrian *iuenga* = Latin *iuvenca*; Umbrian *ander* = Latin *inter*).

The influence of Oscan in Latin inscriptions has been examined by Pisani (1954), and by Moltoni (1954), who is concerned especially with inscriptions in Campania and *Latium adiectum* (Regio I). He picks out numerous examples of *ē* > *i* or *ō* > *u*, of *i* for *e* before *r* (*Valirius*, *Vinirius*), of syncope, of anaptysis and also of *nd* > *nn* (*Verecunnus*), features that are found in Southern Italian dialects. Pisani stresses uses of precocious palatalization (ascribed to Oscan influence) in Latin inscriptions from the same region (especially near Naples): for example, *gj* > *zz*, *dj* > *jj*, *pl* > *pj*, *fl* > *fj*, *gl* > *gj* and *tj* > *z*. In general, whereas Latin is conservative in its treatment of clusters with *j* (unlike Greek), the other ancient Italian languages (Osco-Umbrian, Messapian, Venetic) offer clear examples of features found later in Vulgar Latin (cf. Pellegrini 1954: 419-25).

One well-founded feature is the presence of intervocalic -*f*- in a number of Latin and Romance words, attributed to Osco-Umbrian interference especially by Ascoli as early as 1886 and universally accepted by scholars. The other features are more controversial – they appear in various parts of Romania, more frequently in South-Central Italy, excluding Tuscany, where it is difficult to distinguish, for instance, the typical Italic assimilation, mentioned above, from analogous evolutions in Italian dialects, attested sporadically in regional Latin.

Leaving aside the Latin words that had already adopted Italic -*f*-, there are numerous cases in which the neo-Latin languages and dialects presuppose original forms that have been borrowed from Italic or have undergone Italic influence. A list of 'Italicisms' in the Romance languages has been drawn up by Alessio (1936 and, especially, 1971), where 'pseudo-Italicisms' are also discussed. Well-known examples include *bufalus* (for *bubalus*) – attested in Venantius Fortunatus – which survives as It. *bùfalo*, Prov. *brufol, brufo*, Cat. *brufol*, Span. *búbalo, búfalo*, Ptg. *bufaro*, while *bubalus* gives Rum. *bour;* also well known is *būfo, -ōnis* (glosses) for *būbo*, 'little owl' and '*rana terrestris nimiae magnitudinis* (Serv. ad Verg. g. I, 184)', whence Span. *bubo,* Ptg. *bufo,* Rum. *bufa* Old It. *bufone* 'toad' (14th c.) while north Calabrian has *bufa* 'eagle owl'. Isidore (*Or.* xx, 19, 15) mentions *scofina* (for *scobina*) whence It. *scuffina, scoffina* 'flat file, rasp, (used by tinkers)', Span. *escofina* 'id'; Nonius (531, 2) notes *sifilare* (for *sibilare*), 'to whistle, hiss', whence Fr. *siffler,* Prov. *siflar,* Span. *chiflar,* and (from a *sufilare*) It. *zufolare.* Alongside *bubulcus* we have *bufulcus* > It. *bifolco* and *cuficulum* for *cubiculum* (from *cubare*) 'bed-room', which gives Abruzzi *cufecchjë* 'den, grotto'. Alessio (1971) also picks out some attested or reconstructed Italicisms with reflexes in Southern Italian dialects; e. g. *cafo, -onis* from IE *scabh-* (Lat. *scabo* 'scurvy, mangy' Gk. *skápheus* 'peasant') which gives S. It. *cafonë, cafuni,* 'villein, peasant', now found also in Italian (*cafone* 'peasant, boor'). He also attributes to the Italic (Oscan) strand *lipida* for *liquida* (*aqua*) – similar to the Lat. *quis* : O-U *pis* correspondence – continued in Calabrian *lípida,* Lecce *lípida* 'drop, drip, small quantity'. From an Oscan variant *ustium* for *ostium* 'gate, door' come the Romance forms It. *uscio,* Fr. *huis,* Span. *uzo* and analogously, from *bistia* with *i* for *bestia,* we have It. *biscia* 'snake', O Fr. *bisse* (mod. *biche*) 'hind' (Meyer-Lübke 1920: 179-80; cf. also Devoto 1930 and Felice 1962).

As for the *nd* > *nn* assimilation (e. g. *quando* > *kuanno*) and *mb* > *mm* (*plumbu* > Roman *piommo*) the substratum hypothesis is examined in detail by Jungemann (1955: 244-72), who comes to a relatively negative conclusion. Assimilatory processes of this sort (he includes *nk* > *ng, rt* > *rd* etc.) could be due to the frequent relaxation of occlusivity after sonants. For South-Central Italy it seems to me that we cannot exclude the possibility of continuity of the Osco-Umbrian articulation, through regional Latin to present-day dialects: the Latin inscriptions from Pompei show clear traces of this and if examples are absent from vulgar texts, this is to be explained by the influence of the *scripta.* Although it seems correct to take into consideration the wide diffusion of such changes in different Romance areas, and in particular in Ibero-Romance and Gascon, we are not convinced of the absence of Italic interference in South-Central Italy, which was so impregnated with an Osco-Umbrian regional Latin. The arguments of many Italian scholars especially Merlo (cf. Merlo 1933: 10-11) and the polemic between Merlo (1954: 7-13) and Heinimann (1953: 302-317); cf. also Pisani (1970) give support to the hypothesis advanced originally by

Ascoli (1882: 113), even though it may not be valid for Ibero-Romance and Gascon.

10. The area of expansion of the Etruscan population – whose origins still remain obscure – was fairly vast and not limited to modern Tuscany, but included a good part of Western Umbria, and Northern Latium right up to the gates of Rome (the rôle played by Etruscans in Rome during the monarchy by the Tarquin dynasty (Etr. *Tarχna*) is well known). The large corpus of Etruscan linguistic documents (more than 10 000 inscriptions) is published in the *CII* and then in the *CIE* (in course of publication). As appears from the Pallottino 1954 anthology (*TLE*), they are concentrated in the towns of Caere, Tarquinia, Volsinii, Vulci, Volterra, Chiusi, Perugia, Cortona, Arezzo, Fiesole (near Florence) and in Southern regions, Capua and Nola, while the major centres of Northern Italy are Adria and Spina.

To Etruscan can be attributed some words found already in Latin among which *populus* 'people', *par* 'equal', *subulo* 'piper', *hister* 'actor', *verna* 'slave born in the master's house', *favis(s)ae* 'temple ditch', *mantis(s)a* 'supplement, bonus', *spurius* 'bastard' (lit. 'belonging to the town' – Etr. *spur* 'city'), *persona* from Etruscan *persu* < Gk. *prōsopon* 'mask'; similarly other Greek words entered Latin through Etruscan e. g. *groma* 'instrument for measuring fields' < Gk. *gnômon* via Etr. *cruma*, or *sporta* < Gk. *spírida:* note also Etr. *utuste* < *Odysseus* (Devoto 1944: 78-9, Simone 1968-70).

11. For the Romance linguist it is more interesting to pick out the few words, used principally in Tuscany and not attested generally in Latin, that can be traced back to Etruscan. Such are the plant-names investigated especially by Bertoldi (1936) and Alessio (1937), among which e. g. *gìgaro* 'Arum italicum', which in its Late Latin form *gigarus* is attributed to the Etruscans by Pseudo-Dioscorides. Also notable is It. *mucchio* from regional Latin *mutulus* 'Cistus, rock-rose', which corresponds to Calabrian *múnduci*, *mutaca* and Sardinian *mudégu* is from Etruscan *mútuka*, according to Hubschmid (1950a). To the question of Etruscan lexical relics Rohlfs (1969b) has also made a contribution, although he is usually hostile to substratum hypotheses (in the realm of phonetics). He starts from Alessio's list of plant-names of probable Etrusco-Mediterranean origin and illustrates with the name *rhadia*,

radia 'Smilax aspera', which became *raźa, raǧa* 'spiny thicket' (note the name of the fish *razza* 'ray, skate'). Obviously, the Tuscan place-names of apparent Etruscan origin are numerous: Pieri (1928), basing his hypothesis on particular suffixes, has suggested that a whole range of Italian place-names are Etruscan (but the lack of ancient documentation makes his deductions untrustworthy). Less uncertain are the introductory chapters on this topic in Pieri 1898, 1919 (the posthumous Pieri 1969 is more careless).

A much debated question, which remains open, is whether Etruscan has left an imprint on Tuscan phonology. In general, it is recognized that Etruscan had no effect on the evolution of local Latin to neo-Latin, of which Merlo (1927) says that Tuscan (afterwards Italian) "which is heard today in the extreme North-Eastern part of what was ancient Etruria, is nothing other than the felicitous graft, on to the fine Etruscan trunk, of a pure Latin, untouched by Umbrian, Oscan or Sabelline influences". Still sub judice, – given the different opinions – is the problem of the origin of the 'gorgia toscana', the typically Tuscan aspiration and spirantization (with its centre in Florence) of intervocalic occlusives: thus $k > kh$, [h]; $t > th$, [θ] and $p > ph$, [φ]. Nissen (1883: 1, 494) cautiously suggested a possible connection of gorgia with the oscillation in Etruscan texts between surds and aspirates. Merlo (1927) has been the most convinced advocate of Etruscan influence for certain features in Tuscan dialects; others include Battisti (1930), and more recently Castellani (1961), who made a meticulous study of the operation and the spread of each change. He points out that there are two types of 'gorgia' – the spirantization of intervocalic voiceless occlusives characteristic, to a greater or less degree, of much of Tuscany, and an overall aspirating pronunciation, found in popular Florentine. The former is determined by the environment, while the latter is emphatic and is the true continuance of Etruscan aspiration, which is attested in all environments. Pulgram (1958: 340-1) and Devoto (1972: 87) are not, on the whole, opposed to the Etruscan hypothesis, but Rohlfs has been consistently sceptical (1930, 1971). In my opinion his rejection of an early dating of attestations, based on the graphy *ch* or *h*, is invalid, as are the Geissendörfer's (1964) deductions from similar graphies in Lucchese documents. Giannelli (1973), in a study of the geographical distribution of spirantization, does not seem on the whole favourable to the Etruscan hypothesis. Hall (1949) is frankly hostile and favours a structuralist explanation. What is certain is that Florence with its outskirts is at the centre of the phenomenon, that it has bit by bit spread to a wide area including eight Tuscan provinces (excluding Massa-Carrara) and that velars were affected before dentals and labials. Opponents of the theory usually advance historical arguments, especially that of the late appearance of the phenomenon in Tuscany, where there is no sure evidence before the fifteenth or sixteenth centuries. The interpretation of graphies in medieval documents as representing aspirate pronunciation has been quite rightly contested (in fact *h* and *ch* represent [k]). Moreover, in Etruscan inscriptions surds are sometimes attested alongside aspirates in identical words, so that we cannot be certain about their true pronunciation. Often aspirates are found in interconsonantal position (*tarcnai/tarχnai*) whereas in Tuscan it is limited to intervocalic position. Weinrich (1958: 105-143) and especially Contini (1961: 263-28) favour a structuralist interpretation. According to the latter, gorgia should be considered as a 'restorative therapy' counteracting the voicing of surds under Southern influence, in intervocalic and even initial position (Contini cites *gattivo* for *cattivo*, *guscino* for *cuscino*, *gosto* for *costo* in Tuscan documents; by combatting lenition (it never did succeed!) Tuscan demonstrates its solidarity with the South-Central Italian type.

12. In Southern Italy the Messapic language is attested by some inscriptions and glosses; this language was certainly in contact with the Balkan region, and is considered as an Italic branch of Illyrian (cf. Parlangèli 1960: 13-16). In the past the designation 'Illyrian' has been abused, as the area covered by the people of this ethnos was limited, according to recent scholarship (cf. Kronasser 1965). The Messapic documents – about 300 texts, some quite long, but known mainly only through copies – are scattered through Apulia and especially in Salento where the pre-Roman texts may be properly ascribed to authentic Messapic (other documents are more properly ascribed to the Peucetii and in the North, in the Foglia province, to the Dauni), which fits in with the historico-linguistic notion of Iapigi (Devoto 1974: 66). The inscriptions, now available in anthologies (besides *PID* 1934, cf. Ribezzo's *Corpus inscriptiorum Messapicarum* in the *Rivista Indo-greco-italica* 6-19 (1922-35)), are examined by Parlangèli (1960), O. Haas (1962),

and Simone (1962, 1964); they are written in an alphabet of Greco-Tarantine origin and can be classified by their calligraphy into archaic, classic, later and final (spanning five centuries, V-I B. C. cf. Parlangèli 1960: 25). The Messapic stratum, of Illyrian origin, probably overlaid (according to Devoto 1974: 67) a broader general 'proto-Latin', perhaps from the eighth century on. The interpretation of the Messapic texts is uncertain, and no less difficult than for Etruscan. Alessio (1962) surveys our knowledge of the texts, based on glosses as well as inscriptions. That the language is Indo-European is beyond doubt, but there are numerous words and forms that lend themselves to divergent interpretations by specialists: let us cite only *daranθoa* (found several times), which O. Haas relates to Greek *gerousía* 'senate' from **geront-ia* (not a nonsensical hypothesis) but Alessio (1962b: 330) thinks it is the Messapic name for *Táras, -antos* 'Taranto', cf. Ligurian *Darant, -asia*.

There are some dialectal Salentine relics which could be Messapic in origin, according to Rohlfs (1958) and Alessio (1962b: 322-8); e. g. Salentine *ariddu*, N. Calabrian *arzella* 'wild garlic' from a Mess. *ardu* (cf. Gk. *skódron*, Albanian *hardhë* 'garlic' from **skorda*). In the Messapic glosses we find *bréndon = élaphon* 'deer' (Hes.) and *bréntion* 'deer's head' (Strab.) with which the name *Brindisi – Brundusium* is often linked (Alessio sees *brent-* 'deer' as a Mediterranean relic). *Baris, Bárioi* – i. e. 'Bari' – comes from *baris, bauria = hē oikía* 'house', *bourio = oíkēma* 'dwelling-place' (Hes.), certainly Messapic words. Up to now, no one has related phonetic features of Salentine dialects to Messapic substratum. It is possible, though, that the greater purity of Salentine, compared with North Central Apulian dialects, is due to the lack of interference between Messapic and Latin (given the dissimilarity between the languages) and the less important influence of Italic which did not stretch as far as the end of the Apulian peninsula.

13. The problems concerning substratum in Sicily are more complex, especially since the discovery of new inscriptions, even though these are pretty fragmentary (Devoto 1974: 374-5). It is usually thought that in Sicily, alongside pre-Indo-European Sicanian (*Sicani*, Gk. *Síkanoi*), related to archaic Ligurian, there was a presumably proto-Latin Siculian. The language of the *Siculi, Síkeloi,* perhaps related to Latin, is attested in few inscriptions but especially in glosses that show definite

affinities with Latin. Their authenticity has been challenged by Campanile (1969), who suggests that some so-called Siculian words are really Greek loanwords. Interpretation of the inscriptions (especially the longest on the *guttis* of Centuripe-Centorbi) is doubtful (cf. Durante 1961, 1964-5). Pisani (1964: 302) concludes his survey thus: "as can be seen, there is little or nothing in these glosses that points to a special affinity between Latin and Siculian".

Piccitto (1950, 1959) has attempted, inconclusively, to show that the difference between Eastern and Western Sicilian dialects, with or without metaphonic diphthongization, can be ascribed to the difference between Siculian and Sicanian substrata: the absence of metaphony in Tuscan would be due to Etruscan substratum. The postulated relationship between pre-Indo-European Sicanian and Ligurian is lent some support from toponomastics, especially by the triad of place-names *Segesta/Sestri*, *Erice* (< *Eryx*)/*Lerici* (near La Spezia), and *Entella* (cf. Contessa Entellina) which is identical with the name of a Ligurian river.

We have already referred to a probable influx of Italici into Sicily (besides the Mamertini) (Parlangèli 1964-5). There is still uncertainty, though, about the linguistic character of numerous graffiti from Segesta, attributed to the Elimi, which Ambrosini (1968, 1970a, 1970b) sees as part of an autonomous linguistic tradition linked with Asia Minor, while Lejeune (1970) distinguishes between 'proto-Elimi' (the prehistoric Asiatics of Segesta) and the 'Elimi' (the 'Italiots' of Segesta in historic times). Any deductions from texts which remain so obscure can only be mere conjecture.

The change *-ll-* to cacuminal *-ḍḍ-* and the like (paralleled, for instance, in Gascon where *bella* > *bero* but *bellu* > *bet* via *beḍḍu) is amply attested in Italy and elsewhere. It is typical of Sicily, Sardinia, Corsica and much of Southern Italy: e. g. Calabria *vaḍḍi* = *valle*, Salentine *capiḍḍu* = *capello*. Millardet (1933) studied this feature using experimental phonetic techniques: he suggests that a 'Libyan' or 'Mediterranean' substratum might be responsible, pointing out that similar phenomena are found in India. The change *tr-* > cacuminal *ṭr* in Sicilian and Southern Italy, (Rohlfs 1966: 371) has similarly been ascribed to 'Mediterranean' substratum influence. Jungemann (1955: 160-189) summarizes the discussion: Rohlfs (1929) seemed in favour of a substratum explanation of cacuminal articulation, but later (1966:

1: 328), while not excluding it, mentions other languages with similar features. Cacuminal pronunciation of -*ll*- is found in Apuania, Lunigiana and Garfagnana (N. Tuscany) where Bottiglioni (1956: 21) discerns Ligurian influence, a hypothesis rejected by Merlo (1957). In fact, there is little firm basis for the hypothesis. Certainly the Southern cacuminals have nothing to do with the acoustically similar coronals of some Alpine dialects (Comelico, Zoldano in the province of Belluno): the phonetic description in Tagliavini (1949/1972: 130) is inexact (for the cacuminals in Abruzzi dialects cf. Giovanni 1970). Politzer (1954a) suggests that the change -*ll*- to -*ḍḍ*- is due to structural pressures in systems where there is a series of voiced geminate occlusives but not of voiced geminate continuants: -*ll*- being isolated as a non-obstruent geminate is drawn into the occlusive series.

14. In Sardinia, the Carthaginian substratum has left rare traces in the lexicon: cf. Wagner (1950: 137-152) who cites mainly plant-names (e. g. Campidanian *tsikkiria* 'dill', and Dioscorides' Punic glosses *sik-kiria = ánethos* 'dill' or *tsípirri* 'rosemary'), Wagner (1957) and Bertoldi (1950: 19-48).

The influence of the pre-Roman, probably even pre-Indo-European, paleo-Sardinian, identified by place-names and in dialectal words, is more important: cf. Terracini (1957), Wagner (1950), Bertoldi (1953), Serra (1960), Hubschmid (1953) and Pisani (1959a: 79-95) who points out that the true nature of the language of the *Ilienses* remains a mystery. Here too mainly place-names and plant-names are cited, and often related to Basque or Libyan-Berber. We note, for example, *anuri* 'hornbeam' (Ostrya carpinifolia) (compare Basque *aurri*), *éni* 'Taxus baccata', *kostike* 'maple'. Hubschmid derives Campidanian *bega* 'fertile plain' from Iberian **ibai* (cf. Basque *ibai* 'river') whence Spanish *vega*, Ptg. *veiga*, and compares Sardinian *buda* 'Typha latifolia', with Berber *tabuda* 'Typha augustifolia', Corsican *buda* 'Butomus umbellata' and Latin *buda* a kind of 'reed', of Libyan origin, etc. Typical Sardinian pastoral terms are also frequently cited – e. g. *sakkayo* 'yearling lamb', *ospile* 'sheep-fold' (compare Basque *ospel*), *idile* 'bog'.

As for phonetic features, we should mention the loss of initial *f*- characteristic of Barbagia, which, together with the use of interdentals, and the prosthesis of *a*- before *r*-, recalls analogous phenomena found throughout the Pyrenean area and thence in Spanish and Gascon. Also typical of some Sardinian dialects (Barbagia) is the glottal stop used instead of some consonants and which is not unlike similar treatments in Hamito-Semitic languages: e. g. *suˀasu* = *kasu, sa vaˀa* = *savakkạ*. For a survey of possible substratal features cf. Wagner 1950: 309-19.

15. Especially relevant to the linguistic history of Romance and Vulgar Latin, Greek substratum is supplemented by a medieval Byzantine parastratum, especially in Southern Italy and Sicily, where possibly the Doric of Magna Graecia survived in isolated pockets, flanked by a well-attested Byzantine element. But most Southern Italian Greek elements filtered in through Latin, as is shown by Battisti (1927), Pagliaro (1934), Alessio (1934, 1938-44), Parlangèli (1953). The debate about the origin of the few Greek-speaking oases in Southern Italy (in Calabria (Bova) and Salento) remains open; their language seems to contain, alongside the usual Byzantine and Modern Greek elements, some archaisms – like *dàfina* 'bay-laurel' < *dāphnē,* Calabrian *nasida,* Messina *nasita* 'strip of cultivated land near a river' < Doric *nāsída* (= *nēsída* from *nēsís* 'islet'), and the word for 'earthworm', Cosentine *kaséntaru, kaćéntaru,* Catania *kaséntaru,* Reggio *kaséntulu, kasentula,* Sicilian *kaséntaru* from *gâs énteron* for *gês-,* a word originating in Magna Graecia and then accepted into the regional Latin of Southern Italy. Rohlfs (1924, 1933, 1950 and 1972: 195-202, 231-245, 246-259, 260-272) is the principal proponent of the idea of continuity in these regions.

The Romans found difficulty in these Greek-speaking areas, unlike elsewhere, in imposing their language, especially where the Greek element was well-rooted (as witnessed by the numerous Greek inscriptions). Indeed, from the earliest times, they borrowed Hellenisms from the South – like *purpura, massa, machina, mālus* (with *ā* betraying a Doric origin in the last three). Cultural and religious loan-words swelled the number: we make no mention here of the Hellenisms, especially in syntax, that penetrated Vulgar Latin.

As for Southern Italian dialects we should note some syntactical interferences, as well as lexical borrowings. One typical feature is the substitution of the conjunction Gk. *na, ina,* neo-Latin *mu* (<MODO) for infinitival constructions (as in the Balkan languages: Calabria *vogghiu mu mangii* = *voglio mangiare* 'I want to eat', *vorría mu sacciu* = *vorrei sapere* 'I'd like to know'). The infinitival construction is not in

popular use in those regions where Greek influence was strongest – in the South of the peninsula and in the North-East of Sicily (Messina). In Calabria the line of greatest Greek influence runs through Nicastro, Catanzaro and Crotone, while in the Salentine peninsula the line runs from Taranto to Ostuni (Rohlfs 1969: iii, § 717). Rohlfs (1964; = a revised edition of Rohlfs 1930a) lists Greek elements in Southern Italian dialects – e. g. *kádos* 'bucket' > Sic. *katu*, Calabrian *katu*, Salentine *katu*, Tarantan *keœ*, Neapolitan, Abruzzi *kadə* 'bucket'; *keramídion* 'small tile' > Catanzaro *ćeramidi*, Cosentan *ćeramile* 'tile', Sicilian *ćaramiti* 'potsherd'; *lákkos* 'ditch, water-hole' > Calabrian *lakku, lakkə* Salentine *lakku*, Lucanian *lakkə* 'well'. Rohlfs (1971a) compares a series of Italo-Greek proverbs with similar texts in marginal Greek-speaking areas.

16. In Northern Italian the substratum languages include pre-Indo-European Ligurian and then Lepontine, which is partly its continuator with some contribution from ancient Celtic immigration (6th century B. C.?). Lejeune (1971c: 121) envisages two Celtic waves in the region with Lugano as epicentre – first that of the Lepontii or Lepontini, and then that of the Gauls from the 4th century B. C. The superposing of the two waves gave rise it seems to a symbiosis of various closely related races (a hypothesis which incidentally is not novel). Gaulish penetrated into North-West Italy in successive waves; Rhaetic, prevalently non-Indo-European in character, covered the East-Central Alpine region and Venetic and Gallo-Carnic was used in the East. The inscriptions in these languages, inadequately edited, are assembled in *PID* 1933-34 and a comprehensive anthology is to be found in Pisani 1964. For Lepontine important studies include Tibiletti Bruno (1966, 1968), Prosdocimi (1967) and Lejeune (1971c). For Venetic we have the bulky work (corpus and studies) of Pellegrini – Prosdocimi (1967), successively updated by Prosdocimi (1969a, 1972a, 1972b), Lejeune (1971a) and Pellegrini (1974b), which examines important new documentation that has come to light since 1967, including lengthy texts from Lozzo Atestino and from Cartura-Pernumia to the South of Padua.

Recently Lejeune (1972b) has discussed how appropriate the designation 'Lepontine' is for these inscriptions (also called Celto-Ligurian) and for features found in North-Western Italian place-names (cf.

Devoto 1962 a for examples like *Aquae Bormidae, Bormida*, where IE *$g^w h$-* > *b-*, *Genua*, and place-names from the *Sententia Minuciorum* (or Polcevera Table) of 117 B. C. (*CIL* I. 2 584) and the *Tabula alimentaria* of Veleia (*CIL* XI, 1147). Without doubt, Lepontine documents which are found round the Lombard Lakes with their centre in Lugano in the Tessin (Lejeune suggests it should be called 'Luganian') cannot be considered wholly Gaulish, even though they have features in common with Gaulish. Prosdocimi's term 'para-Gaulish' is convenient. It extended South as far as the province of Pavia and the inscription from Prestino (Como), which is undoubtedly Indo-European, is of relevance here.

17. More important for the study of substrata in Upper Italy are the Gauls who left few inscriptions – essentially three, from Briona (Novara), from Zignago (La Spezia) and from Todi (bilingual texts mentioned above, coming from Cisalpine Gaul).

Merlo (1938, 1942) discerned Ligurian substratum influence not only in toponymy but also in the phonology of North-Western Padana and Provence – e. g. the substitution of *-r-* for *-l-* as in *ala* > *ára*, Genovese *áa* – but there is little evidence to support this idea. Probably it is better to follow Martinet (1955: 257-96) in seeking diachronic phonological causes. The simplification of geminate occlusives and voicing of intervocalic surds in Western Romania (*t/tt* > *d/t*) was not initially accompanied by a similar reduction of the geminate – single opposition for continuants: eventually N. W. Italy opted for simplification of *ll* and rhotacism of *l* (> *r*). Similarly in Spanish *ll* became palatal, while *l* remained intact (cf. Jungemann 1955: 163-80 and Pellegrini 1974, who shows that the typical Venetian 'evanescent' *l* is probably the result of earlier (12th century) palatalization).

18. The definition of 'Rhaetic' is more uncertain (cf. Pellegrini 1973 a: 21-2 and Prosdocimi 1971). The inscriptions are concentrated in Trentino-Alto Adige, with offshoots as far as Verona, Vicenza, Padua. According to ancient historians the Rhaeti were satellites of the Etruscans but the texts show no close connection between the languages (except e. g. for the verb *tinaχe, ϑinaχe, trinaχe* which recalls Etruscan *zinace*, the well-known preterite of the votive formula). However it is certain that so far no word or linguistic feature has been found in

Rhaetic to explain characteristics of Ladin (or 'Rhaeto-Romance', an unfortunate denomination due to Gartner (1883) that has gained currency): cf. Schürr 1963, and Pellegrini (1972a) who shows that the pre-Romance Rhaetic has nothing to do with 'Rhaeto-Romance', a term disliked also by Ascoli (1880: 567) and especially by Salvioni and Battisti. The few pre-Roman words in Ladin are best labelled 'Alpine' (cf. Hubschmid 1951 for "Alpenwörter", preceded by Jud 1911 and Stampa (1937) who assembled a large quantity of pre-Roman lexical material from the Western Ladin and the Lombardy Alps; also Alessio 1952).

19. Better known, though still in fragmentary fashion, is the language of the Venetii (Venetic), which covered much of North-East Italy. The inscriptions (about 300 of them) are found mainly at Este (ancient Ateste), Padua, Vicenza, Treviso, Oderzo, Cadore and in the Transalpine part of Carinthia and the valley of the Isonzo. Venetic seems clearly to be an independent Indo-European language, with features in common with Latin; we need hardly repeat that any suggestion of affinity between the Venetii and the Illyrii is pure imagination (cf. Hubschmid's earlier works, and Pisani 1959a: 25 n. 1).

If we leave aside toponomastics, it is difficult to find any Venetic influence in present-day Venetan dialects, even in vocabulary. It is mere conjecture to attribute to Venetic substratum the interdentals widely used in rustic Venetan (Pellegrini 1949, Màfera 1957). Words of supposedly Venetic origin require more study: for instance, *ceva* = 'small (of a cow)' in the gloss of *Colum. RR* VI, 245, attributed to the Venetii, cannot be the origin of Venetan *čèo* (as Cocchia thought) which probably is related to Gk. *kúos* = *fetus* (< IE *k'ew*, IEW 592-3) and is continued in Venetian *civéto, tsivéta*, 'young calf', *civeta* 'heifer' (cf. Alessio 1974).

The Carnii or Gallo-Carnii of Friulia have left no inscriptions, except on coins, probably consisting of names of tribal chieftains (Pellegrini 1972a: 285) – e.g. *ADNAMAT, ECCAIO, ATTA, NEMET, COPPO, COGESTILIO* (similar coins have been found in the Pannonian-Danubian region). It is odd that there are no traces of 'Celtic' influence in the phonology of the Friulian region. There is virtually no evidence of the presence of Rhaetii in this region in ancient times.

20. Celtic substratum is of great importance in the differentiation of the Romance languages, because of its wide distribution in Western Romania, and because it had far-reaching effects on Latin pronunciation.

The 'diaspora' of Celtic peoples from Central Europe dates back to the seventh century B. C. or earlier. They penetrated far: note the *Galati* of Asia Minor, *Galicia* in Spain, and the sack of Rome under Brennus, in 390 B. C. As far as Romania is concerned, the substratum was formed by the Gauls in France and Northern Italy, as well as in part of the Iberian peninsula (the Celtiberi and other Celtic peoples in successive waves occupied the West, especially).

When the Romans conquered Gaul in the first century B. C., it had already been Celtic for centuries; similarly Cisalpina (Northern Italy), with perhaps the exception of Southern Veneto and some Alpine valleys, was at the time of Romanisation (2nd-1st centuries B. C.) populated by Celtic tribes who spoke forms of Gaulish. The Celts had penetrated to Ancona on the Adriatic: note the place-name *Senigallia* which recalls its founding by the Gallic-Senones. There are few Gaulish documents of any importance: the hundred or so that exist do not provide sufficient linguistic information for grammatical reconstruction (especially of verb forms). One of the most interesting is the calendar from Coligny which gives us names of months, but little else. For textual studies cf. Dottin (1920), Whatmough (1970) and Lejeune (1955, 1968-9, 1974) who, with great philological skill and acumen, has examined especially Spanish inscriptions – like that of Botorrita (Saragossa) – and the few Northern Italian inscriptions.

In spite of the scarcity of inscriptions (to which should be added the brief fifth century 'Vienna' glossary and the Gaulish formulae inserted in the *De medicamentis liber* of Marcellus Empiricus of Bordeaux), we have some knowledge of the language thanks to the numerous place-names of obviously Gaulish character (and transparent etymology), to some glosses and, especially, to the rich seam of Gaulish words laid down in the Romance languages. According to Devoto (1972: 96) the Latin imported into Gaul was impregnated with local elements, in spite of the influence of schools. Gallo-Latin was prestigious enough to be imitated elsewhere, especially in Northern Italy (Devoto 1974: 69).

21. Among the phonological features often ascribed to Gaulish substratal influence (but today frequently contested) we mention:-

a. the change $\bar{u}$ > [y], which occurs in much of the territory populated by the Gauls;

b. the development of tonic free *a* to *e* which is characteristic of French, but is found also in the Alps and also further south – even in Romagna, the Northern Marches and part of Umbria (Ascoli 1882: 105).

c. vowel nasalization, found especially in French, and the change of final -*n* to velar [ŋ] in Northern Italy and Ladin.

d. the palatalization of -CT- to -*it*- (*FACTU* > *fait* etc., whence Spanish *hecho*).

e. voicing of intervocalic surds which traditionally (Wartburg 1950) is supposed to stop at the Spezia-Rimini line dividing East from West Romania.

f. strong stress on tonic syllables, causing weakening and even loss of atonic syllables, and hence shortening of words.

In recent years the primary role of substratum in the occurrence of these features has been disputed. Best documented is the -CT- > *it* change which is found in all Western Romania (*FACTU* > Fr. *fait*, Ptg. *feito*, Gascon *heyt, het*, Sp. *hecho*, N. Italian (not Venetan) *fait, fač*). An intermediate phase would be -χ*t*- which is attested on Gallo-Latin inscriptions and coins (*Luχterios* alongside *Lucterius, Atectorix/Ateχtorix, Divicta/Diviχta* and the *Rectugenus/Reχtugenus/Reitugenus* quoted by Thurneysen). Welsh also has *lait* < *LACTE* and Old Welsh *noid*, Irish *nocht* < *NOCTE* (French *nuit*). Ascoli (1881-82: 1-71) was convinced that substratum influence was responsible, and many other scholars agree: that the feature is found sporadically elsewhere does not invalidate the hypothesis. A parallel development is seen in -*ks*- > -χ*s*- > *is*: *LAXĀRE* > Fr. *laisser, AXE* > Fr. *ais*.

22. More reservations have been expressed about the substratum explanation for the change $\bar{u}$ > [y] not only by traditional historical grammarians (e. g. Meyer-Lübke 1913, 1920), but especially more recently by structuralists (Lausberg 1947, Haudricourt – Juilland 1949: 100-113, Martinet 1955: 52-3). In fact the comparatively recent appearance of [y] from $\bar{u}$ in French, can be seen as a reduction of a *Mehrlautphoneme ui*, determined by a displacement of back vowels.

When [o] in blocked syllables became [u], *ou* – e. g. *RŬPTA* > *route* [rutə] – the functional load of [u] < Latin *ū* and Romance [o] became excessive, so that *ū* acquired a palatalizing articulation, and the resulting vowel acted as a catalyst for the formation of the parallel phoneme /ø/. The confusion of [o] and [u], leaving a case vide, was favoured by the narrow possibility of differentiation of velar vowels which are articulated within a restricted space at the back of the mouth; the shape of the oral cavity conditions asymmetry between front and back vowels. The change *a* > *e* can also be explained in structural terms, due to a lengthening *a* > *aa* in tonic free syllables, with subsequent differentiation to *ae* and closing to *e:* the evolution can also be conditioned by a juxtaposed palatal (cf. Haudricourt – Juilland 1949: 38-49). The tonic free-syllable lengthening affects other vowels and results in descending diphthongs: *e* > *ei, o* > *ou:* not only in French but also in some Italian dialects. The lengthening could be connected with a strengthening of tonic stress, which may be due to Celtic substratum.

West Romance 'lenition' of intervocalic surds could also be due to Celtic influence (here we leave aside the isolated examples found elsewhere, including those found among the Pompeian inscriptions). Mohl (1899: 273) plausibly suggested that Gaul was the centre of diffusion of this phenomenon: Meyer-Lübke (1920: § 239) contested the idea but others (including notably Tovar 1949: 126-8, 1952) have espoused it. The voicing of intervocalic single surds instigated the simplification of geminates *pp, tt, kk,* while the single/double opposition was maintained for continuants (cf. Pellegrini 1974a).

23. The vigesimal number system of French, of which a trace remains in *quatre-vingts* (also Old Fr. *treis-vinz* 'sixty', *sis-vinz* '120') could be an echo from Celtic (even though such a system is used elsewhere). The lexical contribution of Celtic to Gallo-Italian and Gallo-Roman dialects, especially French, is more certain. Bolelli (1941-1942) drew up a list of Celtic words in *REW* (see Appendix I for reference), and Campanile (1965) surveyed the contacts between the Celts and the Romans. Some Celtic words were borrowed into Latin and are used throughout Romania: e. g. *camisia* > Fr. *chemise*, It. *camicia*, Sp. *camisa*, Rum. *cămăşă; braca -ae* > Fr. *braies*, Sp. Ptg. *bragas*, It. *brache*, Rum. *brace; camminus* 'road' > Fr. *chemin*, It. *cammino*, Sp. *camino* etc. Latin borrowed numerous Celtic words for vehicles: *carrus, car-*

pentum (from which was formed Fr. *charpentier,* Prov. *carpentier),* *petorritum* 'four-wheeled cart'. In similar semantic spheres we can mention also *paraveredus* > Fr. *palefroi,* Prov. *palafré,* It. *palafreno;* *ambactus* 'servant' whence *ambactia* > Prov. *ambaisada* (It. *ambasciata,* Fr. *ambassade).* More numerous are those Gaulish words unattested in Latin, that may have survived from pre-Roman times, whose reconstruction is based on modern Celtic languages: examples cited by Bolelli (1941-2) include **barros* (*REW* 967) 'thicket' > Venice, Trieste *baro,* Parma, Ferrara *ber,* Bologna *bär,* Friulian *bar, baráts;* **crama* (*REW* 2294) 'cream' > Piedmont, Como *krama,* Engadine *grama* etc.

24. There can be no doubt that the way French stands out from the other Western Romance tongues (Vidos 1956: 363) is largely due to the intensity of its Celtic substratum, compared with lateral areas like Iberia and Veneto, where the phonetic identity of the word was better preserved: compare Fr. *eau* [o] < *A(C)QUA* with Sp. *agua,* Old Venetan *aigua, aiva* etc.

25. In the Iberian peninsula we can distinguish three types of substratum that have undoubtedly contributed to the formation and characterization of Ibero-Romance dialects (including Gascon). Here we have the unusual situation that one of the substratum languages has survived till today in the Western Pyrenees – Basque, or *Euskera* to use the Basque term which is properly an adverb. Especially in the nineteenth century, until Humboldt's study appeared (1821), it was believed that Basque could be identified with ancient Iberian, attested in a hundred or so undeciphered inscriptions (edited by Hübner in 1893), now supplemented by new discoveries. In fact now archaeologists distinguish Basque (or Aquitaine) from Iberian as being two different cultures (Bosch-Gimpera 1944). After Gómez Morena (1949) deciphered the Iberian documents and Tovar (1951) had classified them and examined the lexicon, it was obvious that Basque could bring no clarification of Iberian monuments (of which the longest is at Alcoy, near Alicante, inscribed on lead, with 342 letters in Greek script).

Some scholars (Trombetti 1925b, Lafon 1952, Bouda 1949, 1952, Tovar 1950) see a connection between Basque (originating with Aquitaine peoples, *Vascones, Cantabri, Astures*) and Caucasian languages. Iberian, on the other hand, seems almost certainly related to

North African languages, brought especially into the East and South of the peninsula. One of the Southern cities, populated by Iberians, was *Iliberris* > *Elvira* (Granada) which can be linked with Basque *iri, ili* 'town' and *berris* 'new' – thus 'Newtown, Neapolis'; it is notable that a cognate name *Elne* < *Iliberris* occurs in the East Pyrenees. Iberian and Basque represent two pre-Indo-European substrata that came from opposite directions and met (and influenced each other) on Spanish territory. These were overlaid, especially in the West and Centre by a layer of Indo-European Celtiberici: their presence is well-documented by ancient historians, archaeology and inscriptions which contain traces of Indo-European declensions (Tovar 1961: 76-90, Lejeune 1955). In phonology, Celtiberian seems to preserve the labiovelar k^w (enclitic -*que* = Latin -*que*), and the diphthongs (*Seiuoreigis, Luguei, Calaitos,* but *eu* tends to *ou*, except in *Teuta*). Noteworthy is a genitive of ŏ-stems in -*i* as in Latin and Venetic. As for declension, I cite the ŏ-stem paradigm: nom. sg. *Turos, Calaitos, tiaso* (< -*os*), *uiros;* gen. *Tiatunei;* dat. *Tigino, Turou, ueisui* (sometimes -*oi* > *ui*); acc. *ueramom;* loc. *Eniorose, Tiatunei;* neuter nom-acc. *Meduainum;* plural nom. *Araticos;* gen. *Abilicom, Abulocum, Contebacom;* dat. *Aregoraticubos.*

For the pre-Roman languages of Iberia, and especially the distribution of characteristic place- and person-names cf. Untermann (1961, with maps) and Schmoll (1959).

26. Leaving aside toponomastics where it is easy to pick out the strata, we can attribute to pre-Roman languages some words in Ibero-Romance and in Gascon (sometimes also in Occitan). We note especially pre-Latin suffixes, like -*rro, -rra, -rdo, -rda:* Sp. *izquierdo* 'left hand' corresponds exactly to Basque *esquer*, Gascon *esquerr*, while *guijarro* 'pebble', *pizarra* 'slate', *becerro* 'calf', *perro* 'dog', *zorro, zorra* 'fox' (cp. Basque *zugar* 'astute'), *cazurro* 'taciturn', *cachorro* 'puppy', *cama* 'bed' (attested in Isidore 8.6) are all pre-Latin words. Other such words are found also in the Alpine region and even in Sardinia.

27. Jungemann (1955) amply covers the Ibero-Romance phonological features that have been attributed to substrata, and gives a full bibliography.

The feature that is most characteristic of Spanish and Gascon is the change *f-* > *h-* with loss of aspiration in many regions (it is kept in the

South): e. g. *FARINA* > Sp. *harina*, Gasc. *hario*, *FACTU* > Sp. *hecho*, Gasc. *het* etc. It is notable that Spanish has kept *f-* before *ue* and *r* (*fuego* < *FOCU*, *frigidu* < *FRIGIDU*) but that Gascon has *h* (Old Bearnese *hoec*, Gasc. *ret*). The Spanish development is typically Castilian and appears to have spread from Old Castile where it is attested early (before 863 *Ortiço*, 973 *Hortiço* < *FORTICIUS*, a personal name); it is possible that *f-* was also used for [h]. Although the feature is found elsewhere (Sardinia, Calabria, Upper Veneto) the Spanish and Gascon development must be related to Basque where *f-* was originally unknown, so that Latin loan-words with this critical phoneme show *b-*, *p-* or *ph-:* e. g. *FAGUS* > *bago, pago, hago; FESTA* > *besta, phesta; FICUS* > *biku, piko, iko*, alongside more recent *fiko* etc. It is probable that Latin *f-* was pronounced in Basque as [Φ] which was unstable and opened to [h]. Jungemann (1955: 372-416) surveys the interminable controversy on this question, showing that even structuralists are not opposed to the substratum hypothesis (cf. Martinet 1955: 304-11). The collapse of *b* and *u* into [β], and the more general fusion of voiced occlusives with fricatives are other features that can be linked with Basque (where there are no labio-dentals): it is assumed that the features radiated out from the Pyrenean region. Perhaps Basque also had a hand in the conservation of intervocalic Latin occlusives in Bearnese and Upper Aragonese (cf. Elcock 1938): Basque *bake, pake* < *PACEM; cleto* < *CLETA* show that the Latin surds were identified with their Basque counterparts and that in this region, perhaps bilingual for a long period, 'Celtic lenition' was resisted.

28. A more controversial hypothesis (e. g. Menéndez Pidal [1929] 1950) is that which ascribes to Italic (Oscan) substratum the assimilation of *mb* > *m(m)* and *nd* > *n(n)* (and also voicing of the type *nk* > *ng*, *rt* > *rd* etc.): e. g. *LUMBU* > Sp. *lomo, MANDARE* > Cat. *manar, ROTUNDU* > Gasc. *arduno, CAMBA* > Gasc. *camo;* several scholars (esp. Rohlfs 1930: 43-44) dispute it, on the grounds that these are widespread phenomena and that there is no sure evidence of Oscan settlement in Iberia (the place-name *Huesca* may be pre-Roman). In any case, Ibero-Latin *-nn-* would have to have had two different pronuciations, as Latin *-NN-* > Sp. *ñ* [ɲ] and Latin *-ND-* (> *nn*) > Sp. *n*.

The prosthesis of *a* before *r-* in Gascon (e. g. *RAMU* > *arram, ROTA* > *arrode*) is attributable to Basque (Luchaire 1877: 28-31,

Menéndez Pidal 1950: § 40,1) as this language has no word-initial *r-* or *rr-*. But it could also be a consequence of the reinforcement of initial *r-* in face of the lenition process, when the single/double opposition was maintained for continuants and the geminate type was used in initial position (cf. *LŪNA* > Cat. *lluna*).

29. In the Balkan peninsula, Latin overlaid various ancient languages which are poorly attested. The process of Romanisation has on the other hand been carefully studied and regional Latin features are well-known (Mihăescu 1960, 1971-1974, Stati 1967).

Illyrian is assumed to have covered a wide area (cf. Pellegrini – Prosdocimi 1967, 2: 247-248) and probably is continued by modern Albanian, though this is thought by some to be Thracian, or at least Thraco-Illyrian (cf. Tagliavini 1949/1972: 188 and, for Albanian, Çabej 1964). Little is known of the Dacian language, except through a few glosses, place and personal names and apparent lexical survivals in Rumanian, which correspond to Albanian or widespread Balkan words.

30. To substratum can be attributed some of those features shared by the widely differing Balkan languages (Romance, Slavonic, Indo-European): cf. Sandfeld (1930), Rosetti (1962), Çabej (1967), for the postulated Balkan linguistic areal grouping.

Perhaps it is no accident that -*MN*- becomes -*un*- in Dalmatian, Rumanian and Latin inscriptions of the Liburnican region: cf. *Volsouna* (*CIL* III, 3149) etc. which corresponds to the common personal name *Voltjomnos* in Venetic inscriptions (Pellegrini – Prosdocimi 1967, 2: 207-16), with -*tj*- > -*s*-, and -*mn* > -*un*- as in Dalmatian *duvna* < *DOM(I)NA, kelauna, kelomna* < *COLOMNA,* (Serbo-Croat *kelovna*). To these examples we can add the Bosnian place-name *Dúvno* corresponding to *oppidum Delminium, Delminum* (through *Dulmensis, Dumnensis*), as well as Rumanian *daună* < *DAMNA, scaun* < *SCAMNU* (Pellegrini 1957: 53-58, 1969: 252-254). The fact that there are examples of the same feature elsewhere in Romania (Gasc. *dauna* < *DOM(I)NA,* and in some Norican place names (Prosdocimi 1969 c: 279-292)) does not invalidate the hypothesis.

31. Mayer (1957-9) contributes a description of what was traditionally called 'Balkan Illyrian'; Krahe's studies (esp. 1955) are now largely

out-moded, and in later works he substitutes for 'Illyrian', the designation 'Ancient European' (rather an all-embracing term!). To Detschew (1957) we owe a comprehensive commentary on evidence about Thracian – a language which almost certainly had some rôle in the formation of the Rumanian language. We note some lexical correspondences between Albanian and Rumanian which almost surely date back to pre-Roman times: e. g. Rum. *mal* 'bank, shore' / Albanian *mal* 'hill', which is echoed in *Dacia Maluensis*, the name used in Marcus Aurelius's time, which gave way to *Dacia Ripensis* under Aurelianus, and in Balkan names *Maluntum, Malontum* etc. (Rosetti 1960: 57). Rosetti (1962: 106-121) quotes examples of Rumanian-Albanian parallels which suggest pre-Roman origin, whether Thracian, Dacian or Illyrian e. g. Rum. *abur*, Alb. *avull* 'steam, vapour'; Rum. *brîu*, Alb. *brez* 'belt'; Rum. *catun* 'village', Alb. *katunt* 'town, village'; Rum. *jumătate* Alb. *gjymës* 'half'; Rum. *scrum* 'ash', Alb. *shkrumb* 'incinerated'.

To the Thraco-Dacian substratum can be attributed some Rumanian phonological features, especially as concerns vowel phonemes that are similar to Albanian, and occasionally Bulgarian and Macedonian, vowel phonemes. It is notable that Latin atonic *a* (and occasionally tonic *a* also) is reduced to *ă* in Rumanian (*CASA* > *casă*) and *ë* in Albanian *BUCCA* > *bukë* 'bread' (for other correspondences cf. Sandfeld 1930).

Russu (1967) has assembled all the Thraco-Dacian forms and attempted to interpret them in the light of Indo-European: he bases his study on place- and person-names and his attempt is, however praiseworthy, of debatable scientific validity. Reichenkron (1966) has also tried to reconstruct the Dacian language – mainly its lexical features – using Rumanian words of doubtful origin: Pisani (1967a) criticizes his methodology and his excessive faith in reconstruction.

Some characteristic Rumanian suffixes are almost certainly of Thraco-Dacian origin – especially adjectival -*esc* e. g. *bărbătesc* 'virile' *omenesc* 'human', *românesc* 'Rumanian' (cf. Rosetti 1962: 61-3). Some place-names – like *Bucureşti* (from *Bucur*) and *Balaneşti* (from *Balanul*) – were originally formed with pre-Roman suffixes on tribal names. We note the abundance of Balkan personal names with the suffix -*iscus: Ciniscus, Coriscus, Etriscus, Laiscus* and also *thraciscus* 'Thracian' in Iordanes (*Get.* XV, 86).

For Dacian we now have, besides some obscure glosses, an inscription with two personal names (*Decebalus* and *Scorilo*) and the word *per*, probably the appellative 'son' (cf. Daicoviciu 1955: 57, 200-202; Russu 1967: 115; Rosetti 1962: 60; Bonfante 1973: 33-36). An inscription in Greek letters on a gold ring found in Ezerovo (Southern Bulgaria) is now ascribed to Thracian and is of doubtful interpretation (Russu 1967: 39-43).

32. We can also discern, in the Romance dialects, vestiges of even older substrata: they are to be found mainly in place-names and are usually labelled 'pre-Indo-European' or 'Mediterranean'. Already in Latin some lexical elements appear to be pre-Indo-European relics: e. g. *lepus* 'hare', *camox* 'chamois', plant-names like *ilex, larix,* and Gallo-Roman **melix* (Fr. *melèze*), *ficus, lilium, vinum, rosa;* even *urbs* is of non-Indo-European origin (cf. Sumerian-Anatolian *uru*, Basque *uri* 'town'). Notable contributions to 'Mediterranean' studies have been made by Italian scholars, including Ribezzo (1921), Trombetti (1925) – whose conjectures are disputable –, Bertoldi (1931), Battisti (1959), Devoto (1967b: 11-62). Alessio, especially, has made numerous studies of pre-Indo-European relics in Classical languages and Romance dialects (summarized in Alessio 1955). Hubschmid (1949, 1950, 1951, 1953, 1954, 1959, 1960a) is concerned mainly with Basque and the Alpine and Sardinian regions and, although conjectural, his works are a model of rich documentation and meticulous analysis. Hubschmid 1965 is an important survey of the results of comparison between Basque and 'Mediterranean' words, examining etymologies advanced by, especially, Bertoldi and Alessio. He concludes that out of 60 Basque words that have been confronted with those of Mediterranean languages, 42 should be excluded from consideration, seven are doubtful, and thirteen are almost certainly relevant: these include Basque *muga* 'boundary' / Alpine dialects *mugo* 'Pinus Mugo'; Basque *tutur* 'crest, tuft of feathers' / (pre)Latin *tutulus,* Tuscan *tùtolo* 'maize cob'; Basque *kosko* 'acorn cup' / Calabrian (Catanzaro) *cuoscu* 'wall-germander', Cosenta 'turkey-oak'; Basque *pentoka* 'little hill', / Mediterranean *penta* 'ravine, cliff', (in place-names in Corsica, Liguria, S. Italy); Basque *gorri* 'red' / Romagnol *gor,* Istrian *guoro* 'reddish' (of wine); Basque *iturri* 'source, fountain' / OProv. *toron* 'id.' (also found in river names – e. g. *Duero*).

Alessio (1962a) believes some Mediterranean phonological features (leaving aside *-ll-* > *ḍḍ* mentioned above) can be attributed to pre-Indo-European substrata. Among these are the change of nasal or liquid +*j* clusters to nasal or liquid geminates, found in the Aegean and Tyrrenean areas; thus in Sicilian and S. Italian forms *rj* > *rr*, *lj* > *ll*, *mj* > *mm* – e. g. Calabrian *ficarra* < *FĪCUS + ARIA* 'fig', Sicilian and Calabrian *pitarra* 'earthenware jar' < **PITHARIUM* (Gk. *pithārion*) and Sicilian *fillu*, *palla* from *FILIUS, PALEA*.

1.2 Historical phonology and grammar

JULIUS PURCZINSKY

Romance historical phonology

The movement and evolution of research in Romance historical phonology appears to be at a turning-point. It is rare that evaluations of trends in scholarship can be fitted into neat chronological divisions, but we seem to be at one of those critical moments when a whole series of approaches is about to be abandoned, or laid aside temporarily, in the interest of a new line of attack. The school of Structuralism, in its various forms, has so far been the major force in the twentieth century and its dominance has been evident within our discipline. Now this school has already given way, in synchronic studies, to the newer, Chomskyan ideology and it is only a matter of time before the attempt to apply the linguistics of Chomsky to historical questions becomes widespread. We are thus at a happy moment in which some evaluation of past work may be attempted.

The field of Romance linguistics is paradoxical in its wealth and poverty. We are almost overwhelmed by documentation both in the form of primary sources and in the immense accumulation of work done by our predecessors in the field. At the same time, there are vast and critical lacunae (cf. Malkiel 1964). Nowhere is this contradiction more crucial than in the study of historical phonology. We are further vexed with ongoing controversy and a kind of partisanship that does not die with its first proponents, but extends across generations without mitigation of bitterness. Nationalism and ethnic feeling are not removed from our disputes, for some of the Romance languages are the mother tongues of great nations and the bearers of historic cultures, while the study of those very cultures and languages is a vested interest in countries which have historically threatened the importance, or even the existence, of the major Romance-speaking countries. For some, the study of sound change may be invested with spiritual significance, a battle against the forces of materialism, while, for others, the invocation of cultural values is obscurantism. Romance scholarship has rarely taken the lead in creating schools of thought, but has imported into our discipline controversies that have originated outside. These are some of the standing difficulties which challenge us: to make sense of the rich data that confronts us, to fill up the gaps in our tradition with reliable evidence, to find or create strategies for attacking old problems, and to form coherent and probable pictures of earlier conditions that have passed away.

Many will say that the present century has not been productive of great advances toward these goals. Certainly, the great work of the nineteenth century overshadows the less bulky achievements of the twentieth. Yet much solid work has been done and, whether or not the theoretical principles motivating much of it survive, there will remain a core of data assembled and a sum of intellectual formulations that can be used. The great mass of work has been structuralist. That approach has dominated our thinking for the greater part of the century and no analysis of work in historical phonology can ignore the output of the Structuralists as a group. With them, we may classify those whose investigations have seemed to support the conclusions of the Structuralist School, although future researchers may employ these results very differently. Next, may be mentioned those theories which rely upon stratum arguments, insofar as they have dealt with questions of historical phonology. The attempt to establish a relative chronology of sound changes, an undertaking which goes back to the Neo-Grammarians, often in conjunction with the sifting of documentary evidence, has occupied a certain number of scholars, whose research is worthy of consideration and may well prove to be more solid than achievements which depend heavily upon changing linguistic theories. A recent interest in comparative reconstruction, another inheritance from the Neo-Grammarians, also merits discussion, if only as an alternative that has not yet been exhausted. A major figure, Malkiel, who has remained outside the mainstream, will be placed towards the end of the discussion. It also seems good to include a brief notice of certain manuals, which contain at least a set of usable data for the student and represent a practical, if not innovative, contribution to the field. And, last of all,

the few attempts that have so far been made to introduce the Chomskyan techniques into Romance historical phonology will be considered.

Haudricourt's and Juilland's basic monograph (1949) has com-
manded the greatest notice and has won a place as a theoretical model
and a classic of Structuralism. The entire dynamics of Gallo-Romance
and much else is explained through the alleged pressures of successive
systems. Writing under Martinet's influence, Haudricourt and Juilland
disavowed any attempt to discredit historical phonology or traditional
methods. Indeed, they specifically invoked external factors, class
dialects, and stratum influences. (The late preservation of *au* was attributed by them to the more cultured Latin of that area, while the reten-
tion of /k/ before /a/ by Franco-Provençal was claimed to have been
due to a Germanic adstratum.) Yet the importance given to systemic
pressures by these scholars was so great as to render external influences
largely superfluous and their closed structuralist picture of events has
been widely rejected. They bring the chronology of the loss of
phonemic quantity into relation with the monophthongization of Classical Latin diphthongs and thereby seek to explain the different
Romance systems that result. Sardinian preserves a five vowel system
because it lost quantity very early before *ae* and *au* simplified. Rumanian preserved quantity until after *ae* had become a long open *e,* thus
creating an assymetrical system: diphthongization of open *e* was necessary to restore symmetry. French, Central and North Italian, and Spanish lost quantity before *au* became open *o,* but after short *u* became
close *o.* The diphthongizations of other French vowels are precautions
taken to preserve contrasts menaced by danger of loss of distinctions of
aperture after simplification of geminates. *f* became bilabial in Spain
because of the correlation that had developed between fricative and
plosive in series of three homorganic phonemes. Clusters ending in yod
were phonetically liable to rapid palatalization, but *ti* and *ki* were
slowed down in Western Romance long enough to merge with the
reflexes of *k* before *e* and *i.* The fronting of *k* before *a* was
phonemicized, wherever *kua* became *ka,* or *kau* became *k'o,* but Germanic influence prevented this phonemicization in some areas. There is
much that is credible, even probable, in this brilliant analysis. Some of
the factors they invoke, the loss of vowel quantity throughout the
Empire and the simplification of geminates in Western Romance, are
major structural changes, whatever may have occasioned them, and,

once they had occurred, must have entailed major readjustments in the language system, but that the monophthongizations of *ae* and *au*, at different times, could have had such sweeping consequences as Haudricourt and Juilland ascribe to them has not been acceptable to more than a small minority of rather doctrinaire structuralists. Hence, the unique position of their work: admired by all, but only partly believed in. With sufficient step-by-step evidence (which is mostly lacking in our field) and with recourse to external forces to explain the alleged developments – and they have made use of such explanations – this brilliant theoretical work may yet turn out to contain much that is true.

Martinet, while blessing Haudricourt and Juilland's work with an introduction, has largely preferred to explain Romance developments with stratum arguments. Nevertheless, his postulates obviously underlie the work of these former students of his, and Martinet himself has not hesitated to employ structural explanations alone where they seemed to him necessary and sufficient. Thus, having attributed Western Romance lenition to Celtic influence, he then (Martinet 1955) sought to explain the phenomena within Celtic in terms of the structure of those dialects – since no earlier external factor could be discovered. What makes Martinet's explanation highly convincing is his exposition of the phonological structure, attributed to Celtic, as opposed to that of Latin, which lacked the conditions necessary to trigger the development of phonemic lenition. His characteristic diachronic explanation of French *r* (Martinet 1962), in terms of strong-weak opposition and his earlier (Martinet 1949) study of the Gallo-Romance affricate *ts* have gained less notice.

Alarcos Llorach, strongly influenced by Martinet, has traced the development of the Spanish sound system (1950, 1951a) and of the vowels (1960, 1962) and consonants (1957) of Catalan. Although willing to accept substratum theories, he has offered structural explanations for developments in such a way as to make external influences frequently seem unnecessary. In what has often been judged the best structuralist history of the Spanish sound system, Alarcos Llorach (1950), mingled the theories of other structuralists in a cohesive and frequently convincing account. For the vocalism he has relied on Haudricourt and Juilland (1949), but has worked into his survey the insights of Lüdtke (1956) and Weinrich (1958). Rejecting Menéndez Pidal's (1926: 122-127) ill-founded argument that the diphthongs from open *e* and *o* could never have been other than rising diphthongs, Alarcos Llorach (1950) insisted on their character as phonematic units until the time when the elements of what were phonetically diphthongs had become identifiable with other phonemes of the system. Until that stage, they were phonemically "long vowels of changing aperture" (Alarcos Llorach 1951a: 16). For his analysis of Spanish consonant history, he again followed and combined the theories of other structuralists: Haudricourt and Juilland (1949) and Martinet (1952) for sonorization, spirantization, and the simplification of geminates; Martinet (1951) for Basque influence in the passage of *f* to *h*, which did not involve the loss or change of a distinctive feature on the part of *f*, as evidenced by Arabic loanwords in the Middle Ages (Alarcos Llorach, 1951b); for the loss of distinctive voice in the sibilants, Martinet (1951) again. The subsequent differentiation of place of articulation among the voiceless sibilants, Alarcos Llorach explained, for the first time (1950: 275), through the structuralist scheme of four sets of phonemes (labial, dental, palatal, and velar) with three items in each set (voiced, voiceless stop, and voiceless fricative), an insight which was original with him. Although widely regarded as the definitive structuralist history of Ibero-Romance phonology, Alarcos Llorach's work suffers from the same diminished power to convince as do so many largely structuralist explanations. The structural formulations are impressive and clear, the explicative recounting of language history is effectual, but the reader is sometimes left with the feeling that structural changes have been described, not accounted for.

    Among other scholars of similar wide influence, Lausberg, Lüdtke, and Weinrich certainly qualify as structuralist investigators into historical phonology. Their structuralism is independent of Martinet's and has shared with it in the far-reaching triumph of this way of understanding language change. For Lausberg (1947a), the major factor in the disruption of the Latin vowel system was the replacement of quantitative by qualitative distinctions and later developments flow from it. For Lüdtke (1956), it was the development of phonemic accent which disrupted the system of vowel quantity and led to further changes, while according to Weinrich (1958), the interplay of differing syllable types (checked vs. free in syllables having long vowels) has led to loss of phonemic quantity and to further developments in the vowel and consonant systems. (As pointed out by Spence (1965), these explanations are not all mutually exclusive and an analysis which gives some weight to each of them does greater justice to the historical evidence.) Major consonant changes have been attributed to similar factors: Weinrich (1958) explained intervocalic voicing as due to simplification of voiceless geminates which imperiled the opposition between them and simple stops, while Lausberg (1956-1962) regarded the spirantization of intervocalic Latin /b/ as the starting-point for the change of voiceless consonants to voiced and of stops to fricatives in intervocalic position, a view partly shared by Weinrich (1958). To explain diphthongization of open *e* and *o,* these three structuralists have all leaned upon Schürr's hypothesis (1936), with its dependence upon analogical extension of diphthongs arising from metaphony. Thus, Lausberg (1947a) believed that falling diphthongs developed because of the strain created by umlaut phenomena and (1948) that these changes along with subsequent loss of phonological quantity spread from Italy. Furthermore, according to Lausberg (1951, 1968), diphthongization before following high sounds occurred first and only later spread to stressed vowels with nonphonemic length. Similar views were expressed by Weinrich (1958) and Lüdtke (1956). All three seemed to hold that vowel systems of four or five degrees of aperture are not viable and must therefore give place to other systems: thus, Weinrich (1958) and Lüdtke (1956), and, with reference to the fronting of /u/ in Gallo-Romance, Lausberg (1947a). There is also the characteristic concern with the study of the successive vowel systems of Romance dialects, to which these scholars have contributed very solid work: Lausberg (1948, 1951), Lüdtke (1956), and Weinrich (1958). So also, Lausberg (1947b) tried to evaluate the shifting position of Spanish in relation to Italian and (1947c) attempted a structural history of the French vowels. Weinrich (1958) devoted much effort to the study of individual vowel systems of dialects, seeing in degemination a turning-point in the history of Western Romance, while Lüdtke (1956) attributed Spanish and Portuguese developments to the supposed imposition of the seven-vowel system upon areas that had previously had a five-vowel system. Earlier, Lüdtke (1953) had compared, in an otherwise synchronic study, the lengthened vowels of some Portuguese dialects to the Latin ones at its critical period, both being 'languages in transition'. And, of course, it was Lausberg's (1939) account of a five-vowel 'archaic' dialect in Southern Italy that, more than anything else, focused the attention of scholars on the role of competing vowel systems in Romance history and thus determined one of the major preoccupations of the structuralist era.

The next major figure, Schürr, is not really a Structuralist, but has been included here, because his one basic theory, richly argued in numerous publications, is closely related to the questions just mentioned and because there is no other convenient classification. He formulated and, then, defended and elaborated a theory to explain the diphthongization of open *e* and *o,* which he attributed to the influence of umlaut (metaphony) and the action of analogy (1936). (This hypothesis, brilliantly rethought by Schürr, goes back to one of two theories, the Later Theory, of the nineteenth century scholar, Schuchardt, whose Earlier Theory has furnished the basic Neo-Grammarian explanation, which, in turn, was for long the predominant theory within Romance historical linguistics; cf. Purczinsky 1970.) Schürr postulated several stages of development in the area north of Rome. Among these were: "1. conditioned diphthongization; 2. analogical transfer of diphthongs to free and checked syllables, that is, 'spontaneous' diphthongization; 3. restoration of open *e* and *o*" (1936: 284). In a series of articles, Schürr extended this theory to other Romance languages: to French (1940), Rumanian (1949, 1953a), Ibero-Romance (1951), Catalan (1953b), Spanish (1964), and, again, Italian (1965). Although the 1936 formulation is considered definitive, earlier statements go back to 1926 and 1933. In its mature form, Schürr's theory emphasizes the contrast between rising and falling diphthongs and between conditioned diphthongization (before high sounds) and so-called spontaneous diphthongization. 'Spontaneous' diphthongization is associated with length and occurs only in stressed free syllables; it produces falling diphthongs. Conditioned diphthongization appears in stressed checked as well as stressed free syllables before following high sounds and produces rising diphthongs. (Schürr has usually talked as if falling diphthongs could never shift their stress, although he believes in the reverse: the shift of rising to falling diphthongs (Schürr 1951), due to the analogy of triphthongs, which, Schürr believed, had sometimes retracted the stress to the first of their three elements.) Rising diphthongs due to metaphony of the stressed vowel before a following high sound coexist with falling diphthongs due to lengthening of stressed free vowels in Central and Southern Italy.

Where diphthongs are lacking (Portuguese, Sardinian), Schürr assumes remonophthongization before the emergence of the literary languages. In Tuscany and Northern France, the diphthongs that arose from metaphony could not be tolerated in checked syllables because of their length; therefore, they could be used to characterize the free syllable. (But is not the onglide of a rising diphthong part of the syllabic onset and, therefore, not a reason to consider the rising diphthong long?) As a consequence of the development of a quantitative distinction between stressed free syllables (long) and checked syllables (short), which Schürr (1969: 36) believed had spread from a central area in the North of France through Northern, but not Central Italy, a contrast of phonological length (vocalic differentiation) arose in vowels other than open *e* and *o*, which were then brought into conformity with the other vowels by the action of analogy. The principal agency of analogical extension of the diphthongs was the word-initial vowel with hiatus-breaking onglide in postvocalic environments (Schürr 1969). Rumanian and Spanish have extended diphthongization through all stressed syllables (Schürr 1936, 1964). Schürr (1938) denied that the loss of phonemic vowel quantity produced length in stressed free syllables, disregarding the testimony of the ancient grammarian Consentius, but without attempting to explain what Consentius really meant. In that way, he was able to separate the phenomena of diphthongization of open *e* and *o* in French from the similar results in Spanish. Diphthongization through metaphony is older than 'spontaneous' diphthongization, since it goes back to a period when final vowels were intact and hence is older than the effects of the strong stress accent (Schürr 1972). (But does not lengthening of stressed free syllables also imply intact final vowels?) The rising diphthongs due to metaphony are explained by Schürr through a phonetic explanation: because open *e* and *o* are inherently longer than other vowels, metaphony takes the form of an onglide (Schürr 1952). Curiously, Schürr (1970: 200) has denied that he ever said spontaneous diphthongization was due to analogical extension: it would appear that he was referring to the falling diphthongs resulting from vowels other than open *e* and *o*, never to the rising ones from open *e* and *o*, which he attributes entirely to metaphony with later analogical spread.

A number of scholars have attacked Schürr's theory as it relates to various languages. A basic challenge was delivered by Aebischer

(1944) who argued, on the basis of documentary evidence, that diphthongization is older at Lucca than in Central Italy. He pointed to
forms with diphthongization before final *a* (i. e. *buona*, the oldest
example dated 983, from Lucca), which he claimed were more frequent
than those with so-called conditioned diphthongization. In response to
Aebischer's (1944) evidence, Schürr (1956) seems to have modified his
explanation for Tuscany to say that diphthongization entered from the
northwest; earlier (1936), he had said from the south! D. Alonso
(1962) harshly handled Schürr's theory, claiming that Schürr had
invented whole series of changes for which there is no historical evidence. Castellani (1962a, 1962b) argued against its applicability to
Tuscan on the grounds of chronology, documentary evidence, and
geographical distribution. He holds that metaphony was never opera-
tive in Tuscany, citing, in particular the form *lei* (Castellani 1970). A
careful analysis of documents would seem to show that metaphony was
confined to Central and Southern Italy, while 'spontaneous' diphthongization is old in Tuscany and has spread beyond its boundaries at an
early date (Castellani 1952). Catalán and Galmés (1954) conducted a
point by point assault on Schürr's theory as it relates to Spain. While
many of their arguments are questionable, their rejection of the idea of
a sudden introduction of analogical diphthongization (Catalán –
Galmés 1954: 97-98), which reached its present boundaries at once, to
change them no more in seven centuries, is particularly impressive.
Foster (1968), in a rather Neo-Grammarian formulation, concluded
that Italian diphthongization of open *e* and *o* in stressed free syllables is
conservative and, therefore, old. Lerch (1940) came nearest to
attempting a general criticism of Schürr. He held that lengthening of
stressed free vowels was general throughout the Empire and produced
falling diphthongs which are not reflected in surviving documentation,
being written as single vowels except where anticipation of a following
high sound led to raising of the stressed element of the diphthong. (This
is, of course, basically a form of the Neo-Grammarian theory, traceable
ultimately to Schuchardt's Earlier Theory.) Meadows' (1948) study of
hiatus groups, without mentioning Schürr, offers some alternatives to
his theory of the development of triphthongs. Solano (1948), in what is
little more than a rehearsal of the historical reflexes, has, nevertheless,
offered some novel comments on Rumanian developments: his theory
involves opening of close *e* and *o* before following *a, e;* then, falling

diphthongs *ea, oa;* and, lastly, shift of stress to give the rising diphthongs of Rumanian.

Schürr has received support from Ernst (1970), who studied the evidence in Rome. Umlaut was native to the city, distinguishing the reflexes of third person plural forms in -*unt* from first person singulars in -*o*. Hilty (1969) attempted a combination of Schürr's theory with von Wartburg's (1936): The opposition of long vowel to short vowel (German influence) produced falling diphthongs from open *e* and *o*, which then merged, for economy's sake, with Schürr's umlaut diphthongs.

Another major figure whose influence has been very strong among Romance linguists is Malmberg, whose structuralism is of a pure and autonomous kind. He has consistently favored explanations based on the internal influences due to the delicate balance of systemic pressures in preference to any external explanation. Rarely have his theoretical arguments concerned themselves with individual problems of historical phonology, but at least one example can be found. Malmberg (1944) explained pairs of Old French forms which he regarded as doublets by means of a theory of differentiation (Meillet 1913). In Old French, close *o* became *ou*, then *eu*. At the stage *ou*, there was a tendency to fill the case vide, *u*, which had resulted from the fronting of original *u*. The similar diphthong *ǫu*, with open *ǫ*, tended towards *oi*, whence doublets of the type: *blou, bloi; pou, poi*. This rather simple example of structuralist analysis was challenged by Hasselrot (1944-1945) who preferred a more Neo-Grammarian explanation: *poi* is from *paucī*, the nominative plural. Hasselrot opposed the idea of a double development: The alternate verb endings of the types -*oe* and -*eve*, both from -*abam* etc., imperfect, are due to the effects of different preceding consonants of the verb stem. Malmberg (1971) returned to this problem, reasserting his belief in differentiation as a factor, pointing out Hasselrot's (1944-1945) confessed inability to account for *bloi*. To the Old French examples, he added, very tellingly, an exposition of the development of the Portuguese diphthong *ou* to *oi*, which he explained as an example of differentiation in the face of the peril of assimilation. Malmberg has generally rejected substratum theories, preferring available structural arguments: thus, almost uniquely among structuralists, he (Malmberg 1959a) rejected the Celtic substratum theory of Martinet (1952) calling recourse to a Celtic substratum "absurd, risky". A

Basque substratum is also set aside, as unneccessary (Malmberg 1961, 1963b). He has consistently opposed the application of substratum arguments to New World isoglosses (Malmberg 1950, 1961). The change of *f* to *h* in Castilian is explained by redundancy of the labial feature of Pre-Castilian *f* (Malmberg 1958, 1963b). The reduction of geminates is, for Malmberg (1959a), a consequence of a general tendency (in Romance) towards the opening of closed syllables. The key to Malmberg's opposition to most external causes lies in certain of his principles: a general explanation is preferable to a particular one; whenever there is a loss of distinctions or units, we should look for reduction at the periphery of the dialect (Malmberg 1959b). Where Malmberg has applied his theoretical subtlety and phonetic expertise to synchronic phonology the results are impressive; his attack on historical problems is much more modest. The relationships of Western Romance consonants are discussed in terms of strong-weak oppositions (Malmberg 1950, 1961) and specific Ibero-Romance developments (Malmberg 1958, 1962) are explained in terms of the series of three phonemes (voiced, voiceless stop, voiceless fricative) patterning which had been identified by Alarcos Llorach (1950). In a particularly clever argument, modern *yeísmo* is attributed to the lack of the distinctive feature stop-fricative in the voiced series. (But then why do some areas retain *ll*?) Malmberg (1971) sees the development of the Romance languages as the unfolding of tendencies inherent in earlier structure. Spanish and French (and even Italian) share a tendency to reduce the syllabic distension, but this tendency is stronger in French, (while in Italian, it is limited to the assimilation of syllable finals to give geminates). What has been said of other Structuralists is true of Malmberg's work: for all its brilliance, it does not quite convince. We are left wondering whether the structural causes were really responsible for their alleged results.

A number of less influential Structuralists must be mentioned. Badía Margarit (1962) followed Alarcos Llorach (1950) in his explanation of Spanish diphthongization and explained the reflex *ue* (instead of *uo*) as having greater sonority. Bustos Tovar (1960) argued that assimilation and dissimilation are the realizations at a particular time or place of general tendencies that exist at all times. Catalán has generally agreed with Martinet, giving structuralist explanations for Ibero-Romance palatalization of double *ll* and *nn* (1954) and for the evolution of the

Spanish sibilants (1957), but, like Martinet, inclining towards stratum explanations, where the known phonology makes them possible, and seeking to locate sound changes within the sociological context. Granda seems closer to Malmberg (1950, 1961), whose theory of a tendency to reduction of the syllable ending he follows (Granda 1966a), and whose aversion to New World substratum and preference for structural motivation within the Spanish sound system he shares (Granda 1966b, 1969). Guitarte (1955) has extended Alarcos Llorach's (1950) theory of series of three related phonemes to explain the unvoicing of the Buenos Aires reflex of yeísmo. Hall (1955) has outlined the vowel systems of a number of Romance synchronic and diachronic dialects, disentangling unrelated events that had been previously lumped together. His conclusion that typology should not be used to identify genetic relationships is convincing. Earlier, Hall (1942) had argued for ss as the normal reflex of ks in Central and Southern Italy. Haudricourt, as a prelude to his major undertaking with Juilland (1949), authored a number of papers offering Structuralist explanations for Old French developments: the vowel systems (Haudricourt 1946), the merger of en and an (Haudricourt 1947a), and the change of ei to oi (1947b). Manoliu (1963) reacted to Haudricourt and Juilland's (1949) reliance on monophthongization of au as a key factor in the evolution of Romance vocalism, preferring instead alternate explanations based on the tendency towards symmetry in vowel systems. O. Nandriş gave a Structuralist explanation for the survival of weak final vowels in Rumanian (1963a) and argued against pushing palatal and velar varieties of l back into Latin (1962). Politzer (1952) developed a structural theory to account for a large number of phenomena in Romance. The divergencies of structure depend upon the merger or failure to merge of the phonemes b and v. Politzer argued, convincingly, that medial b (from a Proto-Italic voiced fricative) was still fricative at the time of the Romanization of Sardinia and Southern Italy (areas of early merger) and that the fricatization of stressed stops in intervocalic position is due to the pattern of fricative intervocalic b. The special developments of double ll towards occlusive (cacuminal or palatal) pronunciation is to be considered one of the side-effects of merger of b and v in all positions (Politzer 1954a). Politzer (1953) has also considered the labial development of Latin qua and gua in Sardinian and Rumanian: the Rumanian and Sardinian treatments are not related. Romeo (1968) analyzed the development of Romance vowels in a way reminiscent of Haudricourt and Juilland, concluding that "two fundamental pressures interplay in the formation of diphthongs: (1) the degrees of aperture, and (2) the Classical Latin relic diphthong *au*" (1968: 108). In an earlier study of Rumanian diphthongization (Romeo 1963), he had anticipated these arguments while rejecting, correctly, the traditional telescoping of historical processes which he called the 'metachronic' interpretation. Rosetti (1955, 1965a) has given Structuralist analyses of the development of the Rumanian sound system. Sala (1963) attributed changes in Rumanian to a strong-weak opposition. In a manner that recalls Malmberg, Sala (1964) attributed the simplification of geminates in Rumanian to structural factors operating throughout Romance; but there has been no voicing of intervocalic phonemes because of the lack of a Celtic substratum in Rumanian. Spence (1965), after a searching critique of other structuralist theories decided that the changes which formed the Romance vowel systems cannot be explained by systemic pressures with totally predictable results, since they have led to different norms in different areas. He pointed to "one incontrovertible fact: that functional distinctions based on quantity were abandoned all over the Empire" (Spence 1965: 17). Vasiliu (1968a) sketched the diachronic phonology of Daco-Rumanian dialects in an excellent structural study.

The concern for explanations of (*satzphonetische*) phenomena that somehow go back to divergent developments at word-boundaries has occupied a number of Structuralists whose work can receive no more than brief mention here. Most of them have concerned themselves with the coexistence, for a time, of alternate reflexes (voiced and voiceless or fricative and stop) in initial positions and later generalization of one type, in most dialects: so Figge (1966), Hall (1964), and Leonard (1968); for voicing of initial *k* only, Guiter (1940-1945); for reinforcement of initial *l*, Rensch (1968); and for alternation in word-final position, Greive (1968). The treatment of final *s* has been studied by Hall (1962) and Politzer (1947, 1951b).

A great mass of historical and phonological work has contributed material that is at least useful to Structuralists. Alinei (1962) proposed an early assimilation of yod to produce geminates such as the *zz* of certain 'archaic' dialects of Italy. A. Alonso (1946) interpreted the reflexes of Ibero-Romance palatalized *k* in Arabic borrowings to show that the Mozarabic sound did not remain at the *č* stage. His discussions of *yeísmo* (A. Alonso 1951) and of *r* (A. Alonso 1954) provide data for the explanation of American Spanish phenomena within the inherited structural pattern. Alvar López (1953) has given us excellent data for Aragonese phonology, without taking theoretical positions. Avram (1965, 1968) has emphasized parallel reflexes in Rumanian and Portuguese and has refined a rule stating the effect of nasal consonants on vowel reflexes in Rumanian (1969). Doman (1969) concluded that velarization of *f* in American Spanish has not been influenced by the vestiges of Old Spanish *h*. Gamillscheg (1948) traced the development and described the phonology of a Rheto-Romance dialect in a way that favors the absence of dogma. Hart (1955) and Herculano de Carvalho (1962) interpreted the phonetic character of early Modern Portuguese unstressed *e* and *o*, in ways that Naro (1971b) has rejected. Joos (1952) offered structural and phonetic evidence to show that Old French /s/ was retroflex. Klausenburger (1970) has visualized and described the changing prosodic structure from Latin to present-day French. Lombard (1943) explained the double reflex of Latin *d* plus yod (Italian *raggio* versus *razzo*), as due to an early reaction against popular loss of *d*. Lüdtke (1953) described a kind of vowel lengthening due to stress in contemporary Portuguese, without really drawing any implications for historical diphthongization. Merlo (1948) sought to explain references of the grammarians Servius and Pompeius to a 'whistling' pronunciation, which has usually been interpreted as a reference to assibilation of *d* plus yod. Michel (1953) studied the sound *s* in Latin and Romance, not always in a linguistic way. Michelena (1968) argued against the presence of apical *s* in Latin, thus opposing Jungemann's 1953 view. G. Nandriş (1951) gave a somewhat Neo-Grammarian summary of the evolution and structure of Rumanian. Parlangèli (1960a) classified the vowel systems of Southern Italy with conclusions that differ from those of Rohlfs (1949-1954) and Lausberg (1939). Pei (1943) suggested that final *e* gave rise to a double reflex, *i* or *e* in Italian. Petrovici (1970–71) examined the ways in which Rumanian has dealt with hiatus; interestingly, a transitional glide represents the most frequent solution, but diphthongal pronunciation also occurs. Pfister (1960) traced the development of the group *ps*, in accordance with von Wartburg's (1936) subdivision into East and West Romania. Piccitto (1970) described the rise of a new conditioned rising diphthong in Caltanissetta, Sicily, *ua* from stressed *a* after a syllable with unstressed *u*. Politzer (1967) described the phonology of a Rheto-Romance dialect and then (1968) discussed the validity of predictions based on the diachronic data of his previous study. Révah (1958) traced the history of Portuguese pronunciation from the sixteenth century. Schmid (1956) studied the palatalization of *k* and *g* before *a* in Northern Italy and the shift of s̲ to š̲, the latter a North Italian feature that has lost its validity. A few Structuralists, within the realm of historical phonology, have developed the principles of the school beyond the usual analysis of symmetrical patterning and the filling of empty slots.

Four such scholars, Dorfman, Guiter, Mańczak, and Kiss, may well be discussed together. In all four of these, Structuralist thinking has been extended in a sophisticated, often mathematical, way. Dorfman (1968), starting from Martinet's view of correlation of distinctive features as a functional factor in the economy of diachronic phonology, has postulated a tendency toward phonemic paradigms that take the shape of a square, subject to the limitations inherent in the inertia and assymmetry of the speech organs. The core system consists of those phonemes which enter into major correlations (as distinct from certain structurally isolated phonemes or groups of phonemes) and it may be said to form a core-related square to the extent that there is a balance between numbers within two classes of distinctive features: those based on mode of articulation, which Dorfman calls the 'series', and those based on place of articulation, which he calls the 'orders'. When orders and series are about equal in number, a square is formed, which, if bulky enough, may form the core of the phonology of a language. Accepting the validity of external factors where verified, Dorfman asserts that phonological systems change in the direction of core-related squares, and applies this thesis to the evolution of the Latin consonant system through intervening stages to modern Spanish and French. It is hard to see how any Structuralist could refuse this logical working-out of the premises inherent in that school and structuralism must be vindicated or rejected on the basis of ultimate resolutions like Dorfman's. Employing somewhat arbitrary values, as he admits, Guiter (1966) tried to express the character of vowel systems in terms of the frequency of vowel types (front or back, high or low, rounded or unrounded). Each contrast provides an average, a figure which supposedly expresses the general tilt of the system. The figures for the individual Romance languages are then compared to values calculated by applying to the corresponding averages of Classical Latin specific figures corresponding to known diachronic changes. Although he disavows any historical implications, he has obviously noted the correspondence between his mathematically plotted positions and the known genetic relationships among the Romance languages. In what is only tangentially a historical study, Guiter (1969) seeks to establish that certain ratios remain the same in spite of language change: the frequency of usage, number of phonemes, and number of meanings words have are related and these relations retain the same form from one language to another. Thinking along similar lines, Mańczak has attempted to establish the importance of frequency in systemic change. It is essential to Mańczak's hypothesis that frequently used forms must change more than others, must be irregular, as in a set of examples taken from Old French and French (1962). Frequently used words should be shorter; there should be an inverse statistical relationship between length of words and frequency of use, as Mańczak tried to show for French and Spanish (1965). The Old French reflex of Latin short *o* is *ue* in stressed free syllables, except in certain frequently occurring words. The traditional explanation involves alternation of stressed and unstressed forms or so-called syntactic phonetics; instead, Mańczak (1968) proposes a frequency-based explanation: the diphthongal reflexes are due to rapid change in frequently used forms. In further studies, he has attempted to establish the principles governing the effects of frequency as evidenced by Romance developments (Mańczak 1969) and to apply these principles to phonemic change. Two poles govern change due to frequency: both very frequent and very rare phonemes change (Mańczak 1970). Kiss (1972) has applied a statistical test to a structural hypothesis: a tendency to generalize the syllabic type CV has operated in the evolution of Latin towards the Romance languages. Following the ideas of Herman (1970b), Kiss has great faith in the statistical method. Comparing passages from Caesar with others from Suetonius, he claims to have found a structural basis for the *isochronie* of Late Latin. The tendency towards open syllables, implicit in the slight preponderance of such syllables in Classical Latin, and the influence of the stress accent, as evidenced by syncope and by the statistical affinity of the Classical Latin accent for open syllables with long vowels, have alternated in their influence on the language structure. Simplification of implosive consonants has alternated with the creation of new consonant groups by syncope. Here again, we have an extension of Structuralist principles in a striking and innovative way.

Stratum theories have been relatively numerous. Most Structuralists have inclined towards them and the insufficiencies of many structural arguments have led scholars to seek external causes. Togeby's (1960) incisive criticism of internal evidence expresses the attitude of many who are less than dazzled by the circular reasoning and question begging of studies not grounded in history and look to stratum theories to account for the time and place of language change. The most widely accepted stratum arguments are those of von Wartburg and Martinet. Von Wartburg's (1936) theory of a Germanic superstratum influence in the form of strenghthening of stress accent, with diphthongization of stress-lengthened vowels as a result, has been challenged only by those with rival theories and has achieved the highest degree of acceptance of any stratum explanation: cf. Purczinsky 1964 for another attempt to identify Germanic superstratum influence as a fundamental factor in the development of French. Martinet's hypothesis (1952) of a Celtic substratum has also influenced a great many scholars: an opposition of strong-weak was introduced into the Latin consonant system in the Western Romance area, with resulting lenition (voicing or fricatization) of single intervocalic (i. e. weak) consonants. Martinet's (1950, 1951) adstratum theory which seeks to explain, through Basque influence, the change of *f* to *h* in Old Spanish and Gascon, as well as the merger of *b* and *v* and the unvoicing of sibilants in Early Modern Spanish, has generally been well received. The best criticism of stratum theories, in a constructive sense, belongs to Hall (1950a), who has laid down criteria for a credible substratum argument: (1)sufficient contact between languages must be proved for a period of bilingualism to have resulted; (2) the source language must actually have had the features which account for its influence; (3) the phenomena thus explained must be old enough to go back to the period of bilingualism. The theories of Martinet and von Wartburg satisfy these criteria, as do certain others. Jungemann's (1953) criticism of all the stratum theories for Ibero-Romance and Gascon has achieved great recognition because of the credibility of his judgments. Less important, at least in degree of acceptance among scholars, are the theories of Petrovici and Hadlich. Petrovici (1957a, 1957b, 1958, 1959, 1960) argued convincingly for a pervasive Slavic influence in Rumanian. He thus explains: the central vowel series; the palatal-nonpalatal and rounded-unrounded consonant oppositions; and loss of final unstressed vowels. Hadlich (1965) discovered in Vegliote the adstratum influences of Serbo-Croatian and Venetian. The argument depends for its validity on the acceptance of a succession of Vegliote vowel systems as Hadlich has reconstructed them.

The attempt to establish some kind of relative chronology, often utilizing the evidence of documents, has been one of the more productive activities of scholarship. The barest mention may be accorded here to work of this kind, valuable as it is. Aebischer (1944) examined a wealth of documentary evidence to establish facts about the chronology, character and direction of diphthongization in and around Tuscany. Allen (1964), on the basis of spellings *rr, ff, ss* that begin in the tenth century, interpreted the Old Spanish sibilant system as involving a distinctive feature of tenseness, rather than voice. A. Alonso (1955-1969) traced the evolution of Spanish from the medieval to the modern pronunciation, using the testimony of contemporary witnesses. Blaylock (1964) analyzed the available evidence on monophthongization of Latin *ae* with interesting results for Spanish. He distinguished early rural monophthongization from the later urban phenomenon and explained the close *e* reflex as the result of borrowing rural *e* from *ae* before the loss of phonemic quantity. On the basis of datable sources, Díaz y Díaz (1960a) insisted that the Latin of the Iberian peninsula was very conservative, even as late as the seventh century. The characteristics of modern dialects can not be identified in Latin inscriptions (Díaz y Díaz 1960b); nor is there room to speak of a Vulgar Latin of Spain as the source of modern dialects (Díaz y Díaz 1960a), beyond the generalization that the language of the people must, of course, have been a living tongue. Gaeng (1968) studied the evidence of Latin inscriptions, with remarkably moderate conclusions, for Late Latin vocalism. (The seven-vowel system had apparently begun in Italy while Gaul still had phonemic quantity.) Gamillscheg (1968a), on the evidence of place names of Germanic origin, dated the full assibilation of *ti* no earlier than the sixth century. Haudricourt (1946) attempted to place changes, which he explained in accordance with the principle later developed in conjunction with Juilland (Haudricourt and Juilland, 1949), in a relative chronology. Phonemic vowel quantity, datable as due to Germanic influence, preceded the change of *a* to *ae*. In an intermediate zone, early assimilation of *au* accounts for the failure of open *e* to diphthongize and the change of close, short *e* to *o* (i. e., *ei* to *oi*), a view which he repeated (1947b), arguing that the change of *ei* to *oi* is not Francian, but borrowed from East French dialects where every close *e* becomes *o*, to fill the case vide resulting from the fronting of *u*. These views would be more acceptable, if the chronology implied had been established from external evidence. Herculano de Carvalho (1956) argued that the voiceless reflex *ç* from the clusters *ki*, *ti* is older and more popular in Portuguese than the voiced *z*, the latter being borrowed from Spanish. Herman (1965) employed the evidence of manuscripts and inscriptions to attempt a relative chronology of the break-up of the linguistic unity of the Roman Empire. He held that the Latin of the fifth century was not entirely uniform but that differences were slight and consisted mainly in the degree to which certain common directions of change had been realized. Gaul was conservative and 'correct' while the center had advanced further along the path the whole area was traveling. Data based on spelling may often be interpreted more than one way. Jackson (1948) examined British reflexes of Late Latin sounds as attested by loanwords in Welsh. They reveal a correct, but learned, usage: quantity was preserved and *v* was kept distinct from *b*. Křepinský (1950) has offered an interesting approach to a chronology whose roots in Neo-Grammarian method are very evident. His results are interestingly schematized in a kind of horizontal tree so arranged that the relationships of priority are strung out in a series which summarizes his conclusions. Where two reflexes have the same source, he has assigned them to different periods on the basis of the kind of words in which they occur. Kuhn's (1939) argument in defense of an early date for palatalization of *ll* in Castilian, against Rohlfs (1935), may be mentioned here. Rohlfs had argued that early palatalization would have led to merger with inherited palatalized *lị*, as in other dialects on either side of Castilian. Kuhn suggested that different points of articulation were involved. Lüdtke (1961) cited Romance-like innovations from the *Appendix Probi* to dispute the dogma of a uniform Vulgar Latin. Macrea (1965) argues for the relative antiquity of palatalization of labials in Daco-Romance: the phenomenon, though lacking in the dialect which has become official, goes back to common Rumanian. His argument is not accompanied by solid evidence. Menéndez Pidal (1926) in his justly famous *Orígenes,* pointed the way to utilization of documentary evidence, although his intuitive insights have sometimes gone astray. The phonological pattern sketched by this scholar for the peninsula on the eve of the Arabic Invasion is still very widely accepted. Michelena (1964), citing Jackson (1948), sought to establish an early (but imprecise) dating for the monophthongization of *ae* to *e*. Evidence from loanwords in a variety of languages surrounding the Romance area has been invoked, along with some inscriptional evidence. But his use of the latter is far from exhaustive. Pei (1932) studied eighth century texts of Northern France. Politzer, an able structuralist of wide-ranging interests, has frequently drawn upon his study of documentary evidence in several parts of the Romance area. He has defended this evidence most ably (Politzer 1951a), insisting upon the necessity for proper interpretation, which he proceeded to illustrate, using structuralist arguments in a restrained, common sense way. Among the problems amenable to this kind of resolution are the treatment of final -*s* in various parts of the Empire, but particularly its loss in Italy (Politzer 1947), the development by analogy or phonetic change of final *i* where Classical Latin had the plural ending -*ēs* (Politzer 1951b), the chronology of geminate simplification in Northern France (Politzer 1951c), and the voicing or failure to voice of intervocalic voiceless stops in the Aragonese area (Politzer 1954b) and in Northern Italy (1955). The joint work of the two Politzers (Politzer – Politzer 1955) affords an accumulation of chronological data for the advent and triumph of the seven-vowel system, the reduction of geminates, and the fall of final *t* and *s* in Italy, all of it supportive of the conclusions of structuralist linguistics. Pope (1934), in what is one of the greatest monuments of Neo-Grammarian scholarship, included, at every point, an excellent chronology for the evolution from Latin to Modern French. Popović (1960) analyzed the reflexes of stressed Latin *a*, identifying some with Dalmatian and others with Rumanian, with implications for relative chronology. Richter (1934) sought to trace and explain the creation of the characteristic features of the Romance languages; the chronological aspect of this important work is among its more enduring values. Rosenkranz (1955) reviewed the evidence for differing Dalmatian reflexes at various times and places with a view to classification of dialects and to chronological ordering. For Rumanian, Rosetti (1965) presented arguments, mostly structuralist, which often have chronological implications: the central vowels are very old as is palatalization. Rosetti (1968) also attempted a reconstruction of the phonology of Common Rumanian. Sanchis Guarner (1960) investigated the phonology of Mozarabic, stressing the variety of dialects and the overall conservative character of this kind of Ibero-Romance. His evidence supports an early dating for diphthongization, which radiated from Toledo, Menéndez Pidal's (1926) view. The question of the voicing of intervocalic stops, by the time of the Arabic Conquest, is still open. Sanchis Guarner favored a double treatment: the conservation of voicelessness seems to have been most widespread in Mozarabic with sonorization as a trait of the vulgar dialect. (This corresponds, in the main, to the views of Meyer-Lübke (1925) and Menéndez Pidal (1926): the former had held that voicing had not taken place by the time of the Invasion, while Menéndez Pidal had authored the more subtle view which Sanchis Guarner has upheld.) Double *ll* and *nn* had not yet palatalized when the Arabs swept over the Iberian Peninsula, according to Sanchis Guarner, who rejected the examples cited by Menéndez Pidal (1926) to show palatalization of initial *l* in Mozarabic. Skårup (1969) opposed Straka's (1966) over-hasty argument that final unsupported *t, d* fell between the ninth and tenth centuries. Skok, in a series of articles (1926, 1928, 1930, 1934), examined the evidence for a Common Balkan Romance, which he called Balkan Latin. He argued that palatalization is later than the Slavic Invasions (Skok 1926). Skok (1928, 1930) reconstructed the sound laws and features of this Latin. The reflexes nearest the Rheto-Romance area share some characteristics with Rheto-Romance (Skok 1943). Sletsjøe (1959) studied the evidence of Portuguese documents to prove that linguistic boundaries in the North of Spain go back a long way. One scholar whose interests in relative chronology has been most productive, if not always reliable, is Straka (1953, 1956, 1959, 1966). Straka (1955, 1964) posited a general weakening of articulatory energy, as part of a general physical weakness, and attempted to date it by reference to known medieval conditions, a theory which has not encountered much support. Straka's dating of pre-Romance sound changes is generally earlier than that of most scholars (1953, 1956, 1966). His chronology is a relative one and depends very much on theories about the evolution of sounds (Straka 1968). Tovar, basing his evidence on inscriptions in Latin and pre-Roman languages, attempted to establish an early dating for the sonorization or fricatization of intervocalic stops in Spain (1949, 1951a, 1952, 1960, 1964). Tuaillon (1968) used Neo-Grammarian evidence to show that the fronting of *u* is later than nasalization of vowels. His arguments would not be acceptable to Structuralists. Vasiliu has produced a chronology of Rumanian reflexes: the formation of central vowels (Vasiliu 1956), the early date of diphthongization (Vasiliu 1970-71), and the order of vowel changes before nasals (Vasiliu 1969).

A return to the comparative method, with full use of historical reconstruction, and a kind of sound-law methodology, without recourse to metaphysical positivism or determinism, has been advocated (under the name of regularism), by Hall (1963), a confessed admirer of the great Neo-Grammarians, in a scathing attack upon the several schools of idealism, which, he feels, by denying the hypothesis of regular change, would deprive linguists even of the possibility of historical investigation. Earlier, Hall (1950b) had revived a challenge of the Neo-Grammarian Gröber by undertaking to reconstruct the vowel system of Proto-Romance as part of a general tactic to recover, in part, the real structure of the parent dialect. This venture has not elicited the response of extensive imitation, nor has Hall himself pursued this course of endeavor as far as would seem justified by the soundness and productivity of his initial essay. Leonard (1964, 1970) has responded by applying this approach to the area of Gallo-Romance, with results that are highly original. Using the comparative method in a way that is certainly open to challenge, he has reconstructed the vocalism of Proto-Rheto-Romance (Leonard 1964, 1972) and has reached the conclusion that Rheto-Romance is closer to French than to other dialects. In a much more controversial study, Leonard (1970) followed up his initial experiment in reconstruction with a Stammbaum theory based on vocalic criteria alone: this theory divides Hall's Proto-Italo-Western Romance into heterochronic and isochronic divisions, the latter being characterized by short stressed vowels of uniform length: thus, French and Italian are placed in one category and Spanish and Provençal in another, a classification which will hardly find wide acceptance. Mazzola (1970–71), inspired by Hall's (1950) example, attempted the reconstruction of a common stage underlying Sicilian and Sardinian, to be called Proto-Meridional. He starts from a ten-vowel system, which most scholars likely to be interested in reconstruction are certain to reject as unhistorical. It can be argued that reconstruction itself is unreliable and valueless, that an earlier system can never be recovered. This antireconstructionist view has found expression in Roncaglia's criticism (1950) of Hall's attempt (1950): The vowel systems that can be postulated may not correspond spatially to other phonological systems or to morphological or lexical ones and there is a danger of too much pragmatism and eclecticism, of pushing too much back into the protohistory, and of creating starred forms. So also Pellegrini (1973b), in his analysis of the language systems of Italo-Romance, which for him includes Sardinian, Friulian and the dialects of the Po Valley: It is impossible to reconstruct a common Proto-Italo-Romance and he rejects reconstruction on principle. Without going to such extremes of skepticism, we may surely question the value of reconstruction where dialects have remained in geographical contact, as the Romance languages have, and the validity of reconstructed systems which may not really go back all the way to the proto-language. The dogma of the uniformity of Vulgar Latin has rightly been called in question, as, frequently, by Tovar (1951, 1955, 1964).

Malkiel, while making free use of structuralist principles and techniques, has created a rival approach, requiring the application of massive scholarship and attention to detail, as well as the creation of new basic concepts: disturbance, multiple causation, weak sound change. The formulation of this attack is dispersed throughout his numerous investigations which are usually concerned with morphological questions, frequently but not exclusively within Ibero-Romance. In the course of grouping lexical items into families derived from the same root morphemes or of explaining grammatical forms which show reflexes that do not follow the traditional soundlaws, Malkiel has pointed to the recurence of phonological solutions that relate to morphological problems and has examined the systemic consequences of such solutions: a series of these changes can add up to a general sound change (Malkiel 1954a). He has emphasized seemingly sporadic developments, not numerous enough to be labeled regular, and sought out factors which may have blocked the generalization of these developments. Where morphological needs or other pressures have limited an incipient sound change to a few items, it may be termed weak (Malkiel 1962c). The factors that prevent regular developments from being carried out are often paradigmatic (Malkiel 1966, 1971a), but other kinds of disturbance are also recognized (Malkiel 1963-

1964). Although ready to admit norms of sound change where they exist and employing structural technique and the analysis of sound systems into phonemes (Malkiel 1962c), this approach requires a sophisticated awareness of levels and a willingness to see many kinds of phonological factors (Malkiel 1963-1964). For Malkiel, a single causative factor is always less probable than a combination of factors. It seems reasonable to look for the total aggregate of forces whose interaction has pushed a dialect in the direction in which it has gone, rather than to seek a single determining factor to be identified by process of elimination. Hence, Malkiel's preference for multiple causation (Malkiel 1967b, 1969). Two examples, from recent publications (Malkiel 1971a, 1973e), may serve to show how Malkiel has utilized his particular outlook to attack problems of conventional historical phonology. The Old Spanish diphthong *ie* occurred before *ll* in one type of diminutive ending. Because other diminutives had *i,* the monophthong spread to the position before the lateral palatal in the diminutive and then elsewhere; this development influenced the parallel diphthong *ue,* which, accordingly, gave way to *e* wherever an *r* immediately preceded it (Malkiel 1973e). The presence of voiced *z* instead of voiceless *ç* in Old Spanish suffixes has long been a problem recognized by Romance linguists. Malkiel's (1971a, 1973e) explanation invoked the avoidance of *ç* because of its appearance in hypocoristic or humorous suffixes. But this multifaceted scholarship does not neglect even the most traditionalist techniques, but brings to them a new rigor and new outlook. In a study reminiscent of the Neo-Grammarians in their prime, Malkiel (1962d) has presented a sound-law formulation of the vowel correspondences between Latin and Spanish. The traditional presentation, which Malkiel here identifies with Menéndez Pidal (1904) analyzed the environment of the vowels both in relation to the stress (tonic, pretonic, etc.) and to the word boundary (final, medial, initial); Malkiel's refinement classifies environments according to an accentual-syllabic system: Vowels may be tonic, countertonic, moderately weak or weakest and position in the word has little effect on their outcome. The vowel affected by apheresis is shown to be moderately weak or weakest. Malkiel's inclusive reasoning contrasts with the narrowness of many scholars who insist on one and only one cause for what are, after all, historical events, as the historian's thinking does with the laboratory scientist's. (But the past cannot be repeated under controlled conditions and history is the study of probabilities!) It is therefore somewhat strange that he prefers to call his discipline, not 'historical', but 'genetic' linguistics (Malkiel 1967 a).

Posner's (1967) spirited criticism of the regularism of Hall (1963) may be regarded as one kind of defense of this many-pronged approach to historical sound change. Her work on Romance consonant dissimilation (Posner 1961) shows a constant awareness of semantic interference. This is essentially a refinement of the "loi du plus fort" (Grammont 1936), to which task Posner has brought the resources of Structuralism, as exemplified by Martinet, with particular concern to appraise the functional load of distinctive features. Another scholar whose outlook resembles Malkiel's, Urciolo (1965) has produced an interesting and exhaustive study of voicing of intervocalic voiceless stops in Tuscan, which seems to support the view that an incipient sound change may, after all, fail to be carried through: It appears that voiced variants developed, only to be ousted by correction. There are also the accomplishments of those whose work may have been strongly influenced by Malkiel. Of these, not all have dealt with problems of historical phonology, while Blaylock's and Leonard's contributions have already been discussed.

It may be appropriate to name a number of general works that have appeared during the era under consideration insofar as they deal, in some measure, with historical phonology. Most recently, Hall (1974), while not intending to write a phonological handbook as such, has given us a very useful picture of the whole evolution of speech within the Roman Empire. Earlier, Kuhn (1951) surveyed the entire field of Romance studies, in a masterly way, with many solid criticisms of his own. Of no less importance is Lausberg's manual (1956-1962), because of its inclusiveness and massive scholarship. Richter (1934), though now somewhat old-fashioned, contains much that is of importance to the student of historical phonology. Rohlfs' (1949-1954) monumental work in the area of Italian, as well as his encyclopedic manual in Romance philology (1950-1952), are similarly of great value. Vidos (1956) has won a place in the field, while von Wartburg's contribution to the theoretical history of Romance language has made his works (1934, 1936, 1938a, 1943) of fundamental significance. The following general publications may be listed as containing, at the least, the indispensable minimum of historical phonology: Auerbach (1949),

Bourciez (1910-1967), Cavaliere (1949-1950), Elcock (1960), Mendeloff (1969), Posner (1966), Reichenkron (1965), Rohr (1964), Tagliavini (1948).

For French only may be cited: Alessio (1951-1955), Batany (1972), Bourciez (1899-1967), Brunot (1905-1972), Brunot – Bruneau (1933), Cohen (1947), Dauzat (1930, 1939, 1950), Ewert (1933), Fouché (1952-1961), Fox – Wood (1968), François (1959), Holmes – Schutz (1933), Lloyd (1968), Nyrop (1899-1930), Pope (1934), Price (1971), Regula (1955-1956), Rheinfelder (1937), Sauro (1952).

For Provençal: Hafner (1955), Roncaglia (1965).

For Ibero-Romance: Entwistle (1936), Trend (1953).

For Catalan: Badía Margarit (1951), Fouché (1924), Griera i Gaja (1965), Moll (1952).

For Spanish: Alarcos Llorach (1950), Baldinger (1958), García de Diego (1959), Hanssen (1913), Lapesa (1942), Menéndez Pidal (1904, 1926), Oliver Asín (1938), Pottier (1957), Spaulding (1943).

For Portuguese: Williams (1938).

For Italian: Bertoni (1940), Grandgent (1927), Pei (1941), Rosellini (1969).

For Rumanian: O. Nandriş (1963b), Puşcariu (1940), Rosetti (1938-1946), Rothe (1957), Schroeder (1967), Vasiliu (1968).

For Sardinian: Wagner (1941a, 1951).

For Latin: Kent (1932), Meillet (1928), Niedermann (1904-1953), Palmer (1954), Sturtevant (1920).

For Latin inscriptions: Carnoy (1906), Gaeng (1968), Mihăescu (1960), Pirson (1901), Väänänen (1958, 1963a).

Four recent endeavors, all of them impressive, may here be noted as the first fruits of what will doubtless be, in time, an abundant harvest of generative studies. Naro (1971a), seeking to demonstrate the superiority of the generative phonology, applied the characteristic analysis of binary distinctive features to the development of vowels in hiatus within the history of Portuguese. A binary formulation proved to be simpler than a system involving more contrasts, and a kind of primitive version of such a rule had already been formulated by a sixteenth century grammarian whose statement Naro reformulated. Curiously, this rule can be shown to have operated already in Latin. It was only at the Romance stage, however, that it could apply to postvocalic as well as prevocalic position, as the result of the fall of certain intervocalic consonants, thus revealing that it was what generative phonologists call a 'mirror image rule'. (The rule raises unstressed midvowels to high when next to another vowel.) In a further examination of processes of vocalic raising, Naro (1971b) saw the phenomena in terms of pre-sixteenth century conditions with subsequent 'grammar construction' and several mechanisms of generalization. According to Naro, the data turn out to constitute a classic case of 'Sapirian' drift. Citing excellent documentation, he has shown that the earlier belief that final unstressed -*o* was already -*u* in the sixteenth century was in error. Then, in an argument which appears to be very like a familiar structuralist approach dressed up in generative clothing, he argued that raising of close *e* and *o* first appeared before pause and was then generalized at all word-boundaries, not only utterance-final ones. This evolution proceeded independently in Brazil, Portugal, and Ceylon. The patterns which have emerged do not agree among themselves, but Naro has managed to account for them all in terms of rule ordering and the generalization of particular rules to mirror image. In an attempt to understand and utilize the generative system now in vogue, Posner (1971) produced an application of Chomskyan linguistics to diachronic problems: the development of nasalization in French and general evolution of the vocalism from the seven-vowel system of Late Latin to Modern French. She found that the characteristically Chomskyan tack of expressing vowel nasality as a surface feature is awkward for Modern French and that it does not, as is sometimes claimed for such analyses, fit the known and reconstructed data of linguistic history. Schane (1971) set out to restore the phoneme as a viable phonological unit for capturing relevant surface contrasts. His defense of the phoneme within generative phonology and his criticism of the Chomskyan lumping together of distinctions that arise from morphophonemic rules with those that are purely phonetic cannot be considered here. But Schane's use of examples drawn from the historical phonology of Romance justifies including it here. He argued that the historical processes of denasalization in French, depalatalization in Rumanian, and delabialization in Romance are due to surface (phonemic) contrast rather than to statable morphophonemic or phonetic developments. The phoneme must be recognized as a phonological entity, in both synchronic and diachronic statements. Vasiliu (1966) outlined a transformational phonology of the Daco-Rumanian dialects, claiming, as is usual in such studies, that the relationships are expressable in terms of rule ordering and that the historical facts are illuminated by the application of this kind of analysis.

KNUD TOGEBY

Romance historical morphology

1. What is morphology?

The meaning of the term morphology changes with the different trends
and schools of linguistics. Traditionally, for instance in Meyer-Lübke,
(1890-99), morphology is the study of the outer, phonological, form of
inflected and derived words, which is to say, strictly speaking, morphonology, while syntax is the study of the combination of words. The
particles, prepositions, adverbs, etc., are thus treated only in syntax,
not in morphology. All structural schools, in America as well as in
Europe, agree in abandoning the supremacy of the word in favor of the
morpheme, the minimum sign or content element, and thus basic for
morphology: roots (nouns, verbs), flexives, particles, derivatives. To
semantic structuralists (Guillaume, Brøndal), morphology is the inner
form of morphemes, their semantics, considered decisive for their use
in syntax. Between those two extremes, morphonology and semantics,
immanent structuralism has introduced a third conception of morphology, defining morphemes by their constructions and combinations in a
morpho-syntax, where morphology and syntax cannot be distinguished.
In transformational grammar the first and the third conception are
predominant: the morphonological component, and the lexicon containing morphemes defined by their construction. In our discussion
below we must obviously take into account the three aspects of morphology: morphonology, morpho-syntax and semantics.

2. Historical morphology

For the linguistic tradition of the 19th century, morphology is by definition historical. The title of Meyer-Lübke's fundamental work, as well

as of Diez', is simply *Grammatik der romanischen Sprachen,* without any "Historische". Saussure advocated the equal value of synchrony and diachrony, but gave much too narrow a definition of the latter, as the change only of elements. The various structuralisms have pointed out that if synchrony is a structural system, diachrony is the shift from one structural system to another, the description of the first being the prerequisite for describing the second. Von Wartburg (1943) has tried in vain to go back to pre-Saussurean positions. Transformational grammar does not seem, up to now, to have been interested in historical morphology. But one might say that Romance historical grammar is in itself a sort of generative grammar, which follows the transformations from the deep structure, Latin, to the surface structures of the fifteen modern Romance languages. And this deep structure has the advantage of being a linguistic one, not a hypothetical one.

3. Romance historical morphology

The great problem of historical linguistics is that of the causes of linguistic change. To discuss this problem, Romance linguistics is in a most favorable situation. Firstly because the point of departure is well known – Latin, or rather Old Latin. The direct line of evolution goes from Old Latin to Vulgar Latin, while classical Latin is a sort of artificial rhetoric language. And secondly because from Latin the evolution can be followed to no less than fifteen end points in the various Romance languages. To be more than purely descriptive, but really explanatory, Romance historical morphology must necessarily be comparative. The numerous histories of single Romance languages, Nyrop's of French (1899-1930), Menéndez Pidal's of Spanish (1904), Rohlfs' of Italian (1949-54), etc., may risk missing the point because they follow the one and only line of evolution from Latin to one single Romance language. Everything may seem natural in such a one-sided perspective. The comparison with the other Romance languages must be a constant check on all explanations.

That is to say that the best approach to a Romance historical grammar is that of Meyer-Lübke and of Lausberg: comparing all the Romance languages à propos of each grammatical problem. In spite of all the outstanding qualities of Bourciez (1910), his idea of treating each Romance language separately is a bad one, because it weakens the comparison between them.

As for the order of treatment of the grammatical problems, no one seems to impose itself. Meyer-Lübke starts with the nouns, which will also be done below, in accordance with the most widespread tradition. Bourciez starts with the verbs, which may be just as good, and perhaps better, because verbs form the core of the sentence. Bourciez places vocabulary and word-formation before the inflection of verbs and nouns, which seems less natural than the inverse order. The particles are unduly put aside by both Meyer-Lübke and Bourciez, to be treated under syntax.

4. Causes of linguistic change

To a very large extent the different trends and schools of linguistics can be characterized by their attitude to the problem of the causes of linguistic change.

4.1 A basic cause of morphological change, recognized by everybody since Diez and Meyer-Lübke, is the influence of phonological change, which can result in intolerable collisions of forms, a factor which has been particularly stressed by Gilliéron and his followers, mostly in connection with vocabulary, but its importance must evidently be just as great in dealing with inflection and derivation. Faced with the great problem of linguistic change, historical morphology is thus in a better position than historical phonology because it has a solid base precisely in historical phonology.

4.2 Another fundamental factor, in the foreground since Diez and Meyer-Lübke, is analogy. It is governed by a tendency towards simplification, or economy, as are most of the sound laws. In the analogical battle the more frequent forms will be more resistant than the less frequent forms, a principle formulated by Meyer-Lübke in his preface, and particularly represented in modern Romance linguistics by Mańczak (1962).

4.3 To those two internal morphonological causes, phonological change and analogy, various external factors have been added since the beginning of Romance studies. One of them has been generally accepted, namely the importance of history, demonstrated for instance by Diez or by Bourciez. If society is stable, language will be stable. If society is chaotic, linguistic change will be favored, which was the case during the barbarian invasions or during the Reconquista in Spain, or during the Hundred Years' War. But it is a question only of the rapidity of linguistic change. There is no direct influence of society on language, except in vocabulary. The Soviet linguist Marr tried to advocate the thesis of parallelism between language and society, but was criticized by Stalin himself in 1950.

4.4 Direct influence on a language has been supposed to be exerted by other languages through bilingual contact. The importance of the substratum language was seriously taken into account for the Balkan languages by Miklosich in the 1860s, and a general substratum theory was worked out by Ascoli (1878) who has been followed by Brøndal (1917), for whom the tendencies of a given language are due to its substratum, centuries after the bilingual period. The substratum theory has been heavily criticized, by Rohlfs and by Malmberg (1973), for instance, because of this gap between the bilingual period and the change in question, and because, almost always, the substratum language is not well known: Thracian underlying Rumanian, Etruscan underlying Tuscan, Iberian underlying Spanish, etc. An unquestioned case of substratum influence is that of the Italian dialects in the former Magna Graecia in Southern Italy, studied by Rohlfs. But here, in fact, the substratum is perfectly known.

4.5 Superstratum influence, from Germanic, Slavonic and Arab, is obvious in vocabulary, but questionable in grammar proper. Germanic substratum influence in phonology, morphology and syntax has been studied above all by von Wartburg in the 1930s. And Slavonic influence on Rumanian was considered important by Rumanian scholars after the Second World War. A very striking fact is that Arab influence never goes deeper than the vocabulary.

4.6 The main case of adstratum influence is that of Greek on the Balkan languages, described by Sandfeld in his doctoral thesis of 1900 and later in *La linguistique balkanique* (1930). Writing in 1896 his first article on Rumanian and Albanian, Sandfeld supported Miklosich's substratum theory about the Balkan languages, but when he corrected the proofs, he arrived at the conclusion that the Greek influence was more important. The learned influence of Latin on all the Romance languages is also an unquestionable adstratum situation, but it does not go beyond vocabulary and style. One of the great problems of Romance historical morphology is whether Greek has had any influence on the creation of the definite article (see 12.1).

4.7 It would perhaps be natural to take into account a fourth sort of stratum, which might be called constratum, in order to describe the situation of constant bilingualism, which seems to reign in Switzerland, where the Rheto-Romance dialects coexist with Germanic dialects. This makes the mutual impacts very strong. This situation has been described by Weinreich (1953).

4.8 The idealistic school, founded by Vossler (1904) and by Bertoni (1923), considered, like Croce, language as creation, and thus opened the door for influence on language from any spiritual or cultural stream, from the soul of the people, from Christianity, from feudalism, from Cartesian philosophy, from romanticism, from the bourgeois spirit, and so on. Once more, such an impact is evident in vocabulary and style, but most improbable in the inner core of language (Hall 1963).

4.9 The program of neolinguistics was presented by Matteo Bartoli (1925), when he expounded his ideas of the main geographical factors in linguistic change. Isolation and lateral position leads to conservatism. Communication and traffic serve to support radical innovation. This theory should serve to explain the ultraconservatism of Sardinian, the relative conservatism of Eastern Romance and of Portuguese, as well as of Walloon, and the radical development of French. One of the crucial questions is why Rome, once the center of Romania, has become the seat of one of the most conservative Romance dialects. It might be explained by the change of center of the ancient world during the later centuries of the Empire.

4.10 Semantic structuralism as represented by Guillaume (1929) or Brøndal (1940) has tried to describe linguistic evolution as the reorganization of certain logical or psychological schemes under the pressure of general tendencies, the nature of which is not clarified (Warnant 1974).

4.11 Immanent structuralism is faced with serious difficulties in dealing with linguistic change. When language is described as a selfsufficient system it appears immutable. Louis Hjelmslev drew the logical consequence of the priority of synchrony in relation to diachrony and taught, in his first lectures at the university of Aarhus in 1931, that linguistic change is nothing but the realization, under certain historical circumstances, of tendencies already contained in the synchronic system. Unfortunately, those lectures have not been published until recently, and only in Danish (Hjelmslev 1972). Independently of Hjelmslev, this same point of view has been represented in several books and articles by Bertil Malmberg (1947-48, 1973) who, after having observed that American Spanish only continued tendencies already present in medieval and Golden Age Spanish, draws conclusions in the same direction as for the development of Latin in Spain. One general objection must be made to this theory. How is it possible that the same tendencies of the one and only Latin language can have such different results in the fifteen major Romance dialects?

4.12 Purely structural explanations of linguistic change are, however, possible to a very large extent in another perspective. A phonological change can explain a morphological change. A morphological change somewhere in the system can be the cause of a morphological change elsewhere. A morphological change can result in syntactical changes, and those syntactical changes can have consequences on other points of the morphological system. And so forth. Thus, in diachrony as well as in synchrony, "tout se tient".

5. Number
5.1 Latin nouns had two numbers, modern Romance languages also, so there is no change in the inner morphology.

5.2 At first sight, the morphonology of number is also very simple. In Sardinian and in Western Romance languages, where final -s was conserved, it was used to distinguish the plural from the singular. In the Eastern Romance languages, where final -s disappeared, the numbers are distinguished by vowel change: from -o (or zero) to -i, from -a to -e, from -e to -i. The problem is phonological: how can it be that the dropping of the final -s, which was certainly the tendency of Latin (without reaching Sardinia), was carried through in Eastern Romance, generally considered conservative, and given up in Western Romance, where the evolution is in principle more radical? Wartburg (1938) has tried to explain this by the influence of the school in the West, but school never had, even in our days, such a force. It is much more probable that the need of a morphological mark stopped the phonological tendency. Morphological influence on phonology is one of the favorite topics of Malkiel (especially 1968).

5.3 In this context it must be remembered that the fundamental tendency, from Old Latin through Vulgar Latin to the Romance languages, was to use the plural *casas* both for the nominative and for the accusative. This tendency was carried through in Sardinian and in the Western Romance languages, and probably also in the East, where *case* does not go back to the classical *casae*, but to *casas* > *casai*, cf. *amiche*, not *amice* (Aebischer 1960, 1971).

5.4 A new collective plural has been created in many Romance languages, for instance in Italian *le ossa*, in opposition to the ordinary plural *gli ossi* (see 6.3), in French *les yeux* as against *les oeils*, etc. Such a plural did not exist in Latin, and it proves in a curious way that linguistic change does not always go towards simplification, but can also result in complication.

6. Gender

6.1 A general tendency of simplification may explain that, of Latin's three genders in the nouns, the neuter disappeared, generally transformed into masculine. The neuter has been conserved in part of Southern Italy and in Rumania, that is to say in the conservative South-East.

6.2 In the Northern part of Southern Italy, where the difference between final -*u* and -*o* is preserved, the masculine is characterized by -*u*: *lu vientu*, the neuter by -*o*: *lo ferro*.

6.3 In Rumanian, the neuter has taken the form of an ambigenous gender, masculine in the singular: *fir* 'thread', *timp* 'time', feminine in the plural: *fire, timpuri*.

The neuter declension *folium-folia* had no chance of being conserved in Sardinian and in Western Romance, where -*s* had become the mark of the plural. Here *folia* was taken as a feminine singular: *folia* > Fr. *feuille*. But in Eastern Romance with vocalic ending in the plural, -*a* and -*ora* could be accepted as feminine plural endings. In Italy it is almost always a collateral form to the ordinary masculine plural in -*i*, and with a collective value: Tuscan *osso, gli ossi, le ossa,* a type even more common in Southern Italy, and in Northern Italian dialects with the feminine ending -*e*. Structurally it would be more natural to consider these forms as a third number, a collective-plural, than as a third gender (see 5.4).

But in Rumanian, two parallel forms in the plural constitute the exception, the rule being a pure neuter declension, masculine in the singular, feminine in the plural, which is a living reality with a clear neuter meaning (Rosetti 1938-46). This might be explained as a more conservative state of things in the lateral and isolated Rumanian language. Another possibility would be a substratum influence: Albanian has also ambigenous substantives with neuter meaning (Togeby 1953). An influence from the neuter of the Slavonic superstratum, which has been proposed by Graur (1937a), cannot be argued with concrete similarities. Hall (1965a) considers the Rumanian neuter a pseudo-problem. The latest contribution to the discussion has come from Windisch (1973).

7. Case

7.1 The Romance languages as a whole tend towards abolition of case in the nouns. This can be seen as the effect of a general analytical tendency, the synthetic case-forms being replaced by preposition + noun, just as synthetic comparison is replaced by analytic, as simple tenses are replaced by compound tenses, as accusative + infinitive is replaced by verbal clauses, etc. But this general tendency has led to most different results in the various Romance languages.

7.2 Phonological change has perhaps favored the realization of the general tendency, but it does not offer any clue to the differences. One might think so in dealing only with French: any Latin form of *filia* must give *fille*, except *filias* > *filles*, all Latin forms of *murus* must give *mur*, except *murus* and *muros* > *murs*. But in Italy and Spain, and even in

Gaul, the nom.-acc. *casa(m)* and the gen.-dat. *casae* could have been distinguished, as they are in Rumanian, and in the first two territories also *muro* and the genitive *muri*.

7.3 In the East, where final -*s* falls, the only possible case distinction was between nom.-acc. *casa(m)* and gen.-dat. *casae*. This possibility was exploited in Rumanian *casă-case*, but not in Italian. Once more, perhaps, because Rumanian was the lateral, isolated, hence more conservative language? A genitive-dative is also found in Bulgarian, Albanian and Greek, which creates the usual three Balkan stratum possibilities. A superstratum influence from Slavonic (Rosetti) is very unlikely, because Bulgarian is the only Slavonic language to have this system. The substratum hypothesis gains support from the fact that Albanian, which distinguishes a nominative-accusative from a genitive-dative form not only in the feminine but also in the masculine, has the same ending -*e* in the genitive-dative feminine as Rumanian. To Sandfeld (1926) there is no doubt that the model has been given by Greek, where the genitive came into use as a dative during the first centuries after Christ. A purely structural approach might consist in explaining the genitive-dative case ending of the substantive as a secondary creation under the influence of the postposed feminine article *ei*. In fact, the special genitive-dative case-form only occurs in the feminine, *casă-case, cruce-cruci,* not in the masculine, e. g. *tată, munte*. In Old Rumanian are found examples with -*ă* in the genitive-dative, and in Macedo-Rumanian, where the initial *l-* of the feminine article has been conserved: *illaei > lie,* there is no special form for the genitive-dative in the substantives: *mamă, cruce*. The solution of the problem may thus be transferred to the article (12.6).

Phonologically, the Latin vocative *domine* might have remained distinct from other forms in most Romance languages, but obviously not in those losing their final vowels: French, Provençal, Catalan, Rheto-Romance and Northern Italian dialects. But it has only been conserved in Rumanian: *doamne*. This time the isolation of this language can hardly be invoked, since Sardinian is generally even more conservative. The ending -*o* of the feminine vocative *soro* can only be of Slavonic origin, so that here seems to be a case of superstratum influence favoring the conservation of a grammatical category. The vocative is, however, a very isolated case, since it corresponds to a complete sentence.

7.4 The conservation of the final -*s* in Sardinian and in Western Romance made possible the distinction between a nominative and an oblique case both in the singular masculine: *murus-muru(m)*, and in the plural masculine: *muri-muros*. But this system is only a possibility, not a necessity, as Wartburg (1950: 75) thought. And this possibility was only realized in Old French and in Old Provençal, not in the other languages, Sardinian, Portuguese, Spanish, Catalan, Gascon. The existence of an original two-case system in Rheto-Romance has been argued by Gartner, Bourciez, and Schmid (1951), but it seems more natural to restrict this case inflection to the adjectives (8.3).

This conservatism of Old French and of Old Provençal cannot be due to any isolation or lateral position. French is generally the most radically developed Romance dialect, so here we are confronted with a very difficult problem. A Germanic superstratum influence has been proposed by Jud (1907), Meillet (1931), and Väänänen (1950), but this theory applies only to Old French, not to Old Provençal, the limit between them having its origin in the strong Germanic influence in the North, not in the South. The -*ane*-flexion, which Jud attributed to Germanic, but which is rather modeled after the Latin -*one*-flexion, is any how almost non-existent in Provençal.

It has also been proposed to explain the French and the Provençal two-case systems in two different ways, the French one by the Germanic superstratum, the Provençal one as an artificial troubadour usage. The troubadours have certainly conserved the Provençal declension, but they cannot have invented it.

There may have been a substratum difference between Celtic in Gaul, distinguishing nominative and accusative both in the singular: -*os*, -*on*, and in the plural: -*oi*, -*os*, and Celtic in Iberia, where -*os* had the two functions of nominative and accusative. But this explanation cannot apply to Sardinian.

To solve this extremely difficult problem one is reduced to looking for a purely structural clue. This might be found in the accented system of the pronouns, which must be closely related to the substantives, because they represent them (Dardel 1964). The two-case system of Old French and Old Provençal corresponds in fact directly to the existence in the same two languages of the accented oblique cases *illui*, *illaei*, *illorum* in the personal pronoun (14.7), *ecce istui*, etc., in the demonstrative (13.4) and *cui* in the interrogative-relative pronoun (17.3).

7.5 Thus those two languages have solved the problem of the important distinction between the subject and the object. In the other languages of the West, the object is marked, when necessary, by the preposition *a*, not only in Spanish, but also in Portuguese (Delille 1970), Catalan, Gascon (Séguy 1973a), Rheto-Romance, Southern Italian and Sardinian, languages in which the indirect and the direct object thus coincide (Müller 1971, Rohlfs 1971c).

In Rumanian, where a nominative-accusative is opposed to a genitive-dative, the personal object is not marked by the preposition *a*, but, from the sixteenth century only, by *pe*.

The great enigma is Italian, where nothing seems to distinguish the object from the subject. The existence of *lui*, etc., has probably excluded the use of *a*.

7.6 The collapse of the case system in French and Provençal is an ultimate effect of the simplification tendency. The fall of the final -*s* in French about 1300, in Provençal about 1500, is posterior to the breakdown of the case system, which takes place already in the twelfth century in Anglo-Norman and in Provençal. The Provençal system was weaker than the French one, because the articles did not distinguish the cases so sharply (12.4), and was only artifically and temporarily conserved by the troubadours.

Once more, the explanation must be a structural one. The case system disappeared because it was no longer necessary to distinguish the subject morphologically from the object. This function was sufficiently assured by concord, the nature of the substantives (animate-inanimate), the construction of the verbs (transitive-intransitive), the use of the pronouns, word order, etc. (Schøsler 1973).

8. Adjectives

8.1 The neuter disappears in most Romance languages, just as in the nouns. But the nominative-oblique case system in Old French and in Old Provençal made it possible for the neuter to remain distinct from the two other genders in the nominative: masc. *buens*, fem. *bone*, neuter *bon*, a form used in impersonal constructions and adverbially.

8.2 The adjectives have the same case declension as the nouns in Rumanian, and in Old French and Old Provençal. But in the Rheto-Romance dialect Sursilvan, the adjectives, in contradistinction to the nouns, have conserved a case difference between *buns* and *bien*. Historically this is the continuation of the nominative *bonus* and the oblique *bonum,* but those forms have been utilized in Sursilvan for another purpose, to mark the predicate: *il baþ ei buns* 'the father is good', in opposition to *il bien baþ* 'the good father'. Such a system exists nowhere else in the Romance languages. The only possible explanation seems to be the influence of the Germanic constratum, where the adjectives have a particular form for use as a predicate.

9. -mente

9.1 In Latin, adjectives were marked for the adverbial use by the neuter: *verum,* the ablative: *certo,* a particular adverbial case in *-e: male,* or *-ter: graviter.* Except for the languages where the neuter had a particular form (8.1), this system was totally ruined in the Romance languages, so that a new adverbial case of the adjective was created on the base of the absolute ablative *firma mente.* This is a curious case of an evolution from an analytical construction to a synthetic form, like the formation of the future *cantare habeo* (21.3), and of the personal infinitive in Portuguese (30.4). The analytical tendency is not omnipotent in the history of the Romance languages (Kuen 1952).

9.2 But *-mente* was only adopted by the majority of the Romance languages, not by all, not by Sardinian, Southern Italian, Friulian, Dalmatian or Rumanian. The most obvious reason for this is that South-Eastern Romance is the most conservative part of Romania. In this region there is no reformed synthetic future either (see 22.2). Greek influence has been invoked by Rohlfs (1959) but this does not apply to Sardinian or to Friulian. Spitzer (1943) has given an idealistic explanation of *-mente* as a product of Western refined civilization in opposition to the popular culture of the South-East.

9.3 The different degree of agglutination of *-mente* may be explained structurally by the existence or not of the substantive *mente.* In French, where it does not exist, the agglutination has been complete since the first texts. In other languages, where there is a substantive *mente,* the

analytical construction is seen in coordinations, in Italian and Provençal only up to the 13th century, in Catalan, Spanish and Portuguese
even to-day.

10. Comparison

10.1 The synthetic relative superlative -*issimus* has been lost in all
Romance languages. This cannot be explained phonologically but only
as a result of a general tendency towards simplification and towards
analytical construction, a new relative superlative being formed by the
comparative introduced by the new grammatical instrument, the article
(see 12). This use of the article, however, is only slowly generalized.

The synthetic -*issimus* was reintroduced in the Romance languages
as a learned borrowing from Latin but only with the value of an absolute superlative: Old French -*isme*, French -*issime*, Italian -*issimo*,
Spanish -*ísimo*, above all during the Renaissance. It has acquired a
great extension in Italian and Spanish, where other modificatives, like
diminutives or augmentatives, are also frequent, but not in French,
where modificatives are very scarcely used (see 36.3).

10.2 Latin had not only a synthetic comparative *longior*, but also an
analytical one, used with certain adjectives: *magis idoneus*, and even,
since Plautus, with any adjective: *magis aptus*. The synthetic comparative disappeared completely in Rumanian and in Dalmatian, and has
left very few traces in Sardinian and in Southern Italian, where only
meglio and *peggio* are used. In this traditionally conservative zone of
the South-East, the analytical tendency has thus gone further than in
Western Romance. This apparent paradox may have a structural
parallel in the refusal, in this same area, to construct new synthetic
forms like adverbial adjectives in -*mente* (see 9) or a synthetic future
(22.2).

10.3 All the other Romance languages have kept the synthetic comparatives, adjectival and adverbial, corresponding to the four Latin
forms *melior, peior, maior, minor*. But in two languages, Old French
and Old Provençal, many other synthetic comparatives are found. A
Germanic superstratum influence has been invoked, but that is impossible in Provençal. A structural explanation is that these comparatives
have been preserved because of the case declension of the adjectives in
these languages (see 8.3; cf. Malkiel 1973).

10.4 The analytic comparative exists with the original *magis* in Rumanian and in Ibero-Romance, i. e. in Portuguese, Spanish, Catalan and Gascon, while *plus,* which also had been in use since Plautus, but less frequently, has been adopted in Sardinian, Italian, Dalmatian, Friulian, Rheto-Romance, French and Provençal. This enigmatic distribution, for which there has never been an explanation, does not correspond to any of the ordinary divisions of Romania, and does not harmonize with any substratum or superstratum. But it has a curious parallel in *formosus* used in Rumanian and in Ibero-Romance, as against *bellus,* used in the other languages.

A structural explanation should take into account the use of *magis* as a conjunction of coordination (32.1). It might be natural that in the languages where *magis* was used to mean 'but', it gave up its function in the comparison in favor of *plus.* This is in fact the case in Sard. *ma,* Dalm. *mui,* It. *ma,* Eng. *ma,* Fr. *mais,* Prov. *mas.* And the contrary is true of Rumanian, where *iar* and *însă* are used for 'but', leaving *mai* to form the comparative. But the theory does not seem to fit the Ibero-Romance languages, where *magis* is used in both functions. In fact, the situation is more complicated. In Portuguese *magis* has been cut in two, *mais* to form the comparative, and *mas* to coordinate. In Spanish, the different spelling *más* and *mas* reflects a difference of accentuation, but it is perhaps also worthwhile noticing that *pero* has overtaken part of the coordination. The same is true for Catalan.

11. Numerals

The numerals form one of the most resistant parts of the vocabulary. That is why the word *centum* has been chosen as a basis for classification of Indo-European languages. On the other hand, numerals are roots and not flexives, and thus can yield to exterior influence easier than flexion.

11.1 In Rumanian the synthetic numerals 11-19 have been replaced by the analytical forms *unsprezece* 'one on ten', etc. This construction exists in many languages: Slavonic, Latvian, Albanian, Hungarian, Celtic, Armenian (Reichenkron 1958). Consequently, substratum influence has been supposed by Miklosich (1862) and Schuchardt (1900) but nowadays almost all agree with Sandfeld (1926) and Rosetti that it must be the Slavonic superstratum that is responsible.

Rumanian also abandoned the synthetic numerals 20-90 of the other Romance languages to use instead *douăzeci* 'two tens', etc., like the Slavonic languages, and like Albanian.

11.2 The French vigesimal system, *quatre-vingts,* etc., is generally thought to have come from the Celtic substratum (e. g. Bloch – Wartburg 1960). But objections are numerous. The system is also an innovation in Celtic and it is not sure that it existed in Gaul. If it did, why did it not also influence Old Provençal? In the Old French texts we only find *-ante,* while the *vingt*-system comes up in the 12th century and is particularly flourishing in the 13th century. The *-ante*-forms are preserved in the Northern and Eastern dialects.

An influence from the Scandinavian superstratum in Normandy in the 9th century was proposed by Rösler (1910, 1929) and accepted by Meyer-Lübke (1935) and by Rohlfs (1943). But chronology proves the impossibility of this theory. The vigesimal system is not Scandinavian but Danish, and it did not come into use until about 1300.

Reichenkron (1952) argues convincingly for regarding the twenty-system as a commercial way of counting, which may come up spontaneously anywhere.

11.3 While the cardinals are popular and develop regularly, the ordinals are rather technical formations. That is probably why the Latin synthetic ordinals were completely abandoned in the South-East, in Sardinian, Southern Italian, Dalmatian and Rumanian, the same area which did not adopt another suffix: *-mente* (9.2), and did not retain the synthetic comparative (10.2). Sardinian uses article + *de* +cardinal: *su'e unu* 'quello d'uno', etc. Rumanian also uses the article, and even twice, before and after the cardinal: *al doilea, al treilea,* with strong resemblances, as usual, to Albanian and to Greek.

Apart from the first synthetic ordinals, the other Romance languages have chosen different suffixes, in more or less learned forms. Italian and Spanish *-esimo* continues directly the Latin form. The Latin distributive suffix *-enus* has been widely used as *-en* in Northern Italian, Provençal, Catalan and even in Old Spanish *-eno.* Sursilvan has created a new suffix *-avel.* This background might perhaps help to solve the riddle of French *-ième,* cf. *decimus > dîme, -esimus > -esme.*

12. The definite article

12.1 The article existed in Greek, and it has been argued that this was the model for the Romance languages (Lausberg 1962). But it is very unlikely that a cultural adstratum influence should go so far, especially when one considers that the definite article is one of the few Balkan peculiarities where Greek does not seem to have exerted any pressure. On the other hand; it must be admitted that the Latin Bible shows the beginning of the use of the article; cf. Abel (1971).

It would be more natural to see the definite article as a creation due to a general tendency of all Western languages, Germanic as well as Romance. But it would hardly be possible to characterize this tendency as an analytical one. Synthetic case is replaced by preposition + noun, synthetic tense by using auxiliary + principal verb. But the definite article of the Romance languages expresses something which was not explicitly expressed in Latin. It has been said that the article replaces case (Guillaume 1919), but it does not seem to be less used in the case-languages Old French and Old Provençal than in the other dialects.

The most direct and evident clue to the origin of the definite article is the creation, due to the great accent differences, of unaccented bound forms to introduce the nominal syntagms (articles, demonstratives, possessives) as well as the verbal syntagms (bound personal pronouns and pronominal adverbs).

12.2 The first word to be used as a definite article, as can be seen in the *Peregrinatio* or *Fredegar,* was *ipse,* conserved as such in the most isolated and conservative language of all, Sardinian, and in some Catalan dialects. It was rejected, not because the schoolmasters did not like it (Aebischer 1948) but because *(ip)sum, (ip)sa* coincided with the possessives *su(u)m, s(u)a.* This did not stop the use of *ipse* in Sardinian, where the possessive is always in postposition and accented: *su pane suo.* In Catalan, the masculine article was reduced to *es* or *s',* different from the possessive *son,* but in the feminine the confusion seems to have been accepted by the language: *sa.*

12.3 Used as an article, *ille* (and *ipse*) lost its initial syllable, which must be due to the fact that, originally, the article was used, not only after a preposition: *de lo patre,* or after a verb: *ama lo patre,* but also after the substantive: *patre (il)lo.* In the Italian *il,* Rheto-Romance *il,* Catalan *el,* the article is *l'* with a prothetic vowel. The Rumanian *al* is a sort of independent pronoun (12.6). In Spanish *el,* the first syllable has been preserved in order to distinguish three genders in the article, as in the other demonstratives (13.3): masc. *el,* fem. *la,* neuter *lo.* The great exception from the general rule is the formation in Gascon dialects of the articles masc. sg. *et,* pl. *es,* fem. sg. *éra,* pl. *éras.*

12.4 In Old French, the masc. nom. *li* (< *illī) is generally explained by an analogy from *quī.* But the structurally important factor is that thus the two cases could be distinguished. Such an explanation is, however, weakened by the fact that the same solution was not used in Provençal, where a nom. *le, lo* was not clearly different from obl. *lo.* This corresponds to the fate of the personal pronoun *ille,* the nominative of which was influenced by *quī* in French, but not in Provençal (14.7).

12.5 The genders of the article must be expected to be the same as in the substantive. This is true also of the Southern Italian dialects, where the neuter has been preserved and its article is *lo,* distinct from masc. *lu* (6.2). In Rumanian, the neuter article is masculine in the singular, feminine in the plural (6.3).

On the other hand, the article is also a sort of demonstrative, and thus must be expected to have a neuter in the languages where the demonstrative has (13.3). This is in fact the case in Spanish, where the neuter article is used to substantivize adjectives: *lo bueno,* but not in Portuguese, because of the fall of the intervocalic -*l*-: *o formoso.*

12.6 The postposition of the definite article in Rumanian can to a certain extent be seen as a continuation of the original Latin construction (Skårup 1970), and one could point to the fact that the auxiliaries *habere* in the perfect and *velle* in the future have been postposed in Rumanian longer than in other languages. But there must however be a special reason for such conservatism. The isolation is not enough: in Sardinian the article is in anteposition. Many Romanists, even Sandfeld (1926) have pointed to the substratum influence, because of the very striking resemblance with Albanian, not only in the postposition, but also in the creation of a specific article for the adjective: *prietenul cel bun* 'the good friend', alb. *mik-u i mirë.*

A structural explanation, often given by Graur (1937 c), is that the article belongs to the adjective, to which it is anteposed: *omul-l bun*. The construction *bunul om* should then be considered as secondary; the simple *omul* proves even more of an embarrassment to this hypothesis. The problem would then be why the article *-l* originally belonged to the adjectival member in Rumanian, as *al* and *cel* still do. And here the parallel with Albanian imposes itself again.

Another structural explanation might however be sought in the case inflection of the article, which distinguished Rumanian from all the other Romance languages. The genitive-datives *-lui, -ei, -lor,* going back to *illui, illaei, illorum,* are accented forms (14.7) that cannot occur in the unaccented position in front of the nominal syntagm, but must have the independent accented position after, just as the pronoun or possessive *lui, ei, lor,* which is always in postposition, like the Italian *loro.*

This case-inflection of the article, which is the source of the case-inflection of the substantive (7.3), is identical with the personal pronoun of the third person (14.7), and thus the fundamental peculiarity of the Rumanian article is that it is more a pronoun than an article.

12.7 The partitive use of *de* in Vulgar Latin and in the first Romance texts made the creation of a partitive article possible in all the Romance languages. It was only realized in French, Provençal (*de* without the article), Northern Italian and Tuscan, and not until about 1300, that is to say independently. Vossler (1913) attributed the rise of the partitive article to the development of a bourgeois, mercantile, commercial mentality. A purely structural explanation of this combination of the bound preposition *de* with the article might be found in the fact that French and Italian are the only languages to have developed a bound article, while the article can still be an independent pronoun in the Ibero-Romance languages, like Spanish *el que, el de*. A parallel to this use of the preposition *de* as an article is its use as the mark of the infinitive in the same two languages (31.3).

13. Demonstratives
13.1 The Latin system of demonstratives had three positions: *hĭc - ĭste - ĭlle*. As a demonstrative with both nominal and adjectival functions, *hic* disappeared because of its reduced corpus, which made it in fact little fit for adjectival inflection, but it was conserved as a demonstrative

pronoun in various languages (13.3) and as its adverbial case-form in all languages (13.5). Thus the fundamental system for Proto-Romance is *iste* for the here-position, *ille* for the there-position. This system was conserved in Rumanian, Northern Italian, Rheto-Romance, Old French and Provençal, e. g. Old French *cist - cil*. But in other languages the former system of three positions was reconstituted by the introduction of *ipse* as a second position: Sardinian, Southern Italian, Tuscan, Gascon, Catalan, Spanish, Portuguese, e. g. Spanish *este - ese - aquel*. Wartburg (1950) considered this ternary system *iste - ipse - ille* as Proto-Romance, and explained the reduction to two positions as the result of the substratum pressure from the Slavonic and Germanic languages. But many arguments run against this theory. Provençal cannot be explained that way. There are no indications for an early use of *ipse* in the second position, but many for a late one. *Ipse* was originally used as an article (12.2). In Italian, where *ipse* was also used as a personal pronoun *isso,* the second position was formed with *tibi: cotesto.* The situation reminds us of the reconstitution of a synthetic future in some languages, not in others (see 22), but it is difficult to find a reason for this reintroduction of the three positions just in the languages in question, although they are mostly the conservative ones. It might, however, be a significant fact that the two-position languages are the same as the case languages (cf. 7).

13.2 In order to distinguish the demonstrative *ille* from the personal pronoun *ille* (14.5), the former was reinforced by *eccum* (< *ecce eum*) in all Romance languages, e. g. Portuguese *êste - êsse - aquele*. In French, only *ecce* was used: *ecce illum > cel*, because *quel* would have coincided with *qualis* (Kjellman 1928).

From the *ille*-forms, the reinforcement *qu-* spread to the first position in all the two-position languages, e. g. Rumanian *acest - acel,* but was not necessary in the other positions in the three-position languages, e. g. Spanish *este - ese - aquel,* the exceptions being Tuscan, where *iste* had to be the base of the two first positions (13.1): *questo - cotesto - quello,* and Sardinian, where *ipse* was used as a personal pronoun (14.5): *kustu - kussu - kuddu.*

In Catalan, where *ipse* was used as an article, it was reinforced as a demonstrative into *ipsius > ex*, the Old Catalan system being *est - eix - aquell;* cf. Tilander (1946).

13.3 The neuter form of the demonstratives completely changed function from Latin to Romance. Because of the disappearance of the neuter gender in the substantives, the neuter demonstrative could only be a pronoun and not have ordinary adjectival functions as the masculine or the feminine. One might expect Rumanian to be an exception because of the conservation of the neuter gender in the substantives (6.3). But this Rumanian neuter is ambigenous and, characteristically, the "neuter" demonstrative is the feminine: *această se poate* 'cela se peut'.

The Latin neuter of the demonstratives was conserved in the cases where *istud - ipsum - illud* could be differentiated from the masculine, that is to say in the languages conserving the final vowel: Sardinian, Southern Italian, Portuguese and Spanish, e. g. Sp. *este - esta - esto*. This was originally also the case in Italian, but here the masculine *queste* sounded like a feminine plural and was replaced by a new masculine form *questi*, etc., created by analogy with *qui*. The case language Old French could also distinguish the masc. nom. *cil* from the neuter *cel*, but the instability of the case system compromised this distinction.

The languages losing their final vowel (and Italian) use as a neuter *hŏc* > Fr. *o*, Prov. *oc, o*, Cat. *ho*, Gasc. *oc*, or the reinforced form *ecce hŏc* > Fr. *ço*, Prov. *zo, aizo*, Gasc. *aisso*, Cat. *aixo, aço*, Eng. *tshai*, It. *ciò*.

13.4 The case-inflection problems of the demonstratives are the same as for the personal pronouns of the third person (14.5). But the demonstrative has also various other cases.

13.5 The pronominal adverbs *ĭnde* and *ĭbī* are in Latin case forms of the pronoun *ĭs*, but came historically to be attached to the demonstrative as its genitive and locative case forms, in competition with *hĭnc* and *hīc*, which have left traces in various languages. *Inde* and *ibi* only develop into real verb-bound pronouns in the languages with a neuter based on *hoc*, i. e. in French, Provençal, Gascon, Catalan (and Aragonese; Badía Margarit 1947), and Italian, but not in the languages with a neuter form parallel to the masculine and the feminine, i. e. Spanish and Portuguese: *esto*, etc., not in Rheto-Romance, where there are no verb-bound pronouns at all (14.1), not in Rumanian, where the neuter is expressed by the feminine. There is one exception from this rule: Sardinian, where *nde* (or *nke*) and *bi* are widely used without the support of a neuter formed on *hoc.*

13.6 As for the adverbial case forms of the demonstrative, *hīc - ĭstīc - illīc* for location, and *hāc - istāc - illāc* for direction, the three positions are evidently conserved in the same languages as in the demonstrative pronoun adjective (13.1), i. e. Sardinian, Italian, Gascon, Catalan, Spanish, Portuguese, e. g., Sp. *aqui - ahí - allí,* while the system is reduced to two adverbial positions in the languages with two pronominal positions: Rumanian, Northern Italian, Rheto-Romance, French and Provençal, e. g. Fr. *ci - là.*

All the forms of the first position have been reinforced, by *eccum* in Rumanian *aici,* Italian *qui - qua,* Spanish and Portuguese *aqui - acá,* by *ecce* in the languages where it was necessary to avoid the confusion with the interrogative-relative pronoun *qui* (17.1): Fr. *ci - çà,* Prov. *aici, sai,* Gasc. *aci,* Cat. *aci - ça.*

For the second position, only Italian has continued *istīc - istāc >* *costí, costá,* just as the pronoun *cotesto* is based on *iste.* In all the other languages with three positions, *ipse* was used as pronoun, but it had no adverbial case forms. Instead, in Sardinian was used *hūc > huke,* in Gascon *ibi > aciu,* and perhaps also in the other Ibero-Romance languages: Cat. *aquí,* Sp. *ahí,* Port. *aí.*

For the third position, *illāc* has been continued in almost all languages, mostly without reinforcement, e. g. Fr. *là,* but with a tendency to reinforcement in the three-position languages: Sp. *allá.* The collateral form *illīc* has only been preserved in the three-position languages: It. *lí,* Sp. *allí,* etc.

14. Personal pronouns

14.1 As a consequence of the new Romance stress accent, the personal pronoun developed in two different series: the accented unbound pronouns, a nominative and one or two oblique forms, used after prepositions; and the unaccented verb-bound pronouns, originally developed in postposition, only oblique forms, accusative-dative or accusative and dative. The only language to have totally abandoned this system in favor of only one series, namely accented unbound forms, is Sursilvan, but this change took place as late as the seventeenth century, probably under the influence of the Germanic constratum.

14.2 The nominative or subject case was originally an accented unbound form in all Romance languages. And it has stayed so except in French, Franco-Provençal, Rheto-Romance and Northern Italian, where, about 1300, it has become an unaccented bound form. Generally this has been explained by the loss of the final consonants -s and -t, which made necessary the use of the pronoun to distinguish the persons of the verb (Meyer-Lübke, Nyrop, Foulet [1935]). But the generalization of the use of the subject pronoun begins long before the fall of the final consonants (Moignet 1965). The infixing and suffixing of pronouns in Celtic might have exerted a substratum influence (Brøndal 1917), but this is contradicted by the fact that the subject pronoun is not generalized in Provençal. This is on the other hand an argument in favor of the Germanic superstratum, the influence of which has been invoked by Wartburg (1941) and Kuen (1957). A purely internal explanation, based on word order, has been given for French by Franzén (1939) and for Northern Italian by Spiess (1956). How this word order, making almost obligatory from the beginning the use of the subject pronoun in the subordinate clauses and in principal sentences not beginning with another word, was introduced in French, Rheto-Romance and Northern Italian, and not elsewhere, is a question that belongs to syntax.

This generalization of the subject pronoun as an unaccented bound form is probably sufficient to explain in French the form *je* as well as the fact that *nōs, vōs,* instead of becoming **neus,* **veus,* has the unaccented development *nous, vous* (Spence 1973).

14.3 The oblique Latin cases *mē - mĭhī (mī)* and *tē - tĭbī (tī)* tend to develop distinct accented and unaccented forms. In the two most conservative languages, Sardinian and Rumanian, which distinguish the two cases in both accented and unaccented forms, this is done with long forms as opposed to short forms. After the model of *quem* > Sard. *kene,* Rum. *cine,* the forms *mē* and *tē* are changed under the accent to Sard. *mène, tène,* Rum. *mine, tine,* and *mihi, tibi* are not contracted: Sard. *mmimme, ttibe,* Rum. *mie, ţie,* in opposition to the unaccented Old Sardinian *me - mi, te - ti,* Rum. *mǎ - îmi, te - îţi.* The case system has however developed differently in the two languages. In Sardinian, the etymological dative *mmimme, ttibe,* is now used with the preposition *a* as an accusative and a dative, the etymological accusative-ablative *mène, tène* having its function after other prepositions. In Rumanian *mine, tine* have conserved their etymological functions as accusative-ablative after prepositions, *pe* marking the accusative, and *mie, ţie* their etymological function as a dative, without preposition. Rheto-Romance distinguishes the accented accusative *mei, tei* from the dative *a mi, a ti* and from the unaccented *me, te.* In all the other languages there is no case distinction within the accented and the unaccented oblique forms. In Italian, where posttonic *-ī* was preserved (*venti*), *mi* and *ti* became unaccented forms, *me* and *te* accented forms. In the Ibero-Romance languages, where posttonic *-ī* > *-e* (Sp. *veinte*), the unaccented forms became *me* and *te*, and consequently *mi* and *ti* were used under the accent, after prepositons. The same distribution is found in Northern Italian and in Picard. In Southern Italian, where unaccented *-ī* and *-ē* > *-i*, and accented *ē* > *i*, the unaccented *mi, ti* acquired as accented counterparts the enlarged forms *mia, tia.* In French (and in Rheto-Romance), the diphthongization distinguished accented *mei, tei* from unaccented *me, te.* Provençal is the only language to confuse completely accented and unaccented *me, mi* and *te, ti.*

14.4 In principle, the development is the same for *nōs - nōbis* and *vōs - vōbis* as for the singular forms, with the difference, however, that the accented accusative is identified with the nominative: Old Sardinian nom.-acc. *nos, bos,* dat. *nois, bois,* Rumanian nom.-acc. *noi, voi,* gen.-dat. *nouă, vouă,* unaccented oblique *ni, ne* and *vi, vă.* The accented and unaccented forms are carefully distinguished in Dalmatian *noi - no,* Southern Italian *nui - ne,* Tuscan *noi - no,* Northern Italian *nui - ne,* Friulian *nô - nus,* Portuguese *nós - nos.*

In some languages the confusion was avoided by adding *alter* to the accented form: Sp. *nosotros - nos,* Cat. *nosaltres - nos,* Gasc. *nousauti - nous,* Prov. *nosautres - nos.*

The only language not to distinguish the accented form from the unaccented is French, where *nōs* should regularly develop into **neus* under the accent, into *nous* before the accent. This must be due to the identity of the accented form with the nominative (14.3).

The reduction of It. *no* and *vo* led to coincidence with the pronominal adverbs *ne* and *vi* (13.5), which resulted in the replacement of *ne* by another pronominal adverb *ci.*

14.5 The Latin third person personal pronoun *ĭs* disappeared in all Romance languages because of its excessively reduced form. *Ipse* and *ille* were ready to take over. But *ipse* could not be used as an unaccented bound form because it coincided with the reflexive pronoun, *(ip)sī* with *sĭbī > si,* and *(ip)s'* with *s'* before a vowel. It is significant that *ipse* has been conserved as an accented personal pronoun in Sardinian (*isse*),where *ipse* is also the base of the article (12.2), and to some extent in Southern Italian (*issu*) and in Tuscan (*esso*), but never as an unaccented form, a function for which only *ille* is found (14.8).

14.6 The neuter of the personal pronoun has developed like that of the demonstrative (13.3). The neuter *illud* was conserved in languages with a final unaccented vowel, e. g. in Portuguese *êle - ela - elo.* This was originally also the case in Italian: *elle - ella - ello,* but the masc. *elle* sounded like a feminine plural, and was replaced by the acc. *ello* and finally by a new form **illī > egli.* This same form was also used in French to distinguish the masc. *il* from the neuter *el,* which in its turn coincided with the fem. *ele* and disappeared. In the other languages losing their final vowel the neuter was dropped, from the very beginning. In Rumanian the feminine is used for the neuter.

14.7 As for the accented case inflection of *ille,* the Romance languages fall into two groups. In the first one, there is only one accented form of the third person pronoun, just as in the substantives (see 7), the article (12.4), and the demonstratives (13.4), the dative and the accusative being marked by *a.* This form goes directly back to the Latin declension of *ille,* which could yield only one form. *Ille,* not *illum,* which coincided with *illud,* was used in some languages to distinguish the masculine from the neuter: Port. *êle,* Sp. *él,* Sard. *isse* (14.6). In other languages, *ille* and *illum* gave the same result: Cat. *ell,* Gasc. *ét,* Rhetorom. *el,* Dalm. *jal.*

In the second group of languages, where the object was not marked, like the dative, by *a,* in French, Provençal, Italian and Rumanian, there had to be two accented case forms of the third person pronoun. In the plural *illōrum* could be used instead of the weak *ĭllīs,* but in the singular *illī, illō* and *illae, illā* were replaced by *illui,* modelled on *cui,* and by *illaei.* In the two-case languages, Old French and Old Provençal, these forms were necessary to distinguish the two cases. Old French, with the masc. sing. nom *il* (< *illī*), could not use *el* (< *illum*) as an oblique, because this was the neuter (< *illud*), so had to use *lui*. In the plural, three forms became possible: *il - els - lor*, which resulted in a syntactic distribution: *els* after prepositions, *lor* in other oblique functions. In the feminine singular, to the unique form *illa(m)* > *ele* was opposed the oblique *illaei* > *li*, and in the plural *illas* > *eles* and *illorum* > *leur*, with the same distribution as in the masculine. In Old Provençal, the situation was the same: *el - lui, il - els - lor, ela - liei, elas - lor*, but here *lor* was used after prepositions.

In Italian and Old Rumanian, where the substantives have one form for the subject and the object, *lui, lei, (ei), lor(o)* became a genitive-dative, which is true of Rumanian up to this day.

It has been suggested (Lausberg 1956-62, Skårup 1970) that there has been a general influence on *ille* from *quī*, also in a nom. *illī* But this form seems to have been used only to distinguish the masculine from the neuter, and only in two languages. It is found in French *il*, different from *illud* > *el* (but not in Provençal *el*, exactly as in the article [12.4]), and in Italian *egli*, probably for the same reason (14.6) (but not in Rumanian *el*, the neuter being expressed by the feminine in this language).

14.8 As unaccented forms of the third person personal pronoun, all Romance languages developed enclitically an accusative and a dative, e. g. Sardinian sg. acc. *lu - la*, dat. *li*, pl. acc. *los - las*, dat. *lis*. In the East, with the loss of final *-s*, the two datives coincide. This has been avoided in Rumanian by the introduction of the unexplained plural form *lă*, which may be formed by analogy with *nouă, vouă*. In Italian, the confusion has largely been accepted, but in the literary language the accented form *loro* has been preferred, which Rohlfs (1949-54, II: 196) unnecessarily calls a Gallicism. In French and Provençal, the dative plural could not be distinguished from the accusative and consequently was replaced by the accented *lor*, followed by *lui* instead of *li*. In the languages where the dative and the accusative of the substantives were marked by the same preposition *a*, there is a tendency also to confuse the accusative and the dative of the pronouns as in the Spanish *loísmo, laísmo, leísmo*. A consequence of this is that in the combination of an dative with an accusative, the dative has been marked as *se* instead of *le* in *se lo, se le, se la, se los, se les, se las*.

14.9 The original order of two unaccented personal pronouns is dative + accusative, still to be found in the conservative languages: Sard. *mi lo*, Rum. *mi-l*, Sp. *me lo*, Port. *mo*. In the languages where the accented *illōrum* was used to replace the unaccented *illīs*, that is to say in Italian, French and Provençal (14.8), but also in Catalan, the order was changed to *illum illōrum*, and consequently It. *lo mi*, Fr. *le me*, Prov. *lo mi*, Cat. *el me*. But at the end of the Middle Ages, the languages returned to the original order: It. *me lo*, Fr. *me le*, Prov. *mi lo*, Cat. *me'l*. In Italian this was the case in all the combinations, perhaps under the influence of the dialects, where *loro* had not been used instead of the unaccented dative. In French, the change occurs only with the datives *me, te, se*, not with *lui, leur*, perhaps because of the constant association of the subject pronoun with the reflexive pronoun.

15. The reflexive pronoun

15.1 The reflexive pronoun, with its reference limited by definition to the same sentence, has developed as have the first and second persons of the personal pronoun. The unaccented form of the reflexive pronoun has however been conserved in Rheto-Romance, while it has disappeared in the personal pronouns (14.1), because this unaccented form was necessary to form the reflexive verbs. Rheto-Romance *el ei selegraus* has been compared with German *er hat sich gefreut* (Bourciez 1910, § 531), but there are so many differences: the auxiliary *esse*, the use of the only form *se* in all persons: *jeu sun selegraus*, and, above all, the agglutination of *se* to the verb as a reflexive flexion, that it will be simpler to stick to the given structural explanation.

15.2 In the languages where *illōrum* becomes a reflexive possessive in the plural (16.2), there is a tendency to use the personal pronoun instead of the reflexive: Rum. *ziceá într'înşii*, It. *dicevano fra loro*, Fr. *ils disaient entre eux*, but in Spanish *decían entre sí*.

This development has gone even further in French, where *lui, elle* also replace the reflexive in the singular (Brandt 1944), probably because *soi* was felt to be a case belonging to the new pronoun *on* (15.3).

In modern Occitan, where the accented oblique case of the personal pronoun has been replaced by the nominative, the accented form of the reflexive has completely disappeared, leaving all functions to the personal pronoun: *cadun n'aima qu'el-même* 'chacun n'aime que soi'.

15.3 The reflexive construction has to a great extent replaced the lost passive (19.2), for instance to express a general personal subject, *dicitur:* Sp. *se dice,* It. *si dice,* Rum. *se zice.* The reflexive has thus developed into a sort of unaccented nominative in these languages: Sp. *se admira a este hombre,* It. *si legge i libri* (Kontzi 1957). But not in French and Provençal, where a new subject-pronoun *on* was created. This is generally explained as a result of the Germanic superstratum influence (Nyrop, Meillet 1931, Ronjat, Bourciez), but its use in Provençal, and in Old Spanish *omne* until the victory of *se,* testifies against this theory. It is simpler to see *on* as a result of the two-case declension in the two languages and of its collapse (7.4-5).

   The Germanic superstratum theory is also contradicted by the fact that in the Romance language most influenced by Germanic, Rheto-Romance, we do not find *homo,* but *unus > ins.*

16. Possessives

16.1 The possessives are adjectives derived from the personal and the reflexive pronouns. They are used in two ways in the Romance languages: as unaccented possessive articles, and as accented adjectives, usually in a construction with an article, except in kinship terms.

   In the conservative South-East, the possessives are not used as articles, but only as adjectives. In Sardinian and Southern Italian, the possessive is always in post-position, like the adjectives, probably to distinguish it from the *ipse*-article (12.2): Sard. *su pane suo.* In Rumanian, the possessive is always combined with an article, as the adjectives often are (12.6), usually in postposition: *fratele mieu,* emphatically in anteposition: *al mieu frate.*

   In Italian, Spanish and Portuguese, the possessives were originally used without an article before the substantive: It. *suo tesoro,* but with the article when they were in emphatic postposition: It. *lo viso mio.* In the article-like anteposition there was a tendency to develop unaccented forms: It. *madonna,* Old Port. *ma, ta, sa,* but this development was blocked in Italian and in Portuguese by the generalization of the article before the anteposed possessive: It. *la nostra città,* Port. *as suas casas.* In Spanish, this was not the case, and the result was a double system of possessives, unaccented article: *su carta,* and accented adjective: *la carta suya.*

In Northern Romance, in French, Provençal, Gascon and Catalan, the possessives were always in anteposition and developed both as unaccented article-forms: Old French *mes cuers,* and as accented adjective forms after the article: *li miens cuers.*

Rheto-Romance is the only Romance dialect where the stressed possessives are always in anteposition without being combined with the article. A Germanic influence is usually assumed here: *mia casa.*

16.2 In Latin, *suus* was a reflexive possessive, and *illius, illōrum* was used for references outside the sentence. In a first stage, *suus* was generalized as a personal as well as a reflexive possessive all over Romania, as it is today in Sardinian, Ibero-Romance, and Rheto-Romance, e. g. Sp. *quieren a su padre,* Port. *amam a seu padre,* Cat. *amen al seu pare.*

In a second stage, *illōrum* was introduced as a possessive of the plural in the languages where *illui, illaei, illōrum* has been introduced as accented oblique forms of the personal pronoun (14.7), i. e. in French, Provençal, Italian, and Rumanian, e. g. It. *i figli amano il loro padre,* cf. *le place lor.*

Illōrum has thus passed from its function as a personal pronoun to that of a possessive, and not directly from the Latin genitive to the possessive. A fundamental proof of this is that *illōrum* has developed as an accented form everywhere. In Italian, *loro* may still be said to be a personal pronoun and not a possessive, *la volontà loro,* cf. *scrisse loro.* And in Rumanian this is manifestly the case, since we here have in the singular the double construction genitive-dative of the personal pronoun and possessive: *copilul lui, ei = copilul său,* but in the plural only *copilul lor.* This state of affairs has been compared with Greek (Sandfeld 1926), but Ancient Greek used, side by side, possessives and personal genitives in all the persons, and Modern Greek has only conserved the genitive, not the possessive, so the differences are great (Togeby 1968).

17. The interrogative-relative pronoun

All the so-called interrogative and relative pronouns and the subordinate conjunctions are, historically and synchronically, case-forms of only one interrogative-relative pronoun, *qui.*

17.1 *quī* has been conserved as an accented interrogative-absolute and unaccented relative (nominative) pronoun in all the Romance languages, except in Rumanian and Spanish-Portuguese, where *quĕm* has taken its place: > Rum. int. *cine*, rel. *ce;* Sp. int. *quién*, rel. *que;* Port. int. *quem*, rel. *que, quem;* in Rumanian probably because all the substantives and the third person pronoun *el* are based on the accusative, in Spanish and Portuguese because the unaccented relative *quī* developed regularly into *que*. Interrogative *qui* existed in Old Spanish, but was absorbed by *quién*.

17.2 *quĕm* has not been continued as an accented interrogative-absolute except in Rumanian and in Spanish-Portuguese, as just mentioned. It has been conserved in all languages as a relative accusative *que*, and has perhaps fused with *quid* to form the conjunction *que* (Jeanjaquet 1894).

17.3 *cuī* was preserved as a oblique case of the interrogative-relative pronoun in the same languages as *illui, illaei, illōrum* (14.7): French, Provençal, Italian, Rumanian.

17.4 The genitive *cuius* had already in Latin been transformed into an adjective, which has survived in Sardinian, Portuguese and Spanish, that is to say in the languages where *cui* did not survive. It seems in fact natural that the interrogative-relative pronoun must be some form of genitive. Complementary distribution is not, however, complete, since there is neither *cui* nor *cuius* in Southern Italian, Rheto-Romance or Catalan.

17.5 *quĭd* was conserved as an accented interrogative neuter distinct from the animate *quī* in all languages. In Sardinian the two forms would phonologically have coincided, so *qui* was prolonged into *kíe*, and *quid* into *quid Deus > itte*. In Rumanian *quid* and *quem* would also have coincided in *ce*, but *quem* was prolonged to *cine*. As an unaccented relative, *quid* fused with *quem* to *que*.

17.6 *quŏd*, which in classical Latin was used as a causal conjunction after emotive verbs, became in Vulgar Latin the general subordinator, replacing accusative + infinitive after verba sentiendi et declarandi, and *ut* after volitive verbs. In its turn *quod,* which coincided perhaps with *cum,* was replaced by *quid* > *que,* not only in its relative functions but also as a general conjunction. This substitution took place very late (all Vulgar Latin texts use *quod*) and did not reach the conservative South-East: Sardinian, Southern Italian and Rumanian. *quod* was preserved, as *cu,* only in some dialects in Southern Italian and in Rumanian, where *că* is used after emotive and declarative verbs, *să* (< *sī*) after volitive verbs. This system of two conjunctions, *că* + indicative and *să* + subjunctive, has been explained from the Greek adstratum (Sandfeld 1900, 1926), but it is important to see that it is a conservatism, not an innovation.

17.7 *quia,* also in classical Latin a causal conjunction, was used alongside with *quod* to transform the accusative + infinitive into clauses, very frequently in the Vulgate. It has been replaced by *quid* in most languages, but has been conserved as the general conjunction *ca* in Sardinian and in Southern Italian, mostly after declarative verbs, while *che* is used after volitive verbs. In the dialect of Terra d'Otranto, the forms are *ca* + indicative, *cu* + subjunctive. The conservation of this Vulgar Latin distribution may be due to the Greek substratum (Rohlfs 1949-54: 788).

17.8 *quam* coincided with *quia* in *ca* and was replaced by *que,* except in Rumanian, where *ca* is still used for equality–comparisons.

17.9 *cum* (*quum*), extensively used in Latin, disappears, probably because of its collision with the preposition *cum,* with *quod,* and perhaps even with *quomodo* (Melander 1925).

17.10 A new conjunction *quomodo* > *como,* originally comparative, later also temporal and causal, spread to all Romance languages, reinforced into *comme, coma* in some languages, to avoid the confusion with the preposition *cum* > *con.*

17.11 *quando* has been conserved in all Romance languages.

17.12 *sī* has been changed into *se* in all Romance languages, perhaps because it coincided with *sīc,* but above all under the influence of the victorious *que.*

17.13 *ubī* has been conserved, different from *aut*, in Sardinian and Italian. It has been replaced by *unde* in languages where it coincided with *aut* > *o:* Portuguese, Spanish, Catalan, Gascon, Provençal, Rheto-Romance, Southern Italian. In French *ubi* and *aut* have coincided in *ou*, but have been both conserved, and also *unde*, which, enlarged into *dont*, has become a relative genitive, when *cui* was absorbed by *qui*.

18. The conjugations

18.1 Most of the Romance languages have conserved the four Latin conjugations in *-āre, -ēre, -ĕre, -īre*. The conjugations in *-ēre* and *-ĕre* had much in common, but they have fused only in Sardinian and in Spanish-Portuguese. In Sardinian, all the *-ĕre*-verbs have the accent on the root in the infinitive: *fákere, déppere* (< *debēre*), but on the *-e-* in the imperfect subjunctive *fakère, deppère*, so that these forms are distinguished.

The reason for this root-accentuation of the *-ēre*-verbs may be the fact that in Sardinian no weak perfect in *-ui* or in *-dedi* (25.1) was introduced, nor any weak participle in *-ūtus*, accented on the ending. The only Romance language to do so, Sardinian has conserved the perfect participle in *-ĭtus*, e. g. *déppiu*, which has influenced the other infinite form, the infinitive.

In Spanish and Portuguese there were neither *-úi* nor *-ūtus*, but *-dĕdi* and *-ĭtus* (29.1), but this is not enough to explain the generalization of the accented infinitive ending *-er*. But Spanish and Portuguese preserved a set of forms accented like the infinitive *-ar* and *-ir:* the pluperfect *cantara*, the future subjunctive *cantare*, which may have changed the accent in *legeram* > *leyéra, legerit* > *leyere*, and from here the infinitive *leer*. Another possible explanation is that the regular phonetic evolution of the *-ĕre* infinitive would lead to impossible forms like *ler, crel, dir, rel*, etc. (Wilkinson 1967: 17-18).

18.2 In Spanish, the *-er* and the *-ir* conjugations have almost identical endings in all forms, probably because they fused in the perfect *-ió* (24.2). The consequence has not been a confusion of the two conjugations, but a complementary distribution of the root vowels: *i* and *u* in the *-ir*-verbs, *e* and *o* in the *-er*-verbs, a picture smudged by the dissimilation *i* > *e* before accented *i: servir, sirvo, serví, sirvió*, etc. (Togeby 1972).

18.3 In Latin, -*are* and -*ĕre* were the two dominant conjugations. In the Romance languages -*are* is the only really dominant conjugation, except in Rumanian, where -*īre* is just as frequent, because of the great number of new -*esco*-verbs, many of them borrowed from Slavonic, but most of them internal Rumanian creations (Lombard 1954-55, Iliescu 1959).

19. The passive

19.1 The Latin synthetic passive disappeared in all Romance languages, except for the perfect participle. Vossler (1954: 124) considered the passive, the future, the supine, the gerundive, the future participle as expressions of the antique heathen naturalistic idea of destiny, rejected when a new Weltanschauung came with Christianity, Judaism and Germanness. Lausberg (1948: 322) proposed that the passive was unknown to the new romanized peoples. But these explanations are contradicted by the fact that the passive was immediately reintroduced in periphrastic constructions. So the reason for the disappearance of the synthetic passive must rather be sought in phonology: final -*m* and -*r* fell, which compromised all the first persons and a third person such as *amatur* (cf. the perfect participle).

19.2 The passive of the third inanimate person was replaced by the reflexive (15.3), except in Rheto-Romance.

19.3 Later, as a more literary construction, but also in all Romance languages, the passive was expressed by the perfect participle, which, as a predicate, was combined with *esse* in almost all languages, a construction directly inherited from Latin *sum amatus,* with a change of meaning from 'I have been loved' to 'I am loved'. This passive is formed with *venire* in Rheto-Romance, probably after the model of German *werden.* In Spanish and Potuguese the passive value is formally marked by the use of *esse* in contradistinction to the state value of *stare.* The special sense of the two verbs in Spanish and Portuguese is due to the fact that here *esse* and *sedere* fused in one form. This distribution has a systematic parallel in the use of *haber* as an auxiliary of the compound tenses, in contradistinction to *tener* (29.3).

20. The tenses of the indicative

The three Latin moods, the indicative, the subjunctive and the imperative, have passed directly into all the Romance languages, with certain
differences in use and forms.

20.1 The Latin indicative had six tenses, a system which has been
completely reconstituted in Old Spanish and in Portuguese, where the
pluperfect and the perfect are conserved with their Latin values. This
conservatism may be explained bv the lateral position of those languages.

20.2 The usual Romance system, formed in all other Western Romance
languages (except in Sursilvan) and in Tuscan, has five tenses, a present
surrounded by two pasts and by two futures (Guillaume 1929), the only
form lost being the pluperfect, after an ephemeral existence in the old
texts. This system has a striking ressemblance with Old Irish (Moignet
1959: 706), but the idea of a Celtic substratum influence is contradicted by the fact that the system is also found in Tuscan. The reason
for the disappearance of the pluperfect must rather be the introduction
of compound tenses. The compound perfect also takes half of the Latin
value of the perfect, and the compound tenses are a Pan-Romance
phenomenon.

20.3 In Sursilvan, the indicative tense system has been reduced to a
present and a past, as in the Germanic languages.

20.4 The Latin future tenses disappeared in all Romance languages,
but they were reconstituted in Western Romance and in Tuscan from
cantare habeo, while their disappearance was accepted in the ultraconservative South-East, Sardinian, Southern Italian and Rumanian, so
that there we have a three tense system: present, imperfect, perfect.
This system has acquired a fourth member in Rumanian with a pluperfect.

21. The present

21.1 The present and the imperfect are the only two Latin tenses to be
preserved in all Romance languages.

21.2 In the first person plural, isolated Rumanian is the only language to distinguish the four Latin conjugations: *cîntăm - tăcém - bátem - dormím*. In all the other languages, the accent is placed on the ending also in the third conjugation, which gives a regular system with three (or two) endings in Sardinian, Southern Italian, Rheto-Romance, Provençal, Gascon Catalan, Spanish, and Portuguese. But in Italian (and Friulian) and in French (and Franco-Provençal), the system has been reduced to one common ending for all the conjugations.

The French *-ons* has been explained from the Celtic substratum, from the Germanic superstratum, as a phonetic *u*-umlaut in *-amus,* as the velar variant *-umus* of the ending *-ĭmus* (Hermann 1955), but the most generally accepted explanation is still the analogy of *sumus* (Meyer-Lübke), which can be paralleled with that of *sunt* (Schmid 1949). Corbett (1969) presents a structuralist explanation of the analogy.

The Italian *-iamo* has also evident contacts with *siamo* (Meyer-Lübke), but Rohlfs (1949) and Lausberg (1962) prefer to see *-iamo* as a subjunctive having taken the place of the indicative in the first person plural, where the two moods can have almost the same value. An important argument in favor of the influence of *esse* is however that already in Latin *simus* was used for *sumus*.

The analogical pressure of *sumus, simus* may have been particularly strong in French and Italian because *esse* here became an auxiliary (29.3). This was also the case in Provençal, but there *sumus* was replaced by *em*.

22. The future

22.1 In a first stage, the Latin synthetic future disappeared all over Romania. That is the stage represented by the *Peregrinatio Aetheriae*. In Vossler's opinion (1925: 67) this was a most natural evolution: the idea of future is weak and will never belong to the language of the people. But how can it be then that the future was reconstituted in so many Romance languages? For the same reason, a mere tendency towards simplification cannot be accepted as a decisive factor either.

The only possible explanation of this Proto-Romance disappearance of the future is that for phonological reasons it had become impossible to utilize it. In the first conjugation, *cantabit, cantabimus* coincided with the perfect *cantauit, cantauimus,* and in the third conjugation *scribes, scribet* with the present *scribis, scribit.*

22.2 This state of affairs, with no synthetic future, has been accepted in the ultraconservative South-East (and in Sursilvan). In Sardinian and in Southern Italian, the present is simply used instead of the future. In Rumanian, the periphrase *cantare volo* > *cîntá voiu* or *volo cantare* > *voi cîntá* has been introduced, which has been attributed to the Thracian substratum (Weigand 1924), but which is more likely to be related to the parallel development in the Greek adstratum (Sandfeld 1926).

   In Sursilvan, the adoption of the periphrase *venit cantare* > *ven'el cantar* (Ebneter 1973) is probably, as usual, due to the influence of the Germanic constratum: *er wird singen.*

22.3 It is much more difficult to find the reason for the adoption, in Western Romance and in Tuscan, of the periphrase *cantare habeo,* which even agglutinizes into a new synthetic future, the most striking exception from the generally assumed analytical tendency (Valesio 1968, 1972, Butler 1969). The possibility of a Greek influence has been suggested (Löfstedt 1933), but it is improbable, above all because quite another Greek influence is seen in the Balkan language. A Christian influence has also been invoked (Coseriu 1957), but why should it not have extended to all Romania? To solve this problem one might shift the attention to the conditional, for the future *cantare habet* is only found where there is a conditional *cantare habebat.*

23. The conditional

23.1 In contradistinction to the future, there seems to be a conditional in all Romance languages. The conditional in the South-East (and in Rheto-Romance) is, however, a modal conditional, used above all in the hypothetical constructions: Sard. *díat cantare* (< *debebat cantare*), South It. *kantara* (< *cantaverat*), Dalm. *kanture* (< *cantaverit*), O. Rum. *cîntare* (< *cantaverit*), Rheto-Rom. *cantass* (< *cantavisset*). In opposition to this, the conditional *cantare habebat* of Western Romance and of Tuscan is rather a temporal conditional, belonging first of all to the indirect style.

23.2 This view is supported by the early history of the conditional. In the first texts in Vulgar Latin where the new periphrasis is found, that is to say in Tertullian, the conditional is chronologically prior to the future and is found above all in the indirect style. The future of the Old Testament *civitatem exterminabit,* which, in citation, in Classical Latin would have been transposed into accusative + infinitive, is rendered by Tertullian with use of the periphrase: *Daniel praedicavit quoniam civitas exterminari haberet.*

One might thus form the hypothesis that the new conditional was a consequence of the new indirect style replacing the accusative + infinitive. This might in fact explain that *cantare habebat* has only been introduced as a conditional in the West and in Tuscan. In those language all the object-clauses begin with *que,* whatever the governing verb may be. But in Southern Italian and in Rumanian there is a specific conjunction after the verbs directing the subjunctive, and another one after the verbs followed by the indicative (17.6-7). The indirect style is thus sufficiently marked by the conjunction and need not be by the form of the verb.

23.3 Western Romance uses as a conditional *cantare habebat,* but Tuscan *cantare habuit > canterebbe,* and North. It. *cantare habuisset > canteresse,* as a sort of halfway solution between South. It. *cantaverat > kantara* and the Western languages.

23.4 The ending *-(hab)ebat* has become *-ea, -ia* in all Western languages. This irregular loss of the intervocalic *-b-* is easily explained as the result of the transformation of a full verb *habebat* into an ending *-ebat* (Togeby 1964, Posner 1965).

24. The imperfect

The imperfect is, with the present, the most stable form of the Romance verbal system. The three Latin imperfect endings *-ābam, -ēbam, -ībam* ought phonologically to have preserved their intervocalic *-b-* as a *-v-,* but in all the Western languages the result has been *-ava* and *-ea* or *-ia,* with the loss of *-v-* in all verbs outside the first conjugation. This has been explained as a dissimilation in verbs like *habebam* and *debebam,* a theory contradicted by Italian, or as a conjugation pattern, but this development is rather due to the systematic pressure of the parallel conditional endings *-(hab)ebat > -ea, -ia* (23.4; Togeby 1964). In Provençal, Spanish and Portuguese, *-ea* developed regularly into -*ia*. In French, the ending of the conditional -*ea* > -*eie* → -*ais* was generalized in the imperfect, first at the expense of -*ia*, later even of -*abam* > -*oe*, which was a weaker form in French than elsewhere, because it lost phonologically its -*v*- in some dialects. This -*v*- was preserved in Wallon -*eve*, where thus the conjugation was conserved.

In the languages where the conditional was not formed with *habebat*, there was no such system pressure, and hence the intervocalic -*v*- was preserved in Rheto-Romance and Italian -*ava*, -*eva*, -*iva*. In Rumanian the loss of the intervocalic -*v*- is regular: *cantabam* > *cîntá*, etc.

The result has been an imperfect system with three conjugations in Italian, and two in Western Romance. Almost exactly the same distribution of the conjugations is found in the perfect, so that one might see a connection here (cf. Posner 1961).

25. The perfect

25.1 In the perfect, Latin had two weak conjugations, the first -*āvit*, and the fourth -*īvit*. This system was retained in the most archaic Romance dialect, Old Sardinian, and originally also in Southern Italian. In all the others new weak perfects were introduced for the -*ere* conjugations. The first one was -*ui*, the only one to reach another very archaic language, Rumanian. The second was -*dědi*, which characterizes all the other dialects. It has stayed different from the other conjugations in Italian -*è*, -*ètte* (cf. -*i*), Catalan -*é* (cf. -*i*), and Portuguese -*eu* (cf. -*iu*). Catalan and Portuguese have thus three weak conjugations in the perfect, as opposed to only two in the imperfect (cf. 24).

The system has in some languages been reduced to two conjugations, as in the imperfect. In Spanish, the diphthongization developed -*dedit* > -*ieu* > -*io*, which coincided with -*īvit* > -*io*. In French, the first person -*dedi* developed phonologically into -*i*, and the third person -*iet* passed analogically into -*it*.

A much more enigmatic simplification has taken place in Provençal, where -*dedit* > -*et* has not coincided with -*it*, but has been introduced in the first conjugation: *amet*, so that the conjugations in the imperfect and in the perfect do not correspond. This generalization is generally explained by the influence of *dar - dei* and *estar - estei*, but why did they not have the same influence in other languages?

25.2 In the first conjugation, *-avit* existed already in Latin in short forms. The oldest one, *-ait* (cf. *iit*) survived in Old Sardinian. Another one, *-aut*, resulted in It. *-ò*, Sp. *-ó*, Port. *-ou*. A third one, *-at*, is the base of North. It. *cantà*, Fr. *chanta*, Cat. *cantá*. In Rumanian, neither *cantaut* > *cîntau* nor *cantāt* > *cîntá* could be used, because they would coincide with the imperfect. So a new ending was created: *cîntă*.

The ending *-a* has generally been explained by the influence of *habet* > *a*, which could be reasonable, especially if one thinks of the new role of *-a* in the ending of the future *-rá*, a tense which is systematically parallel to the perfect. But this systemic pressure was possible all over Western Romania and in Tuscan: why did it only have consequences in some languages? In French, *-aut* would be impossible because it coincided most impractically with the imperfect *-abat* > *-ot* (24.1). But this explanation does not apply to the other languages with *-á*.

Here one might point to the fact that the languages from Northern Italian via French to Catalan, which show *-á*, are precisely those which lose their final unaccented vowels. A particular reduction of the perfect ending *-avit* may thus have taken place in those languages. A further argument in favor of this theory is that the distribution is the same for *-īvit*, which results in *-i(t)* in the central languages, in *-iu* not only in Port. *-i2u*, Sp. *-io2*, but also in South. It. *-iu*, *-io*, and in Old It. *-ío*.

25.3 Latin had three types of strong verbs, in *-ui*, *-si* and *-i*, stressed on the stem in *díxi, díxit, díximus, díxerunt*, on the ending in *dixísti, dixístis*. The *ui*-type became weak in Rumanian (25.1). The accent stayed on the stem in the first person plural in Rumanian *zíserăm*, just as in the present (21.2). In Spanish and Portuguese, the accent shifted to the ending in the whole plural (cf. the infinitive, 18.1), and Portuguese adopted the open vowel of the *-dedi*-perfect in all forms: *dissęste, dissęmos, dissęstes, dissęram;* Spanish only in the third person plural: OSp. *dixieron*.

The paradigm *dixi - *dicisti*, etc., and *habui - *habisti*, etc., with a simplification of the consonant group before the stressed ending, which is evident in Italian: *disse - dicesti, ebbi - avesti,* has been proposed as a base for all Romance languages by Dardel (1958); cf. Posner (1963).

The perfect is the most vulnerable point of the Romance verbal system. It virtually disappeared in Northern Italian about 1300, in Rheto-Romance about 1400, in Catalan about 1400, in Sardinian about 1500, in French about 1700, in Rumanian about 1800. In some of these languages, the result has been a two-tense system of present and imperfect: Sardinian, Rheto-Romance, Rumanian; in others, a four-tense system composed of present, imperfect, future and conditional: Northern Italian, French, Catalan.

It is natural to see in this the result of a general analytic tendency (Meillet 1926), because the perfect is replaced by the compound perfect *habet cantatum*, but it is difficult to see why this tendency should have turned out stronger in some languages than in Italian, Provençal, Spanish and Portuguese. Another explanation generally given is that the conjugation of the perfect is too complicated (Gilliéron 1919). It is true that the many strong forms are a weakness of the perfect, and that the conjugation has been very much regularized in Provençal, Spanish and Portuguese. In Rumanian, however, the perfect has been completely regularized but has nevertheless disappeared. Because of the late date of the phenomenon, one might look for a particular reason in each language. In Sardinian the position of the perfect may have been utterly precarious because there was no weak perfect created for the *-ere* verbs (25.1). Rheto-Romance may have been, as usual, under the influence of the Germanic constratum. And in French the confusion between the present and the perfect of *finir* may have compromised the perfect (Schogt 1964). In Rumanian it would perhaps not be quite impossible to envisage a style influence from French.

25.4 The perfect has been replaced by the compound perfect, except in Catalan, where the substitute is *va cantar,* a historical present which has taken the place of the perfect because the first and the second persons of the plural coincided: *anam cantar, anats cantar* (Badía Margarit 1951: 327).

26. The pluperfect

26.1 The pluperfect *cantaverat > cantara* was preserved in its original function in the isolated and lateral and hence conservative languages Old Sardinian, Portuguese and Old Spanish. A synthetic pluperfect indicative also exists in another lateral language, Rum. *cantase,* but based etymologically on the Latin pluperfect subjunctive, because the pluperfect indicative had fused with the potential (27.3). In all the other languages, the synthetic pluperfect has been replaced by an analytical one, by virtue of the general tendency.

26.2 With the temporal value of a perfect, the pluperfect existed for some time in Old French; it disappeared, not for phonological reasons, but because it was superfluous.

26.3 Already in Latin, the pluperfect had a modal value in the hypothetical constructions. This value of *cantara* has been conserved in Southern Italian, Rumanian (O. Rum. *cîntare* or *cîntară*), where there is no temporal conditional (23.1), and in Provençal, Catalan, Spanish and Portuguese, along with the temporal conditional *cantare habebat* (Gamillscheg 1913, Mourin 1959).

The pluperfect *cantara* was not adopted as a modal conditional in Tuscan and Northern Italian, because here the other conditional was formed in a different way: *cantare habuit* and *cantare habuisset* (23.3).

And if *cantara* has not been used as a modal conditional in French, that must be due to the fact that here, from the beginnings of the language, the hypothetical constructions were in the indicative, not in the subjunctive (Wagner 1939).

27. The tenses of the subjunctive
27.1 Latin had four tenses in the subjunctive. The imperfect *cantaret* has survived only in the most isolated and hence most archaic dialect, Sardinian, which thus acquired a system of two tenses, present and imperfect, because it gave up the perfect and the pluperfect, just as in the indicative it lost the perfect future and the pluperfect (20.5).

27.2 In all the other languages, the Latin imperfect *cantaret* disappeared, because it coincided with the perfect future *cantaverit*, the perfect subjunctive *cantaverit*, and the infinitive *cantare*. The imperfect was replaced by the Latin pluperfect *cantavisset* > *cantasset*, which had a more marked form, but only in those languages which also had a conditional *cantare habebat*, and a regular indirect style (23.2), that is to say in Western Romance and in Tuscan, but not in Southern Italian, Dalmatian, or Rumanian. In Southern Italian, the subjunctive has been almost completely lost, under the influence of the Greek substratum. In Rumanian, a past is followed by a present subjunctive: *eram să vă spun* 'j'étais sur le point que je vous dise'.

27.3 The future perfect *cantavero, -it* and the perfect subjunctive *cantaverim, -it* coincided in a potential *cantaret,* which was used in some languages as a sort of conditional of the subjunctive. The most complete system of the subjunctive is found in Portuguese and Spanish, just as it is the case in the indicative (20.1), with three tenses, e. g., in Portuguese a past *cantasse,* a present *cante,* and a future *cantar.* Golden Age Spanish even reconstructed a system of four tenses in the subjunctive by using also the pluperfect indicative *cantaverat* as a conditional subjunctive *cantara* (26.3).

27.4 But the general rule is that where *cantaverat* was adopted as a conditional, *cantaverit* was not. This is the case in Catalan and Provençal, which have thus a system of three tenses in the subjunctive: present, past and conditional. In French and Tuscan, neither *cantaverat* nor *cantaverit* was introduced as a conditional (26.3), so there is only a present-past system here.

27.5 In the South-Eastern languages, there was no need for an imperfect subjunctive, but only for a present and a conditional. In Southern Italian the conditional chosen was *cantara,* in Dalmatian and in Rumanian *cantavero, -it* > Dalm. *kanture,* O. Rum. *cîntare.*

27.6 Sursilvan has developed a completely new system of tenses in the subjunctive, with two direct tenses, a present *el levi* and a conditional used in hypothetical constructions *el levass,* and two indirect tenses, an imperfect used in the indirect style: *che el levavi* (different from the indicative *el levava*), and a "conditional" used after the expressions which are followed by the subjunctive in all Romance languages: *che el levassi.* The creation of a special imperfect subjunctive for the indirect style must have its model in German.

27.7 The imperfect subjunctive has fallen out of use in modern French. This may be due to a general tendency towards a purely modal subjunctive without any temporality (Warnant 1974); but this does not explain the great differences between the languages. Another possibility would be to see a connection with the dying out of the perfect (25.3), but there is no direct correspondence. The imperfect subjunctive is still used in Northern Italian, in Rheto-Romance and in Catalan, where the perfect has disappeared. It is only in French that we find this retreat of the imperfect subjunctive, and only in Central French. The two tenses are still in use in North-Eastern Wallon, while in the center and in the West the only form left is the etymological imperfect. A specific French cause for the abolition of the imperfect might be the almost complete formal identity of the present and the imperfect in the *finir*-conjugation.

28. The imperative

28.1 The Latin future imperative *amato, audīto* has disappeared in all languages owing to its confusion with the participle *amatus, audītus*.

28.2 The Latin imperative of the singular *cantā* has developed into Romance imperatives clearly distinct from the indicative and from the subjunctive, even in Eastern Romance, in spite of the loss of the final -*s:* It. *canta* (ind. *canti*), Rum. *cîntă* (ind. *cînţi*).

28.3 The imperative of the plural *cantate* coincided with the indicative in Eastern Romance: It. *cantate*. In Western Romance it remained as a distinct form in the languages conserving the final vowel, but in languages losing the final vowel, *cantate* could not be distinguished from the participle *cantatum,* and so the imperative was replaced by the indicative (rarely by the subjunctive). Thus we have in Portuguese *cantai* (part. *cantado*), in Spanish *cantad* (part. *cantado*), in Engadinian *chanté* (part. *chantô*). But in French *chanté* → *chantez,* in Provençal *cantat* → *cantats, cantau* (Kuen 1950).

28.4 An imperative first person plural has been created on the basis of the present subjunctive: Sp. *cantemos,* etc. In French it has later coincided with the indicative: *chantons,* because the subjunctive changed its ending to -*ions.*

28.5 The Latin imperative could not be combined with a negation. Instead the subjunctive was used in the perfect: *nē cantaveris,* or in the present: *nē cantes,* or the verb *nolo: noli cantare.* This rule has been kept in the Romance languages in the cases where the imperative remained distinct from the other moods. The present subjunctive is used in negative orders in the singular and in the plural in Sardinian,

Spanish, Portuguese, while the negative infinitive is used with an imperative value in both numbers in Rheto-Romance. In the other languages, in Rumanian, Italian, Old French, Provençal, the negative infinitive is used in the singular, where the imperative has its own form, but the negative imperative in the plural, where it is identical with another mood, e. g. It. *non cantare - non cantate.*

This negative infinitive has its origin either in the popular use of the infinitive in orders (Löfstedt 1966), or in the construction *noli cantare,* or in *ne cantaveris > non cantares,* with the final *-s,* however, a problem in the Western languages. An argument in favor of the last theory is the fact that this use of the infinitive is not found in the languages where *cantaret* is used as a subjunctive tense: in Sardinian, Portuguese and Spanish (see 27).

29. The participle

29.1 The perfect participle is the only participle left in the Romance languages, because the future participle *amaturus* disappeared with the future (21.1), and because the present participle ceased to have verbal functions and became a pure adjective (30). The participle followed the conjugation model of the perfect. In Latin, there was only a weak participle in the first conjugation *-ātus* and in the fourth *-ītus,* and this is still the case in Sardinian, just as in the perfect (25.1). In the other languages a weak participle *-ūtus* was introduced, corresponding to the weak perfect *-ui,* but also to *-dedi,* except in Spanish and Portuguese, where there were only three conjugations (18.1), and where neither the weak perfect *-ui* not the participle *-ūtus* was adopted, so that *-ido* became the common participle for the *-er* and *-ir* verbs.

29.2 The compound tenses existed already in Latin: *amatum est,* and from the deponent verbs the form has been directly continued in Romance: *mortuus est, natus est.* An innovation is the use of *habere* as an auxiliary. The generalized use of the compound tenses in all Romance languages can be considered a result of a general analytic tendency (Dietrich 1973).

29.3 The original situation is the use of the two auxiliaries *esse* and *habere,* preserved in Sardinian, Italian, Rheto-Romance, French and Provençal. *Habere* was generalized during the Middle Ages in Rumanian, Southern Italian, Catalan, Spanish and Portuguese. For Rumanian and Southern Italian a Greek influence might be possible. For Rumanian, the substratum influence could also be invoked: Albanian uses only 'to have'. The use of the prepositional accusative (7.4) could have weakened the distinction between intransitive and transitive verbs in Portuguese, Spanish, Catalan, Southern Italian and Rumanian, but this explanation is contradicted by the use of the two auxiliaries in Sardinian and Rheto-Romance. Another possibility would be that *esse,* after having fused with *sedere* (19.3), was less fit to be an auxiliary of the perfect in Portuguese and Spanish, but this fusion did not take place in Catalan, where the generalization of *habere* could, however, be of Spanish origin. The auxiliarization of *habere* could also have been furthered by the concurrence of *tenere* in Portuguese, Spanish (and Catalan), Sardinian, Southern Italian, where characteristically the *-a-* accusative is used.

29.4 In languages having the two auxiliaries *esse* and *habere,* their use may vary from language to language. But *esse* will always be the auxiliary of the reflexive verbs. This is a systematic law which is not easy to explain.

29.5 The agreement of the participle with the object seems to exist in the same languages where there are two auxiliaries, not in those where *habere* has been generalized.

29.6 At a time when the literary passive Rum. *a fi* 'to be' + participle had not yet come into use (19.3), from the Slavonic model, as generally presumed, the use of *a fi* was introduced to form the compound tenses of the active in the future, the conditional and the subjunctive: *să fiu lăudat,* which in the modern form *să fi lăudat* is also the form of the passive.

29.7 The use of the participle as an infinitive or supine after the preposition *de: am multe de făcut* 'I have much to do', has only a parallel in Albanian (Sandfeld 1926).

30. The gerund
30.1 It is a Pan-Romance phenomenon that the adjectival present participle *cantans, cantantem* became a pure derived verbal adjective,

replaced in its verbal functions by relative clauses, a result of the general analytical tendency (Wandruszka 1958). But the adverbial gerund, *cantando,* preserved its verbal functions, and stayed morphologically distinct from the former present participle: Old Sardinian *-ando* (the present participle has disappeared), Italian *-ando* (pr. part. *-ante*), Rheto-Romance *-ond* (pr. part. *-ont*), Spanish *-ando* (pr. part. *-ante*), Portuguese *-ando* (pr. part. *-ante*).

But in the languages which lose their final vowel, in French, Provençal and Catalan, the gerund *-ando* and the present participle *-ante* coincided in the form *-ant.*

30.2 The three Latin conjugations *-ando, -endo, -indo* have been preserved in Sardinian, Friulian, Sursilvan, Gascon, Catalan and Portuguese. The ending *-endo* has been extended to the *-ire*-conjugation in Italian, Provençal and Spanish. And the ending *-ando* has been generalized to all verbs in French, perhaps because here the imperfect has one and the same ending (24).

31. The infinitive

31.1 The Latin perfect infinitive *cantavisse* disappeared because it coincided with the pluperfect subjunctive. The infinitive is generally taken as the basic form of the conjugations (18).

31.2 The reduced use of the Rumanian infinitive has been explained as an influence from the substratum, where the infinitive did not exist (Miklosich 1862, Schuchardt 1900, Weigand 1924). But the positive correspondence with Albanian *me* + participle is seen in Rumanian *de* + an active past participle (29.6).

Most Romanists have accepted the theory that the decisive factor has been the Greek adstratum (Sandfeld 1926, Wartburg 1950, Giese 1952, Rohlfs 1958c). An important piece of evidence is the replacing of the infinitive by *să*-clauses in the subjunctive: *vreá să facă* 'he will that he shall do' = 'he will do', as in Greek. Another is that the same replacement is seen in Southern Italy, under the influence of the Greek substratum.

A structural explanation may, however, also be given. The Greek infinitive disappeared and was replaced by the finite verb because the loss of its final *-n* made it coincide with those finite forms. The same thing has happened in Rumanian, where the original long infinitive *cîntare* was taken to be a noun and preserved as such, because its ending coincided with *-ale > -are*. As an infinitive verb it was reduced to a short form, first in constructions with a postposed auxiliary: *cînta(re) voiu*. Those short infinitives have coincided with various finite forms and thus opened the door to the subjunctive clauses introduced by *să*. But the infinitive has not disappeared in Rumanian, as in Greek. It was protected by an infinitive index *a* marking its nominal function, just as in the Germanic languages (Togeby 1962).

31.3 In French, the position of the infinitive was also threatened when the loss of the final *-r* made *chanter* and *finir* undistinguishable from the past participle *chanté* and *fini*. That is probably why the preposition *de* was introduced to mark the infinitive as a noun in various functions.

But the nominalized infinitive *le chanter* was compromised by this confusion. So, in contradistinction to the other Romance languages it disappeared in French in its real verbal functions, and was also replaced by *de* + infinitive.

31.4 The Portuguese future subjunctive *cantar* (27.3), but not the Spanish *cantare*, coincided with the infinitive, which, combined with the construction nominative + infinitive, resulted in the use of a personal infinitive, for instance after prepositions: *parti depois de terem falado* 'I left after they had spoken' (Togeby 1955).

Exactly the same thing happened in Sardinian, where the imperfect subjunctive (27.1) coincided with the infinitive, which as a result can be used with personal endings: *prima 'e torrarédzis = prima 'e torrare bóis* 'prima di tornare (voi)'. Wagner (1938-39) considers the form as an imperfect subjunctive, while Rohlfs (1958c) viewed it as a personal infinitive.

32. Conjunctions

32.1 Among the conjunctions of coordination, *et* was conserved in all languages, except in Rumanian, where pretonic *e* became most impractically *ă*, so *et* was replaced by *sīc > și*.

Gascon has adopted a series of enunciative particles, *e, que, be, ya*, which are of Romance origin but seem to be used after a Basque model.

The adversative coordinator *sĕd* disappeared in all languages, probably because of its collision with *sī* > *se* (cf. *que*) 'if', and was replaced by *magis*, except in Rumanian, where this word was reserved for the comparison (10.4).

32.2 All Romance conjunctions of subordination can be considered as case forms of the interrogative-relative pronoun (17.5-12).

33. Prepositions

33.1 Many concrete Latin prepositions disappeared. And two very abstract prepositions were created: *de* and *a*, used as case markers in all languages (7.1), *de* as a partitive article in French and Italian (12.7), *de* and *a* as infinitive indices in Rumanian and in French (31.3) (Brøndal 1940).

33.2 No Slavonic preposition was borrowed by Rumanian. An Arab preposition was borrowed by Spanish: *hasta*, but the corresponding Portuguese *até* is a Romance formation based on *tenus*. This proves the sparse influence of the superstratum even on vocabulary.

33.3 *sĭne* was lost in all languages, except Old Spanish *sen*, Spanish *sim*, with an unexplained vowel, and Portuguese *sem*, perhaps because *sine* sounded too much like *sī* → *se* 'if'. It was mostly reinforced into *absentia* > It. *senza*, Fr. *sans*.

33.4 *sŭb* was also lost in all languages, except in Spanish *so* (old for *bajo*) and Portuguese *sob*, probably because it coincided with the possessive. It was replaced by the adverb *subtus* > It. *sotto*, Fr. *sous*.

33.5 *per* and *pro* have fused in one preposition in all languages except in French *par* and *pour*. The distinction has been recreated in Spanish *por* and *para*.

33.6 *cum* was preserved as *con* in all languages, except in French, Provençal and Catalan, where it coincided with *como*, and hence was replaced by *apud* (Melander 1925).

33.7 *in* + the article resulted in various collisions in French, Provençal, Rheto-Romance, and Northern Italian, and was consequently reinforced by the use of *intus* → Fr. *dans*, etc.

33.8 *inter* has been preserved in all the Romance languages, except in Italian, where *intra* > *tra* and *infra* > *fra* were preferred because of the parallelism with *trans* > *tra, de ab* > *da,* and *sopra.*

34. Adverbs

34.1 The Latin constructions with many negative words, *nemo, nihil, unquam,* etc., were replaced in all Romance languages by a unique negation *non* combined with various positive words, another aspect of the general analytical tendency. Only in French and Northern Italian, *non* developed into an unaccented bound negation *ne,* which needed a reinforcing adverb *pas* or *mīca.*

nemo was only preserved in the most conservative languages, Sardinian and Rumanian, but was elsewhere replaced by other words. *nihil* was continued nowhere. Only *nullus* and *nec* survived everywhere.

34.2 The local adverbs have here been considered as case forms of the demonstrative (13.6).

34.3 Among the temporal adverbs, Latin *nunc* disappeared, probably because it coincided with *non,* and was replaced by *horā. tunc* was retained in Rumanian, Spanish and Portuguese, but elsewhere replaced by *illā horā.*

hŏdie and *hĕrī* have survived in all languages, *cras* only in archaic Sardinian and Southern Italian.

34.4 The Latin adverb *sīc* was preserved as *si* in the languages where 'yes' was said in another way (35.2): French and Provençal *si,* but was reinforced in the languages that used affirmative *si*: It. *cosí,* Sp. *así.*

35. Interjections

35.1 In answers, *non* was already used as a sort of interjection in Latin and has continued to be so in all the Romance languages.

35.2 But there was no word for 'yes' in Latin, and Dante felicitously decided to use the Romance forms for it as the basis of his classification of the Romance languages. The two most archaic languages, Sardinian and Rumanian, have not changed the Latin situation very much. Old

Sardinian used *emmo*. Rumanian (and Portuguese) have to a large extent stuck to the characteristic Latin affirmation by means of the repetition of the verb. In Rumanian dialects *e* < *est* is still found. Modern Rumanian has adopted the Slavonic *da*.

The other Romance languages fall into two groups: *sīc*-languages and *hŏc*-languages. *sīc* is the first Romance affirmative interjection, used in Italian, Rheto-Friulian, Spanish and Portuguese. In between, in the languages using *hŏc* as a neuter demonstrative (13.3), *hŏc* was also used for direct affirmation, while *sīc* was reserved for the affirmative answer to a negative question, the result being a system of three interjections in French, Franco-Provençal, Provençal, Gascon and Catalan. In Catalan, the modern use of *sí* is secondary. In French, where *hŏc* was reduced to *o*, which could be confounded with various other words, the subject pronoun was added to clarify the meaning: *o je, o il* > *oui*.

36. Prefixes

The fourth type of morphemes, after roots, flexives, and particles, comprises the derivatives. Prefixes were very scarce in Latin. They became very frequent in the Romance languages, but mostly as learned formations based on the lost Latin prepositions. In French *con-* is a prefix, but in Italian and Spanish *con* is a preposition, which can be used in various compounds.

Prefixes can be borrowed. In Rumanian the negative prefix *ne-* (instead of *in-*) comes from Slavonic, and also *răs-*, which to some extent has been mixed with *re-*. In French *mé-* may come from Latin *minus* or from Germanic *miss-*. An argument for the last theory is that it is found above all in French, scarcely in Provençal and Italian, not at all in Rumanian.

37. Modificatives

The suffixes which, just as the prefixes, do not change the word class status of the root to which they are added may be called modificatives, for instance the diminutives, the augmentatives and the absolute superlatives.

37.1 Diminutives are widely used in the Romance languages and are characterized etymologically by an expressive gemination of consonants. Latin had *-ellus,* which is still found in all Romance languages, and which is the only diminutive known by Sardinian. The next wave brings *-īccus, -ūccus,* which are found in Rumanian, Southern Italian and Friulian. A third wave brings *-ittus,* which is most popular in Tuscan and Western Romance. It has been ascribed to the Celtic substratum (Hasselrot 1957). French has to a large extent given up the use of diminutives, probably because *-et,* losing its final *-t,* was no more a distinct diminutive, and because *-ellus* coincided with the ordinary suffix *-alis* in *-el.* The consequence has been an increased use of *petit* (Hasselrot 1972: 89), which may have resulted in other chain reactions in syntax.

37.2 Augmentatives did not exist in Latin nor do they in Sardinian. The suffix *-one* was introduced in most languages, but not in French, Provençal, Catalan, where only *-aceus* > Fr. *-asse* came into use, perhaps because *-on* in French and Provençal was the ending of the oblique case of some substantives, e. g. *baron* (cf. 7.4).

37.3 The learned absolute superlative (10.1), unknown to Sardinian and Rumanian, has been favored in the other Romance languages with many diminutives and augmentatives, but not in French where those modificatives were dying out.

38. Suffixes
38.1 Curiously enough, the verbal suffix which has had most success in Romania is the Greek *-idiare,* which, introduced with Christianity, did not reach Sardinian, but created in Rumanian a particular variant of the first conjugation, with 1500 verbs: *salvá-salvez,* etc.

38.2 A new ultrafrequent deverbal adjectival suffix was created by the reduction of the Latin present participle to a simple adjective, except in Sardinian and Rumanian (30.1), with an ending in *-ante* or *-ente* following that of the gerund. In Rumanian it has been replaced by *-tor: lucrător* 'working'.

The suffix *-bilis* has been adopted neither in Sardinian nor in Rumanian. The forms *-ēbilis, -ībilis* have developed regularly into It. *-évole,* but *-abile, -ibile* are learned formations, like the corresponding forms in French and Spanish.

38.3 The deverbal substantival suffix *-ātus, -ītus* has been little used, because of its collision with the past participle, but this has on the contrary fortified its position in Rumanian, where the past participle can be used as a verbal substantive (29.6): *făcut* 'action', etc.

The deadjectival substantival suffix *-ia* was preferred by Christian authors as a means of nominalizing adjectives in *-ens: clementia*, etc. This *-entia* is the only form known in Rumanian: *credinţă*, where the present participle was not preserved (30.1). In the other languages, the new adjectives coming from the present participles: *-ante*, etc., introduced *-antia* (Malkiel 1945).

39. Synchrony and diachrony

In proclaiming the equal value of synchrony and diachrony, Saussure minimized in reality the importance of diachrony, which had been dominant up to his time. Since then synchronic studies have been flourishing at the expense of diachronic. But the time seems to have come for a revival of diachrony. There are great possibilities in a new diachrony based on the enormous progress in synchronic studies. For methodologically diachrony presupposes synchrony. For each step forward in the synchronic description of the system involved, we will be able to give a better diachronic clue to the change from one system to another. So, the new inspiration which has come from generative or transformational grammar will certainly also one day have a fruitful impact on Romance historical morphology.

PETER F. DEMBOWSKI

Romance historical syntax

1.1 Anyone contemplating trends in historical syntax must ask himself
what is meant by that category. The very term 'syntax' is of course
problematical. In fact, what syntax designates – and this is also the case
with its close relatives 'morphology', 'grammar', and even 'semantics'
and 'stylistics' – must be determined with respect to the disciplinary
orientation of those who use it. The problem of delimitation of syntax
was seemingly simple only in times when one could make and maintain
a clear-cut distinction between grammatical entities arranged according
to their formal properties in descriptive, normative groups (morphology), and these entities seen in their normal linguistic function, i. e., in
their normal place in speech (syntax). One does not, as a rule, maintain
such a distinction now. The nature and function of linguistic
phenomena are, in our days, constantly merged, or better: the nature
tends to be explained in terms of function. For example (and to over-
simplify a little): the tradition in American linguistics is to deal with
linguistic entities in terms of syntagmas, whereas European, Saussurian
tradition(s) deal(s) with paradigmatic constructs. Obviously, what in
one of these traditions is 'syntax' or 'morphology' depends on these
basic approaches in dealing with linguistic distinctions[1].

1.1.1 As a result, the increasingly popular terms 'morphosyntax', 'morphosyntactic', etc. do not necessarily reflect the often deplorable trend
to coin new terminology for its own sake, but correspond to a realization that the distinction between morphology and syntax is not a distinction of essence but rather a result of different ways of considering
linguistic reality. The term 'morphosyntax' acknowledges the funda-

mental affinity between these two ways. Both 'syntax' and 'morphosyn-tax' I shall therefore take to mean the varied disciplinary approaches taken by modern linguists and philologists.

1.2 The term 'historical' as applied to Romance syntax may require elucidation. One of the distinctive features of Romance languages (at least of the best known and most thoroughly investigated ones among them) is the practically 'unlimited' availability of documents from the earlier stages, as well as the existence of a rich body of opinion concerning these documents. It is therefore natural that very many 'historical' studies in Romance are explicitly so. They are concerned with the presentation and/or explanation of linguistic change. Very often, they present the Latin 'etymological' background, the parallel development in different Romance dialects, and the modern results. Many Romance studies, however, are 'historical' in a different sense. They do not examine a cross-temporal development explicitly but rather they concentrate on a given point in the past referring implicitly to the modern situation. Whereas the very numerous studies of modern syntax of Romance can be rigorously synchronic, and usually are so, a strictly synchronic analysis of the linguistic data taken from the past constitutes a real exception[2].

1.3 The study of syntax presents affinities with other branches of linguistic and philological inquiries. A considerable number of students of syntax, both synchronic-modern and historical, base their approaches on semantic considerations. Whether or not 'syntax' does in fact become in their work a subdivision of 'semantics' is not essential here. What is important is that the morphosyntactic explanations that they offer depend on the semantically defined oppositions[3].

1.4 Finally, syntactic inquiries come, in certain modern practices, very close to stylistics. It does not really matter here whether for certain linguists and philologists the borderline between syntax and stylistics can be established clearly, or whether syntax can be subsumed under a larger category of stylistics[4]. What matters really are the various degrees of emphasis on the individual, literary, artistic aspects of the materials studied, which are given in various syntactic inquiries. The importance of more or less explicitly stylistic approaches in historical syntax for the Romance field stems from the very nature of that field. More perhaps than other areas the Romance languages are endowed with very rich and varied, especially literary, documents. They possess also a long and proud philological tradition of analysis and interpretation of these documents not only in terms of language history but also in the light of literary conventions. Such a tradition accounts for a 'natural' interest in stylistic approaches to syntactic inquiries, as well as for the existence of a somewhat ill-defined borderline between syntax and stylistics[5].

1.5 It is important for the understanding of the current trends in Romance linguistics and philology that we bear in mind that syntax studies occupy a rather ill-defined territory between morphological, semantic, and stylistic inquiries[6]. Such a position implies, of course, the interdependence of historical syntax studies and morphological, semantic and stylistic insights and approaches. The dependence of historical syntax on other modes of perceiving the linguistic facts varies with different schools and with different linguists. It has to be clearly understood, because, very often, it is neither acknowledged nor explicit. It makes an inquiry into the field of Romance historical syntax quite difficult, but also, as we shall see, it can be helpful in distinguishing the basic intellectual trends and fundamental methodological approaches in this field.

2.1 Modern linguistics, particularly after 1957, has had an enormous impact, in the first place, on all kinds of synchronic studies. It has also influenced some aspects of historical studies, particularly phonology, where the ground had been well prepared by various structural schools, but it has not as yet seriously affected morphosyntactic studies of Romance. There are many reasons for this, some of which will be mentioned later. For the present, I wish to point out that the relatively weak position of syntax vis-à-vis other historical inquiries is also a heritage of the past. One must agree with King (1969: 140) when he observes that "Syntax has always been a stepchild in the family of historical linguistics. A language cannot get along without syntax, but that it can is exactly the impression one might get from reading the average 'handbook' on the historical development of a language. There have been no great 'breakthroughs' in historical syntax comparable to the Law of Palatals, Verner's Law, or the discovery of Indo-European laryngeals." It must therefore be said that research in Romance historical syntax occupies, relatively speaking, a modest position in the enormous mass of studies devoted to other branches of Romance linguistics. Although the editors of the recent *Readings in Romance linguistics* are careful in pointing out that their miscellany is not "a complete reflection of Romance linguistics since the 1950's" (Anderson–Creore 1972: 7), I am inclined to believe that the assignment of space to the items treating historical morphosyntax does reflect grosso modo the quantitative importance of diachronic morphosyntactic studies vis-à-vis other branches of Romance linguistic research. Out of twenty-seven articles only four deal with diachronic morphology and syntax[7]. It is, therefore, difficult to share an optimistic assertion made by a contemporary linguist, that "the substantial core of agreement about the form and substance of transformational grammar is certainly enough to support its application to Romance historical [syntax] problems. This application began in the 1960's and promises to be extremely fruitful" (King 1969: 141). It suffices to observe that its applications to Romance historical syntax have not as yet been 'extremely fruitful'. Romance linguists of the post-1957 persuasions do not, as a rule, choose historical syntax as their field of activity. Let us take another 'statistical' example. In the extensive bibliography appended to Casagrande – Saciuk (1972) one finds that out of some three hundred items treating Romance linguistics either in a generative or in at least a 'modern' perspective, only about fifteen could be classified under the rubric of historical syntax.

2.2 For the history of Romance studies, there is nothing surprising in such a state of affairs. Historical syntax is difficult, and this difficulty is reflected in the general output of Romance linguistics and philology during the 'Golden Age' of those disciplines, i. e., from about 1880 until the Second World War. If we look closer at that output we notice that historical syntax occupies only a modest position in the total production. The great historical studies of the 'Golden Age', i. e., the studies which have served as traditional scientific background for the current situation, do not stress, on the whole, specifically syntactic problems. It is true that a classic such as Meyer-Lübke (1890-1902) is divided into three parts: *Lautlehre, Formenlehre* and *Syntax* (1899), followed by an additional volume containing an Index. Volume 3, *Romanische Syntax*[8] is, as far as I know the only extensive work (815 pp.) devoted exclusively to the comparative historical syntax of Romance languages. Far less insistent on syntax are other 'classical' historical grammars. Thus, for example, the widely consulted Bourciez (1910, [4]1946)[9] which is divided into chronological and geographic compartments (*Le latin, Phase romane primitive, Ancient français et provençal,* etc.), offers less information concerning historical syntax than Meyer-Lübke (1899). Each compartment organized as a chapter offers: (1) brief *faits historiques,* (2) *les sons* (the longest section), (3) *les mots* (borrowings and word-formations), (4) *les formes,* and (5) *la phrase.* The information concerning historical syntax must be sought not only in the last subdivision, but also in the section on forms, since Bourciez follows quite systematically a morphosyntactic approach defining the forms presented by means of their functions. He seems to have systematized the principles generally followed in the monumental collective work under the general editorship of Gröber (I, 1888, [2]1904-1906)[10], where the *Lautlehre* receives the lion's share, and where usually there are no separate sections dealing with syntax as such[11]. The extensive morphosyntactic data must be culled from the *Formenlehre* sections.

2.2.1 The relative importance of historical syntax can be deduced, if we consult the way historical grammarians for individual Romance languages arranged their materials during the 'Golden Age'. The tripartite mode (phonology – morphology – syntax) adhered to by Meyer-Lübke (1899) was maintained and extended to include other subdivisions by various 'classics'. Nyrop (1899-1930) is divided into six volumes, two of which, V (1925) and VI (1930), deal with syntax[12]. Brunot (1905, [4]1933)[13] preserves the three facets of linguistic analysis interspersed with others (spelling, vocabulary, latinisms, etc.). Brunot and Bruneau (1933, [4]1949)[14] maintain also the tripartite organization.

2.2.2 Even more important for our purpose is the presence or absence of historical syntax treatment in more modern, or modernized historical grammars and language histories. These works, certainly heirs (i. e., continuators or revisionists) of the great compendia of the 'Golden Age', can be divided grosso modo into two groups. The first maintains (or, often, expands) the tripartite division, in either case assigning (a) significant part(s) of the work to the explicit discussion of historical syntax. Such well-known works as Rohlfs (1949-1954)[15], Moll y Casanovas (1952), García de Diego (1951, [3]1970), and others offer an autonomous treatment of historical syntax. This is true even in such culturally slanted language history as Silva Neto (1952, [2]1970).

2.2.2.1 But a large number of standard reference works in Romance historical linguistics belong to the second group. These works, different as they are in scope, depth, theoretical assumptions, intended public, etc. share one fundamental trait. They are organized along general bipartite lines (phonology – morphology). A great amount of information and commentary on historical syntax can, of course, be found in the morphological part, but such avoidance of specifically syntactic problems, treated as such, by some very well-known and widely consulted works[16] seems to confirm more than anything else King's (1969) pessimistic appraisal of syntax as a stepchild in the family of historical linguistics.

2.3 There are reasons, nevertheless, to indicate that an excessive pessimism even with regard to general historical manuals is not in order. Certain more recent works, more conscious of theoretical problems do stress the importance of syntax. We need only consider here two grammars (both good examples of 'haute vulgarisation'), Kukenheim (1968)[17] and Moignet (1973) to realize that the diverse efforts to reconsider methodological bases do lead to emphasizing the importance of syntax. The same emphasis is seen in such 'Introductions' as Iordan-Manoliu Manea (1965)[18]. The section important for us (*Morfosintaxa*) was written by Manoliu Manea, a modern linguist at home in traditional historical linguistics as well as in current structural and transformational theories[19]. She has since recast the 1965 volume in her *Gramatica comparată* (1971)[20]. The importance of syntax is also evident in the methodologically slanted, concise and frankly pedagogical Pottier (1958, [2]1960), where syntax and morphology are seen as an organic whole in the light of Pottier's own brand of psychosystématique. Tekavčić (1972) is a more extensive and ambitious ideological descendant of Pottier's manual. The solid position occupied by historical syntax in such modern works as the above indicates, incidentally, a healthy persistence of historical grammars.

2.4 If I have dwelt at length on the position of historical syntax in general historical grammars and language histories, it is because such syntheses have always had a profound influence on current trends in historical linguistics. They introduce and, more often, confirm these trends. They can serve as good indicators of the general state of our discipline. But in order to understand the background to present-day trends in historical syntax, we must also remember that in the Romance field the most extensive work in historical syntax has been carried out in studies devoted exclusively to the history of syntax, rather than in various types of historical grammars. Here again Romance and particularly French present-day research can rightly boast about a distinguished tradition going back to the later years of the 'Golden Age'. I have in mind extensive, sometimes multi-volume ventures into historical syntax representing either continuations, or, often, various reactions to the neo-grammarian doctrine. It was in historical syntax that linguistic 'idealism' of the 1920's and 1930's found its clear expression. The insistence on psychological, creative, and artistic bases fitted very well into the explicatory system of syntactic change. In Sneyders de Vogel (1919, [2]1927), Lerch (1925-1934), Ettmayer (1930-1936), and Gamillscheg (1957a)[21] historical syntax, approached with different degrees of theoretical involvement, is conceived as a 'Ding an sich', rather than as a section of a bi-, tri-, or multipartite grammar or language history. A pioneering work in Portuguese, Epiphânio de Silva Dias (1918, 1959) and a recent 'traditionalist' Spanish work by M. Alonso (1962) should also be mentioned here[22].

3. The works described up to now constitute a kind of foundation upon which most of the research in Romance historical syntax in the last forty years or so has been constructed. The studies carried out in the framework of this research deal with countless aspects of individual morphosyntactic problems. They range from a book-length monograph to a page-long mise au point. It would be impossible to list most of them. It would be impossible even to mention those which I might, from my personal point of view, consider the most significant. Rather, let me distinguish several categories among them and offer examples of each. These categories illustrate the most significant current trends in historical syntax. They correspond to various modes in which syntactic

research is conceived. Like most categories they represent an oversimplification.

3.1 A fundamental practical distinction between various approaches to historical syntax, a distinction which implies also an ideological position, is that between the 'text-centered' and 'problem-centered' approach. The 'text-centered' study must almost always be a stylistic one. The student concentrates upon the analysis of syntax, or more often, on certain syntactic phenomena, in a restricted and clearly defined corpus, such as a single text, author, or genre. The 'first' aim of such studies is stylistic, since they attempt to elucidate the syntactic phenomena specific to the corpus, by contrasting them, frequently in a tacit manner, with corresponding modern phenomena. Only 'by extension' do they contribute to the general store of knowledge of historical syntax by, first of all, presenting more refined data, and, above all, confirming, weakening, or rejecting a given tenet. Numerous studies in this category remind us again about one of the fundamental features of Romance historical linguistics. Most of the materials dealt with by historians of Romance languages are explicitly literary. This means that syntactic phenomena in this category are, if not exclusively, at least predominantly literary. These phenomena may very well have belonged to conventional literary habits rather than to 'real' linguistic patterns used by ordinary speakers of a given language.

3.1.1 Many studies such as Sandmann (1953), Lope Blanch (1956), Dąbska-Prokop (1965), Körner (1968), Flasche (1969), Yvon (1960) (as well as other similar analyses by this linguist), treat a single author or a single work. They are stylistico-syntactic. Like other 'text-centered' studies, they are pertinent for historical syntax (apart from their 'factological' value) only insofar as their explicatory virtues remain within the linguistic domain.

3.1.2 The same is true in regard to the stylistico-syntactic research focusing not on a single work but on a genre or a subgenre, as for example: Corti (1953), Segre (1952), Stefenelli-Fürst (1966) and others.

3.1.3 The precarious balance between syntax and stylistics in the 'text-centered' research tends to be tilted in favor of the latter in the numerous analyses which concentrate upon such relatively free syntactic feature as word order: Crabb (1955), Clifford (1973); metre: Scaglione (1967-1968); articulation of sentences (sentence beginnings): Rychner (1970); or various narrative devices: Dardano (1969). It is obvious that stylistically-minded historical syntax studies mentioned in 3.1.1, 3.1.2, and 3.1.3 represent a rich lode of contemporary research[23]. They are doubtless varied not only in regard to national traditions (Italian scholarship, for example, seems especially to favor such studies), but in relation to real theoretical and methodological approaches. The advantage of 'stylistic' historical syntax lies in its concrete philological nature. The exact definition and delimitation of the corpus enhances this concrete character and guarantees against using examples to fit the theory[24]. The danger of the approach lies in the often displayed tendency to slight the importance of theory, and also in the dispersion of efforts inevitable in any kind of 'pointilism'.

3.2 In comparison to much 'text-centered' research, 'problem-centered' studies with their own sub-categories follow a more properly linguistic approach. They study a history of a given phenomenon in a usually large number of documents representing a considerable chronological and/or geographical expanse. Their aim is not so much to explain this or that aspect of the documents but to elucidate the diachronic trajectory of a given linguistic, morphosyntactic phenomenon, or to illustrate historically a given theoretical tenet. This aim may be called therefore the creation of a section of a historical grammar.

3.2.1 A great number of studies, varying in scope, can be listed here. The first category which may be established includes those which deal with various syntactic problems confined to one language. They examine often one thorny question of that language (not necessarily, as so often happens in Romance, without implicit comparisons with 'mother', 'daughter', or 'sister' languages). A good example is the varied research papers dealing with the problem of the Portuguese infinitive, such as: Meier (1950), Sten (1953), Togeby (1955), J. W. Martin (1960), and a book: Maurer (1966), etc. Some of the studies in this category can be very extensive. They are often defined notionally, for example: Heinimann (1963), and Ehrliholzer (1965). More typical, however, are the studies whose object is defined formally. They examine syntactic function and its evolution in a morphological category conceived either paradigmatically, for example: Sá (1953, 1954), Ageno (1964), Macpherson (1967), and Reiner (1968), or syntagmatically, for example: Reichenkron (1951), Schellert (1958), and Leão (1961b). This last work, which could also be classified with Heinimann (1963) and Ehrliholzer (1965), was greatly inspired by Wagner (1939), not so much in its theoretical assumptions as in the manner of its presentation.

3.2.1.1 Works such as Kröll (1952), Andersson (1952), Henry (1968), etc. constitute a distinctive class of this category; they concentrate on the syntactic functions in their fine, semantically perceived nuances of a particular, usually very common, linguistic form. But Deutschmann (1959), while belonging to the same class, stresses, and this is rather rare, the popular, modern dialect usage, as well as the historical antecedents of the French adverb in -*ment*.

3.2.2 As it could be expected from the very nature of the field, the studies in which historical syntax is cast in explicitly comparative terms are also numerous. The following quite extensive studies can be considered as illustrations: Badía Margarit (1953), Ramsden (1963), Beckmann (1963), Herman (1963), Referovskaja (1964), Löfstedt (1966), etc.

3.2.2.1 In a fashion similar to the fundamentally monolingual studies, there exist a number of comparative syntactico-semantic works which examine specific 'idiomatic' expressions in their historical perspective: Gazdaru (1949), Väänänen (1951), Baldinger (1953), etc. The research in such a mode can, of course, treat very central questions of Romance historical syntax when, as in the case of Berchem (1973) the expressions analysed are the auxiliary verbs *to go, to have,* and *to be.*

3.2.3 Contrary to synchronic studies, those concerned with Romance historical syntax are relatively lacking in explicit preoccupation with language theory. It would be incorrect, however, to think that the theory is completely neglected. Feldman's (1964) modest article uses the Portuguese verbal system as a point of departure of what is basically a theoretical discussion of analytic versus synthetic structure.

Similarly Manoliu (1965) tests the validity of the structural approach to the analysis of the Romance nominal group, and Heger (1963) applies a kind of 'inhaltsbezogene Grammatik' to French and Spanish conjugations. (A propos of this work, see Klum 1968-1969.)

3.3 But by far the most important category in the 'problem-centered' research of historical syntax, one in which it is easy to perceive an explicit theoretical involvement, is constituted by modern, chiefly French, studies. They are associated (in very different degrees of faithfulness) with the 'psychomechanical' or 'psychosystemic' teachings of Gustave Guillaume (1960). The importance of this category for the current trends in historical syntax cannot be exaggerated. It would be fair to say that most of the scholars working in France on diachronic (and to an even greater extent on synchronic) syntax have been significantly influenced by the philosophical and methodological works of Guillaume (1919 and 1929, [2]1965), as well as by his personal teaching in the Ecole des Hautes Etudes. It is not my role here to discuss the theoretical aspects of 'Guillaumianism' but it is important for the purpose of this report to stress two points. Guillaume shares with the French tradition, seen in the monumental grammar Damourette–Pichon (1930-1956) and others[25], a marked and systematic preference for semantic, 'psychological' explanation of a syntactic state or change. This predilection is of utmost importance to the theory of the Guillaumian 'school', or more properly 'schools'[26]. Less important for language theory is my second point. The strict or less strict followers of Guillaume share the general respect of the basic French tradition for the philological facts and for judgments about these facts made by past generations of scholars. This respect for the meticulous sifting and presentation of philological materials, certainly 'inherited' also from Guillaume himself, has allowed the Guillaumians to be the most active one among other definable groups in Romance historical syntax.

3.3.1 The important contributions of this 'school' include, first of all, a series of dissertations: R.-L.Wagner (1939), Imbs (1956), Stefanini (1962), and R. Martin (1966). The dissertation of Jonas (1971), a student of Albert Henry, can very well be defined as belonging to an independent 'wing' of the 'school'.

3.3.2 Gérard Moignet, probably the most active and also most explicitly Guillaumian of the linguists doing research in historical syntax, is a student of Guillaume and of R.-L. Wagner. He is the author of numerous morphosyntactic studies both synchronic and diachronic. The most important of the latter category are: his dissertation on the Latin and French subjunctive (1959), *Les signes de l'exception* (1959b, [2]1972), *Le pronom personnel* (1965b), as well as articles such as (1958), (1965c), (1966), (1967).

3.3.3 Nothing seems to indicate any imminent weakening of this 'school' in its dealing with historical syntax. Much in accord with the still prevailing French, intellectual traditions, it continues to flourish, as can be seen in such diverse works as R. Martin (1967), Stefanini (1970), Wilmet (1970, 1971; this latter is a discussion of Henry 1968). It is interesting to note that the historical syntax research in the Guillaumian mode is apparently confined, unlike its modern synchronic counterparts, mostly to French; see however the Italian venture of Tekavčić (1972) mentioned above (2.3).

3.4 At the beginning of this report (cf. 2.1), I mentioned that the important event in the history of linguistics in the last twenty years, i. e., the 'break-through' effected by generative grammar has had as yet only a limited impact on the study of historical syntax in Romance. I also mentioned that the hopes of certain transformationalists (King 1969) that generative grammar could be applied fruitfully to the analysis of historical syntax, have proved, in the Romance area at least, overly optimistic. I know of only one published, serious attempt to use the generative mode in Romance historical syntax. I am speaking here about Robin T. Lakoff, *Abstract syntax and Latin complementation* (1968). This difficult study is, like a great many Guillaumian works, panchronic, i. e., it treats certain aspects of the subject synchronically, but it offers also the explicitly diachronic Chapter 6. In this chapter, Lakoff analyzes the problems of changes (from Latin to Spanish) in the complement system (in which, incidentally, she upholds the influence of the Greek adstratum in Hispanic Latin). The work is important, not only because it is a rare venture of a transformationalist into the domain of Romance historical syntax, but also because it is a contribution to the generative theory of syntactic change expounded, up to now, chiefly in the history of English. But her work was not followed by a flurry of similar studies. In fact, it seems that she herself has abandoned inquiries into the cross-temporal problems of Romance syntax. (Cf., nevertheless, her paper [1972] which deals only incidentally with Romance.)

3.4.1 The reasons for such a state of affairs are multiple. The most important are related directly to the very theory of generative grammar as applied to historical linguistics in general (with the possible exception of certain kinds of phonological analysis). The conference on historical linguistics and transformational theory held at UCLA in 1969 certainly reflects that view. The editors of the recently published *Essays* of this conference remark: "It is clear . . . that the idealized [Chomskyan] model of language acquisition as an instantaneous process is less likely to be 'fruitful' in diachronic linguistics, since it excludes many possible explanations. It is therefore necessary in studying linguistic change to investigate somewhat less idealised approaches to the writing of grammar" (Stockwell–Macaulay 1972: viii). The theory of language acquisition, as well as other facets of transformational grammar, such as syntactic synonymy and redundance, kinds of rule-changes, etc., are doubtless responsible for the theoretical difficulties in applying transformational analysis of syntax in a diachronic perspective. This is, of course, not the place to discuss these difficulties[27]. But what should be mentioned here are some non-theoretical causes of the practical nonexistence of cross-temporal Romance generative syntax studies. I am thinking here only about the 'heartland' of transformationalism, i. e., about the American scene. The mostly bright and often young modern transformationalists are faced with a post-Sturm und Drang period of the doctrine. They have branched out in fields other than the syntax of spoken English. They are looking for new fields of studies, they have diversified their theoretical insights. But they do not seem to be committed as yet to making the overly 'idealized' linguistic models[28] more fruitful in our domain. The important reason for it is the fact that they have inherited from their predecessors the American linguist's suspicion of philology, suspicion, I may add, richly justified by the long history of anti-linguistic attitudes displayed by many American philologists. In the late 1950's and in the 1960's this 'traditional' anti-philological turn of mind was further strengthened by certain trends inherent in the early stages of generative grammar. There are signs that the situation is changing. Many transformationalists of various kinds are far more open now to new ideas and, what is more important here, also to some old ones. The reductivist cry 'This is not linguistics!' which used to greet practically any statement not à la mode, is heard less. But an anti-philological turn of mind seems to persist. I am sure that if we are going to witness a genuine progress in generative Romance historical syntax, it will have to come from the Romance countries themselves. There, I hope, philological traditions can coexist with generative approaches to historical syntax.

4.1 Anyone trying to arrive at even tentative conclusions as to the present and future trends in Romance historical syntax must concern himself precisely with the relationship between philology and linguistic theory. It is easy to see that research in Romance historical syntax, whether of the traditional, not overtly 'ideological' kind (both stylistically and linguistically slanted) or of Guillaumian persuasions, is absolutely dependent on the abiding respect for philological traditions, with all the corollary demands of multilinguism, long apprenticeship, and a friendly understanding of the literary world. Future developments in Romance historical syntax are inexorably bound up with the persistence of philological research.

4.2 But the future of Romance historical syntax is also tied in with developments in language theory. No branch of linguistics remains forever immune from philosophical or methodological developments in another branch. If it does, and there is a danger that certain kinds of syntactic research find themselves in such a situation, they cease to influence other branches of linguistics, they cease to find a linguistic audience. Language theory, either tacitly accepted, or explicitly expounded is essential. It determines what the student is able to perceive in the great mass of historical facts. It determines also what questions he is likely to ask of those facts. One of the most obvious conclusions which can be drawn from looking at the current trends in Romance historical syntax is that much of it is not explicitly concerned with language theory. Much of it lives largely on theoretical 'capital' accumulated in the 'Golden Age'. This doubtless accounts for its weakness vis-à-vis, for example, synchronic syntax. This is not a satisfactory situation since, in the long run, the development of Romance historical syntax research depends on the harmonious coexistence and collaboration of theoretical linguistics and philology. The 'health' of this research will be, as it always has been, an indication of 'health' in both linguistics and philology.

1. The paucity of modern discussions concerning the nature of syntax (as opposed to its functions) is symptomatic. A Romance linguist dealing with historical syntax studies in the last several decades would still profit from the ideological and methodological insights of Ries, *Was ist Syntax?* (1894, ²1927). Cf. also Regula (1951). For views on the dichotomy morphology-syntax in the mid-1950's, see Llorente (1955). Chevalier (1968), discussing the history of the notion of complement, contributes greatly to the understanding of the modern notions of syntax itself.
2. A recent example of a consciously synchronic treatment of Old French is Hollyman (1968). The avoidance of diachronic and comparative references borders here on an obsession.
3. One of the clearest expressions of the dependence of morphology and syntax on semantics and psychology, and the concomitant interdependence of morphology and syntax, is to be found in the first volume of the opus magnum of Damourette and Pichon (1930-1956): "Le langage est, avant tout, chose psychique; tous ses phénomènes sont dominés par des raisons sémantiques, si bien qu'en dernière analyse aucune partie de grammaire ne peut être examinée avec fruit que du point de vue problème mental qu'elle pose. Ce serait donc de notre part une faute de méthode que de vouloir envisager séparément la morphologie et la syntaxe, celle-ci étant la raison d'être de celle-là" (I: 111). This seven-volume *Grammaire* contains a wealth of information concerning historical syntax of French. It draws its illustrations from all epochs of that language (which incidentally, includes also Provençal).
4. And of course the basic affinity between syntax (language) and stylistics (individual expression) has had its theoretical exponents, scholars who have profoundly influenced studies in Romance linguistics. I have in mind here Benedetto Croce and Karl Vossler who have championed the 'idealist' primacy of the creative, individual act over the collective in linguistic explanations. The role of such students of Vossler as Eugen Lerch and, above all, Leo Spitzer in 'stylistic' approaches to historical syntax cannot be overestimated.
5. Note, for example, that many items of Hatzfeld (1953) and Hatzfeld – Le Hir (1961) could very well be listed in a bibliography of syntax.
6. For the sake of 'symmetry', let us add that it is also adjacent to phonology. Cf., for example, French liaison, accent d'intensité. etc.
7. Anderson and Creore (1972) republished six essays under the rubric of diachronic morphology and syntax, but Pulgram (1967) deals only in part with French morphosyntax (with its future, possible developments), and Coseriu (1965) does not treat historical syntax at all.
8. French translation by Auguste Doutrepont and Georges Doutrepont (1900).
9. The 4th edition revised by the author's son, Jean Bourciez (1946), was reprinted several times.
10. *Grundriß*, unlike many great German works of the 'Golden Age', was not translated in toto into any Romance language.
11. This is the case of the chapter on Rheto-Romance by Theodor Gartner, on Italian by Francesco d'Ovidio and Meyer-Lübke (published separately later in Italian), on

Catalan by Alfredo Morel-Fatio and J. Saroïhandy, on Spanish by Gottfried Baist, and on Portuguese by Jules Cornu. Only the chapters on Rumanian by Hariton Tiktin and French and Provençal by Hermann Suchier (each of them, like the other chapters in vol. I of *Grundriß*, a veritable concise historical grammar) contain specific sections dealing with historical syntax.

12. Between vols. I (1899) II (1903) (treating historical phonetics and morphology) and vols. V (1925) and VI (1930) (dealing with historical syntax) Nyrop has inserted vol. III (1908) (word formation) and vol. IV (1913) (semantics). Nyrop's work on phonology and morphology appears to be more authoritative than his later volumes, including the ones on historical syntax.

13. The new edition (1966) with a preface by Gerard Antoine and a bibliography by Jean Batany is a reprint of the fourth edition (1933).

14. This is a recasting of Brunot (1887).

15. Syntax shares vol. II with Formenlehre and vol. III with Wortbildung.

16. As, for example, the famous *Manual* of Menéndez Pidal (1904) – the last revised edition republished several times in the sixth (1941); Nunes (1919, [3]1945); Regula (1955-1956); Rothe (1957); Pellegrini (1966). Grandgent (1927, [3]1940) and other *From Latin to* . . . also follow a bipartite approach: Pope (1934, [2]1952); Williams (1938, [2]1968). Occasionally it is difficult to know whether such an approach results from an anti-syntactic attitude or simply the unfinished state of the project. Such is the case of the widely consulted Schwan–Behrens ([3]1898) particularly well-known through its French recasting by Bloch ([4]1932).

17. It follows *Les parties du discours* (1967).

18. Spanish elaboration by Alvar (1972).

19. See her *Structuralismul lingvistic* (1973), especially Chapter 5, "Structură şi geneză: 'fire' şi 'devenire'" (156-190).

20. An Italian 'aggiornamento e adattamento' of both Iordan–Manoliu Manea (1965) and Manoliu Manea (1971a) appeared in 1974 in one volume.

21. In spite of this late date of publication the *Syntax* belongs undoubtedly to an earlier era, not only because of Gamillscheg's conservatism, but also because the first draft of the work was burnt in 1944. The 1957 version represents a recreation of this draft.

22. Although far less ambitious, originally planned as a simple and a purely practical manual, Foulet's *Petite syntaxe* (1919, [3]1930) should also be counted in this category. Based on a relatively restrained number of Old French verse compositions, this manual is very authoritative.

23. Very important for this kind of study are the well-known stylistic and especially semantic works of Stephen Ullmann. Clifford (1973) was a student of Ullmann.

24. Cf. Dembowski (1966-1967).

25. Above all, Le Bidois (1935-1938, [2]1967).

26. The term 'school' fits synchronic research better than the less extensive and more diversified diachronic studies in the Guillaumian mode. Theoretical insights of Guillaume and his continuators are applicable to synchronic, diachronic and comparative approaches. Herein lies their methodological strength. See the theoretical statement by Valin (1964).

27. I wish to thank my colleague Maria Manoliu Manea for letting me read her interesting, unpublished 'provisional' version of "Grammaire transformationnelle et linguistique romane: Le changement syntaxique". I hope that the final version of this paper will be published soon.

28. Overly idealized, i. e., too formal, too far removed precisely from that kind of linguistic realities that a linguist confronts constantly in Romance historical syntax.

1.3 Historical lexical studies

REBECCA POSNER

Historical Romance lexicology and semantics

With lexical studies Romanists are most in their element: perhaps significantly this is the area in which the lines between synchrony and diachrony, and between linguistics and philology are most difficult to draw. Even for one individual, vocabulary is virtually limitless and ever-changing, and between individuals within a linguistic community there is wide variation in use and comprehension of words. This is the aspect of language that gives fullest rein to individual creativity and expressivity. The lexicon – in the sense of the stock of lexical items shared by speakers of the same language – defies definition: dictionaries may list as many as half a million words in an attempt to be comprehensive, though most current dictionaries confine themselves to less than 50,000. Yet it can be maintained – as we shall see – that a mere 5,000 words can be considered as the 'basic' lexicon of a language.

Modern structural and generative linguistics, seeking regularities and formulating rules, is nonplussed by the complexity and apparent chaos of the lexicon, regarded as an unordered repository of idiosyncrasies and irregularities. As such, lexical study is more the domain of the philologists, who are concerned with texts ('parole', 'discours') and with 'vocabularies' (the lexical items used by individuals or special groups) rather than with the lexicon of the langue. The philologist's approach is necessarily synchronic even when he studies old texts, but unlike the synchronic linguist of present-day languages he cannot tap speakers' intuitions (although admittedly he sometimes has access to contemporary commentaries and dictionaries). Thus he is largely confined to statements about performance, not competence. His dia-

chronic insights come from comparing and contrasting one performance with another (and with present-day competence): new items are
borrowed or created, old ones change their scope, or are lost.

As it is obvious that to some extent lexical 'creation' (word-formation) is rule-governed, generative linguistics has recently sought
methods to describe the regularity (cf. especially Aronoff 1976); difficulties arise because rules have only limited productivity and because
morphological forms are not consistently matched with semantic
interpretations. However, the assumption of filter devices that block
generation of regular, but non-existent, forms can alleviate some difficulties. Surely a better solution is to recognize that between competence and performance there is room for a social convention, like the
'norme' Coseriu posits between langue and parole, limiting the potential output of the system and fossilizing some forms. It is the norm that
will interest most the diachronic linguist, for it is here that change is
most readily discernible. If generative linguistics has little contribution
to make to lexicology, it has even less to say about historical semantics.
'Interpretive' semantics of the Chomskyan type does little more than
formalize traditional dictionary entries and harmonize lexical 'readings'
to reveal the meaning of the sentence as a whole: in Saussurean terms,
it is a method for discovering which signifié a given signifiant is mapped
on to. 'Generative' semantics even denies the existence of 'lexeme-
sized chunks of meaning', seeing a lexeme as an arbitrary abbreviation
for certain semantic configurations, which may have little or no connection with each other. Such an approach surely leaves no scope for
diachronic study: there is no synchronic polysemy – merely homonymy
– and no change – merely substitution.

For some linguists, extension of meaning is the simplest kind of
derivational process – using a familiar form for a novel semantic configuration: Leech (1974) lists among his 'lexical rules', 'conversion'
(change of category) and 'semantic transfer', alongside derivation and
composition. Carroll and Tauenhaus (1975) suggest that a 'Minimax
Principle' operates, by which the speaker minimizes the surface complexity of his utterances while maximizing the amount of information
he effectively communicates to the listener: by this principle 'lexicaliza-
tions' will be preferred according to the following hierarchy: 1) existent
form (e. g. semantic transfer, change of category), 2) derived form, 3)
compound form, 4) coining (or borrowing?). In a 'functionalist'

framework of this kind semantic transfer will be taken for granted and attention will be riveted on why new forms are introduced to fill 'semantic gaps', where it might have been simpler to extend the meaning of existing forms (cf. Polge 1962 who distinguishes 'imposture lexicate', 'adaptation lexicale' and 'innovation lexicale').

The idea of 'lexical' or 'semantic gaps' is implicit in most studies of neologism and merits further investigation (cf., in the Romance context, Ducháček 1968 and 1974, Posner 1975, Geckeler 1974). It would be circular to argue that the introduction of a neologism proves that a 'gap' previously existed: the definition of 'well-formed concepts' on to which lexical items are not mapped (signifiés without matching signifiants) is also hazardous. A model that recognizes no polysemy, viewing each variation in use of a form as a different lexical item, would point to a very large (infinite?) number of possible concepts (or, at least, of semantic configurations), many of which would represent a semantic gap in any given language. That these may in practice be plastered over by the use of existing forms would account for the vagueness of much everyday language: the speaker may have in mind a perfectly 'well-formed concept', but the hearer may not be able to guess what it is, as the form evokes for him another 'well-formed concept' (if he is familiar with the form, that is!). It is presumably when such misunderstanding becomes pathological that recourse is made to a new form, to give surface expression to the difference between the concepts.

Such models permit the study of lexical history, but hardly of historical semantics. It is not surprising then that Saussurean linguists, particularly those influenced by Hjelmslev and Guillaume, have made a much greater contribution: the theory of the sign, with its indissolubly linked signifié and signifiant, places, surely, 'semantic gaps' outside the scope of linguistics, and pays attention, at one and the same time, to lexical form and meaning.

But pride of place in lexicology and historical semantics must go to more traditional philologists, lexicographers and linguistic geographers who have collected and analysed an enormous amount of material from all Romance dialects. Little of this work is primarily comparative – it is concerned mainly, as I have said, with 'performance' by one writer or in one community – but it provides ample data for comparison, both between different languages and between different stages of the same language. Particularly valuable are the French computerized projects – the *Trésor de la Langue Française* at Nancy, the *Centre d'Etudes du Vocabulaire Français* at Besançon, the *Centre de Recherche de Lexicologie Politique* and the CREDIF projects at Saint-Cloud (for description of these cf. especially Guilbert 1969). They derive ultimately from the Matoré-type 'lexicologie' of the fifties, which I discuss later. Besides statistical data on occurrence and frequency of words, they provide us with more accurate dating of the first use of neologisms in texts (cf. Quemada 1959–).

Lexicographical history is of particular interest in that it may provide insights into the competence of our predecessors, with respect to word-meanings. Again, it is in France that such studies are most pursued – cf. Matoré (1968), Quemada (1968), R.-L. Wagner (1967, 1970), Rey-Debove (1971) and the Besançon analysis of 18th and 19th century dictionaries currently being published by the CNRS under the title *Mots et dictionnaires*.

It is obviously impossible to survey the vast amount of lexicographical work that has been done in Romance – not only the great 'languages of culture', but also hundreds of minor dialects have been documented. A summary of trends and a bibliography is to be found in Quemada 1972; cf. also Malkiel 1958-60, 1962. Etymological dictionaries are discussed in the Craddock et al. article in this volume: Malkiel 1976 is a more extensive examination and Baldinger 1974 is particularly valuable for French. (For dictionaries cf. Appendix I; for bibliographies cf. Appendix II.)

Onomasiological studies – also mentioned in Craddock et al. – are often a restricted type of dictionary, listing and contrasting words used in particular domains – especially for animals, plants and agricultural activities, in the Word-and-Thing tradition (cf. Quadri 1952, and Gorog 1973-4 in Appendix II, to which we should add some more recent works – Schuchard 1970, Trujillo 1970, Fossat 1971, Nagel 1972, Koenig 1973, Grafschaft 1974, Vilela 1974, García Hernandez 1977, Gorog 1977; Heger-Baldinger onomasiology is discussed later, as a branch of structural semantics).

The Craddock et al. article also fully discusses the 'history-of-a-word' type of etymological study, in which semantic and lexical history are intimately intermingled. It is in such studies that Romance philologists delight most: the word-indices of the principal periodicals

(Romania, Revue de Linguistique Romane, Zeitschrift für Romanische Philologie, Romance Philology and others concerned with individual languages) provide a guide to contributions about individual words (cf. also the bibliographies in Appendix II). The etymologist is concerned with semantic history, but also with the provenance of his chosen word or word-family, and the dating of its introduction: he tends to neglect the 'obvious' – the basic inherited words with a dull uneventful history.

The introduction of neologisms particularly fascinates the philologist and historian of language because they are revelatory of social and cultural upheavals. The most salient changes in vocabulary are those that result from language contact – borrowings from foreign languages and from social or geographical dialects or specialized jargons. Traditional Romance philology abounds in loan-word studies, with a theoretical dimension added by the investigation of bilingualism and contact between languages: this area is discussed in T. E. Hope's article in this volume, which is principally concerned with the lexical interchange between Romance languages. Although many monographs are devoted to borrowing from non-Romance languages (including 'substratum' and 'superstratum') the extent of such borrowing is far outstripped by inter-Romance borrowing and by borrowing from Latin ('learned forms' or 'cultisms' – cf. eg. Bustos Tovar 1974, Greive 1976, Wright 1976). Thus the lexical coherence of the Romance languages remains firm – in spite of contacts with non-Romance, and even non-European, languages in the course of history. We can laugh at purist over-reaction to the incursion of foreign words (today most flamboyant in French abhorrence of 'franglais'), but perhaps this is one of the factors that have preserved Romance as a closely-knit group of languages.

Another aspect of the study of neologism as a branch of social history is amply exemplified in the French school of lexicologie whose manifesto was Matoré 1953, and which, in the fifties, inspired a number of monographs investigating specialized terminology at different periods (eg. 19th century art, Matoré 1951, 1953; feudalism, Hollyman 1957; railway terms, Wexler 1955; medical terms, Quemada 1955) with an attempt to identify 'mots-témoins', around which a lexicological structure is organized, and 'mots-clés', which express a social ideal of the period. The method is obviously philological, involving the careful sifting of textual evidence, rather than linguistic: its diachronic insights spring from a comparison of different synchronic stages rather than from a study of the mechanism of change. A. Rey (1977), for instance, sketches out a couple of examples – *sarabande* and *roman* (of architecture) – pointing out that progress towards a linguistic treatment is yet to be made. For some discussion of the method cf. Ullmann 1972, Quemada 1972, Picoche 1977 and Spence 1961, a critical account which lumps the Matoré method together with more linguistically oriented semantic field studies. A bibliography, Schmitt 1972, is mentioned in Appendix II; other recent studies in this tradition include Peter 1969, Burgess 1970, Johnson 1973, Dumonceau 1975, Picoche 1976.

Linguistic geography and 'Word-and-Thing' lexical studies are often also concerned with socio-cultural distinctions and the way lexical differences hint at social history (cf. particularly the chapter 'Le nuove metodologie dello studio lessicale' in Vàrvaro 1968: 249-286). Rohlfs' studies on lexical differentiation within Romance (1954, 1971 d, e), Redfern 1971 and Lüdtke 1974 are in the tradition. Not dissimilar to such studies – if sometimes more rigorous – are those that use the lexicon to delve into the past, uncovering the deepest layers that must have been laid down during the Imperial period, and using lexical differences as a basis for classification. C. Schmitt (1974, 1976), a pupil of Bodo Muller (1971 b, 1974) is particularly concerned with Gallo-Roman dialects and uses statistical data. Šabršula (1966), a pupil of Křepinsky (1958), warns against taking too much account of mere existence of words and neglecting their function; he emphasises the importance of external factors, as distinct from structural pressures, in lexical change. Other comparative studies, with a statistical bias, include Sergijevskij 1946 and Uhler – Vlasák 1959. There are numerous studies of the lexical composition of individual languages: Rumanian has received particular attention (cf. Giuglea 1909, Domaschke 1919, Macrea 1941-3, Teodorescu 1946, Buescu 1953-8, Şiadbei 1957, Bonfante 1959-60, Bahner 1971, and the chapters on Balkan Latin (Fischer) and Proto-Rumanian (Coteanu) in Academia RPR 1965-69). Among recent works on other languages we should mention Fisher 1976 (Vegliot), Colón 1976 (Catalan), Frago-García 1977 (Aragonese), Chaurand 1977 (French).

The most current neologisms in Romance are more frequently formed from native sources than borrowed from other languages, though productivity varies between languages and periods. The study of word-formation is particularly fruitful in Romance, as can be seen, for example, from the number of papers presented in this subject at Congresses: cf. Lloyd's bibliography (1963-4) in Appendix II, also Craddock 1965. While many traditional studies do little more than simply list processes and morphemes (composition, derivation by prefix or suffix, change of category etc.), more recently attempts have been made to give more explanatory descriptions of lexical creativity.

Here possibly the most important name in Romance is that of Yakov Malkiel, whose own interest in the topic is stimulated by the way it bridges grammar and lexicon, between the fixed, structured and regular and the open-ended, amorphous and creative, as well as between morphological form and semantic content (cf. Malkiel 1966a). Malkiel's own studies are essentially philological in method and bound up inextricably with his etymological research (for which cf. Craddock et al. in this volume), but his awareness of modern linguistics leads him to formulate general hypotheses that take account of complex reality. He insists on the necessity of meticulous collection of data, including anomalies and residues, and of attention to scholarly traditions, while seeking causal explanations. These will probably be many-pronged – semantic or functional need, holes-in-the-pattern, phonological habits, convergence, borrowing, diffusion, contamination, differentiation and sheer exuberance have their place in his schema. It is clear to the practising philologist that there may be disproportionate proliferation of derivatives in some communities and that some processes are abortive, or 'stunted', that sometimes derivational processes are identifiable only in diachronic projection (as for 'suffixoids', to use his term) and that account must be taken of polygenesis of forms. For a fuller discussion cf. Posner 1970 and for a bibliography, Malkiel (– Rico) 1969 in Appendix II; more recent works are listed in the bibliography of this volume.

Malkiel's pupils at Berkeley – including Blaylock, Butler, Craddock, Dworkin, Georges, Lloyd, Tuttle – have between them enriched the field with many new and illuminating studies, always models of traditional philological scholarship, with an eye kept open for new linguistic insights; for a bibliography cf. Posner 1970: 439 to which we should add Butler 1972 (for his bibliography 1975 cf. Appendix II), Blaylock

1975, Jasanoff 1975, Kvavik 1975, Lopez Morillas 1975, Fleischmann 1976, A. Allen 1977. Outside the sphere of Malkiel's direct influence, but in the same tradition is Pattison 1975.

More specifically linguistic studies of word-formation are rarely historical and comparative – we might mention Ettinger 1974, inspired by Coseriu's theories, Thiele 1978, and the work of French linguists like Dubois, Guilbert, Rey, Corbin who are more sympathetic to generative techniques. Among recent works that compare word-formation processes in different Romance languages, we should mention Hasselrot 1957, Alsdorf-Bollet 1970, Gauger 1971, Reinheimer-Rîpeanu 1974, Giurescu 1975, J. Lüdtke 1978.

As we have seen, lexical studies are more frequently synchronic in character and philological in method, to such an extent that it is hard to see how they integrate into historical linguistics, as distinct from language history (cf. eg. Lecointre – Galliot 1971). This is particularly true of semantics, which, though originally concerned with change of lexical meaning, has for some time been grappling with the problem of how to describe the content of utterances – perhaps more a philosophical or psychological problem than a linguistic one (cf. Ullmann 1972). Traditional historical semantics is barely distinguishable from history-of-a-word etymology on the one hand, or synchronic study of polysemy and stylistic extension (metaphor, metonymy, etc.) on the other. Awareness of the pitfalls in describing meaning, even at a synchronic level, has averted scientifically-minded linguists from such studies, especially as generative theory leaves no place for lexical history except in the wasteland of accident and idiosyncrasy. Werth (1973) does attempt to describe semantic change in terms of Katz – Fodor componential analysis, using some French examples – cf. also Voyles (1973) – but there has been no follow-up of his ideas.

In so far as historical semantics has progressed it has been a spin-off from the developments in Saussurean semantics that are discussed in Vasiliu's article in Volume 2 of this series. Baldinger, a disciple of Wartburg's and a lexicographer and philologist of the good old school, has imbibed the theoretical ideas of Heger, producing insightful onomasiological studies. His examination of *se souvenir* and its field (in e.g. Baldinger 1970) is a model. The 'concept' is summarized in the formula $P\psi \ (A_p; M_B)$ (the psychic presence P of something in the past A_p; in the memory of a living being M_B), and the various syntactic frames in which this occurs in modern and old French are examined. Thus the 'transformation'

$$[cP\psi \ (A_{\overleftarrow{p}}; M\gamma; C) + 2c \ [C{\rightarrow}A_{\overleftarrow{p}}; M\gamma] + t + (A \neq C)$$

(where C evokes the memory of A, with ellipsis of M_B) is represented in modern French as eg. C *rappelle* A; C *évoque* A, C *parle d'*A etc. and in Old French as C *remembre* A, C *recorde* A, C *(r)amentoit* A. In Old French the *re-* prefix seems to have more semantic impact than in the modern language. The change for the transformation

$$P\psi \ (A_{\overleftarrow{p}}; M_B) + 2 + t \ (A \neq B)$$

(where A is recalled by B) is from the impersonal type

$$me \ \frac{sovient}{membre} \ de \ qch$$

to the personal reflexive

$$je \ me \ \frac{souviens}{rappelle} \ \frac{de \ qch}{qch}$$

(with *se rappeler* denoting a more voluntary action – but taking over more and more the domain of *se souvenir de*).

Alongside such onomasiological studies Baldinger approaches change from the viewpoint of semasiology. For instance, he schematically contrasts the semasiological history (based on polysemy) of Provençal *trebalhar*

'to work'   'to be in torment'   'to be in pain'
                     'to become fatigued'
                     'to labour'

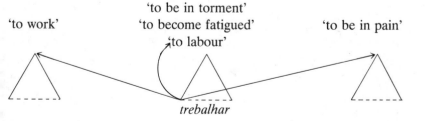

trebalhar

with the onomasiological history (based on synonymy) of the concept
'to work':

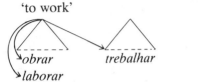

'to work'		'to be in torment'
		'to become fatigued'
obrar *trebalhar*		'to labour'
laborar		

Ullmann attempted a classification of changes on the basis of a Saussurean sign, distinguishing changes that result from shifts in relationships
between signifiés and those that originate in shifts in relationships between signifiants, but added little in the way of new data. Benveniste
(1966) sketches out the way in which related signifiants can develop
differentiated signifiés, using the examples of *amenuiser* 'to reduce' and
menuisier 'joiner', but can conclude only that much remains to be done
on the theoretical plane.

Coseriu is the only linguist who has specifically tackled the theoretical question of meaning change (1964), which must be treated on the
level of relationships between signifiés within a 'functional language'
(not an 'historical language' which is necessarily an amalgam of several
functional languages). When one signifiant replaces another without
change of signifié (eg. *tuer* replacing *ocire*) then no semantic change has
taken place, merely a sort of borrowing – it is a fact of language
'architecture' not 'structure'. Change takes place only when signifiés
change their relationship to each other: as, for instance, when the
signifié of old French *chef* is split between the modern signifiants *chef*
and *tête* (cf. also discussion in Vasiliu's article in vol. 2). One difficulty
in Coseriu's 'lexematic' approach is how to identify signifiés: we are
told that difference of signifiants implies difference of signifiés (i.e.
there is no total synonymy), but one signifiant can have more than one
signifié (polysemy). Recall that for Heger this latter is not so, but the
signifié may be composed of more than one 'sememe', conjunctively (in
polysemy) or disjunctively (in homonymy) linked (cf. on this question
Vasiliu's article in vol. 2). Presumably, for Coseriu, signifiés are, to a
large extent, intuitively identified – but for past periods of a language,
present-day intuition is defective, and it may be impossible to delimit
'functional languages', as distinct from individual uses in texts, when
commutation and collocation criteria are used.

Another difficulty is in delimiting the data: Coseriu regards it as legitimate to concentrate on only sections of the lexicon, semantically delimited. Thus in practice (exemplified mainly by Geckeler but cf. also Osswald 1970, Pacquot 1976) there is little difference between Coseriu's diachronic lexematics and the Trier-type lexical field studies treating concepts rather than signifiés proper (cf. Spence 1961, Ullmann 1972, Coseriu and Geckeler 1974). Geckeler 1976 contrasts his own Coserian study (1971) with Trujillo's more traditional onomasiological (1970), pointing especially to his own more systematic analysis of the lexical field, as sharing an 'archilexeme'.

Thus

Content $= \Sigma$ Archilexeme $+$ [dimension(s) $\times$ seme(s)] $+$ classemes eg. *ancien* $= \Sigma$ adj. designating age $+$ [historico-temporal classification $\times$ relatively far back in time] $+$ [for animates $+$ for non-animates]

(for a different use of the term 'classeme' cf. the discussion of Greimas' conception of 'isotopie' in Vasiliu's article in vol. 2).

Another type of Saussurean semantic field-study that can lend itself to diachronic analysis is developed by Duchaček (for his own bibliography cf. Duchaček 1971 in Appendix II; for a survey of works inspired by him cf. Duchaček 1976: most notable are Ostrá 1966, 1967, 1976 and Vrbková 1971) – though here again it is more a question of comparison of synchronic states than of analysis of change, so that the method is more properly described as a kind of synchronic onomasiology than of historical semantics.

The Pottier-Greimas type of study, with analysis into semes, discussed by Vasiliu in Volume 2 of this series, lends itself even less to diachronic treatment and most studies in this tradition are synchronic in scope (– e.g. Mounin 1965, Renzi 1973, Bidu-Vrănceanu 1974, Meya 1976, also Alinei 1974).

A comparative approach to semantic differentiation based on lexical fields is favoured by some Soviet Romanists (Budagov 1963, Berejan 1971, cf. Weinreich 1963 and in Appendix II Borodina et al. 1962), and Klein (1961, 1968) looks to synonyms for clues to the mechanism of differentiation.

Posner (1973, 1975) goes so far as to suggest that diachronic semantics is not an autonomous field of study at all: 'semantic change' is in fact synchronic (within what Coseriu calls a historical language) with extension and restriction of meaning determined by context, and vivid transfers being part and parcel of the striving for effective, and affective, communication. What alters the system is lexical change – most easily discerned in the entry of new items or the loss (partial or complete) of old, occasioning shift in the semantic relationship between items, when the speaker may detect differences of meaning between synonyms, or understand a polysemic item as a series of homonyms.

Such shifts are most likely to occur at the stage of the speaker's acquisition of items (which in the case of the lexicon is a lifelong process) but is limited by the need to understand and be understood. What determines the acceptance into the 'norm' of what may have been originally simply errors, is one of the prime questions a linguistic historian should ask. Comparison of the meaning of cognate forms in the different Romance languages can provide material for the study of the problem. One important factor may lie in the mechanism of lexical loss – a topic popularized in Huguet 1935 but otherwise somewhat neglected in comparison with the much studied question of neologism, (but cf. Candrea 1932, Bahner 1968, Goosse 1973, Baldonado 1975). Although, as I have pointed out, 'semantic transfer' can in many cases be seen as the simplest type of lexical creation ('lexicalisation' to fill a 'semantic gap') this is not always so. Frequently there is competition between near-synonyms which may result in the loss, or restriction in use, of one of the competitors, while the victor takes over some of its meanings, even though these were previously adequately 'lexicalised'. Sometimes indeed the loss of an item may leave a gap that has to be filled by circumlocutions (cf. Posner 1975).

Comparison of dialects in which an item has been lost with those in which a cognate item has been retained may reveal the conditioning of loss – elimination of homonymic clashes, as suggested by Gilliéron, or avoidance of irregular morphological items, is obviously part of the story, but so are swings of fashion (that favour perhaps now foreign words, now native derivatives) and other sociocultural factors. The influence of educators and lexicographers cannot be ignored – lexical meaning (as distinct from reference) is apparently recognized quite late in the language acquisition process, when the child is subject to social pressures from superiors and peers (if only through fear of mockery).

Not only may there be feedback from performance, in which syntagmatic environment modifies the purport of an item, to competence, leading to change in the speaker's idea of what a word means, and even of whether one form is envisaged as one or more words, but there can also be contamination between lexical items, so that similar forms may acquire similar meanings (originally malapropisms) or words with similar meanings may acquire similar formal features, or even blend together. This is the sort of change successfully described by Guiraud, which occurs especially in those areas of vocabulary that escape the control of lexicographers and other arbiters of language. Craddock et al. discuss Guiraud's work; cf. also Posner (1970: 450).

It can be seen that the vast amount of lexical data collected by Romance philologists still awaits a theoretical treatment that will supply answers to some of the questions of historical linguistics: in what ways do forms come to be given new interpretations, or concepts come to be associated with new forms, and how and why do some items fall out of use, sometimes being replaced by others and sometimes apparently leaving a lexical gap? Are there universal semantic primes that are arbitrarily combined into lexeme-sized bundles, which can change their composition through time? Or are the basic semantic units actually lexical items (signs), learned early in life for simple needs, to which other items are later related?

Another question that remains to be answered is what constitutes the lexicon of a language (and indeed of a family of languages like Romance) and how it can change through time. This question has received a good deal of attention from linguists of statistical bent, for whom new information has been made available in computerized projects – of which the most ambitious is that directed by A. Juilland at Stanford University under the title *Romance languages and their structures*. This project includes the publication of frequency dictionaries of each of the Romance languages (cf. Appendix I) giving data about the 5,000 most frequent words that constitute more than 95 per cent of usage. Two Stanford dissertations successfully examined the Spanish data, from the point of view of genealogy, chronology, function and syllabic structure: their conclusions are set out graphically in Patterson–Urrutibéheity 1975, using pie-charts. Thus we learn, for instance, that an estimated 81.31 per cent of Spanish usage is made up of 'inherited' (mainly Latin) words, while borrowed Latin words account for another 8.99 per cent, with 'created' words making up another 8.07 per cent, and borrowings from other Romance languages 0.96 per cent. The non-Romance borrowings, to which so much attention is often paid, occupy very little of discourse: 0.25 per cent for Arabic, 0.35 per cent for Greek, 0.07 per cent for others. Of borrowings, some 35 per cent of those used in present-day texts entered the language in the 13th century: the 12th and 13th centuries were most productive of frequently-used created words (21.96 per cent and 22.38 per cent of usage respectively) even though more words were actually created in the 15th century (24.70 per cent of members of the present-day lexicon, making up only 17.13 per cent of usage).

Similar exercises have been performed especially for Rumanian, perhaps motivated by the desire of Rumanian linguists to demonstrate the essential Romanceness of their native tongue, in spite of the incursion of Slavic, Magyar and Turkish words (cf. Graur 1965, also Poghirc's contribution to the Etymology article in this volume). Here not only frequency, but 'circulation' value is to be taken into account : cf. e.g. Vintilă-Rădulescu (1974) and Coteanu (1958) who points out that *urzi* 'to hatch' or *vultur* 'eagle, vulture' may be heard infrequently but are still part of the basic vocabulary; a similar discovery was made in the formulation of *français élémentaire* when it was found that many essential everyday words did not occur in the conversational samples analysed.

Maneca has made several contributions to the study of basic lexicon, showing, for instance (1966, 1967), in considering a base of 6,231 words, that about 70 per cent of modern literary Rumanian texts is made up of inherited Latin words (in the works of Eminescu this rises to 83 per cent) with French words constituting another 18.20 per cent (41.63 per cent of members) and creations 11.52 per cent (25.90 per cent of members); as might be expected Latinisms are less numerous than in Roman Catholic countries (only about 3 per cent of texts and members). Tudose (1965) examines 16th century Rumanian texts, analysing 5,211 different words in translations and 879 in documents: of these 60.16 per cent are inherited from Latin, with 10.46 per cent native creations; Slavic words are more numerous than in modern Rumanian (19.01 per cent of members, compared with Maneca's figure of 6.99 per cent). We may compare Chelaru and Şoşa's analysis (1970) of the first original Rumanian document (1521) in which they contrast Rumanian with other Romance languages: of the 112 lexical units, 67 are Latin and 6–8 are Slavic. Comparisons have also been made between Rumanian and Spanish (Sădeanu 1968, 1972), between Rumanian and French (Nedelcu 1976), between Rumanian and Italian (Maneca 1969, 1971) and more generally between a number of Romance languages (Şandru-Maneca 1973).

The works of D. Messner, concerned with what he calls 'lexicochronologie', are also comparative and historical in their orientation: his studies concern Spanish, Portuguese, Catalan and French, showing when items in the modern lexicon (which he numbers at around 25,000 'characteristic' items) made their first appearance. Thus in French (Messner 1975) 49.42 per cent of the 13,581 words that he examines are of Latin origin, of which 13.50 per cent were not attested till the 16th century: the most receptive periods for neologisms were the 14th and 16th centuries. (Dubois 1965, examining only words beginning with *h-*, finds that about one-third of present-day words were not attested till after 1750.) Messner 1974 starts from the 28,747 Portuguese words listed in his DILP (cf. Appendix I) and compares them with corresponding words in the other languages (using, note, dictionaries rather than texts) showing the periods of greatest convergence and interchange.

This type of lexicochronology differs from glotto-chronology and lexicostatistics of the Swadesh type, which has had rough handling from Romance linguists (Rea 1958, 1974; Coseriu 1965). This attempts to establish a basic list of lexical meanings (most notoriously one of only a hundred items) of the sort that are learned early in life; the items that lexicalize them are assumed to be least likely to change over time and so can be criterial in recognizing genetic relationship. The great degree of interinfluence within Romance, and the preference for Latinisms, so skews the evidence that this method is obviously of little use in dating the separation of Romance languages for which in any case we have historical and textual evidence. However, the establishment of what may be considered a basic lexicon is useful, not only for pedagogical purposes (as in *le français fondamental*), but in order to allow meaningful historical study of the lexicon as a whole, as distinct from individual words, which, though fascinating, permits little in the way of insights into the mechanism of language change. The foundations have been laid for a study of semantic change in terms of lexical acquisition and loss; by limiting the list of items considered to about 5,000 for each language, and by taking into account the semantic needs of everyday communication and avoiding excessively culture-bound concepts, we may at last get a grip on the elusive problem of lexical change. The Romance languages have similar enough lexicons to permit isolation of differences and variables. Quantitative investigation is an essential prerequisite, but more qualitative and substantial study is required for general hypotheses to be made, taking account of psycholinguistic theories of learning, which have so far made little progress in so far as acquisition of word-meanings is concerned.

Thus I believe that, in spite of the wealth of Romance lexical studies available to us, there is everything yet to be done to draw together the different strands and bring coherence to the domain. The paucity of linguistically-oriented studies in historical semantics and lexicology can be explained by the daunting complexity of the material, which provides a happy playground for the philologically-minded, and which discourages theorists and methodologists. If, however, any progress is to be made in the field, more attention must be paid to defining the data, refining methodology and formulating theory – which will probably then lead to re-examination of the material. This is one field of linguistics to which Romanists can make a particularly valuable contribution, by virtue of the scope for comparison that is presented by the Romance languages and dialects both on the synchronic and the diachronic plane.

One crucial question that must be asked is whether there is a lexical semantics of langue (or a native-speaker competence that embraces lexical items and their meaning) which is accessible through the examination of parole (or performance). Furthermore, can the kaleidoscopic philological studies that make up so much of the literature in this field, confined as they are to parole (performance), contribute to our overall knowledge of the way language works – and changes? My own view is that it is misguided for theoreticians to ignore this material, confusing and chaotic though it appears at first sight.

JERRY R. CRADDOCK, STEVEN DWORKIN,
CICERONE POGHIRC*

Romance etymology

1. Introduction

In the last few decades, a number of crucially important etymological dictionaries have been composed or brought to completion (for bibliography cf. Appendix I). Among these the *FEW* (for Gallo-Romance) is most important (Wartburg 1922-); it lacks only portions of the volumes [21-23] devoted to words of unknown origin, while a new and throughly revised edition of the first volume is in progress. Also important are the *DES* ([Sardinian] Wagner 1957-64), the *DCE* ([Spanish] Corominas 1954-57), and, on a somewhat more modest scale, the *DER* ([Rumanian] Cioranescu 1958-66). Other important dictionaries have undergone new editions, for instance the *EWFS* (Gamillscheg 1966-69, 1st 1928), the DELF (Bloch – Wartburg 1968 [5th], 1st 1932) and Dauzat (1964 with Dubois and Mitterand, 1st 1938) in the Gallo-Romance domain; a whole spate of Italian etymological dictionaries of somewhat lesser calibre has appeared (the *DEI* by Battisti – Alessio 1948-54; Prati 1951; Olivieri 1953, 2nd edition 1961; Migliorini – Duro 1950, 4th 1964 and, most recently, Devoto 1966, 2nd 1968); last, and very much the least, are Machado (1952-59) for Portuguese and the *DEEH* (García de Diego 1955) for Spanish.

In the major and minor learned journals etymological literature continues to pour off the presses. Whether by design or by coincidence, 1968 turned out to be, as it were, the valedictory year for an earlier generation of etymologists; Wartburg, Gamillscheg and Rohlfs were all honored with impressive homage volumes. H. and R. Kahane, Meier, Piel and Tovar have since been similarly honored, just to name a few of the stellar figures (cf. the bibliography under these names). Finally, new and very ambitious dictionary projects have been commenced (cf. Appendix I): Vàrvaro 1975 [Sicilian], Pfister 1973 [Italian], Baldinger – Gendron – Straka 1971- [Old French], and Kramer 1970- [Rhaeto-Romance, i. e., Gadertal, a dialect of "Dolomitenladinisch"], Baldinger 1975 [Old Occitan, Gascon].

The foregoing makes it abundantly clear that in the Romance field the amount of etymological information available to the erudite public has reached truly awesome proportions since World War II, an abundance that perhaps explains the apparent abandonment of all attempts to bring the *REW* (Meyer-Lübke 1935 [3rd]) up to date (see Piel 1961) or to initiate a new comparative Romance etymological dictionary (cf. in Appendix I Alsdorf-Bollée – Burr 1969, Schwake 1970). In any case, it seems unlikely that any other language family can boast such extensive coverage of its lexicon, nor such a large group of first rank scholars who continue to cultivate a linguistic discipline that in some quarters is one of the least glamorous (besides those already mentioned, Aebischer, Graur, Guiraud, Hubschmid, Malkiel [for his bibliography see in Appendix II Malkiel – Rico 1969(-71)] and Tilander (1973) stand out among very many others).

2. The genres

Much of our presentation will be given over to the discussion of dictionaries. Besides being the best known and most easily accessible form of etymological publication, they have, in the Romance domain, reached such outstanding levels of methodological sophistication that they represent, far better than was the case before World War II, the current state of the art. The truly outstanding examples provide a landmark from which further progress can be conveniently measured and, in most instances, have themselves been a spur and incentive to further etymological efforts. Still one must bear in mind that the dictionary entry must of necessity contain no more than a distillate of the relevant documentation and argumentation.

The highest form of the etymologist's art is no doubt the monograph or article dealing with a single word or word family. The author is under no compulsion to stint either his presentation of sources or his discussion of previous conjectures, and can paint for the reader a leisurely mural of deduction and proof that the vast scope of etymological dictionaries can ill afford. We have attempted to survey the most salient specimens that have come to our attention, but, despairing of anything like exhaustive coverage, have opted for presenting a brief anthology of recent etymological essays in order to give some idea of the intense activity that continues to flourish outside the specific compilation of lexica.

If the sheer number of titles were the decisive criterion, one would have to concede that the dominant form of etymological publication is the brief note, sometimes as little as a paragraph in length. Since these notes characteristically present little more than a bare conjecture, one which would no doubt require detailed investigation in any case before gaining general acceptance among etymologists, I sometimes wonder if they are really worthwhile. I suppose that many scholars, having been struck by some unpredictable intuition analogous to the Newtonian apple of legend, make haste to publish forthwith their etymological brainstorms in order to stake claim, as it were, to the discovery in the fear that some other sleuth might happen upon it before the "no trespassing" signs are posted. But unless the author at a later juncture or someone else performs the necessary corroboration, these brief and often schematic conjectures risk becoming an exercise in futility.

The literature that is self-consciously etymological in nature falls far short of exhausting the sources one must consult in search of etymological information. Nearly all diachronic linguistic studies tend to touch on etymology in some way, either because new solutions are proposed within the framework of, say, a complex phonological issue, or because in the course of such work previous etymologies are refurbished or shown to be impossible or at least unlikely. Our original intention was to survey such contributions as well, but it soon became apparent that any account aspiring to such a degree of inclusiveness would assume monographic proportions. Regrettably we have had to trim our sails, and will take up only self-confessed etymological investigations. However, I must mention the genre that impinges most immediately on etymology proper, that is, diachronic lexicology; only the exceptional onomasiological study would entirely disdain etymological considerations. Usually such works are chock full of speculations on word origins. Fortunately, we can refer the reader to an excellent, and recent, bibliography of general Romance and Gallo-Romance onomasiology (Gorog 1973-4 in Appendix II; for good recent examples of the genre cf. Söll 1967 and Hubschmid 1970, a monograph-length critique, also Baldinger 1975a, b).

3. Theory and method

Etymology is a discipline that involves little theory and much method. There is no point in repeating here what can be found in any general treatment of the subject (for instance, Anttila 1972: 322-334, Baldinger 1958-59, Guiraud 1964, Iordan 1972, Malkiel 1968a: 175-256, Palmer 1972: 300-340, Pisani 1967, Ross 1958, 1965, Ullmann 1958-59, or Wartburg 1970: 114-121). The entirely pointless dispute between the 'phoneticians' and 'semanticists' (nicely summarized by Roques 1905) subsided well before the period that interests us here (since World War II). It is now recognized on all sides, if not always put into practice, that the ideal etymological study should take full account of every linguistic and extra-linguistic fact that might buttress the solution proposed, including not only phonological and semantic data, but also all relevant morphological and syntactic details. Even a brief perusal of recent literature makes it evident that scholars do indeed strive more energetically than before to provide plausible explanations of the semantic shifts experienced by a form in its transmission from one language to another (excellent remarks on this score in Benveniste 1954). However, in favor of the residual 'phoneticians' among us, it must be said that there still is no unimpeachable theory of regular diachronic semantic laws to which one may appeal (for an attempt along these lines consult Ullmann 1959: 236-298); the investigator is perforce limited to establishing semantic connections that are intuitively satisfying.

One controversy of long standing has endured into the contemporary scene, though the two opposing positions seem a bit old hat by modern standards; I refer to the strenuous polemics between 'substratists' like Hubschmid and 'reconstructionists' like Meier. Neither extreme represents what is most admirable in the field for reasons that are not far to seek. Both operate almost entirely within the realm of the hypothetical, the former preferring to term their reconstructions 'pre-Roman, pre-Indo-European, Mediterranean,' or the like, while the latter would have us attribute to 'Vulgar' or 'Spoken Latin' their often bizarre concoctions. The soi-disant etyma thus "discovered" are far too often mere abstractions derived from the phonological and semantic properties of the words under study.

There are two basic considerations whose import, if taken seriously by practising etymologists, would provide a salutary element of restraint. Let us start from the presupposition, which few would dispute, that the discipline is far better served by well documented and solidly argued hypotheses than by hasty conjectures. That premise accepted, the first axiom is: nothing is more worthless than an erroneous etymology. This is not to say that the erudite vehicle, i. e., the article, monograph or dictionary that contains the unfortunate etymology is necessarily valueless, for after all much interesting material may have been presented in the pursuit of a misconceived goal, but rather that the irreducible core of the etymology, that is, that word *x* < etymon *y,* is, I repeat, worthless if erroneous. The important feature of this quite obvious point is the corollary one must draw from it: authors who fail in their etymological essays to strive to the utmost to piece together a convincing or compelling case are indulging in a frightful waste of time and effort.

Before about 1950 it would have been unnecessary and presumptuous to write the foregoing. Since that time, however, beginning, more or less, with his article "Mirages . . ." (1952), Meier has strung together an enormous number of conjectures, some of which are in the last analysis not bad; for a bibliography, cf. Meier 1971: 575-586, in Appendix II. Besides directing the journal *ASNS* since 1962, Meier has founded two monograph series, the *RVV* (since 1956) and, more pertinent to my present concerns, *Romanische Etymologien,* of which I have seen the first three numbers: Meier – Roth (eds) 1968, Bork 1969 and Greive 1970 (cf. Genaust 1972 for a review of the latter). Meier 1975 a, b are two recent monographs. Yet even his occasional bright idea (I am thinking, for instance, of his suggestion Sp. *conchabar(se)* 'to gang up' < *confābulāri* 'to converse together' [1972]) is all but useless to other researchers since he offends so drastically against the corollary to my first axiom. He seems to believe that suggesting an etymon is the same as proving one, or making it appear plausible, even though the latter part of the etymologist's task, i. e. the work of proof and confirmation, is far and away the more difficult and is, in fact, what tests an etymologist's mettle. More important, it is incumbent on the etymologist to bring some really new elements into the discussion other than his conjecture pure and simple. Only well established, or at the very least compellingly plausible, etymologies represent an advancement of knowledge and can be put to other linguistic (e. g., as a datum for historical grammar) and non-linguistic uses. Trivial and transparent cases aside, it is often agonizingly difficult to establish convincing etymologies, and the chances of failure are very great indeed. Surely, then, it is only reasonable to expect that the practitioner reveal original findings about the word (family) under analysis so that something will nevertheless be gained, in the likely event that his conjecture proves to be mistaken. The new material frequently constitutes the key to his solution, so that this requirement is no more than standard operating-procedure for all competent etymologists.

Meier relies on standard reference works, dictionaries and historical grammars; little, if any, of the conscientious perusal of archival material, little, if any, of the broad practical experience or 'Sachkenntnis' that have made Romance etymology renowned. The only salvageable part of his essays are usually the analyses of previous conjectures where telling criticisms are made against other points of view.

Meier in general starts off with the perception of a semantic similarity between Romance and Latin forms. The morphological and phonological distance between them usually remains very great, so he brings into play two assumptions: 1) that one may extrapolate on the basis of almost unlimited productivity derivational affixes that do indeed exist, especially the verbal types *-icāre, -itāre, -ināre,* and the like, the nominal types *-ul-, -ell-, -ill-,* etc., the prefixes *re-, ob-, de-, dis-,* etc., or, at last, any combination of them *(-iculāre, -itillāre,* etc.); and 2) that one may extend any diachronic irregularity (in phonology, normally) observed elsewhere to the case at hand, say syncope before voicing, assimilations, metatheses, etc. Then one selects an apposite combination of morphological and phonological hypotheses to form the diachronic bridge between the Romance forms and the putative Latin basis. Needless to say, all this allows one to prove just about anything, and the delightfully cockeyed formula *haricot < faba* would seem perfectly at home in this schema. The modus operandi just outlined strikes one as a rather mechanical process that requires but a very modest degree of ingenuity. Meier never seems to take the vast number of hypothetical intermediaries he posits seriously enough to attempt to establish in some fashion their reality; it suffices him to quote one or two allegedly parallel cases in unrelated word families.

The second axiom I would like to advance is the following: there is no philosophically perceptible difference between saying that a word is of unknown origin and saying that a word comes from an unknown language. If one claims that the cognate set $x = y = z$ descends from a prototype $*a$ belonging to a pre-Latin language for which there exists no independent evidence, then he might just as well say that the cognate set derives from prototype $*a$ of unknown origin. There simply is no empirical difference between the two statements. It follows from this that the most important part of the substratists' work is not the attribution of a given form or set of forms to some more or less chimerical stratum, but rather the identification of the cognate set in the first place. It is very interesting to know that forms x, y and z of dialects X, Y and Z must be related and that there can be found no convincing Latin base, nor a base in any extant or recorded language, to explain their relationship. The further allegation that the prototype of the forms involved belongs to a "Hispano-Caucasian" layer or the like seems gratuitous and transfers the whole issue from the pure radiance of science to the misty fumes of hocus-pocus. Scientific probity would be much better served by a formula such as $x = y = z < *a <?$.

Hubschmid is the most obvious example of the 'substratist' group: cf. Malkiel 1962, 1971 and Craddock 1969: 29-47.

Philosophically the two sides of the issue under discussion (substratists vs. reconstructionists) are not as far apart as the individual combatants may imagine. They both operate almost purely on reconstructed etyma; no reconstructed etymon is stronger than the cognate set that supports it. In the absence of further corroborative data to tip the balance one way or the other, it matters not a whit whether an etymon, once reconstructed, is labeled 'spoken Latin' or 'substratum' (except that it would be better, of course, to maintain a prudent silence on the matter). All one ends up knowing for certain is that a group of words is no doubt related by way of a common ancestor, which is exactly what he knew before bothering to set up the hypothetical etymon. In fact, the writings of extremists of both camps bear unmistakable resemblances. Veritable constellations of asterisks sparkle on the pages written by these earnest souls; the letters of the alleged bases are so scrambled, shuffled about and rearranged as to convince the bemused observer that skill at anagrams is the ideal intellectual equipment of the etymologist.

In the last analysis, this controversy is no longer very current. Each side has gone its own way, while a pervasive laissez-faire attitude seems to prevail among editors of journals. I miss very much the sort of severe yet even-handed criticism that much contemporary etymological literature would have elicited in the past, especially between the two world wars. Though I don't approve of the way some American linguists prowl around the groves of academe forever ready to leap at the jugular vein of their adversaries, the remarkable critical passivity that now dominates the field of Romance etymology carries with it a graver danger: that the debased coinage will drive out the hard currency.

The dominant model of etymological research in the Romance domain has been established by Wartburg's *FEW* where the primary emphasis is laid on careful and exhaustive attestation of every form in every dialect attributable to a given etymon throughout the entire historical span of Gallo-Romance. The concretely etymological considerations bring up the rear of each entry, almost as an afterthought. It is this dictionary, above all, that best reveals the fabric of Romance etymology, where the originally disparate strands of phonologically based correspondences, Wörter and Sachen realia, dialect study, both geographic and monographic, and diachronic semantics are woven together. (Though I will ignore as belonging to an earlier epoch Wagner 1943, Wartburg 1931 and Spitzer 1925, I do not at all wish to suggest that those excellent papers lack relevance at the present time.)

Wartburg's most brilliant disciple Baldinger now represents, more than any other single scholar, that mode of lexical research. So much so that he has become an advocate of "étymologie-histoire du mot" as opposed to "étymologie-origine" (1958-59). He accordingly places much greater emphasis on the chiefly semantic vicissitudes that words and word families experience within a given language rather than on their points of origin. His chief operating principle is two-sided: semantically similar words tend to become more alike formally, and formally similar words tend to coalesce semantically (for a concise statement see Baldinger 1965; at greater length 1973). This can, in the long run, lead to frightfully tangled skeins of interlocking word families that require the ultimate in etymological expertise to unravel. Baldinger's curiosity has led him into some fascinating areas (for instance, the terminology of the tobacco industry [1969]), while his collaboration in the *FEW,* his new venture on Old French (with Gendron and Straka 1971), and his numerous etymological articles bear ample testimony to the fact that he continues to honor 'étymologie-origine' as well. See Schwake's bibliography (Baldinger 1969), in Appendix II. I would only quibble with Baldinger's terminology, while recognizing the legitimacy of his approach. First of all, word history may be attempted, is in fact just as necessary for diachronic description, when the etymon is unknown as when it has been established to everyone's satisfaction (*pace* Szemerényi 1962:178). On the other hand, it is by now all but truistic to affirm that the pursuit of difficult etyma requires the pursuer to investigate in great detail the history of the words at issue. Secondly, the contrasting binomial 'étymologie-origine' (on this notion see Sandmann 1973:17-33), besides being tautological, in reality represents something of a polemical straw man since so few contemporary etymologists actually cleave to the outdated 'phoneticist' line advocated by Thomas in his well known debate with Schuchardt (see Roques 1905).

All the methodological innovators, Baldinger included, that have come forth since World War II share a common striving: to allow far greater scope to the analysis of the semantic elements in a given etymological equation. Vendryès (1953) envisioned a species of synchronic etymology, or 'étymologie statique' whose fundamental task would be (I translate) "to define the place each word occupies in the mind (esprit), circumscribing its meaning and usage, calculating its frequency, estimating its evocative force and noting the relationships that link it to other words". Though absolutely essential as a preliminary operation, I fail to see how it can be considered part of etymology per se rather than of synchronic semantics (cf. Malkiel 1968a:175).

Quite independently of Vendryès a species of synchronic etymology has cropped up in descriptive linguistics under the guise of 'synchronic cognates'. Generative phonologists feel obliged to provide synchronic phonological rules that relate such pairs as Sp. *anexar* 'to annex'/*anejo* 'supplement', *octavo* 'eighth'/*ocho* 'eight', and so on (see, e.g., J.W. Harris 1969:169 and Craddock 1973). I consider the utilization of such cognates to form synchronic rules in a descriptive grammar an ephemeral aberration. In any case, since each pair's relationship must necessarily be transparent, the whole tendency can be of little interest to serious etymologists. The coexistence of *octavo* and *ocho* proves exactly the opposite of what generative phonologists would deduce, i. e., that in Modern Spanish there is in fact no synchronic rule that converts [kt] into [č]. Bakel (1968) uses the phrase "transformational etymology" in a sense unrelated to what is here under discussion. For a view equating a word's etymon with its transformational deep structure see H. Kahane (1975).

That part of Vendryès' program dealing with the relationships among words can take on a diachronic dimension as demonstrated by Maher (1971), who attempts to reconstruct the original semantic bonds linking putative, and certainly no longer transparent, derivatives of Lat. *aqua* 'water': *aquila* 'eagle', *aquilus* 'dark' and *aquilo* 'northwind'. He has distinguished methodological predecessors in Ernout (1956) and Trier (1952) (cf. Malkiel 1968:209, 217). His originality lies in his insistence that any thoroughgoing linguistic description must include this particular chapter of diachronic lexicology.

Under the label 'étymologie organique' Vidos (esp. 1957 and 1965 a) has launched a minor methodological innovation based on the supposition that terms pertaining to a tightly integrated semantic field may very well betray a like or similar origin; his most convincing illustrations have to do with French nautical terminology of Italian and Dutch provenience. Words associated with certain cultural complexes tend to migrate along with the objects, artifacts or conceptual structures they designate, so that one often finds clusters of loanwords in specific semantic fields, like Gallicisms in English legal jargon, Arabisms in Medieval Spanish military parlance, and the like. So as a working hypothesis Vidos' notion offers some advantages, unless the researcher falls into the trap of assuming aprioristically a given word must stem from a given source because the former occurs among a set of forms safely attributable to the latter (see Colón 1962 and Höfler 1966 a). 'Organic' etymology in no way frees one from the task of proving the etymology of each individual word on its own terms.

The interaction of form and meaning, likewise an operating hypothesis in Baldinger's recent work as noted above, has received its greatest theoretical development as a linguistic principle in Guiraud's concept of 'morpho-semantic fields', i. e., formal and semantic matrices within a language that tend to integrate words of heterogeneous origins into paradigms, that is, clusters of forms sharing formal and semantic properties. The task of identifying such paradigms belongs to what he calls 'internal' etymology as opposed to traditional 'external' etymology that concentrates on extralinguistic criteria (chronology, geo-graphic distribution, and the like).

The importance of these paradigms for etymology is twofold. First, they are to a certain extent productive insofar as they motivate new forms based on familiar patterns. One cannot help recalling at this point Şăineanu's 'sources indigènes' (1925-30, 1935), however superior Guiraud's methods may be to his predecessor's. Second, and perhaps more important, the paradigms may help explain just why a particular loan word was adopted and why it subsequently prospered in the borrowing language. Guiraud's views (see especially 1956, 1964:88-125, 1967) bear strong resemblance to certain notions developed in the study of word formation, especially derivation. Note, for instance, Malkiel's suggestion that suffixal gamuts may generate structurally parallel suffixal types (1970:58, 77-78).

Guiraud regards his 'internal' etymology as complementary to, rather than a substitute for, Wartburg's traditional approach (see their gentlemanly exchange [Guiraud 1960, 1967:125-141, Wartburg 1964] about Gallo-Romance forms containing the sequence *chic-*). The phenomenon in question was hardly beyond the ken of most skilful etymologists. Guiraud's contribution perhaps lies more in having sys-tematized the study of morpho-semantic fields than in having dis-covered them: cf. Posner 1970:447-451 and, for criticism, Meier 1969 and Höfler 1968.

Most, if not all, of the scholars heretofore mentioned accept without reserve the legitimacy of etymological study, apparently unconcerned with the impact their particular interest may have on the progress of linguistics in general. Conversely, they seem very slow to take advan-tage of new insights gained in the broader field. One investigator who has consistently striven to affirm and illustrate the necessary inter-dependence of etymology and general diachronic linguistics is Malkiel. Three of his most pertinent essays are now available in his recent miscellany (1968a:175-256); rather than summarize those earlier pieces, I can refer the reader to his recent paper (1975a) where he warns that "a reconciliation between spatio-temporal linguistics and etymology must occur because without it, either discipline is doomed to slow extinction." Malkiel also brought out a typology of etymological dictionaries, not limited to Romance (1976). Compare Kiparsky (1959) and Picoche (1970, 1971b).

In sum, the imposing edifice of Romance etymology has admitted only gradual and measured shifts in theory and method in contrast to the somewhat frenetic vicissitudes of descriptive linguistics. The most recent movements in the latter domain, focusing as they do on meaning and word structure, may, however, prove to have far greater implications for etymology than its immediate predecessors. Let us hope that the work of 'onomatologists' and semanticists may soon permit the development of canons of semantic change analogous to diachronic phonological rules; such a result would represent an immense gain in scientific rigor for a discipline that despite its brilliant achievements still too often falls into erudite frippery. We might here mention one minor current that is now enjoying a certain vogue: the rehabilitation, or at least the assessment of the contributions pioneers have made to the field. On Diez we have Sykorra 1973; Poghirc 1968 a memorializes Hasdeu; and there is a recent dissertation on the etymological research of Gilliéron and Şăineanu (Hillen 1973). Medieval and Renaissance etymological activity is analyzed by Klinck 1970 (12th c. Latin Renaissance), Niederehe 1968, 1969, 1974 (Leomarte, Boccaccio, Alfonso el Sabio, resp.), Burke 1968 *(Libro del cauallero Cifar)*, Coseriu 1972 (Giambullari), and Sánchez Regueira 1971 (anonymous 16th c. Spanish etymologist). Here at Berkeley the work of Gilles Ménage will receive searching scrutiny (Holtzmann in preparation).

4. Critical anthology

Most introductory treatments (e. g. most recently Kiparsky 1966, Lohmann 1966, Sanders 1967, Kohler 1970, and for Indo-European Szemerényi 1962), for all their intrinsic interest, leave the beginner rather unprepared for what he will actually find in recent etymological literature. Their somewhat abstract disquisitions frequently operate with words or word families whose origin is hardly a matter of controversy, e. g., Fr. *cuisse* 'thigh' < *coxa* 'hip', while the very essence of etymological work is the attack on the unknown. It is, for instance, far more instructive to observe Malkiel the etymologist at work (say, 1974 and 1967-68) than Malkiel the theorist and historian of etymological research (1968a:175-256) though the latter triad of refurbished essays makes for very agreeable reading. Consequently, I would like to survey some recent etymological papers, commenting on the methodological problems they present and the cogency of the solutions proffered.

H. and R. Kahane (1968) study the origin of Fr. *risque* (> Eng. *risk*),
It. *rischio,* Cat. *risc,* Ptg. *risco,* Sp. *riesgo,* It. *risico,* Prov. *rezegue,*
OCat. *reec* (< **rezec*) and Medieval Lat. *ris(i)cum.* To all appearances
this is a typical Romance cognate set ('panromain sauf roumain'). The
principal authorities *(REW, FEW* and *DCE)* accept, with some misgiv-
ings, a reconstructed **resecum* 'cliff', allegedly derived from the verb
resecāre 'to cut off', whose chief or only Romance descendant, other
than the words meaning 'danger', is OSp. *riesco* 'cliff' (> *risco).* Cliffs
are dangerous places for ships and sailing boats, to say nothing of
unwary hikers, so a metaphoric transfer is envisaged: 'cliff' > 'danger'.
The obvious semantic model is, of course, *scopulus* 'rock, cliff, crag' >
'difficulty, danger, harm, evil', one of Cicero's favorite clichés.

I note, first of all, that the base is reconstructed and that the meaning
is simply extrapolated from Sp. *risco.* The problems the Kahanes perceive are the following: 1 (phonology) – the [z] of Prov. *rezegue* clashes
with the [s] of the putative source verb *ressegar;* 2 (morphology) – the
Sp. verb *arriesgar* 'to risk' is certainly secondary, observe in particular
the failure of the root vowel to alternate, whereas the head of the word
family, if it does indeed stem from *resecāre,* should have been OSp.
resgar 'to tear, rip' (> *rasgar* × *rascar* 'to scratch'), yet there is no
evidence of the slightest contact between *riesco/riesgo* and that verb
within the history of Spanish; 3 (semantics) – outside Spanish there
seems to remain no vestige of the meaning 'cliff'.

The first two of those objections could be somewhat allayed by arguing that Prov. *ressegar* and Sp. *arriesgar* are in fact irrelevant to the
problem of origins, being relatively modern 'recompositions' rather
than organic descendants of *resecāre,* and assuming, in addition, that as
the metaphoric meaning of **resecum* came to predominate it became
irretrievably isolated from its source well before the appearance of the
earliest Romance documents. The third, on the other hand, seems to
weigh very heavily against this etymology, since there is no evidence
that the other Romance forms are borrowed from Spanish, a most
awkward theory in any case, since Sp. *ri(e)sco,* as opposed to *riesgo,* is
not known ever to have meant 'danger'.

After considering numerous rival hypotheses, the Kahanes eventually support Arab. *rizq* 'military pay, anything given to you by God and
profitable to you, good luck'. Here we have a known word offered as
putative etymon, and one which can be etymologized in Arabic (<

Pers. *roǵik* 'daily ration, maintenance'). This, I presume, peremptorily eliminates the possibility of a Romance loan in Arabic. It is nevertheless apparent that the phonological and semantic gaps that must be bridged are formidable, but the Kahanes succeed brilliantly in my judgement by bringing into play an expertly constructed word biography. They prove that Arab. *rizq* passed into Byzantine Greek as *rízikon,* especially in the notion 'soldier of fortune', and that from there it appears in Latin documents (first attestation of *risicum:* Venice, 1158, in a document from Constantinople) dealing in particular with seafaring and most often allied to the near synonym *fortuna:* "ad risicum et fortunam Dei maris et gentium". A century later a paroxytonic variant appeared, radiating, it seems, from Pisa (first noted 1264), and it is surely this doublet *risicum/riscum* that gave rise to the Romance cognate set under consideration. The Kahanes are admirably scrupulous in solving the phonological and semantic details of each step in the long journey; their paper is a classic example of the importance of documentary expertise allied to thoroughgoing background information in etymological research.

Baldinger (1968) again demonstrates how crucial hitherto unknown and earlier documentation can be in resolving an etymological dilemma. Fr. *laie* 'ride, a road or way made for riding on horseback, especially through a wood' has been attributed to a Frankish **laida* 'path', whose alleged Germanic cognates include Eng. *lead* and Germ. *leiten* 'to lead' (*FEW* 16:438 [1957]), or, alternatively, to the OFr. verb *lai(i)er* 'to let, allow' < Galloroman **laggāre* based on Gaulish **laggos* = Irish *lag* 'feeble, slack, lazy' (EWFS, cf. App. I). The latter lexicographer's objection to his colleague's etymon is that a Germanic *-d-* should not have disappeared; in his own conjecture, the semantic difficulties seem very great, though one could perhaps arrive at 'path' from the notion 'to let, allow (a way [be opened?] through the woods)'.

However, Baldinger came up with what is no doubt the correct answer by tracing the word's history not only in vernacular texts but in Medieval Latin documents as well. First he verifies what was evidently the original meaning 'mark or incision made on trees reserved for some purpose, especially those selected for firewood'; from there to 'path through the woods marked by blazing, i. e., nicking the bark of trees along the way' and finally 'path cut through the woods' constitutes an intuitively satisfying sequence. In the Latin material he studied, the frequent form *laya* represents no more than a Latinization of the vernacular term; but he also discovered the decisive forms *lachus/laha* in documents reaching back to Carolingian times (770 A.D.), they too merely Latinized versions of, in this instance, Germanic vernacular designations. As the author gleefully puts it, "Damit . . . fällt die Etymologie wie eine reife Frucht vom Baum", i. e., Frankish **lākan* 'to blaze', a form with abundant Germanic cognates, including Germ. *Lache* 'notch (made in a tree), blaze', and which provides an exceptionally neat semantic and phonological fit to Fr. *laie*. Though in this case we must still deal with a reconstructed etymon, the gain in overall plausibility is very great indeed; improved documentation provided the essential key to the solution.

Phonological criteria can become entirely inoperative for etymology in certain unusual circumstances, for instance when two bases in the source language present unexceptionable phonological fits to presumptive descendants. Malkiel (1974) considers just such a case, i. e., the sequence *sañ-* in Sp. *saña* 'wrath, ire', *ensañar(se)* 'to become wrathful', and *sañudo* 'wrathful', which from the strictly phonological point of view, may match either *insānia* 'madness' or *saniēs* 'bad blood'. Semantically either form likewise constitutes a plausible starting point, but Malkiel proves quite convincingly that the latter must have played a central, though not necessarily exclusive, role in the *saña* family by analyzing in thorough fashion the morphological, in this case, derivational, aspects of the problem.

First, and perhaps most important, is the demonstration that the meaning of *saniēs* (var. *sania)* seems far more compatible with the semantic ambit of the suffix *-udo,* indicative so often of remarkable anatomical traits in the person or animal referred to. From 'full of bad blood' to 'wrathful' strikes me as an eminently plausible step, one in fact present in the English phrase *bad blood.* When beside this argument Malkiel adduces the OSp. adj. *sañoso* 'wrathful' which corresponds to Lat. *saniōsus* (← *saniēs*) so perfectly that, as he deftly puts it, they "fit together like matching parts of a broken object", I think the case must be considered closed, though secondary influence of *insānia* (as well as *sanna* 'mocking grimace') should be reckoned with.

Ast. *cabruñar* 'to sharpen (scythes and sickles by beating the blade with a hammer on a special anvil driven into the ground for that purpose)' has been explained (*DCE* 1.265b), on the basis of the variant

(Cespedosa de Tormes) *enclavuñar,* as a derivative of *clavo* 'nail'. Piel (1968) raises two objections to this derivation, first, that the sequence *-uñ-* is left unaccounted for, and, second, that the semantic relationship between base and presumed derivative is unconvincing. One might have added that the phonological process envisaged is also difficult, i. e., that an occidental cognate **cravuñar* (← *cravo* = *clavo*) became *cabruñar* through a hypercorrection triggered by the shift *cabra* > *craba.* Piel fails to note that the shift *cabra* > *craba* seems never to have occurred in Colunga (cf. Vigón 1955 in Appendix I), likewise well to the east of the *cr-/cl-* isogloss. Hence *DCE*'s explanation requires that Colunga *cabruñar* be a western loanword, an assumption that clashes with the fact that *clabuñar* (perhaps a hypercorrect recoil from *crabuñar*) is the western Asturian version of this word, so the geographic pattern also militates against Corominas' reconstruction. Now secondary association with *clavo* 'nail' motivated by the hammering operation involved seems far more likely than a blend with *cabra* 'she-goat' (see on this point Malkiel 1970:42); in sum, this reader finds it easy to acquiesce to Piel's skepticism.

His own conjecture starts from a metaphoric application of the name for the billy goat, **capr-o, -ōnis,* to the allegedly two-horned shape of the anvil in question (the author notes the parallels **bicornia* 'anvil', lit. 'two-horned[object]' and It. *capruggine* 'chimb-notch, notch in a stave for fixing the bottom of the cask' < **caprōne* × **incūgine* < *incūdine* 'anvil' [but cf. *DEI* s. v.]), which would have given rise to a verb **caprōneāre.* This hypothetical verb would indeed explain the suffixoid *-uñ-,* compare the Asturian toponym *Cabruñana* < **Caprōniāna,* no doubt inseparable from the attested anthroponym *Caprōnius.*

One misses, in this brief note, any mention of the current designations of the anvil in question, a crucial point, since Piel alleges its name to have been at one time **caprōne,* if I understand him correctly. The object actually resembles a large nail, i. e., *clavón,* and I believe that W-.Ast. *clabuñar* could correspond to a Cast. **clavonear.* In any case, Piel's is an interesting suggestion, but it suffers from excessively exiguous documentation and confirmation.

Cat. *rost* (adj.) 'steep' and congeners attracted Meier's attention (1968:225-227). The prevailing explanation of this word as originally belonging to the family of Cat. *rostir* = Fr. *rôtir* 'to roast' through the semantic chain 'roasted' > 'fast, swift' > 'steep' (cf. *FEW* 16.685

[1959]) he finds "eine zwar reizvolle, aber übermäßig künstliche Konstruction". He offers instead a VLat. *reobstitu/a, presumptive derivative of *obstitus* 'oblique'. At this point it becomes evident that the reader has seen all the documentation Meier cared to consult: the *DCVB, FEW, REW* and Georges' *Handwörterbuch* (1913). Nevertheless he falls short of reporting all he found in those sources, passing conveniently over the archaic Cat. adj. *rost* 'roasted', given as a synonym of *rostit* by the authors of the *DCVB*. This last point, is, of course, not decisive. We may perfectly well be dealing with a case of secondary homonymy. But how many etymologists of, say, Piel's calibre, would have broached the problem at all with so little in their dossier? Surely it would have been worthwhile to sort out this homonymy, if that is what it is, by a careful examination of Old Catalan texts, to say nothing of Old Provençal, where an identical situation prevails, i. e., *raust* 'steep'/'roasted'. Perhaps this investigation would have revealed some missing link in the conjectural chain Meier sets up.

Now about *obstitus* and its derivative *obstitum* 'oblique direction'; is it sufficient to quote Georges' definitions? The two forms are given as hapax legomena from Apuleius' treatise *De deo Socratis,* hence the meanings attributed to them may (but, of course, need not) be hasty conclusions of the lexicographer. As past participles of *obsistere* 'to stand against, oppose' one would expect *obstitus* to mean 'opposed, opposing'; in Georges, s. v. *obsistere,* one finds that the past-participial adjective can mean 'thunder-struck', i. e., 'subjected to violent heavenly opposition in the form of a thunderbolt', I presume. The reader requires a reasoned account of the semantic changes from 'opposed' > 'oblique' > 'steep'. Neither step seems impossible, but there is no reason to take them for granted (one speaks, for instance, of "opposing" slopes, hills, etc.). There is, as far as I can tell, no hint of the meaning 'oblique' in the Catalan forms; Germ. *schräg,* the word Georges uses to define *obstitus,* unfortunately means both 'oblique' and 'sloping'. One wonders whether Meier hasn't been victimized by some purely lexicographical imprecision.

As for the morphology of the reconstructed etymon, the etymologist should motivate the prefixation with *re-*; what Meier offers is no more than the fatuous statement that "nach ihrer Bedeutung waren [*obstitus* and *obstitum*] zu einer Präfigierung mit *re-* 'entgegen' geradezu prädestiniert". Readers are prepared to accept all sorts of possibilities; the whole point is to move from what is possible to what is probable. Now neither Georges, Souter (1964; App. I), the *FEW* nor the *REW* contain any entry beginning with the sequence of prefixes *re-ob-*. This circumstance alone demands particularly thoroughgoing investigation, rather than reliance on predestination.

The VLat. bases **reobstitu/a,* according to Meier, explain effortlessly (mühelos) the Romance forms. Let us see what he means by that. First one must assume a contracted variant **robstitu* to account for monophthongal forms like Cat. *rost,* while the uncontracted base is needed to account for OProv. *raust,* since *eo/eu > au* in that language. Naturally, one would expect Meier to provide a set of correspondences Cat. *o =* Prov. *au < eo/eu* to shore up his argument, but not a single further example is adduced. For the contraction the reader is referred laconically to *FEW* 7.288 [1953], s. v. *obstāre;* there he finds OFr. *roster,* Mid. Fr. *reosté* (p. ptc.) 'to take away again', the almost perfect model for the *re-ob-* sequence I was curious about. Why didn't Meier make more of this apparent support for his notion? The answer may lie in this same *FEW* article where Provençal descendants of *obstāre* showing prefixation with *de-* are listed. Though both uncontracted and contracted forms occur *(dehostar/dostar)* not a single one contains the *au* one might expect if Meier's claim were genuinely tenable. The whole matter suggests a strong disinclination to consider negative evidence, perhaps the most serious single failing that one could attribute to a scientist. It turns out that the Provençal descendants of **deobstāre* are a powerful, not to say conclusive, argument against **reobstitu > raust.*

It would no doubt be better to ignore, like Corominas, these "ocurrencias poco serias" *(DCE* 4.1060) of Meier, were it not the case that he and his students have been generating a bibliographic blizzard in the European journals, much to the discredit of the entire field of Romance studies. It is a waste of time and energy to dissect such trivial and ill-founded notions, but unless serious workers take this disagreeable task in hand, the infection appears likely to spread. For other somewhat less pessimistic appraisals of this school, see Dworkin (in press) and Kahane (1977); in the latter, some flattering generalities paradoxically introduce a devastating critique.

5. *Language-by-language survey*
5.1 Gallo-Romance

5.1.1 Etymological dictionaries
Students of French etymology have at their disposal the *FEW*, the most extensive and detailed etymological dictionary of any Romance language – conceived, directed, and largely written by the Swiss scholar Walther von Wartburg. Its subtitle clearly indicates his aim, a diachronically slanted thesaurus of all Gallo-Romance dialects. It is the first Romance dictionary to regard etymology as the study of a given word's complete history from the time it entered the language to the present or to the moment of its extinction, with careful attention to all semantic shifts.

The origins of the *FEW* antedate the First World War. After disagreements over method and approach led Wartburg and Jakob Jud to abandon their project of a jointly authored Romance etymological dictionary, Wartburg began planning a similar work restricted in scope to Gallo-Romance. He spent the years 1910–1918 copying and cataloguing according to semantic criteria all the material available in French dialect and patois dictionaries. This emphasis on rural speech, which reflects the influence of his teacher Jules Gilliéron, shows through clearly in the opening fascicles (1922-) of the *FEW* where the modern literary language is all but ignored. However, he quickly realized the importance of tracing the evolution of the literary language as well, so adjusted accordingly the design of the remaining volumes (see Wartburg 1929). At the same time the work of Gilliéron, Jaberg and Jud made the author of the *FEW* keenly aware of the interdependence of words belonging to the same semantic sphere; individual lexical items and entire word families could no longer be studied profitably in isolation. Consequently, starting with the 4th volume, Wartburg decided to compose, though not publish, the *FEW* according to semantic groups; for illustrations of this technique, see Wartburg 1952a and 1954.

136 fascicles, comprising nearly all of the *FEW*'s first 25 volumes, appeared before Wartburg's death in 1971 (fascicles 137 and 138 were published in 1973). The first 20 volumes, now complete, contain all formations for which Wartburg felt he could safely establish etymologies. Volumes 1-14 treat principally the Latin and Greek components of the Gallo-Romance lexicon; the Germanic element is

examined in volumes 15-17 (which include revised versions of the Germanic entries in volumes 1 and 3); volumes 18, 19 and 20 deal with Anglicisms, Orientalisms, and borrowings from all other languages, respectively. The entries are ordered alphabetically according to the etymon, which serves as the head-word and is glossed in German. The first part of each entry presents all Gallo-Romance lexical items derived directly or indirectly from the head-word. Morphologically related forms belonging to the same semantic field are grouped together and glossed in French. Meanings are arranged chronologically and a date is provided for initial, and when necessary, final documentation. Dialect formations are localized as precisely as possible. The second segment of each *FEW* article offers an analysis and discussion in German of the data, with special attention to semantic developments as well as to the competition from, and the influence of semantically akin but genetically distinct formations. Appropriate footnotes conclude each entry.

Volumes 21-23 (volume 22, though already complete in draft, still awaits publication) gather together the numerous dialect and slang formations for which no plausible origin has been suggested. The entries, arranged according to the conceptual categories drawn up in Wartburg – Hallig 1952 consist of a presentation of the pertinent data carefully glossed and localized. Only rarely did Wartburg attempt to analyze historically this material. He intended volumes 24 and 25 to serve as a completely new edition of the first half (A) of volume 1, from which he had excluded consideration of the history of the literary language. Three fascicles pertaining to volumes 21-25 have appeared since 1969; cf. also Wartburg 1969 in Appendix I.

According to the statistics in Wartburg 1971:26 (App.I), the 136 fascicles published in Wartburg's lifetime contain 19,844 entries, of which Wartburg personally edited 17,380. Responsibility for the remainder lay with 26 scholars, the most prolific being Hans-Erich Keller, Marianne Müller and Paul Zumthor, who each prepared over 300 articles. Readers can find a complete critical bibliography in App. II (Wartburg 1971:94-101). Observations on the external and internal history of the *FEW* are offered in Zumthor 1955, Wartburg 1961 (App. I) and in Baldinger 1974; for a penetrating analysis of the *FEW*'s structure written from the viewpoint of modern lexicological theory and techniques, see Rey 1970.

Most of Wartburg's scholarly output derives from his work on the *FEW*. In 1957 he abandoned his plan to write a multi-volume history of the French lexicon based upon the research undertaken for the *FEW;* his earlier studies on the names of the days of the week (1949) and the linguistic impact of the Greek colonization of southern Gaul (1952b) represent contributions to this aborted synthesis. At least two book-length ventures can trace their ultimate origins to the *FEW:* Wartburg 1934 in Appendix II, and Wartburg – Hallig 1952. Needless to say, many of Wartburg's etymological articles and notes afforded scholars advance glimpses into the unpublished portions of the *FEW;* for titles, see the bibliography (Wartburg 1971:53-94) in Appendix II.

Two other etymological dictionaries stem directly from the *FEW.* After Wartburg had completed the first volume of his magnum opus, a French publishing house asked him to prepare an abridged etymological dictionary designed for the non-specialist. When Wartburg's many commitments threatened to delay excessively this venture, the collaboration of Oscar Bloch was secured. Bloch singlehandedly prepared both volumes of the *DELF,* which Wartburg revised prior to publication (1932), assisted by Vendryès for the Celtic etymologies. The *DELF* restricted its scope to the lexicon of contemporary Standard French. Each entry is a miniature word history, indicating the etymology, the date of entry into the language, the semantic evolution, and the linguistic and non-linguistic factors which influenced the growth of the lexical item at issue. The *DELF* omits all discussion of previous etymological hypotheses.

After Bloch's untimely death in 1937, Wartburg assumed responsibility for the four subsequent editions (1950, 1960, 1964 and 1968). Financial pressures necessitated the compression of the *DELF* into a single volume. Wartburg revised many entries on the basis of the material prepared for eventual publication in the *FEW,* thus using the *DELF* to preview some of the findings destined to appear in the larger dictionary. In the absence of a complete index to the *FEW,* the *DELF* enables scholars and non-specialists to determine which entry to consult in the *FEW* for a more elaborate presentation of data and analysis: cf. in Appendix I Baldinger 1961 and Pfister 1966, 1971.

The *DEAF* can be classed as a direct outgrowth of, and a supplement to the *FEW.* Five fascicles have appeared to date, three devoted to the letter G, an index and a bibliography. The *DEAF* proposes to examine more than could the *FEW* the history of those word families which constituted the French vocabulary from the *Serments de Strasbourg* (A. D. 843) to the middle of the 14th century. Since the *DEAF* relies heavily on material collected in the *FEW,* Baldinger chose to initiate publication with the letter G while awaiting the revision and updating of the first three volumes of the *FEW* (A-F). The internal structure of the *DEAF* differs in several important respects from the *FEW*. The main word of the Old French family under discussion, not the etymon, heads each entry. As the Medieval language knew no fixed orthographic system, the spelling used in the Francien dialect, which evolved into the literary standard, was chosen whenever possible. Each article begins with a discussion of the head-word's origin and history, as well as a list of orthographic variants accompanied by precise indications of primary and secondary sources. Unlike the *FEW,* the *DEAF* gathers together all meanings of the particular formation under study with copious references to Medieval texts. The same pattern is followed in presenting pertinent derivatives and compounds (see the appraisals by Pfister 1975 in App. I and by Vàrvaro 1974).

Two other etymological dictionaries that still render good service to scholars merit discussion here. Ernst Gamillscheg made his first mark as an etymologist by publishing a series of notes entitled "Französische Etymologien" (1919-20, 1921-22), and by reviewing the opening fascicle of the *FEW* (1923). These early ventures, probably designed as a prelude to a future etymological dictionary, aroused the opposition of his former collaborator Leo Spitzer (1922) who heaped scorn upon Gamillscheg's ultraconservative, neogrammatical conception of etymology as the search for word origins. Conceivably the appearance of the *FEW* caused Gamillscheg to rush into print sooner than he had intended his *EWFS,* which appeared in fascicles from 1926 to 1928.

Gamillscheg chose as his guide to the French lexicon Darmesteter – Hatzfeld – Thomas 1890-1900 (in Appendix I), thereby omitting any neologisms, dialectalisms, or slang formations excluded from that compilation. Certain Old French terms were considered under the corresponding modern word. The concise entries of the *EWFS* concentrate on establishing word origins rather than on sketching compact word histories; the semantic evolution of each form is ignored. Gamillscheg indicates the century in which each lexical item included in the *EWFS* is first attested. The bibliographic references to previous etymological conjectures constitute perhaps the most valuable feature of this dictionary. Its author's unwillingness the declare the origin of a word as obscure or unknown led him to reconstruct numerous implausible hypothetical bases. Rohlfs (1957) took Gamillscheg to task for positing many unjustified Celtic etyma. In a series of articles Brüch (1926-29, in Appendix I) subjected a host of *EWFS* entries to detailed examination. The *EWFS* provoked a strident critique from Spitzer (1926, in Appendix I), to which Gamillscheg acrimoniously responded at length in 1927; for a further assessment, balanced in tone and perspective, of the *EWFS'* deficiencies, see Meillet (1927-29).

The bibliography appended to Gamillscheg 1968 (649-670) discloses that the study of individual etymological problems represented only a small portion of that scholar's output since 1928 (see also Malkiel's necrology (1973-74), esp. at pp. 176f.). In his final years Gamillscheg authored a revised and expanded two volume edition of the *EWFS* (1966-68). Despite many changes of detail, the new version of the *EWFS* brought with it no innovations in Gamillscheg's approach to etymological research (cf. Pfister 1972, in Appendix I).

Dauzat 1938 (in Appendix I) is essentially a commercial venture sponsored by the Larousse publishing house. It includes more technical neologisms, rural and slang formations than the *DELF*. Dauzat claims no originality in matters etymological; for cruxes, Dauzat indicates (without bibliographical references) the most plausible hypotheses, or wisely states that the word's origin is unknown. No attempt is made to trace word histories; the century and the author of the text in which each word appears for the first time is indicated. Dauzat prefaces the etymological component of his dictionary with an introduction to problems of historical change written for the layman. Each edition of the *Dictionnaire* contains a *Supplément lexicologique* with corrected etymologies and references to lexical items omitted from the body of the dictionary, and a *Supplément chronologique* with revised datings.

Dauzat's *Dictionnaire* went through many printings before his death in 1955. It served as the foundation for Dauzat – Dubois – Mitterand 1964 (in Appendix I), with an increase in information provided, even though less regionalisms are discussed. In addition to the etymon, each article traces the semantic evolution of the head-word, provides a date for the first attestation for every meaning and for every derivative listed, and documents more secondary formations than Dauzat (1938).

The forematter contains a sketch of the internal and external history of the French language, a list of learned Latin and Greek prefixes and suffixes employed in French word-formation, and the sources used to establish the date of a given word's initial appearance: cf. Pfister (1966) and Höfler (1970) in Appendix I. Picoche (1971, in Appendix I) has introduced a new, and not very successful, wrinkle by organizing her etymological information on the basis of the most remote, usually Indo-European, root form (compare Devoto's like concern for ultra-Romanic origins [1966]). For a crushing appraisal of her effort, see Genaust (1972, in Appendix I).

5.1.2 Monographic endeavors

The period under consideration in this survey has seen the publication of scores of monographs, articles and notes devoted to single Gallo-Romance lexical items and word families. The traditional concept of etymology as the search for word origins continues to flourish; in the last thirty years several long-standing cruxes have been thoroughly investigated (though not necessarily resolved) by competent, well trained scholars (e. g., Deutschmann 1947, Corréard 1958, Tilander 1955). Several specialists in French etymology have further developed and refined the tradition laid down by Schuchardt, Gilliéron and Wartburg by envisaging their discipline as the study of complete word histories in which the establishment of a given formation's genealogy received less attention than its semantic evolution or the means and reasons for its entry into the Gallo-Romance lexicon. The leading practitioners of this approach today are Baldinger and his disciple Höfler. The former's contribution to etymology has been analyzed above; see also his bibliography, (1969) in Appendix II. Höfler (1967b) has concerned himself primarily with textile names based on toponyms and with the transformation of toponyms into common nouns, a theme reminiscent of Migliorini (1927; cf. Craddock 1971–72).

One facet of word history has grown into an autonomous subdiscipline – the dating of a given formation's first documented appearance in French. Such investigations, which demand the careful scrutiny of hundreds of non-literary and literary texts and documents, have been carried out with vigor and enthusiasm by such lexicologists as Quemada, Arveiller and Rey; for further discussion and useful bibliographical hints see Höfler 1969, Schwake 1968 and Gebhardt forthcoming. Straddling the hazy border between etymology proper and diachronic lexicology are the numerous onomasiological studies devoted to French, many of which discuss and take a stand on controversial etymological problems. Onomasiology has enjoyed tremendous popularity, especially among European scholars. Gorog's bibliography (1973) of Gallo-Romance onomasiological studies, which claims to be exhaustive, lists 364 titles (cf. Appendix II). For one example, rich in etymological analyses, prepared by a North American scholar, see Livingston's monograph on the designations of skein-winding reels in Gallo-Romance (1957) and Malkiel's detailed commentary (1958–59).

Since the pioneering investigations of Gilliéron and Sainéan (Şăineanu), etymologists have displayed considerable interest in the spontaneous creation of lexical items within French, i. e., in the process which Guiraud (1967) labeled 'étymologie interne'. Most work in this domain focuses on colloquial, slang, scabrous, metaphoric and onomatopoeic formations usually coined in rural or dialect speech. Guiraud's hypothesis of the role played by 'morpho-semantic' fields in the genesis of lexical items represents the most important (though not necessarily convincing or successful) attempt to systematize this approach to the study of word origins; for discussion and analysis, see the latter part of section 3 above.

This aspect of etymology has given rise to the notion 'étymologie populaire' (Ger. Volksetymologie), a process by which a word's phonetic or semantic development could be altered in unexpected ways through (genetically unjustified) association in the minds of speakers with phonetically or referentially similar formations. Some scholars have deemed the term 'étymologie populaire' inaccurate. The incorrect association of unrelated words is not limited to the untutored masses. Such mistakes, when committed by the learned and semi-learned, deserve Gougenheim's (1948) derisory label 'fausse étymologie savante'. Although Orr spoke of 'associative etymology' in 1939 (see Orr 1953:96), that designation did not appear in a later paper (1954) devoted to, and entitled "L'étymologie populaire". The semanticist Ullmann (1966:34) cited the phenomenon at issue as a prime example of synchronic or 'static' etymology, a qualifier first used by Vendryès (1953, see above, section 3) and criticized as paradoxical by Malkiel (1968:175). Compare now also Baldinger 1973.

5.2 Hispano-Romance

5.2.1 Spanish

Juan Corominas' monumental *DCE* (Appendix I) stands out, in its scope and coverage, as the most ambitious individual project in Hispanic etymology. The appearance of its four volumes between 1954 and 1957 marked the culmination of more than twenty-five years of study, research and writing by its author, a direct disciple of Menéndez Pidal and Jud. In 1929, Corominas began to collect material for an etymological dictionary of Catalan (his native language); a few early fruits of this venture appeared during the thirties in Griera's *Butlletí de dialectologia catalana*. Ten years later, Corominas decided to concentrate on the preparation of a Spanish etymological dictionary. Throughout the forties and early fifties, he offered his fellow scholars a preview of his magnum opus in a string of articles and etymologically slanted book reviews (partial list in *DCE* 1.xxxix). These papers sought to pinpoint the origin of a given lexical item, viewed in isolation. Corominas was a pure etymologist; relevant side issues of historical grammar entered the discussion only to strengthen a new hypothesis or disprove an earlier conjecture. At no time did Corominas commit to print the theoretical and methodological assumptions underlying his etymological investigations.

The years 1947-51 were devoted to the uninterrupted writing of the *DCE,* avowedly to endow this work with a high degree of homogeneity (see *DCE* 1.xvii and xxvii; for a severe assessment of Corominas' failure to attain this goal, see Malkiel 1956:39-41). Breaking with the practice followed in the *LRW, REW* and *FEW,* Corominas arranged the entries alphabetically according to the word studied, rather than according to the suggested etymon, thus skirting the difficulties of classifying formations of doubtful or unknown origin. Many entries also included discussion of other members of the head-word's family, as well as genetically distinct but semantically akin items and formations from other Romance and non-Romance languages whose history might shed light on the particular Hispanic problem at issue. To a large extent, the *DCE* is pan-Romanic in scope and merits consultation by scholars working outside the domain of Spanish etymology. Indeed, it is still the most reliable tool available to students of Catalan and Portuguese word origins. Within the confines of Hispano-Romance, the

DCE extends beyond the modern literary language to include numerous Medieval, Classical, dialect and modern technical formations.

Each article in the *DCE* assumed the same basic shape, offering the reader:

1. Corominas' suggested etymon and the date of the word's first-known appearance in a written text. In many difficult cases, the author realistically qualified the etymon as probable, uncertain, or admitted that no plausible solution had yet been proposed. Corominas also indicated the vernacular, semi-learned or learned status of native Hispanic formations (an oversimplified division assailed by Malkiel 1956:42);

2. a discussion, often sarcastic and acrimonious in tone, of the merits and weaknesses of earlier conjectures and the presentation and interpretation of data extracted from texts and dialects. Unlike the author of the *FEW,* Corominas failed to separate rigorously facts from analysis;

3. a list, with minimal, if any, discussion of derivatives and compounds;

4. footnotes, in which certain points receive further elaboration, and additional bibliographic material is cited and evaluated.

Corominas displayed a balanced attitude in assessing the various layers of the Spanish lexicon. Although he perhaps exaggerated the contribution of Catalan, he refrained from rashly assigning genetically obscure items to one favorite source such as substratum or superstratum languages, reconstructed Vulgar Latin etyma, or onomatopoeic formations. The richness of the documentation and discussion, and consequently the length of each entry, varied according to the etymological opacity of the word at issue. Those of transparent or learned background received little attention, despite the light they might throw on broad phonological, morphological, and especially semantic trends in the development of Hispano-Romance. Corominas espoused the segregation of etymology from historical grammar, evincing no interest in applying his lexical findings to broader questions of diachronic Hispanic or Romance linguistics.

The appearance of such an important reference and research tool provoked a large number of detailed critical assessments and reactions (see *DCE* 4.897-898), the most original being Spitzer 1956-59 (Appendix I). Amidst the general acclaim, I note only that Corominas' excursions into the domains of Sardinian and Gallo-Romance met with harsh criticism in the reviews by Wagner (1957) and Wartburg (1959, Appendix I), the leading experts in those respective fields. The latter's closing statement represents one of the severest judgments passed upon the *DCE:* "Quant à la partie purement hispanique du livre, je n'oserai pas me prononcer ne disposant pas du temps nécessaire pour l'examiner. Mais ma confiance est fortement ébranlée par les expériences faites par rapport aux excursions de M. C[orominas] dans le domaine galloroman."

Several scholars devoted their analyses of the *DCE* to revising the dates of initial documentation provided by Corominas or to adding Spanish formations (usually derivatives) absent from the *DCE;* for pertinent bibliographic clues see *BDE:* 10 (Appendix I) and Malkiel 1968b: 206 n. 101. These workers made no attempt to show how their earlier datings might further clarify the origin or history of the chosen lexical item.

Three experts in lexico-etymological research dwelled upon the structure of the *DCE:* cf. (in Appendix I) Baldinger (1956-58), Colón (1962) and Malkiel (1956). Their criticisms touched upon the polemic tone of many of its entries, the excessive discussion of previous conjectures, the author's discursive style, scanty documentation provided for etymologically transparent formations, and failure to exploit recent etymological literature. Malkiel also reproached Corominas for his cavalier dismissal of the relationship between etymology and historical grammar, particularly with regard to such problems of word-formation as anomalous derivational patterns and the formation of diminutives. The Berkeley scholar likewise voiced his dismay at Corominas' indifference to the phenomenon of lexical extinction.

As a sequel to his *DCE,* Corominas prepared for a wider audience a single-volume abridgement (1961 = *BDE)* from which he deleted most regionalisms, obsolete or rare technical terms, and words peculiar to the Medieval language. Each entry provides the date of the chosen word's first appearance and a summary of its origin. Unlike the *DCE,* the *BDE* furnishes a date of initial documentation for most derivatives listed, while all discussion of earlier conjectures, textual citations, and the bibliographic apparatus were eliminated. The *BDE* often represents an advance vis-à-vis the parent publication; Corominas was able to cite (BDE:15) 38 entries that had undergone major changes. Significantly, almost all these items are of non-Latin origin; cf. in Appendix I Hubschmid 1962. Apparently Corominas does not intend to issue a revised edition of the *DCE;* the 1971 reprint contains no up-dating of any sort.

Of considerably less importance and value is *DEEH.* The work epitomizes almost forty years of etymological research devoted primarily to the rural Castilian lexicon. García de Diego can be characterized as the Spanish representative of the idealistic school, which stressed word meanings and the association of ideas by speakers, over the workings of sound laws in the search for word origins. Underlying most of this scholar's etymological writings is the assumption that those numerous lexical items which fail to obey the so-called sound laws reflect blends of semantically associated formations: note especially García de Diego 1920, 1922, 1928; the brief introduction to García de Diego 1923, originally designed as a Spanish supplement ot the *REW;* and his inaugural address to the Royal Spanish Academy (1926).

The *DEEH* falls into two parts: an alphabetic repertory of Spanish formations with an etymon and a reference number to the second part, in which the etyma are arranged alphabetically and numbered. Each entry in this second section gathers together the alleged progeny – extracted from the literary language, dialects, Galician-Portuguese, and Catalan – of the base at issue. The wealth of dialect material is one of the positive features of this work, although the author often fails to localize and specify the source of many of these formations. Few references, if any, are supplied to earlier discussions of controversial etymological problems; almost no illustrative passages are provided from literary texts. Essentially the *DEEH* is a species of etymological checklist.

García de Diego treated at greater length some of the entries from the *DEEH* and criticized the corresponding *DCE* articles in a series of papers entitled "Notas etimologicas" (collected in book form in 1964). Corominas' devastating and vituperative assessment of the *DEEH* *(DCE* 4.898 and 899-1092, passim) prompted García de Diego's bitter rebuttal (1958). He attempted to defend many of his etymologies on the grounds that they had been first suggested by such venerated masters as Diez, Gamillscheg and Meyer-Lübke. Between 1963 and 1967, García de Diego published several articles dealing with 'etimologías naturales' – expressive and onomatopoeic lexical formations created within Spanish – an interest that culminated in García de Diego 1968 (in Appendix I), concerned with sound symbolism not only in the author's native tongue, but also in many other languages. He thus ranks as the chief intellectual heir of Şăineanu still active at present. This last compilation, like all the author's production since the '20's and '30's, betrays the same slipshod methods and trivial conclusions that drew forth Corominas' barbs.

Of the numerous scholars who channeled their entire etymological production into monographs, articles and notes, one of the most prolific, thorough and innovative has been Yakov Malkiel. Although this scholar has by no means restricted the scope of his lexico-etymological investigations to Hispano-Romance, we shall here refer only to those studies which deal directly with this linguistic domain. His most recent theoretical and methodological papers. outgrowths of his work in Hispano-Romance, have been alluded to above.

For Malkiel, etymology encompasses the history of word families as well as the search for individual word origins. Several features of his method and approach to this field distinguish him from the bulk of his predecessors and contemporaries. Each paper characteristically offers: (a) a careful presentation of all previous opinions stated on the origin of the formation(s) at issue, with a discussion of the weaknesses and merits of each hypothesis; (b) abundant documentation and semantic analysis of all pertinent formations and variants in order to segregate primary, original meanings from secondary developments; (c) consideration of the chronological, geographical and social stratification of the lexical item(s) under study; (d) examination of the linguistic, cultural and social factors which may have contributed to the genesis or extinction of a given word; (e) discussion, with numerous examples localized as to source, of all points of historical phonology, morphology, word-formation and syntax relevant to the elucidation of the chosen problem(s); (f) a statement of the theoretical and methodological lessons which Romance and general linguistics can derive from the particular word history. A similar approach to etymology can be seen in the writings of several of Malkiel's students: see Craddock 1967-68, 1974; Dworkin 1971-72, 1973-74, 1974-75; Harris 1969-70, 1971; J.F. Levy 1973-74 and López Morillas 1973-74.

Most of Malkiel's contributions to Hispanic etymology treated some facet of the documented Latinity of the Iberian Peninsula (for a partial balance sheet, see Malkiel 1955b:63-68), with occasional ventures into the realms of hybrids involving non-Latin stems and Romance formatives (1946, 1947). Entire word families were subjected to close scrutiny in an effort to highlight the effects of the regional distribution and multi-leveled transmission of genetically akin lexical items, and of the rapprochement of historically related and unrelated formations. Illustrative of this approach to word history are the monographs, articles and notes devoted to those Hispanic formations traceable to the family of Lat. *pes, pedis* 'foot', see Malkiel 1954 and the related studies therein cited, p. iv. Malkiel did not strive in every paper to establish new Latin-Spanish etymological equations; often he presented new data or a fresh analysis to confirm an earlier worker's conjectures (1952b, 1966, 1974), to reconcile divergent yet plausible hypotheses (1955a), or to clarify some linguistically important aspect of an etymologically transparent formation's development (1973a). In addition to the resolution of etymological cruxes, many of Malkiel's studies were designed to illustrate the workings of certain factors capable of altering the straightforward evolution of individual lexical items and whole word families, such as lexical polarization (1951, 1952a), lexical blends (1953a, 1961), homonymic conflict (1952c, 1953b), diachronic hypercharacterization (1957-58), as well as novel methods and techniques of etymological analysis (1950a, 1958, 1968-9, 1973a, 1974).

As noted above, Malkiel has been keenly aware of the indifference to etymology displayed by linguistic theoreticians and methodological innovators. He has striven to revitalize and rejuvenate Hispanic (and Romance) etymology by elaborating new methods and links to the mainstream of linguistic thought. Since the turn of the century, scholars have debated the relative weight to be assigned to form and meaning in the resolution of an etymological puzzle; for Malkiel's view, see 1966:182f. He has added a new dimension to the discussion by suggesting that greater attention be paid to patterns of derivation, inflection and composition in etymological investigations. He labeled this technique 'morpho-etymology'; for two examples of its application to Luso-Hispanic material, see 1973d and 1974.

Limitations of space preclude a detailed survey of the monographs, articles and notes of varying scope and quality on problems of Hispanic etymology authored by several dozen other scholars of the past three decades. Their ranks include such veteran Romanists committed to the study of word origins and history as Aebischer, Colón, Hubschmid, H.

and R. Kahane, Meier, Menéndez Pidal, Oliver Asín, Rohlfs, Spitzer, Steiger and Wagner. I shall attempt here to characterize succinctly the contributions of some of these experts to Hispanic etymology and to pinpoint whatever trends may be observable in the diachronic analysis of the Spanish lexicon.

Not all the specialists named in the preceding paragraph have devoted the bulk of their output to Spanish. That language played a subordinate role to Catalan, Southern Italian, and Sardinian in the etymological investigations of Colón, Rohlfs and Wagner, respectively. Most focused the greater part of their attention on a chosen stratum or strain of the Spanish lexicon: substratal languages (Hubschmid, Menéndez Pidal, Rohlfs), documented Latinity (Aebischer), reconstructed spoken Latinity (Meier), Arabic or Arabized elements (Oliver Asín, Steiger and Wagner, who also examined the Gypsy component of Spanish slang), Hellenisms, especially those transmitted from Byzantium, and migratory Mediterranean nautical terms of Romance and non-Romance origin (H. and R. Kahane).

Scholars have not recently formulated many new plausible correspondences between genetically obscure Spanish formations and documented Latin bases. At least one specialist asserted that there remained few Latin-Romance etymological equations to be established (Wagner 1953:358). In that portion of his output devoted to Spanish, Aebischer traced the path followed into or within Hispano-Romance by selected lexical items, usually of Latin origin, without suggesting novel etymologies; for examples, see Aebischer 1948a, 1948b, 1951. A careful study of conservative rural dialects may yet yield new information on the composition of the Hispano-Latin lexicon. No competent etymologist has investigated this domain in a systematic fashion. One of the most active explorers of this field was Wagner, who examined some of the Latin and Arabic elements observable in the rural speech of Spain (Wagner 1941, 1948, 1952, 1953); for one assessment of Wagner's performance as a practitioner of Hispanic etymology, see Malkiel 1955-56 and Wagner's bitter riposte (1956).

Despite the inherent dangers (cf. Malkiel 1950b), a few workers continued to operate with hypothetical Latin etyma of dubious validity (Alessio 1953, Janner 1949, Lüdtke 1956a, Lecoy 1953-54, Tilander 1958). This practice has been carried to an extreme by Meier, as noted above. Several young German workers have followed in Meier's footsteps by substituting highly suspect Latin bases for non-Latin etyma; for examples see the studies in Meier–Roth 1968.

Various Romanists have devoted considerable effort to unearthing those elements of the Hispanic lexicon directly traceable to the pre-Indo-European and Indo-European languages spoken in the Iberian Peninsula prior to the Roman conquest and settlement. The most prolific investigator of these archaic strata has been Johannes Hubschmid, one of Meier's severest critics. He seeks to establish genetic links between Hispanic formations that often denote configurations and features of the terrain, flora and fauna, and referentially similar items allegedly of pre-Indo-European origin, scattered throughout Europe and Northern Africa. An analytic bibliography of more than thirty studies by Hubschmid which treat Hispanic material appears in Baldinger 1958 (1972:339-349). Hubschmid's three contributions to the *Enciclopedia lingüística hispánica 1* (1960), synthesize his probings into pre-Latin relics preserved in the Hispanic lexicon and onomasticon. Other individual Hispanic words of pre-Roman origin have been discussed over the last three decades by, among others, Cocco, Corominas, Rohlfs and Tovar (Baldinger 1958 [1972:326-385]). One American worker (M. R. Harris 1970, 1971) has recently devoted two lengthy papers to such formations.

Arabisms have continued to interest practitioners of Hispanic etymology since 1945. Besides the scholars identified by Baldinger 1958 (1972:62-91), see Skelton (1970a, 1970b, 1971) and Walsh (1967). One particular aspect of the Hispano-Arabic lexical symbiosis – the alleged influence of Semitic models on the semantic development of Romance formations – has sparked a lively debate. The examples first adduced by Lombard (1936) and Castro (1948, 1950-51) were dissected by Coseriu (1961), Lapesa (1949), Spitzer (1949) and Wagner (1950). Additional instances of such calques have been suggested by Aebischer, Giese, Tovar and van Wijk (Baldinger 1958 [1972:82-85]) and recently by Latham (1968) and Kontzi (1970, 1976).

Three other experienced etymologists deserve brief mention here. Although the husband-and-wife team of Henry R. and Renée Kahane cannot be accurately classified as Hispanists, they have devoted a fair share of their scholarly activity to many of the nautical terms diffused throughout the Mediterranean basin, and to Hellenisms – especially the Byzantine layer – that entered Hispano-Romance. In these studies the Kahanes succinctly described the historical and cultural conditions which led to the spread of the lexical items in question; for samples of their work treating Hispanic material, see the bibliography in Kahane 1973. In addition to dealing with problems of Catalan etymology, Colón concentrated on intra-Romance lexical relations, especially Spanish loans from southern Gallo-Romance and Catalan (Colón 1958, 1962b, [anent Vidos 1957], 1966, 1967a, 1967b).

5.2.2 Galician-Portuguese

Galician-Portuguese remains among the least favored Romance domains in terms of major etymological projects. Machado's inexpert compilation (1952-59, in Appendix I) is very disappointing, though one of its most glaring defects, entirely inadequate dating of first attestations, has been to a large extent remedied by Lorenzo (1969); still useful are the U. S. dissertations of Ruiz y Ruiz (1964) and Clemens (1949), cf. App. I; note also Messner's 'lexicochronological' analysis of Portuguese (1974-75) and Nascentes (1932). Machado's dictionary has attracted only a modest amount of criticism; see in Appendix I the "anotações" of Cunha (1956-60) and Pico (1961-67), alongside the deservedly severe reactions of Wagner (1953-55), Piel (1960) and Lorenzo (1968:i-vii). The author himself brought out a collection of emendations (1965-66) and a second edition of the dictionary has been launched or at least announced, though I have yet to see the result.

Buschmann 1965 (in Appendix I), a student of Meier, is the initial portion (A-F) of a planned etymological dictionary of Galician. Modelled on the *REW,* the entries are an alphabetical list of etyma, among which one will recognize not a few of the reconstructed bases so beloved of her mentor (e. g., 2052a *collugicāre* [sic; the -*u*- should be marked long] 'afligirse juntos' > ? *calucar* 'impacientarse'). The author includes a good sampling of derivatives with a reasonable quantity of references to relevant literature. Datings and word history are omitted, while etymological explanation is held to the barest minimum. The present version lacks indices; no doubt the complete work will contain this indispensable aid to the general reader and the specialized researcher (see Colón 1967, in Appendix I).

The safest guide to Galician-Portuguese etymology remains unfortunately Corominas' *DCE* (an index of Galician and Portuguese forms occupy pp. 4.1117-1134); much less reliable, but occasionally useful, is

García de Diego's *DEEH.* From there one must move to the specialized literature, for which we have Gorog's handy bibliography (1967, in Appendix II), for the years 1950-65 (includes reviews and boasts a word index [2:102-110]) and Santos' more discursive account (1966, especially section 8 "Lexicologia", pp. 75-100) covering the period 1945-60. Among foreigners, Piel must be regarded as the doyen of etymologists operating on Luso-Romance, cf. in particular his 1953 miscellany beside scores of articles (e. g. 1958, 1963, 1965, 1967; see the bibliography to Piel 1969). Though they concentrate more often on Spanish or some other Romance language, the roster of important contributors must include Hubschmid, Malkiel, Meier, Tilander and Wagner. Machado's dictionary and reactions to it aside, the etymological discipline has not flourished among Portuguese scholars since World War II. Some recent work by native sons on Galician seems very promising, for instance Pensado Tomé (1965) and Lorenzo (1969). The less said about the nonsensical conglomerations that Otero Álvarez jumbles together (1967, 1949-71), the better.

5.2.3 Catalan

There exists as yet no etymological dictionary of Catalan (as opposed to dictionaries with etymologies), though Corominas in his *DCE* (1.xl) went so far as to employ an abbreviation *(DECat)* for a *Diccionari Etimològic i Complementari de la Llengua Catalana* "que el autor . . . tiene en preparación avanzada". I am unaware of the reasons that may have deflected him from his evident intention to follow up the *DCE* more or less immediately with the *DECat.* Criticism of the former has been occasionally severe, but no one could argue that the general reception it obtained was unfavorable. As is true for Portuguese, the first and best available source for Catalan etymologies is the *DCE* (see the index of Catalan forms, 4.1135-1154). Beyond this, scholars possess one of the finest descriptive and historical dictionaries of any Romance language in the monumental *DCVB* (Alcover-Moll 1930-62, in Appendix I). Since it includes a rich harvest of historical (with verifiable citations) and dialectal material as well as brief etymological indications, the *DCVB* renders essential assistance to the professional etymologist and the layman alike.

For individual work in Catalan one may consult Badía Margarit (et al.)'s survey of the field (1970:52-55); from there it appears that one of the most active investigators of Catalan vocabulary, since Corominas has of late concentrated more and more on Catalan toponymy, is Colón: see his recent discovery of vernacular descendants of Lat. *indāgāre* 'to search, explore' in Catalan (1973), as well as the other essays collected in his recent book (1976).

5.3 Italo-Romance

As noted above, five etymological dictionaries of Italian have come out since World War II. None, however, was designed to meet the needs of specialists; the authors were infected by an unjustifiable bias in favor of the layman and amateur. Dictionaries conceived for a broader public than linguistic technicians remain, no doubt, necessary and useful, but only those based on a specialized dictionary genuinely fulfill the purpose they are meant to achieve, as, for instance, the *DELF* (in close rapport with the *FEW*) or Corominas' *BDE* (abstracted from his *DCE*). The Italianists' own best interests have so far been defeated by their strange refusal to face up to the essential task at hand.

Of the five, the least pretentious is Migliorini–Duro 1950 (in Appendix I), whose very title *Prontuario* leaves no doubt as to their fundamentally pedagogical intent, i. e., to present to non-specialists the results achieved by specialists. Consequently, their lexicon provides very little beyond a bare listing of etyma. Olivieri 1953 (Appendix I) was more ambitious than the afore-mentioned team in that he includes considerable dialectal material, Romance and Indo-European cognates and numerous references to toponomastic reflexes. Still, the strictly etymological portion of each entry is nearly as laconic as in the *Prontuario*. Prati 1951 (Appendix I) differs from both the preceding in offering his readers allusions both to literary sources and to some linguistic literature. By consulting the index of cited authorities, one can derive from the former a rough dating, but the references are not otherwise verifiable; the latter are exiguous indeed. Devoto 1966 (Appendix I) avers he felt "imprisoned" by the infra-Romanic limitations observed by his competitors (this, however, is not always the case with Olivieri 1953 or the *DEI*), so his chief innovation is to pursue etyma beyond the immediate source languages. He has, nevertheless, been extremely selective in this effort, so that the reader in no way feels relieved of the burden of tracing these etyma on his own in the etymological dictionaries of the languages in question.

The most complete, as regards the sheer number of entries, is the *DEI* (Battisti-Alessio 1950-51, in Appendix I); it is also the most disappointing. Following the fatal inclination to remain accessible to non-specialists (p. 1.xx), the compilers have produced a dictionary all but useless to the specialist, indeed, yet so voluminous as to stand beyond the economic means of all but the most devoted non-specialists. Dating of head-words and derivatives is exhaustively attempted, but the information cannot be verified. Again, as so often, the etymological portion of their work involves nothing but the stark presentation of likely source forms (for an advance sample of the *DEI,* see Battisti 1949-50).

Let us see what can be learned from each of them concerning a randomly selected word, *gromma*. Olivieri (1953) defines the word as 'tartar (in a wine cask)' and mentions two derivatives, *grommare* and *grommoso,* left undefined. Tacitly adopting the information provided by *REW* § 3884, he hesitatingly refers the base word to Swiss Germ. *grummele* 'cicciolo ('greaves, the sediment formed when animal fat is melted down for tallow')'; he compares the cognate Germanic base *griubo* 'greaves' (source of Eng. *greaves* and Germ. *Grieben)* that apparently gave rise to OIt. *gréppola* and Veron. *griopo* 'tartar' (as per *REW,* loc. cit.).

This is about the barest minimum one could demand of an etymological dictionary, yet Devoto (1966) provides still less, since he omits definitions, other members of the word family, and possible cognates. His conjecture, on the other hand, seems original: a VLat. **grumma,* fem. form of *grum(m)us* 'piccolo tumulo ('little grave, burrow, sand hill')' taken as a collective 'insieme di grumoli ('collection of small clots or lumps [in a liquid]')'. He sees no further etymological connections, but refers the reader to *gruma* 'incrustation, tartar of a wine cask' < **grūma,* a collective of the selfsame *grumus* we met before, except that it has shed its optional geminate consonant, hence *gromma/gruma* are clearly variants of the same base. The comparison immediately causes one to wonder why Olivieri failed even to mention the synonym and near homonym *gruma* apropos of *gromma*. Upon returning to his dictionary, one finds, astonishingly enough, that neither form appears s. v. *grumo.*

At this point the reader is left to guess at a reasonable semantic progression, since Devoto's indications are quite informal. The starting point, Lat. *grūmus* 'mound of earth', was evidently applied to 'clots, lumps (in a liquid)', then a derived feminine collective became the term for 'wine tartar'. Devoto does not seek to account for the *gromma/ gruma* duality. Neither author offers the slightest hint to the word's history nor to any etymological literature that may have been devoted to the words in question.

Migliorini–Duro (1950) remain faithful to the *REW*'s etymon, though referring the reader to *gruma,* described as "lo stesso che *gromma*". Apparently they believe both forms unrelated to *grumo.* The only new material here provided are slightly longer lists of undefined derivatives.

Prati (1951) omits *gromma/gruma* but has an entry for *grumo;* he gives datable literary references and several allusions to linguistic literature, as well as various members of the word family. There is a 16th century attestation of *grumo* in the meaning 'flower bud' and one in the 17th as 'blood clot, milk curd'. The diminutive *grumetto* is on record in the same century, while *grúmolo* occurs in a 16th c. agricultural treatise as 'heart of lettuce, cabbage'. He also notes the toponym *Grumo,* used, he claims, for places located on hills. It should be observed that Olivieri provides cognate forms both in the Italian dialects and in the other Romance languages, a richer harvest of derivatives (some have blended semantically with offshoots of *rūmināre),* and several vaguely localized toponyms.

In the process of consulting these authorities, our attention has been diverted from the original goal: *gromma* 'wine tartar'. Now the *DEI* dates this word already in the 14th century. The author (in this case, De Felice) adds a small set of derivatives with their corresponding chronological notes and attribute to the base word the Swiss German etymon discussed above, without referring to *grumo* (was Olivieri a tacit source for the *DEI* in this case?). *gruma,* however, is explained as a blend of *gromma* and *grumo.* The compilers are led to this conclusion, without saying exactly why, by the meaning 'blood clot' attested in the 16th c. (Olivieri's reference is repeated) for the latter.

As for *grumo* the *DEI* also claims it for the 14th c., deriving it from Lat. *grūmus,* tentatively identified as a "Mediterranean relic" cognate with Gk. *krōmax* 'heap of stones'. They believe the diminutive *grumolo* learned, though Lat. *grūmulus* has survived in some Romance vernaculars. They allude to Romance cognates without citing them, but do list a few Italo-Romance congeners. Their most interesting contribution is the very early dating (1003) of *grumello* 'fine wine (from Valtellina)', originally a toponym.

It would be inaccurate to say that the reader is left no wiser than when he began this multiple consultation; however, he not only fails to receive a firm answer, something that frequently happens in the best of dictionaries, but much worse, if he wishes to pursue the issue, he must start almost from scratch since so few of the data provided by these dictionaries can be traced to their sources. Datings cannot be verified, since even in Prati no page references appear. Meanings are given in an entirely helter-skelter fashion. The etyma are simply announced with no attempt to justify them. Devoto, the distinguished Classical scholar, by carelessly omitting macrons, manages to convey the impression that **grūma* has the aberrant vowel quantity rather than **grumma*. He alone seems to be aware that alongside *grūmus* there occur in mss. variants containing geminate *-mm-,* a fact of considerable potential relevance available to scholars in the 1st volume of the *LEW* (Walde – Hofmann 1938-56): The *gromma/gruma* dichotomy could be explained by Weinrich's theory of inversely proportional vowel and consonant length (1958); this particular case, however, he fails to consider. Devoto ignores the possible Indo-European connections (to say nothing of the *DEI*'s substratal suggestion) the last-mentioned authority perceives (including Eng. *crumb),* cf. also the *GEW* (Frisk 1960-72), s. v. *gruméa* 'bag or chest (for old clothes)'.

None of the five dictionaries here sampled bears comparison with the other major etymological dictionaries in the Romance domain, i. e., the *DES, DCE, FEW* and *DER.* A swift perusal of these four failed to reveal any immediate solution to the *gromma/gruma* problem, but they do present, always with verifiable references, a host of further reflexes of Lat. *grūmus,* some of which happen to have an *-o-* root vowel and feminine gender (Ast. *gromo* 'branch of furze, gorse', Ptg. *gomo* 'bud, sprout', dial. *goma* 'rebentos novos do mato' [Figueiredo]). The Germanic section of the *FEW* (16:87-88 [1955]) unfortunately does not go into any possible relationship between Swiss Germ. *grummele* and It. *gromma,* but it would on the surface seem just as likely that the former is an intruder from the south rather than the source of the Italian words, if the two forms are indeed genetically related.

I am happy to report that there is a silver lining to this gloomy assessment (similar appraisal in Lurati 1972). Pfister (1973, Appendix I) has recently announced a massive new *Italienisches etymologisches Wörterbuch* planned along the lines of the *FEW*. His announcement contains ample entries *(abiēs* 'fir tree', *apis* 'bee', and related bases) and they are all the most demanding linguist could desire. I would, however, question the wisdom of using German as the medium of communication. Romance specialists normally read German, but there would, I assume, be real advantages, both economic and intellectual, in reaching a wider audience in Italy.

Pfister's *IEW,* like the *FEW,* may require 50 years or more for its completion, so what can one do in the meantime? If Italian lacks a serviceable etymological dictionary, it possesses, on the other hand, far and away the best linguistic bibliography of any Romance language (Hall 1941, 1958, 1969 and 1973, in Appendix II). The lexical portions of Hall's superb efforts provide a scope and depth of information that cannot be matched in any other Romance domain; it is, in fact, indispensable for work outside Italo-Romance, since he systematically includes all relevant material dealing with the Romance languages in general that happens to touch in any way on Italian linguistic problems. Italian also boasts the finest historical dictionary (Battaglia, 1961-) available for any Romance language. It is progressing at a reasonable rate (7 vols., A-Ing, at last count) and bids fair to equal the monumental *OED.* All references are retrievable, and the bibliography of authors cited, besides constituting an indispensable research tool in itself, provides both chronological and geographical data about each author or text. Hence the interested etymologist can piece together the beginnings of a word history and the record of previous conjectures by consulting Battaglia and Hall as supplements to the available dictionaries. For instance, though Hall records no study of *gromma/ gruma,* Battaglia (7.56-57, 82-83) provides a crucial datum: alongside every form in *grum-,* one in *gromm-* is extant, i. e., *grommo/grumo, grommolo/grumolo,* etc., a fact that surely militates in favor of those who regard the two stems as variants.

The writer's hand trembles as he broaches the subject of etymology with regard to the Italo-Romance dialects; the field is so rich, so much has been done, so much remains to be done, that what he says here can have only a fleeting resemblance to the actual state of the art. Overall, one of the most important events since World War II must be the appearance of Jaberg–Jud's 1960 etymological *Index* to their linguistic atlas of Italy and southern Switzerland *(AIS,* Jaberg–Jud 1928-40). It is, of course, an instrument that only specialists can make full use of; no explanatory material is provided. Rohlf's excellent *EWuG* (1930) has appeared in a second, and much enlarged edition (1964) with a high-falutin Latin title; the text, mercifully, remains in German. Though ostensibly a lexicon of non-Romance – Hellenic – forms extant in the dialects of southern Italy, it is nevertheless central to the linguistic study of that region (cf. in Appendix I, H. and R. Kahane 1966-67 and Hubschmid 1971). A posthumous collection of Prati's Venetian etymologies made its debut in 1968. Beyond those high points, I must refer the reader to Hall's bibliographies.

As for individual work, the chief clearing-house for etymological conjectures has for a long time been the journal *Lingua nostra.* Each year scores of new "noterelle" grace its pages, often as little as a paragraph in length. My own preference is for longer and fewer etymological papers, but I must confess my amazement at Alessio's production (including 2 sets of "apostille" to his own *DEI* [1957-58 and 1962]); the man is a veritable machine à etymologies. The most distinguished current practitioners include Pellegrini, witness his two-volume venture on Arabisms in Romance and Italian (1972; cf. Contini 1973), and Cortelazzo (Byzantine influence in Venice; see H. and R. Kahane 1973-74).

5.4 Rhaeto-Friulian

The Romansh sector of Rhaeto-Friulian boasts one of the most ambitious lexicographical projects ever undertaken in the Romance field: the *Dicziunari rumantsch grischun* (Pult et al. 1938- in Appendix I; 1972 saw the completion of vol. 5, D-E). No other dictionary, not even the *FEW,* offers the expert so much: preliminaries containing a list of dialect abbreviations with a map showing their location, as well as an exhaustive bibliography; entries that provide careful phonetic transcriptions of variant forms, enormously detailed semantic descriptions with each subentry supported by verifiable literary citations (which are translated into German), concise etymological discussion with careful attention to the linguistic literature; finally, truly remarkable indices that cover etyma, concepts (onomasiological and semasiological), and historical grammar (phonology, morphology, syntax, derivations, lexicology [words categorized as to origin, i. e., substratum, Germanic, etc.]). I know of no other lexical work that attempts so thoroughly and successfully to integrate its findings into the broad spectrum of linguistic research. For other lexical projects in Romansh, Widmer 1966 and 1968 are useful guides; cf. also Kramer 1970 (App. I) and Francescato on Rhaeto-Friulian in Volume 3.

5.5 Sardinian

The completion of Wagner's *DES* (1957-64) was a signal event not just for Sardinian linguistics but for the entire Romance field, since few would dispute that this culmination of his life-long devotion to one of the most out-of-the-way dialect groups stands among the very finest results obtained in Romance etymology; for his bibliography, cf. Appendix II. Particularly useful to the Romanist is the volume of indices (edited by Urciolo) that bring together 1) Sardinian variants, 2) a sort of Italian-Sardinian thesaurus, i. e., an alignment of Italian and Sardinian (near)synonyms, extremely useful for onomasiological ventures, and 3) more traditional lists of words in other languages discussed à propos of a Sardinian form, including under "Latin" a massive list of attested and reconstructed etyma (Wagner 1957-64:3.411-454). Of course, like any such vast undertaking, the *DES* is not without its faults; these have been most sensitively appraised by my late good friend Jonathan Butler (1970-71). Wagner closed the second volume of his magnum opus with his own addenda et corrigenda together with vigorous responses to his critics (2.604-618; see also his presentation of the *DES* in 1958), while the excellent lexicologist and bibliographer Atzori (cf. 1953, in Appendix II) has published numerous "apostille" (most recently, I believe, in 1964-65; for a convenient list of other reactions see, in Appendix II, Butler 1967-68:535).

Before his tragic death, Butler was engaged in preparing an inverse index to the *DES;* as a useful innovation he had planned to include words treated in Wagner's previous work but omitted from the *DES.* The project has been taken over by Edward Tuttle of UCLA.

Recent periodical bibliographies seem to indicate a considerable slackening of activity in Sardinian etymology, whereas the appearance of the *DCE* and the long progress of the *FEW,* if anything, quickened interest in etymological research in the domains they surveyed. Of course, one must reckon with the vastly greater number of scholars that concern themselves with Gallo- and Hispano-Romance as opposed to Sardinian, one of the most esoteric subdisciplines within Romance linguistics.

5.6 Balkan Romance
5.6.1 Dalmatian

Elmendorf's unpublished etymological dictionary of Dalmatian (cf. Appendix I) has had little resonance, not only because of its inaccessibility, but also because its entries are most often trivial and unoriginal. Muljačić 1969 (Appendix II) is an excellent guide to what has been published on this corner of the Romance world between Bartoli's 1906 description of the dialect of Veglia and the year 1966. However, the sole active etymologist specializing in this domain that I am able to cite is Vinja (1957, 1959, 1967 and 1972-73, in Appendix I). His efforts are directed toward recovering Romance relics in the present-day Serbo-Croatian dialects of the Dalmatian coast. In the first three articles just mentioned (the third contains a word index for all three) the proposed etymological connections are brief to the point of laconism. They are organized in the form of entries that supplement those of the *REW*. It is my guess that a careful sifting of this material would be required, in particular a thorough investigation of possible alternative Slavic sources, before they could be adopted for the purposes of comparative research.

5.6.2 Rumanian

[I have adapted and translated freely Professor Poghirc's account of Rumanian etymological research, attempting never to betray his thought. I was, however, compelled to trim some parts of his excellent exposé when it became apparent that the original outline agreed upon would produce far too extensive a text. For an unadulterated sample of his research in Rumanian etymology see Poghirc 1968b as well as his mimeographed bibliography cf. 1969 listed in Appendix II. J.R.C.]

The motley sources of the Rumanian lexicon (vernacular descendants from spoken Latin, recent loanwords from literary Latin or from the other Romance languages, substratum elements, borrowings from Ancient, Byzantine and Modern Greek, from ancient Germanic tongues [Goths and Gepids] and modern literary German as well as the 'Saxon' dialects spoken in Transylvania, numerous Slavic borrowings of varying date and provenience, beside Hungarian, Turkish and other Oriental words) and the quite late appearance of the language in written form (2nd half of the 16th century) give rise to particularly difficult problems that do not crop up in the other Romance domains to the same extent and explain why it is that approx. 10-15% of the Rumanian vocabulary is of uncertain or unknown origin (Poghirc 1968b: 206).

These peculiar circumstances also seem to be responsible for the special attention that was accorded to methodology even by pioneers such as B. P. Hasdeu (1836-1907; for a description of his admirable statement of principles see Poghirc 1968b:203). The dispute over reconstructed vs. attested bases, a chief concern of Hasdeu in his statement of principles just mentioned, continues to attract the interest of Rumanian etymologists, witness Mihăescu's recent contribution (1965) à propos of Graur's judicious treatment of the question (1934). Widespread abuse of reconstructed bases provoked Şăineanu into formulating his famous concept of the 'sources indigènes' (1925-30, 1935); his example, insofar as it constitutes a healthy corrective to overly narrow concentration on external etymology, has found contemporary adepts in Hristea (1971) and Király (1973).

Rumanian scholars have been predominantly responsible for two innovations in etymological theory that have proven quite fruitful. First is the notion of word currency ('circulaţia cuvintelor') expressed in the last century by Hasdeu (1887-98:1.xlvi-lix) and taken up recently by a series of investigators (Graur 1954, Macrea 1941-43, Maneca 1966 and Schroeder 1965, among others). By word currency we allude to the greater fundamental importance of living etymological structures as opposed to lexical statistics in determining the basic typology of a language. The recent interest in this problem arose as a reaction against researches that tended to exaggerate the relative importance of the non-Latin elements in Rumanian.

Secondly, exclusive concentration on the most immediate and obvious sources of Rumanian vocabulary at the expense of a genuinely sensitive comprehension of the manifold possibilities of lexical transmission has received an effective antidote in Graur's extremely useful theory of 'multiple etymology' (1950). Alongside such well-known phenomena as lexical contamination, popular etymology, linguistic calques, and the like, Graur has observed that a given word may have entered the language from various, in this case, convergent, sources either at the same time or in different periods. For instance, in the eighteenth century a word may have been borrowed from Greek, later the etymologically identical form may have penetrated from Italian, but at last the final victor may turn out to have been the cognate French word. Other words, after careful inspection, reveal successive Greek, German or Russian strains in their pedigree. Thoroughgoing phonological and morphological adaptation often obscures any isolable traits of these various starting points, so that only the most delicate historical research succeeds in fully elucidating this remarkable phenomenon.

Before World War II, Rumanian lacked an etymological dictionary that was both complete and reliable (cf. Appendix I for references to dictionaries). The pioneering work of Cihac (1870-79) preserves only historical interest; Hasdeu's *Etymologicum Magnum Romaniae* (1887-98), after almost 4,000 pages, remained incomplete at the word *bărbat*. Puşcariu (1905) and Candrea–Densusianu (1907-14) surveyed exclusively the Latin elements surviving in Rumanian; the latter effort was broken off at the word *putea*. Consequently the appearance of Cioranescu's *DER* (1958-66) was most welcome. Though not exhaustive, neither as to the number of forms treated nor to the linguistic literature cited, it nevertheless constitutes a convenient guide to the most important etymological conjectures regarding a very large number of Rumanian words.

Cioranescu's original etymological contributions are, however, relatively few and at times insufficiently substantiated though interesting suggestions are not lacking. For instance, he systematically replaces substratum conjectures with Slavic or Romance hypotheses that are often anything but convincing, a result of his belief, correct in principle, but which leads to errors through injudicious and excessively absolute application, that "ce substratum cher aux philologues ... semble appelé à dissimuler complaisamment toutes nos ignorances" (Cioranescu 1959:199). This reservation aside, the *DER* constitutes a useful instrument, especially for investigators located outside Rumania who are unable to consult original sources.

Excellent both with regard to method and to wealth of documentation, since the author has utilized a full chronological gamut of texts that extend back to the earliest known and has analyzed exhaustively earlier linguistic literature, is Tamás' historical and etymological dictionary of the Hungarian elements in Rumanian (1967). As some reviewers have noted, this book practically renders the consultation of the earlier bibliography useless. I would only have wished for a stricter delimitation between words of Hungarian origin that have become quite generally accepted in the language and those that are dialectal or limited to the speech of Transylvanian bilinguals.

I understand that a team of West German researchers, in collaboration with Rumanian experts, has undertaken the preparation of a new etymological dictionary of Rumanian, destined to take its place alongside to *FEW, DCE,* and the like.

Finally I should mention that in order to form a well rounded etymological picture of Balkan Romance one can consult with profit Elmendorf 1951 (mentioned above) and in particular the results of Çabej's systematic investigation of Albanian etymology (for instance, 1962a) as well as his (1962b) and Mihăescu's (1966) work on the Latin elements of Albanian, sometimes labeled a 'quasi-Romance' language.

Among older Rumanian dictionaries with etymologies the best and most complete is Tiktin (1903-1925). As for more recent dictionaries, *Dicţionarul limbii române moderne* (Academia R. P. R. 1958) indicates too often merely the language of origin without specifying the precise etymon. It has received well deserved criticism (Brîncuşi 1961, Hristea 1960, among others) not only for erroneous etymologies but above all for the considerable number of words left unetymologized, sometimes with no apparent justification. Later printings, in which Hristea revised the etymological information, show marked improvement.

The dictionary-thesaurus of the Rumanian language *(DLR),* directed by Puşcariu until 1949 (Academia Română 1913-), has been continued from the letter M since 1965. In its earlier form the *DLR* offered abundant etymological discussion; the fascicles printed in the new series, however, limit themselves to brief etymological indications with various laconic estimates of the paths followed by words on their way to becoming part of the Rumanian lexicon as well as comments on the degree of certainty attributable to the etyma suggested, including only rarely references to solutions proposed elsewhere. Apparently obeying a desire to avoid detailed analysis the editors have declared the "origin unknown" for more words than is strictly appropriate. One quality that confers a decided advantage to this dictionary over its predecessors stems from the adoption by the collective entrusted with elucidating word origins *(Colectivul de etimologie)* of the theory of 'multiple etymology' (see above), so fruitful for the analysis of Rumanian etymological sources. Consequently, in appropriate cases the etymological statement includes all foreign words that have constituted the basis of the Rumanian word at different times and on varying socio-economic levels, ranged chronologically or according to their intrinsic importance for the history of the word at issue. It would be desirable, for that reason, upon revising the earlier portions of the dictionary with a view to correcting some of the outdated etymologies on the basis of more modern information, not to impoverish excessively the discussions mentioned above, which often retain even today great interest for etymological research. In any case, the renewal of this great lexicographical project has revived both lay and scholarly fascination with etymology, dormant for so long after World War II. The appearance of each fascicle stimulates the publication of numerous additions and corrections, usually in the journal *Limba română (LbR)*.

The useful dictionary of the Arumanian dialect brought out by Papahagi (1963) regularly provides etymologies, often superior to those supplied in Pascu's etymological lexicon (1925).

Two books of a general character have been devoted specifically to Rumanian etymological problems since World War II. Following his interesting work on the basic nucleus of the Rumanian vocabulary (1954), which touches on several important etymological cruxes, Graur (1963) begins on a methodological note, rounding out his theory of multiple etymology mentioned above, then takes up certain curious forms occurring in rhymed formulae, various rather complex prefixes and suffixes, the elucidation of whose origin and structure clarifies the provenience of an entire series of words. The second part comprises a long alphabetical list of etymological notes that bring together additional documentation, emendations or explanations of previous etymologies as well as novel etymological conjectures. Hristea's (1968) suggestions about word origins are grouped around, and interwoven with, significant methodological discussions concerning, for instance, internal etymology, lexical borrowing, linguistic calques, popular etymology, hypercorrection, etc. The two works highlight the methodological superiority of monographic investigations compared with the concentration on isolated etyma inherent in dictionary projects.

The best studied portion of the Rumanian vocabulary is, as one might expect, that of Latin ancestry. Besides general works, two etymological dictionaries (Puşcariu 1905, Candrea–Densusianu 1907-14) have concerned themselves exclusively with the Latin elements in Rumanian; the same is true of Candrea 1902, 1932, Domaschke 1919, Giuglea 1909 and Graur 1937. In the last thirty years, these researches have been carried forward in a more profound and nuanced fashion. The importance and specific nature of the Rumanian vocabulary derived from Latin has received close attention in various essays dealing with the place of Rumanian in the Romance family of languages, among which Bonfante 1959-60 and Macrea 1954 are the most interesting from the lexical point of view.

Research into Balkan Latin (Mihăescu 1960, Stati 1961) has failed to lay bare essential lexical cleavages from western Latinity. More revealing in this regard have been recent works on the Latin elements in Albanian (Çabej 1962b, Mihăescu 1966a). The outstanding contemporary work on the lexical peculiarities of eastern Romance is without doubt Bahner 1971 (see also Şiadbei 1957). Unusually important are likewise the chapters on the vocabulary of Balkan Latin (Fischer) and Proto-Rumanian (Coteanu), based on the comparison of dialects lying both to the north and south of the Danube, to be found in the 2nd volume of the Academy's history of the Rumanian language (Academia R. P. R. 1965-69). Finally, among works that treat the subject under discussion with a certain amplitude I should mention Teodorescu (1946) and Buescu (1953-58), though neither effort is entirely free of exaggeration and errors of method.

After the promising investigations into the pre-Latin substrata of Rumanian carried out by Hasdeu in the last century, the first half of the twentieth century witnessed the predominance of an almost absolute scepticism about the validity of such work, a point of view associated most directly with Densusianu. In the last forty years, however, the successes of Rumanian archaeologists in ferreting out the autochthonous cultural heritage coupled with the significant progress realized in the study of the ancient languages of the Balkans have revolutionized the field. For a long time the lone paladin in this difficult domain, I. I. Russu (see among recent items 1959 and 1962) has been followed by an entire generation of younger followers; we can mention, as regards the more general problems inhering in the study of substratal vocabulary, Brîncuşi (1963, 1966), Çabej (1965), Giuglea (1944), Poghirc (1967, 1973), and Vraciu (1963-64). Major, and strictly etymological investigations include: Reichenkron (1966), criticized, justifiably, for his hazardous reconstructions and for his exaggeration of the role Armenian is supposed to have played in the substratal configuration of Rumanian; Poghirc (1968 b), who attempts to classify Rumanian substratal elements according to whether a) they are attested in the ancient languages of the Balkans, b) they are shared exclusively by Rumanian and Albanian, or c) they are deduced through comparison with other Indo-European languages (Armenian, Balto-Slavic, Indo-Iranian); and Russu (1970), the second part of which (pp. 131-216) constitutes an etymological dictionary of substratum elements that offers numerous and interesting original contributions by the author, though some have aroused opposition on the grounds that they represent an abuse of 'root etymology' ('Wurzeletymologien'). [For a useful critical bibliography of this subdomain, see Russu 1970:14-47. J. R. C.]

The importance of pre-Indo-European (Mediterranean) strata in the Balkans, no doubt overstated by some scholars, has been, particularly in the light of the decipherment of Linear B and the demonstration that numerous pre-Hellenic survivals in Greek are nevertheless Indo-European, almost entirely denied by Georgiev (1961). The post-war period has seen, on the other hand, an extreme exaggeration of allegedly Mediterranean material in the Balkan languages by Lahovary (1954-55), whose work, though occasionally offering useful lexical comparisons, is methodologically dilettantish and fanciful. That pre-Indo-European elements must exist among Rumanian substratum survivals has been demonstrated by Hubschmid (1964).

Much of the etymological work in Rumanian is devoted to tracing the source and chronology of borrowings from other languages: as Hope's article in this volume is devoted to a discussion of this question, here only a summary account will be attempted, with reference made only to recent work. On Germanic, we have Bahner 1963, Coterlan 1965, Arvinte 1965, 1967, 1968, Isbăşescu 1969; for Greek, Poghirc 1971:8-9, Mihăescu 1966 b; for Slavic, Petrovici 1938, 1965, 1966, Mihăilă 1960, 1965, Pătruţ 1970, 1971; for Turkish, Şăineanu 1900 has not been supplanted by Wendt 1960 (cf. Drimba 1950, 1957, 1964); on Hungarian, Tamás' dictionary (1967) remains fundamental, though we should mention contributions by Király (1964, 1967, 1973) and Kelemen (1971). A large proportion of the modern Rumanian vocabulary (about 40%) has been borrowed from Western Romance, most often from French; the topic of 're-Romanicization' of Rumanian has been usefully reviewed by Sădeanu (1973).

Note

* The authors' division of labor is as follows: Dworkin undertook the survey of the French and Spanish sections of this paper, and Poghirc's illuminating description of the etymological field in Rumania was translated, edited and, alas, abbreviated by myself. It is important to emphasize that each party is responsible for the statements made in his portion only. This refers particularly to the polemical portions of the introduction, which neither my colleagues Dworkin and Poghirc nor the editors necessarily support and for which they bear no responsibility whatsoever.

We are extremely grateful to Ruth Holzmann for an excellent critical appraisal of the manuscript and to Keith Karlsson for catching several typographical slips. [J. R. C.]

THOMAS E. HOPE

Interlanguage Influences

1. Introduction

There is as yet no universally accepted field of study to which the name
of 'interlanguage influences' may be applied, whether in the Romance
area or elsewhere – accepted, that is, in the sense that it might appear
as a heading in a manual of Romance linguistics, or as the title of a
basic university course. "Interlanguage influences" is a blanket term
whose edges are not well tucked in, and no one can say with assurance
what it should cover and what it should not. There is nevertheless a
widespread feeling that many of the things which happen when languages come into contact are in reality individual facets of a more far-
reaching phenomenon, both linguistic and cultural in its nature, to
which they all belong; and that for this reason they are best studied in
conjunction one with another. Within this general area some of the
topics are traditional and have provided material for research since well
back into the last century. There will be for example an important
lexical ingredient in any overview of contact influences: borrowing or
interference at the lexical level in the form of loan-words, calques,
loan-translations, creations and the other accepted categories of transfer which fall beneath the head of lexis[1]. Etymology, the matter of the
previous chapter, is relevant here too. Romance etymologists from
Diez onwards have had a lot to say about the movement of lexical items
between one language and another. Perhaps too much for a more
sceptical and demanding age like ours, as anyone can judge for himself
who glances at Meyer-Lübke's venerable *REW* or the maps accompanying Rohlfs 1954, where arrows denoting lexemes sweep across
frontiers with the confidence of a patriotic newspaper indicating the

progress of a battlefront. As well as traditional topoi, there are traditional problems. In the outlying areas of our subject serious difficulties of definition and delimitation arise. They are acute on the borderline with comparative/contrastive studies[2], and also in the area of overlap with dialectology, since the thorny question of characterising any Romance tongue and locating it in spatial terms has a direct bearing on our field of study when it comes to identifying and assessing mutual influences. But all domains of research have their boundary disputes, and this is no reason for neglecting the subject and failing to exploit the possibilities which the underlying phenomenon of interference affords, by allowing this promising corpus of related facts to lose its identity and be dispersed among a number of adjacent disciplines.

The emphasis of this short survey will be on picking out what is typical, rather than trying to be complete. Some four hundred titles in the bibliography go with this chapter, but they are no more than a goodly sample of the material available. It could not be otherwise, given the increasing volume of literature in the past few years. A recent bibliography covering no more than a modest sub-section of our field – foreign influences on Rumanian vocabulary – lists no fewer than 365 items (Goddard 1977, in Appendix II). Mackey 1972 (in Appendix II) ran to 11,006 entries; and though some of the items listed deal with topics marginal to the business of the present chapter the impression of intense scholarly activity one gains from this indispensable work of reference is not exaggerated. So there is in the first place a purely logistic explanation why our overview must remain incomplete, provisional. It is not the only reason, however. Despite their long history inter-Romance studies are still in the process of being realised. One might say without anticipating too much on what follows that hopes expressed and programs of research laid down early in the present decade have produced a rather disappointing response among students of the neo-Latin languages. To identify current trends is therefore only a part of what needs to be done. It will be at least as important to show where progress so far has been uneven, what there is still left to do and where new developments are likely to occur in the future.

Another ambition of this survey will be to substantiate the claim that in spite of its disparate nature our subject does indeed possess the underlying unity referred to in our opening paragraph, as well as a body of doctrine worthy of independent status and of an accredited title to go with it. One factor that makes for unity is purely practical: contact phenomena provide a useful point of entry into a wide range of sub-disciplines and research specialisms bordering on the central core of linguistic studies – structural semantics, neologism and the diffusion of newly-created linguistic signs, the relation between plurilingualism and pluriculturalism, effects of diglossia, and many other topics relating to language loyalty which have a foot securely placed in the sociolinguistics camp and for that reason alone are well worth cultivating[3].

Three analytical articles published in *Current Trends in Linguistics* are to be considered essential preliminary reading for this chapter. Two of them bear the title "Bilingualism" (Di Pietro 1968; Oksaar 1972). Oksaar's synopsis is broadly based and takes in the western European languages as a whole, though it is particularly at home with the Germanic group (including English) and the work of scholars associated with Germanic traditions. Written from the standpoint of the general linguist or linguistic scientist, it is invaluable for its insights into the body of bilingual/contact theory as it stood at the beginning of the 1970s. The year 1970 can be said to mark a climacteric in the development of these studies[4]. By that date a new generation of re-searchers was beginning to profit from the lead given by Weinreich (1953), who consolidated and interpreted in terms of theory the result of much field-work on American minority languages, checking it against the author's own personal experience as a Yiddish/American English bilingual and his early researches in a European context[5]. For perfectly legitimate reasons Oksaar's testimony is thin in respect of Romance, and it is in this area that most gaps remain to be filled. The third survey is by Haugen (1973), following on from his well-known monograph on American Norwegian (1953) via other notable publications in the same field. Within the setting of an extensive survey of North American immigrant languages Haugen works his way through the history of research into bilingualism and language contact leading up to the early 1970s. He too assesses it in the light of his own research, both practical and speculative, which at that time could look back already over a period of more than twenty years. On the way he does a good deal to update Weinreich, whose investigations were carried out simultaneously with his own, each working on parallel lines with mar-kedly different languages. Weinreich 1953 remains a pivotal work of scholarship, of course, occupying as it does a position in the domain of language contact analogous to that of Chomsky's *Syntactic structures,* published four years later, in respect of syntax. Though its detailed findings are being gradually overhauled as new bilingual situations are explored, *Languages in contact* will remain important because it disposes our minds in favour of an uncompromisingly social approach.

Di Pietro (1968) maps out another spacious tract of relevant enquiry. His "suggested typology for bilingualism and multilingualism" (p. 408) has outstanding methodological value. The article as a whole, though not long, concerns us more closely than those already mentioned because it concentrates on the Ibero-American and Caribbean areas, where the languages upon which bilingual situations are imposed are in most instances Spanish and Portuguese. Here however it becomes necessary to make certain distinctions which among other things can help us in pin-pointing what the role of the traditional or typical Romance scholar ought to be within the general ambit of bilingual studies. For the plain fact is that any scientific or 'core' linguist who wished to find out more about the mechanism of bilingual activity and develop models to codify it by would not direct his attention – at least, not in the first instance – to contact situations which arise between one Romance language and another. He would quite probably stay clear of Romance territory altogether. On the other hand he might make a compromise and look for situations where Romance and non-Romance meet and begin by investigating creoles and immigrant languages in an area such as the one under scrutiny in Di Pietro, where French, Spanish and Portuguese have a special standing. Nevertheless it is true to say that in an entirely unrestricted research project the role assigned to Romance languages would tend to be a secondary one. In this connexion it is instructive to grade in order of importance the areas of investigation which have generated discussion on bilingualism – and on contact theory – in the past and seem likely to do so in the future. Such a grading might run as follows:

1. Immigrant languages in North America, for the reason that these have been studied most intensively. Here the basis is of course American English, and the most fertile bilingualisms, as we have observed already, are those which involve a symbiosis of English and one of a widely representative spread of Germanic languages. Yet Romance comes an honourable second, and there are monographs on Italian,

Spanish and Portuguese-speaking immigrants which have long been classic[6].

2. Creoles and mixed languages, both in the Western world and elsewhere (cf. the articles in vol. 2 of this series). Four-fifths of the world's creole speakers live in the Caribbean area (Di Pietro 1968:405); of these French-based creoles form the most important group (Haiti, Martinique, Guadaloupe, as well as Louisiana in the U.S.A.). Spanish and Portuguese form a mixed creole in Papiamentu. The alternation of standard French and French creoles in the former French Caribbean colonies has received so much attention that it has come to be cited as the classic example of diglossia. Despite this, English-based creoles continue to make the running as far as theoretical enquiries are concerned, and will go on doing so in these areas, e. g. Africa, where many promising situations still have not yet been probed fully. These include some where English and Romance creoles are in competition – in Cameroon, for instance.

3. Interference studies relating to established Romance languages in a non-European context (cf. the articles on these questions in volumes 2 and 3 of this series). Effects on Spanish in Central and Southern America, on Portuguese in Brazil; the status of 'substratal' Indian languages; but above all the language loyalties of immigrant communities in the major urban centres. The latter are still mainly of European origin (German, Italian, Polish, Serbo-Croat) but have come increasingly from territories other than Europe since the second world war (Hindi-Urdu, Japanese, Arabic). These later trends are certain to provide a new growth point for interference studies during the coming decade, no doubt integrated with research on Labovian lines into the social patterns and problems reflected in changing urban dialects.

Under these three heads so far the question of bilingualism between one Romance language and another has scarcely arisen: but at this point we need to take cognizance of a promising sector of Romance/Romance contact for which the same prognostication of future growth may be made. Little has been published on it in the past; yet the Italian colony in Argentina (to cite the most obvious example) has been established for upwards of a century. To the five works mentioned by Di Pietro (1968:401) we may add Donghi de Holperin 1925, 1958 (cf. also Wagner 1928); Meo Zilio 1958, 1960; and Meo Zilio – Rossi 1970. French is involved to a much lesser degree; but see Cassano 1972 for French/Spanish interference in bilingual communities in the area of the River Plate (a short article, but with good, clear-cut examples of phonological adjustment and integration observed in the field).

In North America French-Canadian studies have known a period of remarkable expansion since the 60s, as a result of a new socio-political awareness and the contribution of a number of gifted scholars on the contemporary scene. A key article here is the very full contribution by Vinay (1973), followed by Dulong (1973) and Haden (1973), in the same volume. Much of the success in this area is due to the work done at Laval University and especially by the *Centre International de Recherche sur le Bilinguisme,* directed in the first instance by W. F. Mackey, and more recently by Jean-Guy Savard. Special mention must be made of the many publications of the *Centre International,* including the master bibliography (Mackey 1972, in Appendix II). A good augury for increasing expansion in this sphere is the greater interest taken in Québec and its problems in the last few years – including that of the standard language – as a result of pan-Canadianism in general, and in particular to the politically inspired shift of emphasis by tertiary education towards native French (i. e. Canadian) culture as opposed to that of metropolitan France (see Gendron 1974a and Vinay 1973, especially 377-84, 389 ff.).

The remaining sectors can be named briefly. Taken as a whole these are the ones which have proved less productive of theory and methodology in the past:

4. The mutual impact of Romance and non-Romance in a strictly European setting[7].

5. Mutual influences in Europe between the Romance languages themselves.

In a prefatory note Haugen referred to his 1973 report as "bilingualism revisited" (505). This present chapter is not a fresh visitation. Haugen took the discussion of principle so far forward, and the subject has proved so centrifugal since then that the time is not yet ripe for re-assessing basic postulates. Re-assessment will take place in due course; there can be no doubt of that. Since the period of codification and planning represented by the early 70s most of the trends recognised then, together with some that have emerged only during the last few years, have gone forward with increasing momentum. Some old wine has been successfully decanted into new bottles. Overtly or otherwise, standardisation of languages – literary languages, that is, or languages of culture – was the chief concern of Romance philologists in the first half of this century. Their conception of the magnum opus was a meticulously documented 'history of the language' in n volumes, a genre ideally represented by Brunot, Menéndez Pidal, or a little more recently, by Migliorini 1963b (1st edition 1958). Since then interest has shifted towards the contemporary scheme of things, either to describing the present state of vernaculars which already exist as recognised standards or aspire to do so (cf. Price 1976); or else towards the issue which complements this one, namely the fate of minority languages (see in Appendix II Price 1969, 1972). From this kind of interest it was a natural step to add the element of directivism one finds so readily on the modern intellectual scene and create the new practically oriented technique of language planning, of which sociopolitical necessity provides the motive force and multilingualism the raw material.

Among practical investigations with a practical spin-off we may also cite attempts to quantify bilingualism and so make it amenable to mathematical processes (statistical, computational). The outstanding publication to date is by Mackey (1976), who takes the relative patterns of French and English as his basis[8]. Quite apart from the question of how widely the actual formulae generated are acceptable or applicable – and one notes that in these regions where scientific analysis is applied to societal phenomena it is easier to criticise than to offer viable alternatives – Mackey's volume is a practical handbook to a whole range of bilingual studies, which must be a basis for all new research in this field. The 'languages across cultures' approach, developed mainly by applied linguists for pedagogical purposes, has made itself felt increasingly. Contrastive studies in the Romance sector show no signs of losing impetus. Above all, bilingual/diglossic theory has become an accepted part of sociolinguistic doctrine and work on it has prospered proportionately with the ever-increasing expansion of sociolinguistics.

It is clear from what has just been said that Romance scholars in the past have stood a little aside from the main stream of research into bilingual theory, if one means by that research governed by strictly linguistic canons. We have also indicated that research in this area consonant with the aims of 'core' linguistics is at present expanding more rapidly and often on different lines from what was envisaged in pioneering reports and programs of the sixties and in the early seventies. What seems to be needed at this stage is not greater abstraction but more information; limited reports, largely descriptive but with some tentative theorizing, in those domains which have not been covered by surveys so far or where there is need for re-assessment in more modern terms. Contact between Romance languages in Europe is such a domain (that is to say category 5 above). External influences on European Romance (category 4 above) will, however, need to be considered on various occasions. The external pressure of non-Romance languages has been so active in generating linguistic/cultural exchanges during the past and – what is more important – is so closely relevant to the fortunes of Romance in the European area at the present day that it cannot be ignored.

The rest of this chapter will be presented under the following headings:

2. Achievements past and present
   2.1 Preliminaries
   2.2 The historico-cultural mode
   2.3 Interference other than loanwords
   2.4 The socio-contemporary mode
   2.5 Purism. Non-Romance influences
3.0 Desiderata and conclusions

But first a note on instruments of research. Since the traditional historical approach (which Oksaar deprecates and characterises pejoratively as "historicism" (1972: 477)) is still the one most commonly met with in our domain, etymological dictionaries continue to be a valuable source of information. Corominas's *DCE* and the body of critical discussion arising out of it are as important for our purposes as they are in other respects; while the "Indices", as Diego Catalán has pointed out, provide an easy orientation to loanword problems in Spanish (Catalán 1972: 1022 n. 496). Perhaps even more productive, though still incomplete, is Battaglia 1961 (in Appendix I), which avoids the puristic bias which so often leads Romance lexicographers to be selective in what they admit; so that the wealth of textual examples it incorporates extends to *barbarismi* and *forestierismi* as well. From a different standpoint, puristic dictionaries, a remarkably productive genre in Italian, French, Spanish and Portuguese since the 16th century, still provide rich veins of information, though they have been worked a good deal recently[9].

The monumental *FEW* has been greatly improved from our point of view by the detailed work of revision and amplification carried out in recent years under the guidance of Baldinger[10]. Manuals and reference books are seldom to be cited for purposes so specialised as that of the present chapter. But an obvious exception must be made in the case of Migliorini 1963b which devotes ample space to contacts at the level of lexis, in line with its author's predilections. The same applies to Muljačić 1971, which earns our gratitude for the short but meaty chapters on foreign elements in Italian (rubric 2.23) and the diffusion of Italian elements in other languages (2.33). Câmara 1964, though still wider in scope, has a useful section on loan-words (pp. 253-88: "Empréstimo e la sua amplitudine; Aspectos linguísticas e sociais do empréstimo")[11].

Though Mackey 1972 (in Appendix II) bears most directly on contact studies, there are others which have a more general coverage yet include works on interference as an important constituent, e. g. Hall 1958, 1969 for Italian. Spanish is well served by the articles on borrowings in *ELH*[12].

Deroy 1956 remains the most extensive overall survey of contact phenomena written by a scholar in the European tradition. Though so inclusive in its approach that it sometimes becomes diffuse, it is valuable – perhaps for that very reason – as a repertoire, a point of departure for the study of contact problems at all linguistic levels and in widely differing cultural contexts.

Certain periodicals have always been receptive to papers on interlingual topics, notably *Lingua Nostra; Le Français moderne; Romance Philology* and the *Revue Roumaine de linguistique. La Banque des Mots,* a periodical founded more recently (1971), has an obvious importance because it is the official mouthpiece of a state planning board set up to deal with an interlingual problem.

2. Achievements past and present

2.1 Preliminaries

It is in the nature of 'inter-' or 'linking' disciplines that their content readily arranges itself in a series of opposites or polarities due to the disparate nature of the phenomena subsumed, the different disciplines brought provisionally together under one head. Between each polarity – each pair of extreme standpoints – runs a gradation or cline on which topics may be located according to the relative importance of one parameter or the other. Interlanguage studies are rich in dichotomous patterns of this kind. Micro versus macro, in the sense of total language community contacts as opposed to minority groups or élites (or, from a different perspective, contacts ranging from extensive special vocabularies or semantic categories down to individual items at the phonological level (e. g. unfamiliar consonantal groups) or that of lexis (e. g. semantic creations)); structural or nonstructural factors; the involvement of cultural/literary languages as opposed to language of use; degrees of purism or liberalism; bilingualism and its differential relationship with biculturalism – these are only a sample of many analogous instances which might be identified. In respect of methodology, a distinction may be drawn between analysing interference as it is seen to affect a bilingual person's idiolect (often by introspection), or to take as one's point of departure the received language, the langue, which is subject to interference owing to the speech-habits of a bilingual minority. Upon all this is superimposed the inescapable duality which is common to all paralinguistic or perilinguistic studies, that of linguistic factors on one hand and extra-linguistic (material, social, cultural) factors on the other.

In practice a number of these parameters tend to occur simultaneously and with a certain regularity, which has the effect of sorting out or classifying published investigations within the Romance area into two over-riding groupings. The first group is historical, deriving its contact material typically from former states of the language. It therefore necessarily draws evidence from written sources which in the main – though not exclusively – indicate a cultural or literary language. Most of the evidence consists of loanwords and is therefore lexicological. In opposition to this large historical, lexicological and cultural cluster stand works based on contemporary usage, implying that they principally have to do with everyday, spoken language – the language of use – or at least the reflex of that language as it appears in the mass media whether spoken or written. The facts described and inferences drawn are sociological by nature rather than cultural in the wider sense of that term. The latter grouping may therefore be described aptly if somewhat elliptically as 'socio-contemporary', while 'historico-cultural' is a handy label to designate the first group by. We can use this widely applicable distinction as a framework on which to classify achievements so far and identify present trends. It hardly needs to be pointed out that the historico-cultural end of the polarity represents in a general way methods which are traditional in the Romance field, while research to which the title socio-contemporary is appropriate on the whole is inspired by more modern approaches and could be taken to indicate how far inter-Romance research has fallen in with recent trends in other linguistic domains, or has neglected to do so. It will of course be understood that the purpose of these terms is primarily mnemonic: they only hint at the content on which a more precise taxonomy might be based.

2.2 The historico-cultural mode

Inter-Romance publications began to appear well back in the nineteenth century with large-scale monographs located squarely at the historico-cultural end of our gradation. Typically they were accounts of loanword influences upon the major standard languages with lexical examples loosely related to known historical circumstances: Nannucci 1840 (Provençal on Italian); Baralt 1874 (French on Spanish); Demetresco 1888 (French on Rumanian); Meyer 1904 (French on Italian); Croce 1895 and Zaccaria 1905 (Spanish on Italian); Schmidt 1914 and Ruppert 1915 (Spanish on French). They were inspired by the even more numerous undertakings of the same kind outside Romance, or in category 4 as we defined earlier: Mackel 1887 (German on French and Provençal), Claussen 1904 (Greek on French); Behrens 1924 (German on French) and so on. Catalogues listing the total influence of foreign vocabulary on a given language were not uncommon (e. g. Berger 1899). Pan-cultural surveys cast in the same ambitious mould continued to appear down to much more recent times (cf. Boulan 1934). Their golden age fell between the two world wars.

Loanword studies compiled according to this time-honoured recipe bore the brunt of criticism from practically all those who during the past twenty years have tried to promote some form of linguistically-centred bilingual analysis. It must be recognised that many of the griefs alleged against the earlier approach are valid, not least that of an excessively idealistic approach in the manner of Benedetto Croce, Karl

Vossler or Eugen Lerch (see Vossler 1926, 1953; Lerch 1930). Perhaps some of the anti-historical bias of a decade ago followed naturally from a constructive desire to push the discipline in an entirely new direction – a work of reform which has in fact succeeded. For all that it would be misleading to assume that the historico-cultural approach has become a dead letter, and more misleading in Romance than elsewhere. Scholarship moves on continually, and lexicologists have gone a long way in the last few years towards putting their house in order[13]. In terms of greater factual accuracy, for one thing. Most of the older sources have been re-examined and incorporated into revised accounts which are at once more complete and more objectively controlled. Croce 1895 and Zaccaria 1905, 1927, along with other earlier authorities on Spanish-Italian borrowings, are taken into account by Beccaria (1968); Gamillscheg 1934-6 is being re-worked at the present time by scholars interested in Germanisms within the northern Italian dialects, in particular Mastrelli (1965, 1974), whose approach qualifies equally well to appear under our second rubric. In the well-cultivated field of Italian influences on French, Wind (1928) improved signally on Kohlmann (1901), Klemperer (1914), Saya (1905), Tracconaglia (1917) and is developed in turn together by Bezzola (1925), Boulan (1934), Schiaffini (1937, 1953) and others by Hope (1971a).

As a result of painstaking scholarship and a fervent regard for detail which is perhaps the most valuable legacy of an earlier, positivistic era, a bountiful harvest of information has been garnered over the past eighty years. Yet rather surprisingly large areas of inquiry still lie fallow, even in the three most influential languages of culture, French, Spanish and Italian, where the most intensive work has been done, as one might expect. For all that the amount of attention devoted by academics to the historico-cultural sector has decreased, possibly in a kind of inverse ratio to the increasing effort which has been expanded on questions of theory and the more obviously sociolinguistic preoccupations mentioned earlier. Or possibly because of the sheer cost of time and labour required, especially if, as Vidos insists, these culturally based investigations need to be carried out by a single individual rather than a team (Vidos 1965a:313).

It will be convenient to indicate what has been achieved to date (and consequently to show up the areas of thin coverage) by representing diagrammatically how each of the major languages has taken part over a long period in a process of constant exchange with the others (fig. 1).

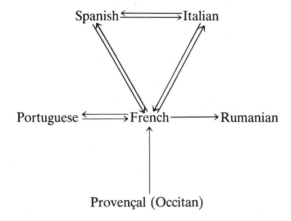

Of the triad of mutual influences – Italian, French, Spanish – which provide a nucleus round which other interlingual movements group themselves, the long and intensive exchange between Italian and French has something of a classic status. Viewed in terms of 'transfusions of culture'[14] the flow of innovation between France and Italy reverses and finally returns to its previous pattern over a period of about a millenium. Bezzola (1925), a perfect example of the genre, deals with the Old French lexical influence corresponding to the typical manifestation of mediaeval and feudal civilisation[15]. Legal, political, aesthetic and ethical conventions from many different sources were codified in France and disseminated from that country together with the literature that reflected them. Bezzola draws no sharp distinction between the langue d'oïl and the langue d'oc and so he leaves open the opportunity for someone to write a corresponding essay on the dissemination of Provençal, which would probably not limit itself to terms exported in the direction of Italy (or Sicily, in the first instance) but would extend to Galician Portuguese and would profit from literary historians' work on courtly terminology. At the other end of the time scale the nineteenth-century vocabulary explosion brought about by the Industrial Revolution, in which French played a foremost role as well as acting as an intermediary to other European languages, has gone largely unnoticed except to a certain extent in respect of Italian (Hope 1971a:548-58). On the other hand French performed a similar double role of originator and go-between with regard to linguistic usage associated with the Enlightenment, which as far as Italian is concerned has been copiously documented by Schiaffini (1937 and 1953:71-115) and Hope (1971a:375-441), backed up by a number of articles on specialised categories of the lexicon (Finoli 1947-8; Zolli 1965 and the more substantial Zolli 1971 which discusses effects on the Venetian dialect[16]). The corresponding influence on Spanish has seemed less worthy of study (but see Krauss 1967 on the fortunes of the key Gallicism *civilización* in that period). It was admittedly received with less enthusiasm in Spain than beyond the Alps[17]. Where the impact of French on Spanish amounts to something is in the Middle Ages, that is in respect of the cultural hegemony just referred to, which affected Spanish to a similar degree, both in literature and the terminology of actual institutions. This aspect was investigated by de Forest (1916) but could bear looking at again in greater detail.

A good deal could be done by way of a commentary on the unidirectional influence of Spanish on its northern neighbour, even though several researchers have chipped away at it from time to time, e. g. Goddard (1966) for the Golden Age; Kidman (1969) for the earlier period; Boulan (1934) for the second half of the 17th century (though the latter is very superficial). Herbillon (1961) discusses Hispanisms in Walloon and adjacent areas[18].

Where the linguistic empire-building of the Spanish Golden Age has been worthily evoked is in Beccaria's studies (1964, 1966, 1968) of Hispanisms in Italian during the sixteenth and seventeenth centuries. His book (1968) has several methodological modernisms which deserve to be taken up elsewhere. It achieves the breadth needed by its panoramic sections, while retaining depth by spotlighting a few key words and semantic families (a whole chapter, for instance, on the Piedmontese Hispanism *creada*). Interest in Spanish-Italian contacts outside the *Siglo de Oro* centres mainly upon the fate of Hispanisms in southern Italy, especially Naples. Here two articles have a special relevance: by Mondéjar (1967) on relations between the Hispanic peninsula and southern Italy and by Vidos (1974-5), which applied itself to certain points of etymological detail but included bibliographical references applicable to the contact situation as a whole[19].

The greatest European secular movement of all times, the Renaissance, has generally received the detailed attention it deserved. Its impact on Spanish was interpreted through the medium of lexical contacts some time ago by Terlingen (1943)[20]; see also Castello 1954 and Terlingen 1967. For France's debt to the Italian Renaissance Wind (1928) remained the standard work on this focal period of French lexical history for forty years, but it is now superseded by the reassessment by Hope (1971a:148-273).

The historico-cultural triad is surrounded by a nebula of publications which bear directly upon this central area. Many of these overlap with etymological studies and are really just word histories which involve an unusual amount of to-ing and fro-ing across languages frontiers. Sometimes an individual lexeme is discussed, as by Burkart (1937), Bertoni et al. (1939), Vidos (1954, 1959, 1969a, 1970), Oostendorp (1966), Pariente (1970), Dworkin (1971-1972). Others examine a particular semantic category or structurally related group: Dauzat 1946 (foreign sources of thieves' slang); Ramalho 1951 (couture); Ciureanu 1951-1953 (commercial terms), Caravalheira 1953 (culinary terms); Zavatti 1959, 1963, 1965 (a series of articles on polar terminology – a sphere of marked international activity); Giacalone Ramat 1967 (terminology of colours – a traditional semantic field); Peter 1969 (an important essay in the terminology of railways) and 1971 (on Savary's dictionary of commercial terms); Cagnon – Smith 1971 (architectural terms in general). Often the lexicon of an individual work or author comes under scrutiny: Mazzoni 1939 (Gallicisms in Machiavelli); Setti 1953 (Gallicisms in Algarotti); Rosellini 1967 (Montaigne); Price 1967 (Spanish, French and Occitan elements in Brantôme); Vidos 1971-73 (Jal's *Glossaire nautique*); Lapesa 1972 (Provençalisms in a Spanish fuero); Vidos 1977a (Lusisms in Christopher Columbus) and 1977b (Hispanisms in Pagafetta's account of Magellan's voyage round the world).

There is something reassuring in the fact that interest in restricted languages and technical vocabularies continues to gain ground, a trend which runs counter to the slackening of activity within the historical area as a whole. Vidos was a pioneer in applying to borrowed vocabulary the 'Wörter und Sachen' techniques which had already proved their value in the larger 'world-field' studies of a type associated with Jolles or Ipsen. He chose nautical terminology as his special preserve and has never fallen out of love with it since. Vidos 1939 was a monumental work by any standards and it reached farther than its title suggested. "Basandomi sul linguaggio nautico", he admitted later, "spero di aver potuto far vedere l'importanza metodologica che i termini marinareschi di natura migratori possono avere per la soluzione dei problemi della migrazione delle parole in genere" (Vidos 1965a:353). The movement of nautical terms from Italian to French was seen as a kind of corridor through which passed items of technical usage from the Levant and from Eastern and Southern Europe to spread as far northward as the region where oceanic navigation begins to take priority, and which has Dutch rather than Italian as its etymological pivot. After his appointment to Nijmegen Vidos added a second expertise to the former in the terminology of textiles, especially those originating in the Low Countries and exported to Romance-speaking lands. Both these interests were brought together in a bumper volume (Vidos 1965a) which is the fullest commentary so far on technical borrowings and a springboard for future research. Nautical terminology in Romance is also the field of Bujenița 1966 (the French contribution to Rumanian). The textile industry was by far the largest and richest until the later eighteenth century. Though some work has been done on its terminology already there are many angles still not yet considered. The same is true of more recent technological and scientific vocabularies. Military vocabulary achieved international status from the very beginning, thanks to the sad realities of the human condition, yet strangely enough it has never found a Vidos and remains virtually unexplored (but see Deschermeier 1923 and Heinimann 1946 for indications on two specialised aspects). Perhaps the subject is repugnant to Europeans since World War II. It remains available for future research.

The sea is even more obviously a means of contact between peoples, as Kahane (1951) reminded us, and the Mediterranean Sea perhaps more than any other. Certainly until recent times the concept of a unified Mediterranean area made more sense than that of a single unified Europe. This being so it was a natural reaction for scholars to want to trace these affinities through the medium of their own languages; and the result of this impulse has been to leave us with a rich legacy of books and articles. Among older authorities who carried great weight in their day are König (1940-41) and Dauzat (1943). But special mention must be made of the Kahanes who as Diego Catalán observed (1972:1023), "made Mediterranean linguistics a speciality", and who have both published on that specialism since 1938 (cf. foar bibliography, Kahane 1973). Another doyen is Raymond Arveiller (1949, 1951 and especially 1963), who has kept bright his interest in eastern and near-eastern contributions to Romance vocabulary since the 1940s. The Kahanes have added to our etymological knowledge of most of the Romance languages at one time or another, but their main gift to scholarship is still their work on relations between Byzantine Greek and the West (cf. especially 1965, 1966). The Kahanes and Tietze (1958) together engaged in the perennially intriguing pursuit of tracing the pedigree of the lingua franca, this time from the standpoint of Turkish, incidentally emphasising the part played by Venice in assembling this koine[21]. Venice and the East received the attention of Cortelazzo (1957, 1965) after a series of more specialised articles (1946, 1947, 1948) on the nature of Italian spoken in Corfù. The work of the Kahanes at this point rubbed shoulders with that of Vidos, who spent a long analytical article criticising and re-casting their findings (Vidos 1965a:311-43; originally published 1961).

To dwell any longer on Romance-Mediterranean contacts is unfortunately more than space will allow, but one cannot move on without calling attention to the bustle of activity surrounding the 'grande impresa di solidarità culturale' of the *Atlante Linguistico Mediterraneo (ALM)*[22]. The *Bollettino* of the Atlas *(BALM)* is perhaps more important still. Since Deanović edited the first volume in 1959 it has been a rallying-point for assorted specialists whose research interests include the languages on the Mediterranean littoral – which takes in most of the Romance group. In a sense the *ALM* was the logical outcome of a long process of philological and onomasiological cross-reference centring upon Italy and, in the western Mediterranean, on Catalan. Catalonia's dominant position as a sea-power in the late Middle Ages is betokened by the port of Alghero in western Sardinia, where the speech is still recognisably Catalan, much as it was when Kuen (1932-34) wrote his authoritative description of this linguistic enclave. Among those currently investigating historical contacts between what we might call the quadrilateral of western Mediterranean languages – Catalan, Spanish, Sardinian, Southern Italian – is Vàrvaro who has written on Romance influences in Sicily, with respect to French (1973) and to Catalan (1974 a).

The reader will have appreciated already that a 'cult of personality' is not unknown among inter-Romance researchers in the historico-cultural mode. Vidos has dedicated himself to this brand of inquiry more single-mindedly than anyone else; but one can always expect an awareness of interference phenomena to inform Malkiel's discussions at all linguistic levels, while another elder statesman who ranges widely over the Romance area, but with special interests in Italian, is Hall. The late Migliorini devoted his long editorship of *Lingua Nostra* to historical lexicology, with interlingual issues to the fore at every stage of his scholarly pilgrimage from purism to Europeanism; while Wandruszka's distinguished contributions in the area of multilingualism are well-known.

Portuguese

Historico-cultural relevance here focuses upon the position of Portuguese as an intermediary between exotic languages and others of the Romance group (via French, to a considerable extent). Fonseca occupies a key position with his study over many years of Lusisms in French (1956, 1957, 1957-1966). The earlier articles identify and document words of continental Portuguese origin, but the great majority (1957: 294 onwards) are dedicated to words borrowed from exotic languages, firstly from Brazil, then from Africa and Oriental sources. This intermediary function runs parallel to the similar office performed by Spanish in respect of South and Central America and the languages of Spanish colonial possessions elsewhere in the world; so that this exotic importation hangs together with Greco-Levantinisms on one hand and Arabisms on the other to form a triple pattern of external influences impinging upon the Romance area over a long period stretching from the eighth to the seventeenth century. Lusisms in Spanish have been collected together and characterized by Salvador (1967).

French in its turn acts as an intermediary for Portuguese, as well as an exporter of vocabulary in its own right. There is a special relationship between the two languages which goes back for the better part of three centuries, during which time the Portuguese – meaning of course the educated and informed classes in earlier times – became accustomed to look at Europe through French eyes (cf. Guerra 1957). In secondary education the French language enjoys privileged status as the first foreign language; the 'Romance' course based on French and Portuguese is well-patronised at university level. Boléo's long pamphlet on problems relating to the importation of foreign words with special reference to Gallicisms (1965) is the best point of departure. It provides useful background material, goes into certain significant words more fully, has a good bibliography with comments (including a number of theses prepared at Coimbra under Boléo's guidance) and adds a sprinkling of additional examples to the stock of borrowings already amassed by lexicologists, who include Figueiredo (1902-13), and Michaëlis de Vasconcelos (1932) individual contact problems are taken up by Chaves (1944) with observations on the use of *bar, dancing, chalé, creche,* and Coelho (1955). The main relevance of Boléo's work to current trends (and for that matter of the French-Portuguese contact as a whole) is that it provides a sensibly presented yet stimulating lead-in to research on lexical purism. So far the topic has scarcely been broached, yet it has a great deal to offer and deserves to attract more attention in future; because if properly analysed – and this means in the first instance divorcing it from literary and pseudo-aesthetic preoccupations – puristic movements can become an additional source of socio-psychological evidence and therefore, inasmuch as language in this case is the target for criticism, a source of sociolinguistic material. We shall take up this point again shortly.

Provençal/Occitan

The relation of langue d'oïl to langue d'oc – between French and its southern neighbour, Provençal or Occitan[23] has at last been given the global study it deserved, in Gebhardt 1974 a, which has been well received[24], and in a number of ways stands as a model for historico-cultural exposés. Reviewers have drawn attention to the very full use of statistical data, which present the borrowed lexicon in different lights and tease out a number of underlying verities from what in this kind of study is often a tangle of brute facts. One may think that Arveiller (1976) is somewhat categorical in affirming that "avant lui, tout restait à faire", in view of the spadework done previously by contributors to the *FEW* and material presented incidentally in discussions of regionalisms in French; but it is certainly true that the area is well covered now, and that the gap waiting for a researcher has been filled. Gebhardt

1974b and 1977 are ancillary to the main thesis on Occitanisms. The same scholar (1974c) has added his tithe to the study of Franco-Provençal infiltrations into central French, a subject worked at earlier by Baldinger (1966). For vocabulary migration from the langue d'oc into Spanish we have Colón 1967b.

Other lexicon-based compilations within this general historico-cultural region are the Berkeley thesis by Pratola (1951) on the movement of vocabulary from Italian to Portuguese, which Malkiel commends warmly (1975d: 62 n.1), and two articles drawing attention to the presence of literary Italianisms in the 14th century Troubadour Biographies – Pellegrini 1962-3 and Boutière 1967.

2.3 Interference other than loanwords

The most damning complaint levelled against historico-cultural studies during the debunking period a decade ago was that they dealt almost exclusively with vocabulary and neglected the formal levels of phonology and grammar, i. e. the levels that have more to do with linguistics as a discrete discipline. Oksaar (1972: 479) may be taken as typical. For some people lexical studies were not reprehensible in themselves, though the monopoly they enjoyed was. Others were not prepared to let cultural (or even semantic) studies based on vocabulary come in under the umbrella of linguistics at any price. In this permissive age we tend to forget how rigorous structural descriptivism actually was. With the rise of research into bilingualism already referred to and the change in the climate of opinion which made semantics no longer a "dirty word" this problem has in a sense been overtaken by events. As far as lexical studies and even "historicism" was concerned the pressure was off. But before this happened traditional contact studies had already travelled some distance along the road of change. Non-lexical interference had begun to be taken into account, although studies actually based on phonological or grammatical data were (and are) still rare – predictably, in view of the conservative environment in which inter-Romance studies have their being.

Actually the vogue of loanword studies a generation ago has nothing mysterious about it: on the contrary, it is perfectly logical. The reason why is obvious, but it will bear repeating. Referential/analytical theories of meaning were generally accepted at the time (and still are widely adhered to for practical purposes, though garbed differently).

Words therefore consisted of a form related to a content; this in turn referred to some non-linguistic reality, which could readily be envisaged as some entity in the world ouside. A true representation of the link between language and culture could therefore be achieved by judiciously arranging and interpreting the pattern of semantic groupings presented by a given corpus. Phonology came into the picture as a time-honoured etymological touchstone whereby to confirm that contact had occurred, and that a particular external language was involved.

In recent major works the phonological element is handled in rather different ways. Beccaria (1968a) resorts to phonological criteria in footnotes where necessary (much as Bezzola did), but on the whole leaves it to the etymologists and accepts their findings. In any event his material presents few acute problems of identification. Hope (1971a) makes a polemical gesture and places phonetic/phonological considerations in a separate chapter, emphasising that the way borrowings are integrated at this level is worth discussing for its intrinsic value; but he is unable to avoid some phonological analysis when talking about criteria, in a different section; and a certain lack of articulation is the result. For Gebhardt (1974a) it is fundamentally important that his Occitanisms should be clearly identified, since a lot of controversy has been sparked off in the past by the issue of what words, suffixes and other forms have their origin in Occitan, as opposed to Italian, Spanish, Portuguese or spontaneous native derivation. Gebhardt states clearly that his work is lexical and that he proposes to use phonological interference solely as a criterion, then does so with tact and insight.

To date the total of independent ad hoc articles on non-lexical topics is quite small: much fewer than one finds in categories 1 to 4 above, and almost trivial compared with the rich yield of contrastive and comparative Romance studies. This is to be expected because of the very nature of contact between standard languages. My own feeling is that the number will increase, perhaps dramatically, as research activity intensifies at the opposite, socio-contemporary end of our taxonomy, which we shall consider in a moment. A foretaste of what might be done is the short article by Tătaru (1968), who discovered the odd but thought-provoking fact that students learning English at Cluj often made the mistake of rendering certain English phonemes by what appeared to be French phonemes; and this occurred even when earlier instruction in French had been slight or frankly non-existent (examples: *university* with /jy/ for /ju/; *view* as /vjy/ or /vy/ or even /vjø/. The whole question of accepted equivalents or linguistic stereotypes has hardly been touched on. Yet interlingual contacts between accepted standards like the Romance languages are the obvious place to start looking for this phenomenon. A similar pedagogical hurdle inspired Titone's article (1961) on difficulties experienced by Italian pre-adolescents in perceiving some of the phonological features of English and French.

It is not a coincidence that the country where interest in contrastive studies is greatest, Rumania, is also the one which has produced the only full-dress treatment so far available of levels other than lexis. The series of four admirable articles by Marius Sala (1974-5) together approach the dimensions of a small monograph. Based on the double premise that "limba este o structură: limba este un fapt social" (part I: 583), they are concerned almost exclusively with interference other than that observable in vocabulary; and though in fact part IV is entitled 'vocabulary' it looks at that level from a sophisticated systemic viewpoint, concentrating on such matters as semantic adjustment within the lexicon of the receiving language, and on loanshifts rather than loanwords. Though Sala's title refers to 'aspects of contacts between languages *in the domain of Romance*' (my italics) the wealth of examples cited are drawn mostly from Rumanian and its outlying dialects, together with adjacent Balkan languages and frequent detailed references to Judaeo-Spanish. The latter command our particular attention, coming as they do from the fichier of an internationally renowned scholar in this field (see Sala 1968, 1971; Crews 1935).

That little attention has been given to phonological interference in the austere sense of external pressures causing phonemic systems to be modified is understandable, but there is less excuse for not exploring more fully evidence for shifts in the frequency of use of indigenous patterns under the influence of corresponding equivalents – what might be called the pre-structural or vestigial stages of interference. This is often as far as non-lexical contact goes in the languages of culture which are our preserve. A succinct but dense synopsis of phonemic interference is given by Sala (1974-5, 2: 9-12). Grossman (1969) has useful information about the adaptation of Arabic to Romance phonemic patterns. Functional phonologists occasionally find themselves dealing with an interlinguistic formal shift: cf. Martinet's (1960:

202) classical descriptions of how the Northern French /a/:/ɑ/ opposition receded under the influence of meridional speech habits. See also notes on formal contacts between Italian and French by Hope (1971a: 579-588, 590-595). At all linguistic levels one's impression is of many things touched upon and little sifted out to the limit of its possibilities. Yet opportunities for study in greater depth are there on all hands.

Some of these 'sondages' are:

Influence of stress patterns: Sala 1974-5, 2: 6-7; Hope 1971a: 588-590.

Adaptation of foreign plurals: Dauzat 1935; E. Lorenzo 1966; Sala 1974-5, 3: 111-2.

Shift of gender during and after transfer: Sala 1974-5, 3: 109; Hope 1971a: 595-597; Malkiel 1974: 967-968.

False or pseudo-loans: Hristea 1974 (pseudo-anglicisms in Rumanian; intermediary role of French).

Syntactic calque seems to have triggered off a certain amount of interest – Galmés (1956) and Hottinger (1958; influence of Arabic) with more recently Lorenzo (1966) and especially Estrany Gendre (1970), where the syntactical influence of English in a modern setting brings us near to the sociolinguistic domain. See also R. Harris (1967) on Piedmontese influences in the Val d'Aosta.

This genre of inquiry, however, still has something exceptional about it. One cannot help noticing how much more productive Romance researchers become as they edge back towards the familiar ground of vocabulary and semantics with topics such as the borrowing of idioms and clichés. Lists of these are given by Goldiş-Poalelungi (1973: 285 ff.), but without detailed comment, except for the wise proviso that "les langues romanes utilisent concurremment des constructions identiques que leur nature rend possible et il n'est pas nécessaire d'invoquer l'action de l'une sur l'autre pour en éclairer la genèse" (p. 285). A more important source is Hristea (1977), which gives the subject a thorough airing, drawing together zealously under the heading of 'frazeologisme' several rather heterogeneous elements ranging from idiom proper to loanshifts and compound phrases (e. g. *à frisa ridicolul = friser le ridicule;* or *comunicat de război = communiqué de guerre).*

Two domains which overlap into lexis itself have been particularly well patronised. The first is generally classified under the somewhat ambiguous term of 'calque', which Malita and Vaimberg (1972: 701) define as "toute modification de contenu (et non d'expression) réalisée sous une impulsion alloglotte dans le processus d'interférence de deux langues". Hristea (1967) speaking of 'calque de structure' interprets the term widely as any structural pattern implanted by one language into another, and suggests a fourfold typology of calque, of which one, 'calque lexical' (with the subdivisions 'calque de structure' and 'calque sémantique') is what chiefly occupies his mind. It corresponds to the traditional loan-translation plus loan-rendition (also glossed as 'calque total' and 'calque partiel' respectively). Haugen's equivalents would be 'exact and approximative creations'. He also discusses the second part of his dyad, semantic calque (traditionally called 'semantic borrowing') and suggests that basic distinctions might be made between the Romance languages according to their propensity for one type of calque or the other.

Semantic loans and semantic structure in general have always been discussed widely in the Romance context. Lörinczi (1969) concentrates on semantic problems associated with Arabic loanwords and comments significantly on shifts of meaning accompanying transfer of a lexical item from source to target language. Manoliu-Manea (1971) also calls attention to semantic disparities, this time between French and Italian words which are normally considered as translation equivalents. Darbelnet (1971) makes similar observations about the lack of congruence between English and Canadian French, while emphasising more strongly the cultural divergences which underpin given semantic discrepancies. Both loanshifts and semantic loans in the narrow sense are investigated at length by Klajn 1972 (English impact on Italian). See also Csécsy 1971 and Rizescu 1958. Hope 1960, which draws its material from Italian and French, is still the most detailed theoretical discussion of semantic borrowing in what we have just called the narrow sense, that is 'extension of meaning under the influence of a formally or semantically related lexical item in a foreign language'. (Haugen's labelling here is 'homonymous and synonymous extensions'.)

Interference and style is a tailor-made topic for Romance specialists. The Romance languages are all literary languages. Even the smallest ones numerically – Sardinian and Rhaeto-Friulian – have their poets and novelists who draw inspiration from the land to which they belong, often achieving recognition far beyond their native villages. The use of language as an art-form takes us to the periphery of linguistics and very probably beyond; but we have seen already how typical it is of Romance that many interesting things happen in the borderland where language and life meet and come to terms. Linguists noticed some time ago that borrowed elements of speech often have the power to make a stylistic impact (often possess 'valeurs stylistiques', that is, in the sense defined by Bally); a power which may or may not be consciously exploited by the literary artist, but at least needs to be recognised and described. Elwert's article on foreign usage in Renaissance comedy (1965) is usually cited as a cardinal piece of research in this sector of what since the beginning of descriptive stylistics earlier in this century have been termed 'evocative' values, i. e. those which help to authenticate the portrayal of a particular milieu, social class, type of person or geographical setting. Ullmann (1950, 1951) wrote on the use of foreign words by important French literary figures, usually for the purpose of evoking what for want of a better term continues to be called 'local colour'. Ullmann 1957a also has an initial chapter devoted to foreign usage and local colour in the French Romantics. Beccaria (1968a) rounds off with a very full chapter entitled "Spagnolismo e citazione spagnola come strumento stilistico" which is both circumstantial and perceptive in the way it attempts to account for the popularity of foreign allusions, quotations and seemingly gratuitous interpolations of foreign words in Italian authors during the period which saw the rise and fall of burlesque and also coincided with what is loosely termed the baroque (references to Della Porta, Marino, Piccolomini and later, Redi and the arch-polyglot Magalotti). There is need for a carefully documented typology of the many different expressive effects which may result, e. g. heightening authenticity or immediacy, evoking novelty, modernity or again, anachronism and archaism, portraying snobbery, inducing revulsion, expressing irony, or simply raising a laugh. Cigna (1957) and Lapa (1959) are relevant in this respect; also Badía Margarit (1973b), a dense article with refreshingly precise ideas about the force of Gallicisms in the medieval Catalan chronicler Bernat Desclot ("le but de Desclot n'offre pas de doutes; il s'agit d'apporter au texte une note émotive, qui retombe dans un sens péjoratif sur les Français eux-mêmes" (p. 540)). Other aspects of style are dealt with in Spitzer 1923, Hall 1965 (influence of stress) and Hope 1973 (hypothesis that Dante uses Gallicisms consciously, for various stylistic purposes).

2.4 The socio-contemporary mode

The last three international congresses of Romance linguistics and philology have had 'languages in contact' among their official topics (1971, Québec; 1974, Naples; 1977, Rio de Janeiro). On each occasion the work of that section was an undoubted success both in the supply of copy it produced and in the animated discussions it triggered off. The Naples and Rio congresses added a section on sociolinguistics – diluted a little through being teamed with traditional linguistic geography and dialectology, but taking a growing young lion's share of the attention. Now the first circular of the 1980 Majorca congress has appeared, and it whets our appetite by observing that "Le Congrès aura à accomplir une tâche délicate, aussi bien vis-à-vis de la linguistique catalane – étant donné que le catalan est actuellement le protagoniste d'un procès de normalisation politico-sociale – que vis-à-vis de la Linguistique Romane elle-même, qui se sent interpellée par les sciences s'y rapportant, de la Linguistique Générale à la Sociolinguistique". The emphasis on sociolinguistics will not go unnoticed (nor, incidentally will the chalk-and-cheese opposition it is deemed to make with general linguistics)[25].

The object of this sub-section is to flesh out a little these hints about sociolinguistically conscious contact studies in our area (further discussion of some of these is to be found in volume 2 of this series). From this angle, as before, the vista so far is one of successful research interspersed with lacunae; but in this case the potential areas for research are more open-ended, while what has appeared so far, though of a very high order, has only scratched the surface of what could be done. Here more than anywhere else in Romance inter-linguistics one finds oneself pointing out where the game can be hunted rather than checking off what is already safely in the bag.

Contact studies in the historico-cultural mode presented a picture of stable interchange or transaction, source and target languages reversing their roles from one period to another. Often transfer in a given lexicon as a whole operated in contrary directions at the same time, according to the different semantic categories which happened to be implicated culturally. The socio-contemporary mode is characterized by two further types of contact situation, each differing radically from the other as regards the speakers' motivation, the respective status of each language, and the ultimate historical outcome of the process taking place. The first of these two may be described as reactive, grounded in confrontation between two languages rather than interpenetration.

An example might be the confrontation between Canadian French and English alluded to earlier. It is not an ideal one, however, because the posture of Canadian French is simultaneously one of reaction against English and vigorous interaction with it. An archetypal example which is frequently cited is the linguistic situation in Belgium, with its reactive prise de position by Flemish and Walloon French. Naturally, even in a confrontational situation interference takes place; and not uncommonly the degree of interference – representing practical linguistic realities – is greater than the speakers themselves would wish, or are aware of. Greater, certainly, than those who are linguistically aware would approve of. By 'linguistically aware' in this context one means, of course, those who have made a psychological juxtaposition between a linguistic convention on the part of certain speakers and a politico-social situation which co-exists with it and is roughly co-terminous with it. This is the classical requirement for the formation of a symbol; and thus one rightly says that for such people language itself has become a para-linguistic symbol.

The second contact situation is familiar to those who research in the area of immigrant languages: where the relationship between two languages is highly interactive but unstable, with one moving towards obsolescence in a diachronic shift which may be constrained, but seldom blocked, by language loyalties and other social, psychological and material factors which have been the object of continuous investigation from Weinreich 1953 onwards.

Catalan

Catalan and Occitan may aptly be called the militant minority languages (for more detailed discussion cf. Gulsoy's and Bec's articles in volume 3). From a socio-contemporary standpoint they fit neatly into the 'reactional' niche of the taxonomy just described. The pattern of conflict existing between Catalan and 'the other language' is perfectly well known in its general lines. Basic works are those of Badía Margarit, who has championed the cause of Catalan over many years (Badía Margarit 1966, 1969, 1972, 1973a). He outlines his personal approach to the problem, with a sensitive, strikingly balanced account of its history during the present century (1972). His theme, particularly relevant to our own exposé at this stage, is that whereas in principle and in normal circumstances language and society stand in a relation inevitable one to the other, "langue et société n'arrivent pas à s'identifier en catalan" (1972:263-4). "Cette identité," (he goes on) "si naturelle et si nécessaire d'ailleurs dans n'importe quelle langue, n'existe pas chez nous. Elle n'y existe pas depuis très longtemps . . .". Within the sociolinguistic setting the author shows how a rapprochement was gradually prepared from 1900 to 1936, only to be swept away by the Civil War. Pursuing the analysis on cultural lines, Badía examines the part played by grammarians, lexicographers and intellectual élites in furthering the integration of langue and société, and later in fighting for the language's survival. The impressive survey Badía Margarit 1969 (compiled 1964-5), we learn, was intended to confirm by recourse to informants drawn from all levels of society that Catalan was still fully viable and that Badía's "idée fondamentale de dépasser la fermeture dans une élite" (p. 301) was a practical possibility. All of the articles on Catalan cited in our bibliography were, of course, written while the language still lay under political duress. Now that the political climate has changed dramatically one expects that the history of Catalan will enter a new phase, and that new opportunities for observation and research will come thick and fast. For the present writer a crucial issue will be the light thrown on the 'confrontational' situation itself, especially since a historical contingency in which each language stands its ground, as it were, symbolising an established difference of opinion between two culturally advanced language groups, has not often been analysed in terms of contact studies to date. What we have here is a 'macro-' situation of a special kind. The language is involved as a totality, but there is not total interference. Theoretically the classic or borderline instance would be that in which each language remained divorced one from the other, in a kind of stasis: in which case linguistic evidence of contact would be unavailable. It is indeed felt that a taking-up of positions in this way is largely a political scientist's or sociologist's affair, with analysis confined to numbers of speakers and bilinguals, variation of language usage between social levels, and so on. In fact what becomes manifest in strictly linguistic terms is a series of minor defections from the impassive stance adopted – elements of interference such as the grammatical Castilianisms referred to by Badía (1972:284, 295); and also social defections on the part of those who for reasons of family, ideology, ambition, etc. incline towards the other language – in this case Spanish (p. 277). Or there may be movements in favour of the confronting language: adhesion of immigrant workers to local linguistic conventions, extension of literary activity and also literacy in the threatened tongue, and so on. What makes Catalan so crucial a case is that it is now poised to recoup its losses. In Catalan we have a full-scale socio-linguistic experiment prepared and waiting for lift-off.

Occitan

Schlieben-Lange (1971a: 302) draws an interesting distinction between *une sociologie de la langue* and *une critique d'idéologie au sujet de la langue.* The former has to do with describing "le comportement linguistique des divers groupes sociaux", while the latter does not refer to "des contenus linguistiques" at all, but examines "les éléments idéologiques qui sont à la base de la conscience linguistique et qui conditionnent l'identification de l'individu avec une communauté linguistique". This dichotomy partly coincides with the more radical 'confrontational' model we have just applied to Catalan. It is true that researchers on minorities tend to fall into two groups: the linguists who describe effects of contact in linguistic terms, and others (they too may be linguists) who address themselves to what might be called extralinguistic considerations surrounding the language – its 'purity', the attitude of speakers to their common heritage and such-like topics. Séguy 1950 and Michel 1949, on French spoken respectively in Toulouse and Carcassonne, are examples of the former, as also, though in a very different sphere, is Rostaing 1942. Two markedly different approaches which both come within the second bracket of the dichotomy are exemplified by Nouvel's paper (1974) on one hand, and Schlieben-Lange's (1971a) on the other. Nouvel's essay is a straightforward account of changing official attitudes towards Occitan from the Middle Ages onwards, concentrating on the recent benificent effects of the 1970 décret relating to the langue d'oc as an educational medium. The second scholar concentrates on the much more problematical topic of 'la conscience linguistique des Occitans' and makes a number of specific statements on the subject (pp. 301-302) which include several comparisons of detail with Catalan where, she claims, the 'conscience linguistique' is more homogeneous and securely based, whereas "la conscience linguistique des occitans est une 'fausse conscience' qui n'a pas de fondement dans les données positives que peut constater le linguiste [...] Plus encore, c'est une conscience aliénée quant aux propres activités spirituelles des occitans, conscience aliénée qui ne leur permet pas de s'identifier avec le travail d'esprit qu'est l'énonciation linguistique" (cf. also Schlieben-Lange 1971 b, 1971 c).

Describing linguistically the complex of differing dialects which make up Occitan (or Provençal) has long been a staple pursuit among philologists (since the fourteenth century, to be precise), and it can be expected to continue under the aegis of dialectology and linguistic geography. There is room within this geo-linguistic frame of reference for more studies about the local effects of Occitan interference upon French, like Séguy's, or even about the impact of contemporary French on Occitan, though one notes that Occitanians are not much attracted by the prospect of studying what is in effect the dissolution of their own vernacular.

But what really gives Occitan a rich potential is the open-endedness of the sociolinguistic/ideological trend we have just mentioned. Articles like Nouvel's fall to be considered under this head, but they are still not the most productive vein in the mine. They run true to the form established by enthusiasts writing on minority languages, who stress the need for formal education in the mother tongue, the benefits that accrue from possessing two 'cultures complémentaires' (though some educationists have taken the contrary view that bilingualism is a handicap – see Haugen 1973:550-551) and the link with nationhood or past greatness. There is a parallel here to the search for an Occitanian literary standard – a long quest reaching back to the early nineteenth century, to Mistral and the *Félibrige* (see among other sources Price 1964, Camproux 1967). But both these approaches represent the politico-cultural aspirations of enlightened minorities inspired by moral, aesthetic, folkloristic or philological ends. The motivation of many Occitanians today is much more down to earth. Specifically, Occitan in recent years has developed a turbulent political connection with an ideology that turns to very different account the warm peasant solidarity Mistral loved to contemplate. The present writer is not qualified to comment on the niceties of federalist or more familiar party organisations which have associated themselves to a greater or lesser extent with the langue d'oc and the separate culture it represents. One thing that stands out, however, is that there are significant differences from the corresponding situation in Catalan: the more tangible political reality of a Catalonia than an Occitania; the fact that the link between language and political identity is more contrived in Occitan, whereas in Catalan it is immanent. At all events the scope for research is undeniable and here also one expects that new developments will follow in the next few years.

Portuguese

In one respect Portuguese too has some claim to figure in our catalogue of 'confrontation' interlinguistic attitudes, though in an attenuated way. I refer to the relationship between Portuguese and its immediate neighbour Spanish, in which one may detect a certain lack of attunement, an accepted modus vivendi in which each takes the other for granted. To foreigners it seems strange that educationists in Spain and Portugal pay so little attention to the sister language, and the indifference is equally apparent in everyday life – hardly any Portuguese magazines for sale on Spanish bookstalls, for example, which nevertheless may display a wide range of French, English and German periodicals; and much the same in the opposite direction. The usual explanation that the two languages are felt to be mutually intelligible, with a little give-and-take on either hand. It is true that a native Portuguese speaker with business to transact in Spain will readily throw in a few phonological and morphemic modifications to help communication – adding diphthongs, modifying the definite article and using some lexical equivalents, for example. Linguistic situations like this, which we might characterise as one where 'like poles repel', would until recently have been ignored or considered not worth thinking about; yet they too embody emotive elements and stereotyped attitudes of the kind social scientists and psychologists acknowledge to be a significant facet of interactional behaviour.

Sardinian and Rhaeto-Friulian

Sardinian and Rhaeto-Friulian have a special status as the two minority languages at bay (cf. the articles by Contini and Tuttle and by Francescato in volume 3). Their most important contribution from a contemporary linguistic standpoint relates to discussions which are outside the scope of this article, i. e. specifically sociolinguistic matters and wider problems that have to do with the process of linguistic change. Both languages have been described at greater length in other sections belonging to this series of volumes. However, one or two points need to be made which bear directly on the interference situations involved per se.

All authorities agree that despite the number of its speakers Sardinian (Logudorian) is clearly a language in recession, losing ground steadily in favour of a closely related, external, imposed language, Italian. Contini, whose articles are a shining example of how future work in the area can best be organised, reminds us that "la plus grande partie de la Sardaigne, à l'exception des villes, se trouve actuellement dans une situation de bilinguisme" (1970: 366; another article which concentrates on interference patterns is Contini 1968). Sardinian is therefore an example – the best one in Romance – of what we called transitional or unstable contact in the terminology suggested earlier. Its prospects of future development are by this token closest to those of immigrant minority languages, and the same analytical techniques apply, including that of investigation in the field, which Contini has used to good purpose. Especially interesting are the snippets of evidence drawn from discourse analysis which show Logudorian speakers aware that they are using Italianisms and attempting without success to reach for a native equivalent, or interpolating attenuating glosses in a spirit of self-justification, often where no Italianism has in fact been committed.

The importance of Rumantsch to interference studies, as also to a number of other areas, is that we have in this, the smallest Romance language, one of the 'artificial' interventions cutting across normal linguistic development which characterise the contemporary scene as far as our sector is concerned. Obsolescence is demonstrably retarded when the threatened language is protected by cultural sponsorship and the academic attention appropriate to the fourth national language of a wealthy country; a country, moveover, which is very much aware of its folklore and its responsibility for minorities. There would be room for an evaluatory essay contrasting the crisis in Rumantsch and in Sardinian and linking the differences to specific interference phenomena.

An impressive article in this area is Denison 1971, which hints at a fruitful line of investigation new to Romania, with its field-work on code-switching between German, Friulian and Italian in the Carnian Alps of north-east Italy. The approach is consciously sociolinguistic rather than dialectological; the important thing is the light thrown on diglossia, not dialect boundaries. It would be a valuable exercise to search for parallels in other languages – say between Occitan and regional French.

For further discussion on Rumantsch and Friulian see again, in Appendix II, Price 1969-1972 under Romansh, especially 1969 items 49-53; also Wunderli 1966 and Redfern 1971.

We should also record the service performed by Iliescu (1967, 1968a) in committing to print the linguistic odyssey of Friulian immigrants who have established themselves in Rumania, as well as descriptive work on Friulian itself drawn from personal experience and the evidence which the Rumanian enclaves provide. Arvinte (1964), on 'terminologia forestale' of Rhaeto-Friulian origin in Rumanian, affords useful evidence of contact in specialised areas.

Immigrant or displaced communities in Europe offer possibilities for description at all levels, especially since the Second World War. The outstanding case of Judeo-Spanish has been touched on already. Another parallel research area that promises well for the future is the linguistic interference caused by emigrants returning to their native countries. Rando (1967) has done pioneering fieldwork on the Aeolian island of Filicudi, to which a number of former emigrants to the U.S.A. and Australia have returned and left marks on local usage. Scope for similar studies will increase as time goes on; and what is noteworthy here is that the impact on the receiving language is made at dialect level and is therefore appreciably different in kind from the process of cultural borrowing, i. e. 'interactional' contact in the sense stipulated earlier, which, as the reader will recall, has to do with reciprocal movements between standards. Tropea (1963, 1966) on the fate of Norman-French enclaves in Southern Italy shows us that the disappearance of immigrant languages can be a long-drawn-out affair. A comparison with Weinreich or Haugen's material is irresistible. Whether an immigrant language finally disappears in three or thirty generations is conditioned, we may guess, not so much by the level of civilisation over the period concerned, but by a direct consequence of this, viz., the opportunities available for communication and hence for social contact outside one's own village; together with the scope for individual or group betterment in the sense of achievement beyond the minimal routine of everyday existence.

Rumanian

The natural point of entry to this domain, which is in many ways the most intensively researched of all, lies in the historico-cultural sector. "Nous n'hésitons pas à affirmer que dans le développement de la culture romaine, l'influence française – au début du XIXe siècle – représente un phénomène clé. Nous ne dirons jamais assez de ce processus [et] de ses effets bienfaisants" (Goldiş-Poalelungi 1973: 425). Macrea's figure (1961: 32) of 38.42% for French loanwords in Rumanian is often cited. A useful control to this estimate is Pop's apportionment of vocabulary (1948: 14-16), where the French loans work out at 29.74%, of 11,860 words (derived from Candrea's dictionary 1931; in Appendix I); Candrea uses *Dicţionarul limbii române moderne* (Academia 1958; in Appendix I). Whatever the precise figure may be, a loan-vocabulary of one-third for a single source language is by far the largest transfer of lexical items in Romance and one of the largest ever recorded. Statistical analyses are a favourite with Rumanian linguists, and French loans are referred to incidentally in their frequent attempts to unravel the different strands which make up the Rumanian lexicon; but surprisingly works directly upon the subject of Gallicisms were few until Goldiş-Poalelungi 1973: Demetresco 1888 (language and literature); Gáldi 1940a (early borrowings of verbal forms); to some extent Capidan 1940 and Weinsberg 1967 (discussion of neologisms). Bujeniţă 1966 has been mentioned in connection with a restricted vocabulary (nautical), and to this may be added Haşeganu 1941, for commercial terminology. This chapter of Rumanian linguistic history is by no means closed. Though full of useful lexical information and a fair number of rather isolated observations about lexical replenishment, sources, intermediaries and the like, Poalelungi's thesis still leaves a lot to be done, especially in matters of detail, which are capable of almost infinite further development. Analysing Gallicisms is one element in the central question of how Rumanian came to be established first as a literary language and later as a well-furnished medium of industrial and scientific activity (Macrea 1966; Maneca 1967, 1968). Eighteenth and early nineteenth century politics come into the picture, and this together with the continuing debate about the constructive part played by élites and exchanges between the literary norm and local (dialectal) language of use bring us across into the socio-contemporary sector. Dumistrăcel (1970) has something to say on the relation between literary and popular usage, while the question of élites, their socio-linguistic background and influence is sensitively examined by Niculescu (1974), who also is deeply concerned about the status of Rumanian as a member of the Romance family. To the outsider Rumanian gives the impression of a language that is for ever establishing its credentials, checking that its papers are in order. It is involved in a problem of cultural identity which links present and past. Until recently the lion's share of interlingual research fell to discussions of Slavic influence (cf. Křepinsky 1952, Kovaček 1963, Mihăescu 1967 in our bibliography and in Appendix II Goddard 1977: 174-180 for 108 items), and also to the interference at all levels of German (Dimitriu 1965, Gutschmidt 1967), Hungarian and Greek. The question of romanité (Graur 1965), though always latent, has taken priority in the last decade, keeping step with the cultural and even economic links re-forged recently between Rumania and the West. Niculescu (1976, 1977) returned to the subject of what he termed 'occidentalisme romane', re-assessing the concepts of 're-Romanisation' and 're-Latinisation' proposed by Puşcariu and Graur respectively, and reaching the conclusion that "le roumain est 'autrement roman' que le reste du monde néo-latin. Sa romanité est le résultat d'une très ancienne et constante *language loyalty,* fidélité à la structure latine de la langue d'origine, renforcée par une *culture loyalty* tardive et complexe, fidélité enthousiaste envers la culture latine de l'Occident roman retrouvé" (1977: 16). There is a sense in which the preoccupations of most Rumanian scholars nowadays are sociolinguistic, if one considers their deep motivation. A unity of interest underlies all patterns of linguistic research into Romance and Latin connections, whether historical or contrastive, whether they spotlight interference effects or discuss the formation of the national standard. But at present the socio-cultural history of Rumanian is being acted out rather than commented on. This is the real reason why "la storia socioculturale del rumeno moderno è ancora da fare" (Niculescu 1974: 290).

A similar sense of cultural involvement applies to the second Romance source language in point of numbers, Italian. Italo-Rumanian contacts, the subject of Isopescu (1935), were studied a little more extensively by Gáldi (1939b, 1940b; 'direct' and 'indirect' Italianisms). A reciprocal influence also exists in that there is a substantial Italian infiltration into the Arumanian dialect. Ruffini 1952 was supplemented recently by Carageani (1978), with a critical survey of previous work. Though lexical Italianisms are poorly represented numerically (540, according to Pop, i. e. only one-twentieth of the French importation) the close relationship between Italian and Rumanian is of course a traditional debating-point of Proto-Romance philology; while the nearness of the two languages phonetically and structurally allows Rumanians to make contact with Italians at the expense of a little ingenuity and practice in language equivalents. For very special culturo-political reasons, then, Rumanian has a special relationship with all other Romance languages, with Italian and French enjoying each in its own way a particular psychological and social standing within that relationship.

2.5 Purism. Non-Romance contacts

Language loyalty and the function of language as a symbol of national or group solidarity, a topic developed by Rogers in volume 2, were analysed and described in explicit terms by Weinreich (1953: 99). His interpretation was shrewd and keeps its force today. Of the three sociolinguistic principles picked out by Weinreich – purism, standardisation and language loyalty – the first has been almost totally neglected both by social and theoretical linguists. It happens to be the area in which the link with contact phenomena is the most direct and the most necessary. Furthermore, and this is what brings purism within our purview – it also happens that the Romance languages have a special reputation for being implicated in puristic movements. It is very likely that more printer's ink has been expended on purist tracts, and more mental effort put forth by scholars, politicians and bureaucrats in this area than anywhere in the world. Most of the languages have been affected at one time or another. There was a general animus against Italian in the later sixteenth century, once the achievements of the Renaissance had become common property and had ceased to confer prestige upon Italy alone. Purism has always been endemic in Spanish, mainly at the expense of French (for a sample see the extract from José de Gadalso (late 18th century) cited by Etiemble (1973: 367-371); also Rubio 1937). During the period leading up to the Risorgimento and the decades of self-assertion immediately following it, Italians published at least a dozen purist dictionaries directed against French (with discursive articles on each individual 'barbarismo'), often in more than one volume and several editions – to say nothing of minor works and pronouncements by literary figures including Manzoni (Zolli 1971-2; Migliorini 1963b: 691-694; Hope 1971a: 559-563).

We have said already that not all these 'confrontational' situations concern interference studies directly. Purism comes within our terms of reference at the point where qualified linguists describe it objectively, assess it and pass critical judgements upon it from the linguistic angle.

As far as French is concerned the notorious campaign centering upon 'franglais' and the reaction to it – a campaign without parallel in the long history of attempts to impose normative principles upon language – has not yet produced a major objective work of re-assessment. Some exploratory research has, however, been carried out in other parts of Romania.

Portuguese is a propitious place to begin studying purism because the liberal attitude shown in that quarter helps to bring out the problem in all its aspects. Few of the 'vernaculistas' are totally uncompromising in their condemnation of foreign words, though some favour widespread use of Portuguese equivalents (Nogueira 1936; Chaves 1944; Sequeira 1952; Feijó 1965: especially 141-149). Many speak out against being too censorious and most are prepared to accept borrowings that are "razõável e necessário" (Amaral 1944, in Appendix I). For Lapa "o estrangeirismo é um fenómeno natural, que revela a existência d'uma certa mentalidade comum" (1959: 46) and the author stresses the advantages that borrowings may confer. See also Moreno 1943; Guasch Leguizamón 1951; Coelho 1955; Almeida 1959; and Leão 1961a.

An excellent unpublished thesis by Risk (1976) surveys the official campaign in Italy under the Fascists for the purpose of achieving 'l'autarchia della lingua'. The phrase seems to have been coined by Migliorini, to whom has also been attributed the evocative synonym 'bonifica linguistica', an act of linguistic 'reclamation' analogous, one assumes, to Mussolini's draining of the Pontine marshes. This attempt at linguistic directivism was one of the first in which the eradication of foreign words was enforced by law; 'linguistic counter-sanctions' was the term used, alluding to the oil sanctions imposed on Italy by the League of Nations. Many interested parties were invited to co-operate, ranging from serious academics to political propagandists whose extreme point of view is exemplified by Adami (1935), who insisted that Italian was in reality largely Latin, and adduced as evidence lists of lexemes whose spellings happened to coincide with some flexional form of a Latin word.

Risk worked carefully through the many linguistic arguments put forward at the time for rejecting foreign importations and found them almost all both specious and fallacious. She then inquired into the fate of the native Italian coinages imposed as substitutes for the barbarismi (again, mainly Gallicisms) which had been judged inacceptable, and with the help of a questionnaire submitted to Italian informants confirmed that very few of them had survived until the present day. A number of interesting sidelights were revealed. It turned out that the majority of the substitutes which survived had justified their viability in terms of semantic structure; and that a few of the original Neo-purists were still energetically carrying on the fight, but had switched to entirely new targets – Americanisms: for the most part precisely the same ones attacked by Etiemble (1973) and his followers in a French context. Monelli (1943) was one of these indestructible xenophobes. His many contributions to the *Corriere della Sera* in the late 60s and 70s have titles like "Il vizio di parlare esotico" (28 April 1968: 3) and "Il Watergate della lingua italiana" (22 July 1973: 3). On the topic of Italian neo-purism in its linguistic aspect see also Jàcono 1939, in App. I; Migliorini 1941, 1971, as well as extensive discussions in Migliorini 1964 and 1966, especially Chapter 4, "Purismo e neopurismo" ; Mattei 1942 et seq. Early volumes of the review *Lingua Nostra* abound in similar articles.

The position of Spanish is perhaps the most stimulating issue at present on the program of interlanguage aficionados. Here, as with the franglais controversy, the source of interference is outside Romance, i. e. English. Of all the external forces which have affected the Romance group individually or collectively, the contemporary English influence is in many ways the most striking of all. So important has it grown during the past decade that it has eclipsed in numbers of borrowed lexemes and in terms of socio-cultural repercussions all the inter-Romance contacts taken together.

What makes the Spanish situation so significant is the radical change of direction it represents. After something like three centuries of partial isolation, and a generation of what might be called protectionism in the cultural sphere (and consequently a moratorium on linguistic innovation), Spain has quite suddenly become accessible if not always wholly amenable to all the cultural trends which typify modern European and American life. And with these trends are imported in ever-increasing numbers the Anglo-American linguistic usages which act as their vehicle. Until a decade ago the collecting, description and commenting of everyday Anglicisms in Spanish had scarcely been attempted. Alfaro as a precursor is almost isolated (1948, 1964) and his concern is essentially with American Spanish. Fernández García 1969 did not collect material beyond the year 1936 and so represents the historico-cultural mode rather than the socio-contemporary. The present influx of Anglo-Americanisms, however, is different in kind from the purely inter-relational pattern of contacts which prevailed before, not only because of its scale (as befits an encounter between two world languages) but because it is a token of a pan-European cultural shift which will have repercussions on several languages for a long time to come.

A certain period will have to elapse before we can see clearly what the Spanish analogue of 'franglais' amounts to. But in the meantime steady progress is being made towards providing the factual documentation needed. One or two detailed surveys have appeared in book form; but unfortunately for scholarship in this area most of the recent work consists of theses which are still unpublished. Taken together they present an imposing and suggestive body of research: Bookless 1968 (University of Leeds); Estrany Gendre 1970 (Madrid); Marcos Perez 1971 (Valladolid); O'Hare 1974 (Manchester); Pratt 1976 (Oxford); Bookless 1977 (Leeds). All these have taken as an important part of their basic material samples – often very extensive ones – from the Spanish press, with emphasis on popular registers[26]. Most of the theses cited are of British origin and the product of individual scholars, though I understand that the work at Valladolid is being developed actively by a team of researchers.

Space precludes a detailed analysis of these, but one notes that there is in practice little overlap between the different programs of research followed. Pratt (1976), for example, bases his thesis largely on an analysis of formal evidence, and includes a very full discussion of the sources available (including radio and television), and also of the various formal patterns in which the interference of English manifests itself. Bookless (1977) on the other hand concentrates on the semantic and psychological aspects, making use of a questionnaire designed to elicit information about the social spread and affective attitudes towards Anglo-Americanism in Spain, and to reveal the process of semantic adjustment undergone by borrowed lexical items.

Corresponding research on contemporary Anglicisms has been carried out in respect of Italian, though there the impact is less distinctive, for a number of reasons. In Italy, if one leaves aside the slight recrudescence of neo-purism just mentioned, the attitude of professional linguists, the Press, the powers-that-be and the Italian public at large is far less reactive towards Americanism either in language or life than it is in Spain or France. Indeed the prevailing orthodoxy, which is that of the Società Linguistica Italiana, is very anti-puristic. Influential writers like De Mauro tend if anything to play down the Anglo-American influences and Italian academics as a whole give the impression that people ought not to worry unduly about them. Nevertheless a good deal of research has been carried out recently, and this is to be welcomed. Klajn's weighty and valuable monograph (1972) has a section on the most modern trends. Readers will wish to consult the various articles by Rando (1969, 1970, 1973), which are recommended by their objectivity; Rando 1969 is based on references in Panzini 1905-60 (cf. Appendix I), comparing editions from 1923 to 1960. Rothenberg 1969 is a little less sympathetic. Frequent references to Anglicisms and Americanisms are made by Menarini (1947, 1951), who moved away from his purism of the early *Lingua Nostra* articles while retaining a lively awareness of the foreign word as a symbol of cultural dependence. Because of the subjects treated Anglicisms turn up in a wide range of lexical investigations e. g. Bascetta 1962 (terminology of sport – a traditional topic!), Bascetta 1963 (market research) and Altieri Biagi 1963 (publicity), among many others.

3. Desiderata and conclusions

It is not surprising that the beginnings of interference studies were set in immigrant languages; the opportunity for a new kind of comparative analysis was there in North America at a time when scholarship, immediately after World War II, was well placed to explore new horizons. Almost from the outset these studies developed, took on new guises. Weinreich more clearly than anyone stressed the duality between the mechanism of interference – the description of it in linguistic terms (which in the 1950s meant in terms of structure and system) –

and on the other hand the social environments which gave immigrant language studies their interest and raison d'être. The opposition is crystallised in his table of structural versus non-structural stimuli and resistance factors (1953: 64-5). Weinreich himself remained attached to the first half of his dichotomy. Haugen, who has both experienced and chronicled this era in linguistic discovery, has more than once expressed dissatisfaction about the feasibility of a purely linguistic analysis of these complex, ineluctably *human* relationships. Referring to one of his earlier attempts at codifying grammatical interference (dating from 1956) he made the significant qualification that "it was a question not of structural equivalence as identified by linguists but of bilingual behaviour as observed among actual users of language" (1973: 526). Earlier in this survey we glanced briefly at the movement away from immigrant studies towards bilingualism as a sociolinguistic factor. For the present writer the seal was set on this transition by Fishman, in his celebrated *boutade* to the effect that interference researchers spend their time thinking what structures have 'rubbed off' onto one language from another, "like a housewife looking for smears of wet paint" (1968: 27). Fishman himself began by writing on immigrant languages, and transferred his allegiance to a realm where bilingualism was ancillary to wider social preoccupations, providing a bridge for himself on the way by extending Ferguson's concept of diglossia (1959) to include the diglossic use of two distinct languages. Others followed suit or effected the transition in other ways, and contact studies set off on the long trajectory of change familiar to all who have so much as a marginal interest in the field.

In another context, as we have also seen, many scholars rejected lexico-historical or loanword studies – "the classical playground of dialinguistics", as Haugen aphoristically puts it (1973: 532) – for a number of reasons which are not hard to understand. To them what we have called the lexico-cultural mode seemed lacking in rigour, rather amateurish (the smear 'linguistic archaeology' used to be commonly applied) and more cogently, one suspects, because the mass of data available was not underpinned by a secure pattern of theory. No doubt partly also because detractors, as we pointed out earlier, had quite different irons in the fire and felt the whole approach to be outmoded.

In all this process of on-going change, what is the position of Romance inter-language studies?

The first important characteristic of our area is its diversity. It is not fortuitous that what we have termed the historico-cultural mode gave rise to a succession of major research monographs during the decade from 1968 to 1978. The main trend to be reported in this respect is that there still is a trend. We have seen in which interlingual areas research is still waiting to be done. Apart from total patterns of interchange between one language and another, we noted the almost unlimited number of options open for analysis of technical vocabularies, everyday language, individual semantic categories and the contribution to transfer made by various intermediaries, including individual authors. The practice of picking out culturally significant periods, usually with the aim of drawing a parallel between the borrowed lexicon and long-established details of cultural history needs to be completed by studying reciprocal influences at a given time, or periods in which the tempo of lexical transfer is reduced to a 'datum' or 'residuum' level (for definitions, see Hope 1971a: 273, 366). The importance of a comparative approach cannot be over-stressed. It needs to be applied widely. A comparison of the way in which the same sample of interference elements is received in different target languages can give new insights into etymological processes (see Levy 1965-7) and also into the mechanics of neologism (Hope 1964: 76-82), since a lexical transfer is a neologism with respect to the receiving language, and one moreover which can be identified, dated and specified semantically with an unusual degree of precision.

It seems hardly necessary to add that a comparative/contrastive approach can be applied as advantageously to contemporary situations, at a number of levels. What explains the differing attitudes to Americanism in different Romance areas? Why does the semantic outcome of 'franglais'-type borrowings differ from one language to another? One factor which undoubtedly enters into the equation is the pattern of pre-existing semantic resources in the target language. Recent interlanguage investigators are agreed about the relevance of semantic structure, which is felt to be an indispensable ingredient in any attempt to grasp or codify in theoretical terms precisely what a parallel between language and culture entails. One expects that theory will be refined with this essential fact in mind. As far as methods are concerned the demand for greater rigour will lead future researchers to use statistics more seriously, including word-frequency. As we have seen, Gebhardt

(1974), Risk (1976) and Bookless (1977) among others stress this source of evidence, and it has been exploited for some time by Rumanian scholars (to authorities already mentioned add Maneca 1966, 1967). Among interlanguage theorists referred to in passing during the course of this survey we should like to call attention again to Vidos' analysis (1965: 356-377). Further theoretical discussions appear in Hope 1971a: 681-742 and in K. Goddard 1969, 1976[27].

The second distinguishing feature is hard to hit off in a single word, though 'artificiality' or even 'sophistication' would be near the mark. For a long time linguistic events in Europe in general and the Romance area in particular have tended to be more subject to policy or contrivance than elsewhere; apt, that is, to be moulded by a complex layering of motives in which human intention plays a material part. Impulses of purism and language loyalty applying to the speech community as a whole are often grounded in institutionalised attitudes or fostered for what may broadly be called political motives. Linguistic directivism in any form offers prospects of meaningful cooperation between language and the social sciences. Is it possible in the long run to control language? Are the sophistications of language planners or linguistic nationalists doomed to failure because the nature of language is still not fully understood, and the symbolic intentions of philologically involved minorities do not square with the practical realities of what to the majority is an unconscious reflex? The success or otherwise of artificial interventions in language habits can be judged objectively only by their results in linguistic terms. Here as before the possibility of being able to discover something about human group reactions looms temptingly ahead, together with other by-products of a socio-psychological stamp. But it is important that theory should not run in front of observation and description. The immediate need is to be clear about what is actually happening – for example as regards Anglo-Americanisms in Italy, France, Spain or Portugal; the role of the mass media, of educational systems; how human beings are actually reacting to extraneous influences, and how these reactions become manifest in linguistic usage. Once description has been taken in hand theory will follow naturally.

Bilingualism in itself implies a more heightened awareness of language than is vouchsafed to the average speaker. In Europe bilingualism is common and multilingualism – sometimes in respect of several languages – is by no means rare. Plurilingualism is widespread as a cultural ideal, helped on its way by the prestige of professional linguists such as Wandruszka (1974, 1975). It cuts directly across linguistic nationalism and normative restrictions, and gains ground with every move towards pan-Europeanism that takes place. What in the long run will be the result of these directly opposing tendencies? In France, while legislation lays down norms for scores of thousands of lexical items in the sphere of technical, commercial and even popular usage, young people are learning English itself in ever-increasing numbers. Once again documentation and field-work are the crying needs of the moment. 'Artificiality' and linguistic awareness may be identified at the 'micro-' level too, as for example in stylistic interference or semantic borrowing. It is clear that semantic calque (to pick out a single example) can only originate and be countenanced in societies which are intimately versed in both the lending language and the borrowing language; consider Canadian French *(faire du) magasinage* '(to go) shopping' or *mépris de cour* 'contempt of court'; or French *dada* 'rocking-horse' acquiring the sense of 'hobby, craze, quirk' by an extension from English, in which *hobby(-horse)* had assumed the dual meaning because of Laurence Sterne's famous anecdote in *Tristram Shandy*.

A third characteristic leads on from the first and second. The multifariousness of inter-Romance offers opportunities to look back and re-think along some of the lines established and partly abandoned by the main stream of linguistic research. Its sophistication suggests novel approaches in keeping with the greater complexity and artificiality of linguistic behaviour (and of behaviour tout court) in the world today. The third factor, then, is simply that of open-endedness. The Romance area seems to be the right place at the right time for a new look at interlanguage studies. Each Romance language is as different from its cognates as it could possibly be in respect of size, viability, cultural traditions and the attitude of its speakers. All are jointly entering upon an era of rapid change due to cultural standardisation from within and socio-economic pressure from without. Most of these new situations will have their reflexes in terms of interference and other forms of inter-lingual strategy. Perhaps the time has come at last to give interlanguage studies in Romance the close attention they have always deserved.

Notes
1 There is no need, for the purposes of this article, to refine again on definitions of interference, contact and bilingualism. For the first of these Haugen's distinctions (1973: 531-4) make a good jumping-off point. The present writer will use 'contact' as a superordinate term embracing 'interference', but would not wish to apply so specifically structural a criterion to the latter term as Weinreich does – or claims to do (1953: 1). Oksaar 1972 treats bilingualism very fully (1972: 481-2 and 491 onwards). Haugen's preliminary notes on the theory of bilingualism (1973: 507-9) are clear and perceptive, and they include a valuable paragraph on the attitude of 'bilinguists'.
   Concerning definitions of 'borrowing' (or 'transfer', 'importation' etc.) as an overall concept, and also of the various subdivisions which may be identified within this wider process, see in the first instance Haugen (1973: 534-5) and sources there cited. Oksaar 1972 has a useful side-by-side comparison of the older German system of definitions and those of Weinreich (drawn from 1953: 47-53) and Haugen. Haugen for his part developed his own working definitions by stages from 1950a and 1950b onwards, eliminating as far as possible a classification based on abstract semantic concepts (cf. Haugen 1958). See also Goddard (1969: 338-40) and Hope (1971: 637-9) together with references cited there.
2 Especially contrastive studies by Rumanian scholars, who in the last twenty years have developed this sector to a remarkable extent. Comparisons and contrasts are most frequently drawn with languages which superficially appear to be the more remote from Rumanian in formal or grammatical terms, or most removed geographically, e.g. Portuguese. It is often difficult to see how far an author intends to imply that an actual process of interference has occurred (examples: Avram 1966; Sădeanu 1972).
3 One of the 'paralinguistic' or 'perilinguistic' areas of inquiry which concern us closely is the relationship between linguistic and extra-linguistic phenomena. On the whole this issue aroused little interest in the structural era, though Firth and his successors in the London school, whose approach many would consider the most liberal and the most suggestive of its period, have always kept 'context of situation' as an important item on the agenda. The crucial nature of contextual and semantic considerations in transformational/generative conceptions of core linguistics is of course well known.
4 The early history of bilingual research goes back to around 1950. Details in Haugen 1973: 505-7.
5 Weinreich's bibliography of six hundred items should be taken in conjunction with Haugen's monumental research guide (Haugen 1956, in Appendix II).
6 For an authoritative and easily accessible report on one Romance area see Craddock 1973, which takes note of interference patterns not only in the immigrant Spanish environment but also of Spanish itself on English and Amerindian languages (pp. 487-9).
7 Studies of Germanic influences on French were probably the earliest external-Romance contacts to be investigated, beginning with Mackel (1887) and culminating in Lévi (1950-52; see also Stimm 1968, continuing a long line of inquiries into the contribution of Frankish). Germanic elements in *Romania* as a whole have received detailed attention (e.g. Gamillscheg 1934-6), but previous findings are capable of a good deal of refinement. I understand from Professor Mastrelli that he is at present working on these lines (Mastrelli 1965, 1974). Valkhoff 1931 and Gorog 1958 are classic studies of Dutch and Scandinavian influences respectively. Interference through contact with Slavonic languages has always been a prime topic of Rumanian

historical linguistics - see Křepinsky 1952, Mihǎila 1960, Gamulescu, Zdrenghea and Gutschmidt, all 1967; the latter deals with usages of German origin which reach Arumanian via Slavonic (see also Dimitriu 1965 for German to Rumanian). Goddard 1977 (in Appendix II) has already been mentioned. Most important of all is the impact of English, which will be discussed further at a later point in our exposé. Klajn's scholarly and up-to-date contribution to the study of Anglicisms in Italian (1972) is important here.

8 Mackey was writing on the measurement of bilingualism from 1962 onwards.

9 See in this connection Baralt (1874), Figueiredo (1938), Guasch Leguizamon (1951), Jàcono (1939), Monelli (1943); and especially the analytical article by Zolli (1971-2) for observations about 19th century Italian purism.

10 For example: in earlier volumes – published as much as half a century ago – many of the headwords were set down as borrowings from Spanish or Italian which are now recognised to have entered French from native dialects or directly from Provençal (Occitan). See also Baldinger 1957 and 1966.

11 Cf. also the earlier works: Castro (1924); Ali (1930: 119-153); Boléo (1944: 2-8, 21-35; 1946: Ch. III); Graur (1960: chapter on *cosmopolitismo).*

12 These are by Colón, Pottier, Salvador, Terlingen and Valkhoff (all 1967).

13 Happily, contact studies have long since given up the attempt to link cultural events directly with other linguistic levels, e.g. formal or grammatical: i.e., the attitude which prevailed when Muller solemnly averred that "L'émancipation de l'homme à l'égard des forces de la nature se traduit par la disparition du passif synthétique du latin ..." *(L'Epoque mérovingienne,* cited by Marcel Cohen, who nevertheless still found "une vérité d'ensemble dans de pareilles considérations" (1971: 122)).

14 The phrase was used by Marcel Cohen (1943).

15 Jaberg's review article on this work (Jaberg 1925) is still informative.

16 Fogarasi 1969 fits in here, though a little later in actual chronology (1816 to 1819). The intellectual and bureaucratic Gallicisms discussed are a product of the Revolutionary-Napoleonic period. It should also be borne in mind that the position of French in Italy was widely discussed by Italian contemporaries (see Grana 1965).

17 For reactions against Gallicisms in Spain during this period see Rubio 1937.

18 Hispanisms in French were discussed long ago by neo-grammarian scholars (Marre 1910 – with Portuguese – Schmidt 1914 and Ruppert 1915). Their publications, now quite outmoded, impressed at the time and are still referred to with unseasonable piety by many a manual. They could however provide useful hardcore for a new lexicological edifice.

19 Mondéjar (1970) has also established an interesting specialism in inter-Romance movements relating to older scientific (or pre-scientific) nomenclatures of plants, animals and fishes.

20 Though Vidos (1965: 47) joins Corominas *(Symposium z.* 106-19 (1948)) in criticising Terlingen's thesis, which he considers to be "metodicamente sbagliata".

21 On the part played by Venice, see also Folena 1969-70. For the *lingua franca,* see Fronzaroli 1954 and Cortelazzo 1965.

22 The phrase is Cortelazzo's. See Catalán 1972: 1023 n. 515.

23 I use Occitan as a patently more apposite term when dealing with the post-medieval language. But to indicate the language of the Troubadours the traditional word 'Provençal' - equally inappropriate from a geographical point of view - is still widely favoured, and it would be hard to wean Italien and Anglo-Saxon medievalists from it.

24 Reviews in *RLaR* 80 (1974): 510-511 [R. Lafont]; *SCL* 26 (1975): 78-80 [M. Sala]; *ZRPh* 93 (1977): 209-212 [G. Hilty]; *FM* 44 (1976) 167-170 [R. Arveiller]; *SN* 46

(1976): 345 [Å. Grafström]; *RF* 87 (1975): 687-688 [T. Stegmann]; *RevR* 13 fasc 1 (1978) [Povl Skårup].

25 One of the 'grans seccions' at Majorca will be entitled "Història externa de les llengües romàniques i sociolingüística" - another pregnant juxtaposition.

26 A similar work in Portuguese is Pereira 1949. On Americanisms in the Portuguese of the Azores (an American base in World War II) see Borges 1960.

27 K. Goddard (Queen's University, Belfast) is at present completing a substantial inquiry into loanword theory (1978).

Appendix I:
Selected dictionaries

Abbreviations

References are to items in this Appendix

AIS	=	*Sprach- und Sachatlas Italiens und der Südschweiz* Jaberg – Jud 1928-40.
BDE	=	*Breve diccionario etimológico de la lengua castellana* Corominas 1961.
DAG	=	*Dictionnaire onomasiologique de l'ancien gascon* Baldinger 1975a.
DAO	=	*Dictionnaire onomasiologique de l'ancien occitan* Baldinger 1975b.
DCE	=	*Diccionario crítico etimológico de la lengua castellana* Corominas 1954-57.
DCVB	=	*Diccionari català-valencià-balear* Alcover – Moll 1930-62.
DEAF	=	*Dictionnaire étymologique de l'ancien français* Baldinger – Gendron – Straka 1971.
DEEH	=	*Diccionario etimológico español e hispánico* García de Diego 1955.
DEI	=	*Dizionario etimologico italiano* Battisti – Alessio 1948-54.
DELF	=	*Dictionnaire étymologique de la langue française* Bloch – Wartburg 1932.
DER	=	*Diccionario etimologico rumano* Cioranescu 1958-66.
DES	=	*Dizionario etimologico sardo* Wagner 1957-64.
DLR	=	*Dicţionarul limbii române* Academia Română 1913.
EWFS	=	*Etymologisches Wörterbuch der französischen Sprache* Gamillscheg 1926–28.
EWuG	=	*Etymologisches Wörterbuch der unteritalienischen Gräzität* Rohlfs 1930.
FEW	=	*Französisches etymologisches Wörterbuch* Wartburg 1922–.
GEW	=	*Griechisches etymologisches Wörterbuch* Frisk 1960-72.
IEW	=	*Italienisches etymologisches Wörterbuch* Pfister 1973–.
LEW	=	*Lateinisches etymologisches Wörterbuch* Walde – Hofmann 1938-56.
LRW	=	*Lateinisch-romanisches Wörterbuch* Körting 1901.
OED	=	*Oxford English Dictionary*
REW	=	*Romanisches etymologisches Wörterbuch* Meyer-Lübke 1911.

Selected dictionaries (and reviews of them)

Academia Republicii Populare Române
1958   *Dicţionarul limbii române moderne* (Bucureşti: Ed. Acad.).
Academia Română
1913-   *Dicţionarul limbii române* (Bucureşti: Socec/Sfetea). [Continued by the
   Academia R.P.R. in 1965.]
Alcover, A. M. – F. de B. Moll.
1930-62   *Diccionari català-valencià-balear* 10 vols. (Palma de Mallorca: Gràfiques
   Miramar).
Alessio, G.
1957-58   *Postille al Dizionario Etimologico Italiano* (= *Quaderni linguistici* 3-4)
   (Napoli: U.P., Istituto di Glottologia).
1962   "Nuove postille al Dizionario Etimologico Italiano", *BCSS* 6: 59-110 (= *Saggi
   e ricerche in memoria di E. Li Gotti* 1).
Alfaro, R. J.
1964   *Diccionario de Anglicismos* (2nd edition) (Madrid).
Alsdorf-Bollée, A. – I. Burr
1969   *Rückläufiger Stichwortindex zum Romanischen etymologischen Wörterbuch*
   (Heidelberg: Winter).
Amaral, Vasco B. de
1944   *Novo dicionário de dificuldades da lingua portuguesa* (2nd edition) (Lisboa).
Atzori, M. T.
1964-65   "Aggiunte al *Dizionario etimologico sardo* di M. L. Wagner", *RPF* 13: 263-
   278.
Baldinger, Kurt
1956-58   Review of Corominas 1954-57, *DLZ* 77: 353-357; 80: 316-320.
1961   "Der neue Bloch – Wartburg (Lexikologischer Forschungsbericht 1950-60)",
   ZRPh 77: 85–137.
1964   Review of Bloch – Wartburg 1964, *ZRPh* 80: 517-524.
1975 a-   *Dictionnaire onomasiologique de l'ancien gascon* (Tübingen: Niemeyer).
1975 b-   *Dictionnaire onomasiologique de l'ancien occitan* (Tübingen: Niemeyer).
Baldinger, K. – J. D. Gendron – G. Straka
1971-   *Dictionnaire étymologique de l'ancien français* (Tübingen: Niemeyer/Québec:
   P. U. Laval).
Baralt, R. M.
1874   *Diccionario de galicismos, o sea de las voces, locuciones y frases de la lengua
   francesa que se han introducido en el habla castellana moderna* (2nd edition)
   (Madrid).
Battaglia, S. (ed.)
1961-   *Grande dizionario della lingua italiana* (Torino: Unione Tipografico-Editrice
   Torinese).
Battisti, C.
1949-50   *"Presentazione del Dizionario etimologico italiano"*, *RomPh* 3: 227-238.
Battisti, C. – G. Alessio
1948-54   *Dizionario etimologico italiano* 5 vols. (Firenze: G. Barbèra).
Bloch, O. – W. von Wartburg
1932   *Dictionnaire étymologique de la langue française* (Paris: P.U.F.). [2nd edition
   1950, 3rd 1960, 4th 1964, 5th 1968.]

Brîncuşi, G.
1961   "Observaţii asupra etimonurilor albaneze din DLRM", *SCL* 12: 193-201.
Brüch, J.
1926-29   "Bemerkungen zum Französischen Etymologischen Wörterbuch E. Gamillschegs", *ZFSL* 49: 290-318, 50: 299-355, 52: 393-483.
Buschmann, S.
1965   *Beiträge zum etymologischen Wörterbuch des Galizischen* (Bonn: Rom. Sem.) (= *RVV* 15).
Butler, J. L.
1970-71   "Wagner's Etymological Dictionary of Sardinian", *RomPh* 24: 108-119.
Candrea, I. A.
1931   *Dicţionarul limbii române di trecut şi de astăzi* (Bucureşti: Cartea Românească).
Candrea, I. A. – O. Densusianu
1907-14   *Dicţionarul etimologic al limbii române. Elementele latine* 4 fasc. (Bucureşti: Socec).
Cihac, A.
1870-79   *Dictionnaire d'étymologie daco-romane, I. Éléments latins comparés avec les autres langues romanes, II. Éléments slaves, magyars, turcs, grecs-moderne et albanais* 2 vols. (Frankfurt am Main: L. St.-Goar).
Cioranescu, A.
1958-66   *Diccionario etimológico rumano* (Tenerife: Biblioteca filológica).
Clemens, G. B.
1949   *A tentative Portuguese dictionary of dated first occurrences to the year 1350* (unpublished Ph. D. Dissertation, Univ. Pennsylvania).
Colón, G.
1962 a   "*El Diccionario crítico etimológico de la lengua castellana* de Corominas. Notas de lexicografía y etimología hispánicas", *ZRPh* 78: 59-96.
1967   Review of Buschmann 1965, *VR* 26: 376-378.
Corominas, J.
1954-57   *Diccionario crítico etimológico de la lengua castellana* 4 vols. (Bern: Francke/
Madrid: Gredos).
1961   *Breve diccionario etimológico de la lengua castellana* (Madrid: Gredos). [2nd edition 1967.]
Cunha, A. G.
1956-60   Review of Machado 1956-59, *Revista brasileira de filologia* 2: 264-275; 3: 105-115, 231-238; 4: 99-109; 5: 53-63.
Dalgado, Sebastião R.
1919, 1921   *Glossario luso-asiatico* 2 vols. (Coimbra).
Darmesteter, A. – A. Hatzfeld – A. Thomas
1890-1900   *Dictionnaire général de la langue française du commencement du XVIᵉ siècle jusqu'à nos jours* (Paris: C. Delagrave).
Dauzat, Albert
1938   *Dictionnaire étymologique de la langue française* (Paris: Larousse).
Dauzat, A. – J. Dubois – H. Mitterand
1964   *Nouveau dictionnaire étymologique* (Paris: Larousse).
Devoto, G.
1966   *Avviamento alla etimologia italiana. Dizionario etimologico* (Firenze: F. Le Monnier). [2nd edition 1968].

Elmendorf, J. V.
    1951   *An etymological dictionary of the Dalmatian dialects of Veglia* (unpublished Ph.
           D. Dissertation, Univ. North Carolina).
Frisk, H.
    1960-72   *Griechisches etymologisches Wörterbuch* 3 vols. (Heidelberg: Winter).
Gamillscheg, Ernst
    1926-28   *Etymologisches Wörterbuch der französischen Sprache* (Heidelberg:
           Winter). [2nd edition 1966-68].
García de Diego, Vicente
    1955   *Diccionario etimológico español e hispánico* (Madrid: S.A.E.T.A.).
    1968   *Diccionario de voces naturales* (Madrid: Aguilar).
Genaust, H.
    1972   Review of Picoche 1971, *VR* 31: 214-217.
Georges, K. E.
    1913   *Ausführliches lateinisch-deutsches Handwörterbuch* 2 vols. (9th edition) (Han-
           nover: Hahn) [Reprint 1951 (Basel: Schwabe).]
Graur, A.
    1937   "Corrections roumaines au *REW*", *Bulletin Linguistique* 5: 80-124.
Hasdeu, B. P.
    1887-98   *Etymologicum Magnum Romaniae. Dicţionarul limbii istorice şi poporane a
           Românilor* 4 vols. (Bucureşti: Socec/Teclu).
Höfler, Manfred
    1970   Review of Bloch – Wartburg 1968 and Dauzat – Dubois – Mitterand 1964, *Rjb*
           21: 211-216.
Hristea, Theodore
    1960   Probleme de etimologie în *Dicţionarul limbii române moderne, SCL II:* 235-
           237.
Hubschmid, J.
    1962   Review of Corominas 1961, *ZRPh* 78: 547-553.
    1971   "Lexicalisches aus der unteritalienischen Gräzität", *VR* 30: 264-271.
Jaberg, K. – J. Jud
    1928-40   *Sprach- und Sachatlas Italiens und der Südschweiz* 8 vols. (Zofingen: Rin-
           gier).
Jàcono, Antonio
    1939   *Dizionario di esotismi* (Firenze: Marzocco).
Juilland, Alphonse – Dorothy Brodin – Catherine Davidovitch
    1965   *Frequency dictionary of French words* (The Hague: Mouton).
Juilland, Alphonse – E. Chang Rodriguez
    1964   *Frequency dictionary of Spanish words* (The Hague: Mouton).
Juilland, Alphonse – P. M. H. Edwards – Ileana Juilland
    1965   *Frequency dictionary of Rumanian words* (The Hague: Mouton).
Juilland, Alphonse – Vincenzo Traversa
    1973   *Frequency dictionary of Italian words* (The Hague: Mouton).
Kahane, Henry – Renée Kahane
    1966-67   "Greek in Southern Italy", *RomPh* 20: 404-438.
Körting, G.
    1901   *Lateinisch-romanisches Wörterbuch* (Paderborn: F. Schöningh). [2nd edition
           1907.]
Kramer, J.
    1970   *Etymologisches Wörterbuch des Gadertalischen (Dolomitenladinisch)* (Köln).

Lorenzo, R.
1968 *Sobre cronologia do vocabulário galego-português (anotações ao Diccionário etimológico de José Pedro Machado)* (Fundación Penzol, Colección filolóxica) (Vigo: Galaxia).
Machado, J. P.
1952-59 *Dicionário etimológico da língua portuguesa* 2 vols. (Lisboa: Confluência).
1966 *À margem do meu Dicionário etimológico da língua portuguesa* (Lisboa: Confluência).
Malkiel, Yakov
1956 "Linguistic problems in a New Hispanic etymological dictionary", *Word* 12: 35-50.
Meyer-Lübke, Wilhelm
1911 *Romanisches etymologisches Wörterbuch* (Heidelberg: Winter). [3rd edition 1930-3.]
Migliorini, Bruno – A. Duro
1950 *Prontuario etimologico della lingua italiana* (Torino: Paravia). [4th edition 1964.]
Nascentes, Anténor
1932 *Dicionário etimológico da língua portuguesa* (Rio de Janeiro).
Olivieri, D.
1953 *Dizionario etimologico italiano, concordato coi dialetti, le lingue straniere e la topo-onomastica* (Milano: Ceschina). [2nd edition 1961.]
Panzini, Alfredo
1905-60 *Dizionario moderno* (Milan). [10 editions: 1905, 1908, 1918, 1923, 1927, 1931, 1935; posthumous, edited by A. Schiaffini and B. Migliorini: 1942, 1950, 1960.]
Papahagi, T.
1963 *Dicționarul dialectului aromân, general și etimologic. Dictionnaire aroumain (macédoroumain) général et étymologique* (București: Ed. Acad.).
Pascu, G.
1925 *Dictionnaire étymologique macédoroumain, I. Les éléments latins et romains, II. Les éléments grecs, turcs, slaves, albanais, germaniques, hongrois, néologismes, créations immédiates, obscurs* (Iași: Cultura Națională).
Pfister, M.
1966 Review of Bloch – Wartburg 1964 and Dauzat – Dubois – Mitterand 1964, *VR* 25: 118-127.
1971 "Der neueste Bloch-Wartburg (lexicologischer Forschungsbericht 1964-68)", *ZRPh* 87: 106-124.
1972 Review of Gamillscheg 1966-68, *VR* 31: 144-159.
1973 "Das Projekt eines italienischen etymologischen Wörterbuches (*IEW*)", *ZRPh* 89: 245-272.
1975 "A propos d'un nouveau dictionnaire de l'ancien français", *TLL* 13: 417-430.
Pico, M. C.
1961-67 "Anotações ao *Dicionário etimológico da língua portuguesa* de José Pedro Machado", *RP* 26: 462-470; 27: 5-9, 68-74, 142-144, 164-170, 223-230, 263-268, 319-322, 448-451, 501-505 (1962); 28: 43-46, 112-113, 161-163, 167-173, 252-254, 332-339, 387-392, 487-491 (1963); 29: 39-42, 81-82, 172-174, 230-232, 411-416 (1964); 30: 37-42, 56-61, 108-110, 152-154, 203-205 (1965); 31: 61-68, 114-118, 157-158, 195-197, 254-257, 343-344 (1966); 32: 28-34, 109-112, 259-261, 291-295, 474-477 (1967).

Picoche, Jacqueline
  1971   *Nouveau dictionnaire étymologique du français* (Paris: Hachette-Tchou).
Piel, J. M.
  1960   "Ein neues portugiesisches etymologisches Wörterbuch", *RF* 72: 449-455.
  1961   "De l'ancien *REW* au nouveau *REW*", in: Imbs 1961: 221-239.
  1963   "Beiträge zu einem galicischen etymologischen Wörterbuch", in: *Wort und Text. Festschrift Fritz Schalk* (Frankfurt am Main: Klostermann), 83-100.
Prati, A.
  1951   *Vocabulario etimologico italiano* (Milano: Garzanti).
Pult, C. – A. Schorta – A. Maissen – A. Decurtins – J. C. Arquint
  1939   *Dicziunari Rumantsch Grischun* (Cuoira/Chur: Società Retorumantscha).
Puşcariu, S.
  1905   *Etymologisches Wörterbuch der rumänischen Sprache, I. Lateinisches Element, mit Berücksichtigung aller romanischen Sprachen* (Heidelberg: Winter).
Rohlfs, Gerhard
  1930   *Etymologisches Wörterbuch der unteritalienischen Gräzität* (Halle: Niemeyer). [2nd edition 1964, *Lexicon Graecanicum Italiae Inferioris* (Tübingen: Niemeyer).]
Ruiz y Ruiz, L. A.
  1964   *A tentative Portuguese dictionary of dated first occurrences in certain documents between 1351-1450* (Unpublished Ph. D. Dissertation, Univ. of Pennsylvania).
Schwake, H. P.
  1970   Review of Alsdorf Bollée – Burr 1969, *ZRPh* 80: 373-384.
Souter, A.
  1964   *A glossary of Later Latin to 600 A. D.* (3rd edition) (Oxford: U.P.).
Spitzer, Leo
  1922   "Aus Anlass von Gamillscheg's 'Französische Etymologien' ", *ZRPh* 42: 5-34.
  1926   "Ein neues französisches etymologisches Wörterbuch", *ZRPh* 46: 563-617.
  1956-59   "A New Spanish etymological dictionary", *MLN* 71: 271-283, 373-386; 72: 579-591; 74: 127-149.
Sykorra, W.
  1973   *Friedrick Diez' Etymologisches Wörterbuch der romanischen Sprachen und seine Quellen (= RVV 47)* (Bonn: Rom. Sem.).
Tamás, L.
  1967   *Etymologisches-historisches Wörterbuch der ungarischen Elemente im Rumänischen unter Berücksichtigung der Mundartwörter (= Indiana University Publications, Uralic and Altaic Series 83)* (Bloomington, Ind.: Indiana U.P./The Hague: Mouton).
Tiktin, H.
  1897-1927
          Rumänisch-deutsches Wörterbuch 3 vols. (Bucureşti: Staatsdruckerei).
Vaccaro, G.
  1966-68   *Dizionario delle parole nuovissime e difficile. Supplemento annuale a tutti Vocabulari della lingua italiana* 3 vols. (Roma: Romana libri alfabeto).
Vàrvaro, Alberto
  1975   *Vocabolario etimologico siciliano* (Palermo).
Vigón, B.
  1955   *Vocabulario dialectológico del Concejo de Colunga,* edited by A. M. Vigón Sánchez, *RFE,* anejo 63. (Madrid: CSIC).

Vinja, V.
1957 "Contributions dalmates au *Romanisches etymologisches Wörterbuch* de W. Meyer-Lübke", *RLR* 21: 249-269.
1959 "Nouvelles contributions au *Romanisches etymologisches Wörterbuch* de W. Meyer-Lübke", *SRAZ* 7: 17-34.
1967 "Notes étymologiques dalmates en marge au *REW*", *SRAZ* 23: 119-135.
1972-73 "Romanica et dalmatica dans le premier dictionnaire étymologique croate ou serbe", *SRAZ* 33-36: 547-571.
Wagner, Max Leopold
1953 "Etymologische Randbemerkungen zu neueren ibero-romanischen Dialektarbeiten und Wörterbüchern", *ZRPh* 69: 347-391.
1953-55 "Disquisições etimológicas sobre algumas palavras portuguesas", *RPF* 6: 1-35.
1956 "Entgegnung auf Yakov Malkiels Kritik meiner 'Etymologischen Randbemerkungen zu neueren ibero-romanischen Dialektarbeiten und Wörterbüchern'", *RF* 68: 443-450.
1957 "Das Sardische im *Diccionario crítico de la lengua castellana* von J. Corominas", *RF* 69: 241-272.
1957-64 *Dizionario etimologico sardo* 3 vols. (Heidelberg: Winter).
1958 "Einiges über die Vorgeschichte, die Entstehung und die Anlage des *Dizionario etimologico sardo*", in: Keller, 1958: 843-855.
Walde, A. – J. B. Hofmann
1938-56 *Lateinisches etymologisches Wörterbuch* 3 vols. (Heidelberg: Winter).
Wartburg, Walther von
1922 *Französisches etymologisches Wörterbuch. Eine Darstellung des galloromanischen Sprachschatzes* (Volume I Leipzig: Klopp; later volumes Basel: Helbing and Lichtenhahn).
1929 "Das Schriftfranzösische im *Französischen etymologischen Wörterbuch*", in: *Behrens-Festschrift; Dietrich Behrens zum 70. Geburtstag, dargebracht von Schülern und Freunden* (= *ZFSL* Supplementheft 13) (Jena/Leipzig: Gronau and Agricola), 48-55.
1954 "Le *Französisches etymologisches Wörterbuch:* Évolution et problèmes actuels", *Word* 10: 288-305.
1959 "Remarques sur les mots français dans le dictionnaire de M. Corominas", *RLR* 23: 207-260.
1961 "L'expérience du FEW", in: Imbs 1961: 209-218.
1969 "Specimens d'une nouvelle rédaction d'articles parus dans le premier volume du *Französisches etymologisches Wörterbuch*", in: *Mélanges offerts à Rita Lejeune* (Gembloux: Duculot) 2: 1685-1696.
Zumthor, Paul
1955 "Évolution et structure du *Französisches etymologisches Wörterbuch (FEW)*", *Orbis* 4: 200-213.

Appendix II:
Selected bibliographies (relating to lexical studies)

Atzori, M. T.
  1953 *Bibliografia di linguistica sarda* (Firenze: Valmartina).
Baldinger, Kurt
  1969 "Kurt Baldinger: notice bio-bibliographique à l'occasion de son cinquantième anniversaire", by H. P. Schwake, *RLR* 33: 392-405.
  1975 *Notice bio-bibliographique (années 1969-1974) à l'occasion de son 55ᵉ anniversaire* (Strasbourg: Centre de Philologie et de Littératures Romanes).
Baldinger, Kurt – Bernard Pottier
  1956-58 "Bibliographie des études lexicales", *RLR* 20: 323-8; 21: 138-144; 22: 141-150.
Borodina, Meletina Aleksandrovna – V. B. Chemietillo – Vladimir Grigorevich Gak
  1962 "Bibliographie des études lexicales en URSS (1945-59)", *RLR* 26: 184-223.
Butler, Jonathan L.
  1975 Bibliography in homage issue of *RomPh* 28: 430-433.
Centre national de recherche scientifique
  1966- *Bibliographie des chroniques de langage publiées dans la presse française* (Paris: Didier).
Current Trends
  1972 *Linguistics in Western Europe* (= *Current Trends in Linguistics* 9) edited by T. E. Sebeok (The Hague: Mouton).
Dolç, Miguel
  1951 "Estudios de lexicografía catalana", *Arbor* 20: 212-16.
Ducháček, Otto
  1971 Bibliography, *ERB* 5: 9-10.
Goddard, K. A.
  1977 "Bibliographie des mots d'emprunt dans les langues romanes, I. Les influences étrangères sur le roumain", *RLR* 41: 162-87.
Gorog, R. P. de
  1967 "Bibliografia de estudos do vocabulario português (1950-65)", *LBrR* 4:1. 83-100; 4:2. 95-110.
  1973 "Bibliographie des études de l'onomasiologie dans le domaine du français", *RLR* 37: 419-446.
Hall, Robert A. Jr.
  1941 *Bibliography of Italian linguistics* (Baltimore: LSA).

1958   *Bibliografia della linguistica italiana* 3 vols. (= *Biblioteca bibliografica italica 13-15)* (Firenze: Sansoni).

1969   *Primo supplemento decennale* (= *Biblioteca bibliographica italica* 35) (Firenze: Sansoni).

1973   *Bibliografia essenziale della linguistica italiana e romanza* (Firenze: Sansoni).

Haugen, Einar

1956   *Bilingualism in the Americas. A bibliography and research guide* (Alabama: U.P.).

Levy, R. – L. Poston

1957   "A bibliography of longer French word studies", *RLR* 21: 145-182.

Levy, R. – N. C. W. Spence

1961   "A supplementary bibliography of longer French word studies", *RLR* 25: 144-160.

Lloyd, Paul M.

1963-4 "An analytical survey of studies in Romance word-formation", *RomPh* 17: 736-70.

Mackey, W. F.

1972   *Bibliographie internationale sur le bilinguisme: International bibliography on bilingualism* (Quebec).

Malkiel, Yakov

1969   Yakov Malkiel y Francisco Rico "Breve autobibliografía analítica", *AEM* 6: 609-639.

Muljačic, Žarko

1969   "Bibliographie de linguistique romane: domaine dalmate et istriote avec les zones limitrophes (1906-66)", *RLR* 33: 144-167, 356-391.

Negraru, Maria – Aurora Moţiu-Marcus

1971   *Formarea cuvintelor în limba română. Cercetare bibliografică* (Bucureşti: Bibl. Centrală Univ.).

Poghirc, Cicerone

1969   "Problèmes actuels de l'étymologie roumaine: bibliographie selective, I. Dictionnaires, II. Études" (Mimeographed. Univ. of Bucharest, Summer Session. Sinaia).

Price, Glanville

1969   *The present position of minority languages in Western Europe: A select bibliography* (Cardiff: U.P. Wales).

1972   "A bibliography of the present position of minority languages in Western Europe: First supplement", *Orbis* 21: 235-47.

RFE

1969   *Indice de voces y morfemas de la RFE (1-45)* by Elena Alvar (= *RFE* Anejo 88) (Madrid: CSIC).

Revista Lusitana

1967   *Indices, 1-38: 1887-1943* (Lisboa: Centro de Estudos Filológicos).

RLR

1969   *Table des mots 1-30* by P. Gardette.

Romania

1906   *Table des trente premiers volumes* (1872-1901) by A. Bos (Paris: Champion).

RomPh.

1974   *Bibliographical index* ... by M. G. Littlefield (Berkeley: California U.P.).

Romero-Navarro, Miguel

1951   *Registro de lexicografía hispánica* (= *RFE* Anejo 54) (Madrid: CSIC).

Santos, M. J. de Moura
1966   *Os estudos de linguística românica em Portugal de 1945 a 1960* (= Suplemento bibliográfico da *RPF* 2) (Coimbra: Casa do Castelo).

Schmitt, R.
1972   „Bibliographie de lexicologie française", *RLaR* 80: 421–25.

Tilander, Gunnar
1973   *Gunnar Tilander, Publications 1918-1973. Bibliographie établie en l'honneur du 50ième anniversaire de sa soutenance de thèse* by H. Bohrn (= *Acta Bibliothecae Regiae Stockholmiensis* 5) (Stockholm).

Wagner, Max Leopold
1954-5   "Bibliografia di Max Leopold Wagner" by G. Manuppella, *BF* 15: 39-124.
1967-8   "Supplementary bibliography of the writings of Max Leopold Wagner. A: Corrections, B: Additions to G. Manuppella's List (1954-55)", by J. L. Butler, *RomPh.* 21. 533-536.
1970   *Bibliografia degli scritti di Max Leopold Wagner*, by G. Manuppella (= *Boletim da Biblioteca da Universidade* 29) (Coimbra).

Wartburg, Walther von
1934   *Bibliographie des dictionnaires patois* (= Société de publications romanes et françaises 8) (Paris: Droz). [2nd edition with H.-E. Keller and R. Geuljans.]
1969   *Bibliographie des dictionnaires patois galloromans (1550-1967)* (= *Publications romanes et françaises* 103) (Geneva: Droz).
1971   *Walther von Wartburg 1888-1971. Beiträge zu Leben und Werk nebst einem vollständigen Schriftenverzeichnis* (Sonderheft zur *ZRPh)* (Tübingen: Niemeyer).
1974   "Walther von Wartburg", *Sonderdruck aus Jahrbuch (1971-2) Sächsische Akademie der Wissenschaft zu Leipzig:* 371-417.

Zolli, Paolo
1973   *Bibliografia dei dizionari specializzati italiani del XIX secolo* (Firenze: Olschki).

ZRPh
1910   *Register 1-30* by L. Beszard (Halle: Niemeyer).
1932   *Register 31-50* by F. Zimmerman (Halle: Niemeyer).

Bibliography

Abel, Fritz
  1971 *L'adjectif démonstratif dans la langue de la Bible latine. Etude sur la formation des systèmes déictiques et de l'article défini des langues romanes*, ZRPh Beiheft 125.
Academia RPR
  1965-1969 *Istoria limbii române*, 2 vols. (Bucureşti: Ed. Acad.).
Adami, Vittorio
  1935 *Vocaboli italiani nella lingua francese* (Milano: Tipografia pontificia S. Giuseppe).
Adams, J. N.
  1977 *The Vulgar Latin of the letters of Claudius Terentianus* (Manchester: U.P.).
Aebischer, Paul
  1944 "Les plus anciens témoignages de la diphtongaison de ę et ǫ libres en Italie", *ZRPh* 64: 364-370.
  1948 "Contribution à la protohistoire des articles *ille* et *ipse* dans les langues romanes", *CultNeol* 8: 181-203.
  1948a "GRANICA 'grange' et sa descendance dans les dialectes italiens et les langues de la Péninsule Ibérique", *RPF* 2: 201-219.
  1948b *Estudios de toponimia y lexicografía románicas* (Barcelona: Escuela de filología).
  1951 "*Argentum* et *plata* en ibéro-roman. Etude de stratigraphie linguistique", in Dauzat (ed.) 1951: 11-21.
  1960 "La finale -*e* du féminin pluriel italien", *SLI* 1: 5-48.
  1971 "Le pluriel -*ās* de la première déclinaison latine et ses résultats dans les langues romanes", *ZRPh* 87: 74-98.
Agard, F. B.— J. E. Grimes
  1959 "Linguistic divergence in Romance", *Lg* 35: 598-604.
Ageno, Franca Brambilla
  1964 *Il verbo nell'italiano antico. Ricerche di sintassi* (Milano/Napoli: Ricciardi).
Alarcos Llorach, Emilio
  1950 *Fonología española según el método de la escuela de Praga* (Madrid: Gredos) (4th edition 1965 as *Fonología española*).
  1951a "Esbozo de una fonología diacrónica del español", *Estudios dedicados a Ramón Menéndez Pidal* (Madrid: CSIC, 1950-1951) 2: 9-39.
  1951b "Alternancia de «f» y «h» en los arabismos", *Archivum* 1: 29-41.
  1957 "Algunas consideraciones sobre la evolución del consonantismo catalán", *Miscelánea homenaje a André Martinet. Estructuralismo e historia* (La Laguna: U.P.) 2: 5-48.
  1958 "Quelques précisions sur la diphtongaison espagnole", *Omagiu lui Iorgu Iordan cu prilejul împlinirii a 70 de ani* (Bucureşti: Ed. Acad.), 1-4.
  1960 "La constitución del vocalismo catalán", *Studia philologica. Homenaje ofrecido a Dámaso Alonso por sus amigos y discípulos con ocasión de su 60° aniversario*, edited by Diego Catalán (Madrid: Gredos) 1: 35-49.
  1962 "Efectos de la yod sobre la vocal tónica en castellano", in *Cong*, 10.3: 945-950.
  1975 *Bibliografía* (Mieres: Inst. 'Bernado de Quiros').

Alessio, Giovanni
1934 "Il sostrato latino nel lessico e nell'epo-toponomastica della Calabria meridionale", *ID* 10: 111-190.
1936 "Nuovi elementi italici nel lessico neolatino", *Annali dell'Università di Trieste* 8: 3-13.
1937 "Una voce toscana di origine etrusca", *SE* 11: 253-262.
1938-1944 "Nuovo contributo al problema della grecità dell'Italia Meridionale", *RIL* 72: 109-172, 74: 631-706, 77: 617-706.
1951-1955 *Grammatica storica francese,* 2 vols. (Bari: Leonardo da Vinci).
1952 "Parole oscure del territorio alpino", *AAAd* 46: 547-671.
1953 "Problemi di etimologia romanza (I)", *RLR* 17: 20-75.
1955 *Le lingue indoeuropee nell'ambiente mediterraneo* (Bari: L'Adriatica).
1962a "Sopravvivenza del sostrato pre-indoeuropee mediterraneo dell'ag-geminazione di liquide e nasali ...", *Atti Accademia Pontaniana* 9: 103-127.
1962b "Problemi storico-linguistici messapici", *Studi Salentini* 14: 293-330.
1971 "Riflessi lessicali italici", *Abruzzo* 9: 33-87.
1974 *Lexicon etymologicum. Supplemento ai lessici etimologici latini e romanzi* (Napoli: Liguori).
Alfaro, R. J.
1948 "El anglicismo en el español contemporáneo", *Thesaurus* 4: 102-128.
Ali, M. Said
1930 *Meios de expressão e alterações semânticas* (Rio de Janeiro).
Alinei, Mario
1962 "Di un antico esito di j postconsonantica in italiano", in *Cong.* 10.3: 965-989.
1967-1968 "Evaluation of semantic isoglosses with regard to Romance dialects", *Verhandlungen des Zweiten internationalen Dialektologenkongresses,* edited by L. E. Schmitt (Wiesbaden).
1974 *La struttura del lessico* (Bologna: Mulino).
Allen, Andrew
1977 "The interfix *i/esc* in Catalan and Rumanian", *RomPh* 31: 203-211.
Allen, J. H. D.
1964 "Tense/lax in Castilian Spanish", *Word* 20: 295-321.
Allen, W. S.
1965 *Vox Latina - the pronunciation of Classical Latin* (Cambridge: U.P.).
Almeida, Maria H. M. de
1964 *Castelhanismos na literatura portuguesa do século XVII,* Dissertação de licenciatura (Coimbra, unpublished).
Almeida, V. de
1959 *Aspectos de filosofia da linguagem* (Coimbra).
Alonso, Amado
1943 *Castellano, español, idioma nacional. Historia espiritual de tres nombres* (2nd edition) (Buenos Aires) [1st edition 1938].
1943a "Partición de las lenguas románicas de Occidente", *Miscellania Fabra* (Buenos Aires), 81-101; reprinted in Alonso 1951a: 101-127.
1946 "Las correspondencias arábigo-españolas en los sistemas de sibilantes", *Revista de filología hispánica* 8: 12-76.
1951 "La «LL» y sus alteraciones en España y América", *Estudios dedicados a Ramón Menéndez Pidal* (Madrid: CSIC) 2: 41-89.
1951a *Estudios lingüísticos: temas españoles* (Madrid: Gredos).

1954   *Estudios lingüísticos: temas hispanoamericanos* (Madrid: Gredos) (2nd edition 1961).
1955-1969   *De la pronunciación medieval a la moderna en español,* 2 vols. (Madrid: Gredos).
Alonso, Dámaso
1958   "Metafonía y neutro de materia in España", *ZRPh* 74: 1-24.
1962   "La fragmentación fonética peninsular", in Alvar et al. (eds.) 1960-1962, Supplement 1.
1972-1973   *Obras completas: I Estudios lingüísticos peninsulares; II Estudios y ensayos sobre literatura* (Madrid: Gredos).
Alonso, Martín
1962   *Evolución sintáctica del español. Sintaxis histórica del español desde el iberorromano hasta nuestros días* (Madrid: Aguilar).
ALPI
1962-   *Atlas lingüístico de la península ibérica,* edited by T. Navarro Tomás, R. de Balbín et al. (Madrid: CSIC).
Alsdorf-Bollet, Annegret
1970   *Die lateinischen Verbalabstrakta der u-Deklination und ihre Umbildungen im Romanischen* (Bonn: Rom. Sem.).
Altieri Biagi, Maria Luisa
1963   "Note sulla lingua della pubblicità", *LN* 3: 86-93.
1965   "Studi sulla lingua della commedia toscana del primo settecento", *AMAT* 30: 251-378.
Alvar López, Manuel
1953   *El dialecto aragonés* (Madrid: Gredos).
Alvar López, Manuel et al.
1960-1962   *Enciclopedia lingüística hispánica* (Madrid: CSIC).
Ambrosini, Riccardo
1968   "Italica o anatolica la lingua dei graffiti di Segesta (?)", *SSL* 8: 160-172.
1970a   "Problemi e ipotesi sulla lingua dei graffiti di Segesta", *RALinc S. 8* 25: 461-474.
1970b   "A proposito di una recente publicazione sulla lingua dei graffiti di Segesta", *SSL* 10: 232-237.
Anderson, James – Jo Ann Creore (eds.)
1972   *Readings in Romance linguistics* (The Hague: Mouton).
Anderson, John M. – C. Jones (eds.)
1974   *Historical linguistics. Proceedings of the First International Conference, Edinburgh 1973* (Amsterdam: North Holland).
Andersson, Sven
1952   *Nouvelles études sur la syntaxe et la sémantique du mot français 'tout'* (= *Etudes romanes de Lund* 14) (Lund: Gleerup/København: Munksgaard).
Anttila, Raimo
1972   *An introduction to historical and comparative linguistics* (New York: MacMillan/London: Collier-MacMillan).
Aronoff, Mark
1976   *Word formation in a generative grammar* (= *Linguistic Inquiry* monograph 1) (Cambridge, Mass.: M.I.T.).
Arveiller, Raymond
1949   "Mots orientaux. Notes lexicologiques, nouvelles datations", *FM* 17: 129-142.
1951   "Mots orientaux. Notes lexicologiques", in Dauzat (ed.) 1951: 23-32.

302   Bibliography

1963   *Contribution à l'étude des termes de voyage en français (1505-1722)* (Paris).
1976   Review of Gebhardt 1974, *FM* 44: 167-170.
Arvinte, V.
1964   "Elemente retoromane în terminologia forestiera romînească", *SCL* 15: 643-659.
1965   "Critères pour déterminer les emprunts saxons dans la langue roumaine", *RRLing* 10: 127-132.
1967   *Die deutschen Lehnwörter in den rumänischen Mundarten (auf Grund des rumänischen Sprachatlasses)* (Berlin).
1968   "Zu den altgermanischen Wörtern im Rumänischen", in Meier – Roth 1968: 7-26.
Ascoli, Graziado Isaia
1873   "Saggi ladini", *AGI* 1: 1–556.
1878   "Schizzi franco-provenzali", *AGI* 3: 61-120.
1880   "Versione letterale e annotata del testo soprasilvano 'Barlaam e Giosafat'", *AGI* 7: 365-602.
1881-1882   "Lettere glottologiche: Prima lettera", *RFIC* 10: 1-79.
1882   "L' Italia dialettale", *AGI* 8: 98–128.
1886   "Due recenti lettere glottologiche", *AGI* 10: 1-108.
1929   *Silloge linguistica. Dedicato alla memoria di Graziado Isaia Ascoli nel primo centenario della nascita* (Torino).
Auerbach, Erich
1949   *Introduction aux études de philologie romanes* (Frankfurt: Klostermann). [English translation by Guy Daniels: *Introduction to Romance languages and literature: Latin, Spanish, Provençal, Italian* (New York: Capricorn Books, 1961).]
d'Avalle, A. S.
1965   *Protostoria delle lingue romanze* (Torino).
1968   *Bassa latinità. Il latino tra l'età tardo-antica e l'alto medioevo con particolare riguardo all'origine delle lingue romanze. Vocalismo* (Torino).
Avram, Andrei
1968   "Parallèles phonétiques et phonologiques roumaino-portugaises", in *Cong.* 11. 3: 1067-1078.
1969   "Sur le traitement roumain des voyelles latines accentuées précédées et suivies de consonnes nasales", *Bulletin de la Société roumaine de linguistique romane* 6: 7-17.
1970-1971   "Parallèles romans dans l'évolution des consonnes vibrantes", in *Cong.* 12.1: 299-304.
Bach, Kathryn F. – Glanville Price
1977   *Romance linguistics and the Romance languages: A bibliography of bibliographies* (London: Grant & Cutler).
Badía Margarit, Antonio
1947   *Los complementos pronominalo-adverbiales derivados de ibi e inde en la península ibérica* (Madrid).
1951   *Gramática histórica catalana* (Barcelona: Noguer).
1953   "El subjuntivo de subordinación en las lenguas romances y especialmente en iberorománico", *RFE* 37: 95-129.
1962   "Nuevas precisiones sobre la diptongación española", *RLR* 26: 1-12.
1966   *Llengua i cultura als països catalans* (2nd edition) (Barcelona: Edicions 62) [1st edition 1964].

1969   *La llengua dels barcelonins. Resultats d'una enquesta sociologico-lingüística* (Barcelona: Edicions 62). [2 volumes published to date.]

1971   "Notice bio-bibliographique à l'occasion de son cinquantième anniversaire", *RLR* 35: 182-196.

1972   "Langue et société dans le domaine linguistique catalan, notamment à Barcelone", *RLR* 36: 263-304.

1973a   *La llengua catalana ahir e avui* (Barcelona: Curial).

1973b   "Les morceaux français de la *Chronique catalane* de Bernat Desclot", *TLL* 11: 533-540.

Badía Margarit, A. – J. Massot i Muntaner – J. Molas

1970   *Situación actual de los estudios de lengua y literatura catalanas* (= *Norte* 11.1,2).

Baehrens, W. A.

1922   *Sprachlicher Kommentar zur vulgärlateinischen Appendix Probi* (Halle).

Bahner, W.

1963   "În legătură cu studiile despre elementele germane din vocabulariul limbii române", *CLing* 8: 83-93.

1968   "Le néologisme et le problème de la synonymie en roumain comparé à d'autres langues romanes", in *Cong.* 11.2: 638-639.

1971a   "Cercetarea vocabularului limbii străromâne din punctul de vedere onomasiologic", in *Cong.* 12.2: 1311-1316.

1971b   "Unele observaţii asupra trăsăturita specifice ale lexicului în prima perioadă a istorici limbii române", *LbR* 20: 141-149.

1971c   *Die lexikalischen Besonderheiten des Frühromanischen in Südosteuropa* (= *Sitzungsberichte der Sächsischen Akademie der Wissenschaften zu Leipzig* 115.3) (Berlin: Akademie).

Bakel, J. V.

1968   "Transformational etymology", *Orbis* 17: 435-458.

Balasz, L.

1964   "Accentul în cuvintele româneşti de origine maghiară", *CLing* 9: 67-94.

Baldinger, Kurt

1950   *Kollektivsuffixe und Kollektivbegriff. Ein Beitrag zur Bedeutungslehre im Französischen mit Berücksichtigung der Mundarten* (Berlin).

1953   "Der Begriff 'während'", *ZRPh* 69: 305-340.

1957   "Contribution à une histoire des provincialismes dans la langue française", *RLR* 21: 62-92.

1958   *Die Herausbildung der Sprachräume auf der Pyrenäenhalbinsel. Querschnitt durch die neueste Forschung und Versuch einer Synthese* (Berlin: Akademie). [Spanish translation by Emilio Lledó and Montserrat Macau, *La formación de los dominios lingüísticos en la península Ibérica* (Madrid: Gredos, 1963, 2nd edition 1972).]

1958-1959   "L'étymologie hier et aujourd'hui", *CAIEF* 10-11: 233-264.

1963   [Translation of Baldinger 1958; 2nd edition 1972.]

1965   "La pesadilla de los etimólogos", *RFE* 48: 95-104.

1966   "Les mots lyonnais et franco-provençaux en français", *TLL* 4: 59-80.

1968   "Fr. *laie, layer,* die germanische Waldwirtschaft und eine neue Etymologie", in Gamillscheg 1968: 49-56.

1969   "Zur Entwicklung der Tabakindustrie und ihrer Terminologie", in Piel 1969: 30-61.

1969a   "Notice bio-bibliographique à l'occasion de son cinquantième anniversaire", *RLR* 33: 392-405.

304   Bibliography

1970   *Teoría semantica. Hacía una semantica moderna* (Madrid: Alcalà). [2nd edition 1977; French and English translations to appear.]

1973   "A propos de l'influence de la langue sur la pensée: étymologie populaire et changement sémantique parallèle", *RLR* 37: 241-273.

1974   *Introduction aux dictionnaires les plus importants pour l'histoire du français* (Paris: Klincksieck).

1975   *Notice bio-bibliographique à l'occasion de son 55ᵉ anniversaire* (Strasbourg: Centre de philologie et de littératures romanes).

Baldonado, Joanne Martin
1975   "Problems in New World lexical 'survivals'", *RomPh* 29: 229-240.

Baralt, R. M.
1874   *Diccionario de galicismos, o sea de las voces, locuciones y frases de la lengua francesa que se han introducido en el habla castellana moderna* (2nd edition) (Madrid).

Barić, H.
1954   "Istočnogermanski i langobardski elementi u rumunskom jeziku [Proto-Germanic and Langobardian elements in the Rumanian language]", in H. Barić, *Lingvisticke studje* (= *Naučno društvo NR Bosne i Hercegovine, Djela,* knj.1; *Odjeljenje istorisko-filoloških nauka, Djela,* knj.1) (Sarajevo).

Bàrtoli, Matteo
1906   *Das Dalmatische: altromanische Sprachreste von Veglia bis Ragusa und ihre Stellung in der appennino-balkanischen Romania* (= *Kaiserliche Akademie der Wissenschaften, Schriften der Balkan-Kommission, Ling. Abt.* 4-5. *Romanische Dialektstudien* 2: 1,2) (Wien: Holder).

1925   *Introduzione alla Neolinguistica* (Genève: Olschki).

Bascetta, Carlo
1962   *Il linguaggio sportivo contemporaneo* (Firenze: Sansoni).
1963   "Il linguaggio delle 'ricerche del mercato'", *LN* 24: 13-20.

Batany, Jean
1972   *Français médiéval* (Paris: Bordas).

Battisti, Carlo
1927   "Appunti sulla storia e sulla diffusione dell'ellenismo nell'Italia meridionale", *RLiR* 3: 1-91.
1930   "Aspirazione etrusca e gorgia toscana", *SE* 4: 249-254.
1949   *Avviamento allo studio del latino volgare* (Bari: Leonardo da Vinci).
1959   *Sostrati e parastrati nell'Italia preistorica* (Firenze: Olschki).

Beardsmore, H. Beatens
1971   "A gender problem in a language contact situation", *Lingua* 27: 141-159.

Bec, Pierre
1968   *Les interférences linguistiques entre gascon et languedocien dans les parlers du Comminges et du Couserans* (Paris: P.U.F.).
1970-1971 *Manuel pratique de philologie romane* I (1970), II (1971, with collaboration of O. Nandriş and Z. Muljačić) (Paris: Picard).

Beccaria, Gian Luigi
1964   "Alcuni ispanismi", *LN* 25: 102-105.
1966   "Ova misside", *LN* 27: 10-12.
1968a   *Spagnolo e spagnoli in Italia. Riflessi ispanici sulla lingua italiana del Cinque e del Seicento* (Torino: Giapichelli).
1968b   "Luoghi comuni e tramiti letterarî dell'ispanismo in Italia: It. *vigliacco*", *Omaggio a Benvenuto Terracini* (Milano), 39-56.

Beckmann, Gustav Adolf
1963   *Die Nachfolgekonstruktionen des instrumentalen Ablativs im Spätlatein und im Französischen* (= *ZRPh* Beiheft 106) (Tübingen: Niemeyer).
Beeler, Madison S.
1952   "The relation of Latin and Osco-Umbrian", *Lg* 28: 435-443.
Behrens, D.
1924   *Über deutsches Sprachgut im Französischen* (Giessen).
Benveniste, Emile
1954   "Problèmes sémantiques de la réconstruction", *Word* 10: 251-264.
1966   "Comment s'est formée une différenciation lexicale en français", *CFS* 22: 15-28.
1975   *Langue, discours et société: pour Emile Benveniste* (Paris: Seuil).
Berchem, Theodor
1973   *Studien zum Funktionswandel bei Auxiliaren und Semiauxiliaren in den romanischen Sprachen. Morphologisch-syntaktische Untersuchungen über 'gehen', 'haben', 'sein'* (= *ZRPh* Beiheft 139) (Tübingen: Niemeyer).
Berejan, S.-G.
1971   "Sur l'étude comparée des microstructures lexicales dans les langues apparentées", *BRP* 10: 140-148.
Berger, H.
1899   *Die Lehnwörter in der französischen Sprache ältester Zeit* (Leipzig).
Bertoldi, Vittorio
1931   "Problèmes de substrat. Essai méthodologique dans le domaine préhistorique de la toponymie et du vocabulaire", *BSL* 32: 93-184.
1936   "Nomina tusca in Dioscoride", *SE* 10: 295-320.
1950   *Colonizzazioni nell'antico Mediterraneo occidentale alla luce degli aspetti linguistici* (Napoli: Liguori).
1953   "Contatti e conflitti di lingue nell'antico Mediterraneo", *La parola del passato* 33: 417-448.
Bertoni, Giulio
1923   *Programma di filologia romanza come scienza idealistica* (Genève).
1940   *Profilo linguistico d'Italia* (Roma: Istituto di Filologia).
Bertoni, Giulio - F. Torrefranca - B. Migliorini
1939   "A proposito di 'ouverture' et di 'suite'", *LN* 1: 166-170.
Bezzola, Reto R.
1925   *Abbozzo di una storia dei gallicismi italiani nei primi secoli (730-1300). Saggio storico-linguistico* (Heidelberg: Winter).
Bidu-Vrănceanu, Angela
1974   "Modalités d'analyse structurale de lexique. Le système des dénominations des animaux domestiques", *RRLing* 19: 525-547.
Binder, S.
1965-1968 "Contributti la studiul elementelor germane în lexicul graiurilor populare romanesti", *Analele Universitatii din Timişoara. Seria şţiinte filologice* 3: 103-122, 6: 189-202.
Bjerrome, Gunnar
1957   *Le patois de Bagnes (Valais)* (Stockholm: Almqvist & Wiksell).
Blass, B. A. - D. E. Johnson - W. W. Gage
1969   *A provisional survey of materials for the study of neglected languages* (Washington, D.C.: Center for Applied Linguistics).
Blaylock, Curtis
1964   "The monophthongization of Latin AE in Spanish", *RomPh* 18: 16-24.

1964a "Hispanic metaphony", *RomPh* 18: 253-271.
1975 "The Romance development of the Latin verbal augment *-sk-*", *RomPh* 28: 434-444.
Bloch, O.–W. von Wartburg
1960 *Dictionnaire étymologique de la langue française* (Paris: P.U.F.).
Bloomfield, Leonard
1933 *Language* (New York: Holt).
Boileau, A.
1946 "Le problème du bilinguisme et la théorie des substrats", *RLaV* 12: 113-125, 169-193, 213-224.
1960 "Les procès sémantiques de l'emprunt populaire observés à travers quelques verbes wallons d'origine germanique", *Bulletin du Dictionnaire Wallon* 23: 81-99.
Bolelli, Tristano
1941-1942 "Le voci di origine gallica nel REW di Meyer-Lübke", *ID* 17: 131-194; 18: 33-74, 203-217.
1974 *Studi linguistici in onore di Tristano Bolelli* (Pisa: Pacini).
Boléo, Manuel de Paiva
1944 *Defesa e ilustração da língua* (Coimbra).
1946 *Introdução ao estudo da filologia portuguesa* (Lisboa).
1965 *O problema da importação de palavras e o estudo dos estrangeirismos (em especial dos francesismos) em português* (Coimbra).
1974-1975 *Estudos de linguística portuguesa e romanica* (Coimbra: Acta Universitatis Conimbrigensis).
Bonfante, Giuliano
1959-1960 "La place du roumain parmi les langues romanes", *RER* 7-8: 251-256.
1973 *Studii romeni* (Roma: Soc. Accad. Romena).
1976 *Scritti in onore di Guiliano Bonfante* (Brescia: Paideia).
Bookless, Thomas Charles
1968 *The language of the Spanish press, 1965-1966* (unpublished M. A. thesis, University of Leeds).
1977 *The phenomenon of English loan elements in Spanish and other Romance languages* (unpublished Ph. D. diss., University of Leeds).
Borges, N. O. da C.
1960 *Influência anglo-americana no falar da ilha de S. Miguel (Açores)* (= *RPF* Suplemento 2) (Coimbra).
Bork, H. H.
1969 *Die Familie von lateinisch* quatere *im Romanischen* (= *Romanische Etymologien* 2) (Heidelberg: Winter).
Bosch-Gimpera, P.
1944a "El problema de los orígenes vascos", *Eusko-Jakintza* 3: 39-45.
1944b *El poblamiento antiguo y la formación de los pueblos de España* (Mexico).
Bottiglioni, Gino
1954 *Manuale dei dialetti italici* (Bologna).
1956 "L'Apuania", *QIGUB* 1: 17-23.
Bouda, Karl
1949 *Baskisch-kaukasische Etymologien* (Heidelberg: Winter).
1952 *Neue baskisch-kaukasische Etymologien* (Salamanca).
Boulan, Henri R.
1934 *Les mots d'origine étrangère en français (1650-1700)* (Amsterdam).

Bourciez, Edouard
1899 [1967] *Précis historique de phonétique française* (Paris: Klincksieck). [9th edition 1958; revised by Edouard Bourciez and Jean Bourciez, 1967: *Phonétique française: étude historique.*]
1910 [1967] *Eléments de linguistique romane* (Paris: Klincksieck'. [4th edition 1947; revised by Jean Bourciez, 1967.]
Boutière, Jean
1967 "Les italianismes de 'Biographies' des Troubadours. Les emprunts au vocabulaire", *Mélanges de littérature comparée et de philologie offerts à Mięczysław Brahmer* (Warszawa: PWN), 93-107.
1971 *Mélanges de philologie romanes dédiés à la mémoire de J. Boutière 1899-1967* (Liège: Soledi).
Brandt, Gustav
1944 *La concurrence entre* soi *et* lui, eux, elle(s) (= *Etudes romanes de Lund* 8) (Lund).
Brîncuşi, G.
1963 "Über die einheimischen lexikalischen Elemente im Rumänischen", *RESEE* 1: 309-317.
1966 "Les éléments lexicaux autochtones dans le dialecte aroumain", *RRLing* 11: 549-565.
Brøndal, Viggo
1917 *Substrater og laan i Romansk og Germansk* (København: Gad). [Reprinted as *Substrat et emprunt en roman et en germanique* (Bucureşti/København: Munksgaard, 1948).]
1940 *Præpositionernes teori* (København: Munksgaard). [Reprinted as *Théorie des prépositions* (København: Munksgaard, 1950).]
Brummer, Rudolf
1974 *Sprache, Literatur, Kultur. Romanistische Beiträge* (Bern/Frankfurt: Lang).
Brun, Auguste
1946 *Parlers régionaux. France dialectale et unité française* (Paris/Toulouse).
Brunot, Ferninand
1887 *Précis de la grammaire de la langue française, avec une introduction sur les origines et le développement de cette langue* (Paris: Masson).
1905-1972 *Histoire de la langue française des origines à nos jours* (Paris: Colin) (13 vols., vols. 12-13 by Charles Bruneau).
Brunot, Ferdinand – Charles Bruneau
1933 *Précis de grammaire historique de la langue française* (Paris: Masson) (4th edition 1956).
Buck, Carl D.
1933 *Comparative grammar of Greek and Latin* (Chicago: U.P.).
Budagov, Ruben Aleksandrovič
1963 *Sravnitel'no-semasiologičeskie issledovanija (Romanskie jazyki)* [Comparative-semasiological studies (Romance languages)] (Moskva: U.P.).
1972 *Obščee i romanskoe jazykoznanie* [General and Romance linguistics] (Moskva: U.P.).
Budinsky, Alexander
1881 *Die Ausbreitung der lateinischen Sprache über Italien und die Provinzen des römischen Reiches* (Berlin).
Buescu, V.
1953-1958 "Survivances latines en roumain", *RER* 1: 109-115; 2: 102-113; 3-4: 147-169; 5-6: 139-157.

Bujeniţă, M.
  1966 "Din terminologia nautică românească. III. Termeni marinăreşti de origine francesă", *LbR* 15: 3.

Burgess, Glyn Sheridan
  1970 *Contribution à l'étude du vocabulaire précourtois* (Genève: Droz).

Burkart, R.
  1937 *"Truchement,* histoire d'un mot oriental en français", *Romanoloji Semineri Derghisi* 1 (Istambul).

Burke, J. F.
  1968 "Names and the significance of etymology in the *Libro del cavallero Cifar",* *RR* 59: 161-173.

Burr, I.
  1975 *Lateinisch-romanische Konsonantenverbindungen mit Liquid. Untersuchungen zur Lautgeschichte und Etymologie* (= *RVV* 51) (Bonn: Rom. Sem.).

Buschmann, S.
  1965 *Beiträge zum etymologischen Wörterbuch des Galizischen* (= *RVV* 15) (Bonn: Rom. Sem).

Bustos Tovar, Eugenio
  1960 "Estudios sobre asimilación y disimilación en el ibero-románico", *RFE,* anejo 70.

Bustos Tovar, J. J.
  1974 *Contribución al estudio del cultismo léxico medieval* (Madrid: BRAE Anejo 28).

Butler, Jonathan L.
  1969 "Remarks on the Romance synthetic future", *Lingua* 24: 163-180.
  1972 *Latin -ĪNUS, -ĪNA, -ĬNUS and -ĪNEUS from Proto Indo-European to the Romance languages* (Berkeley: University of California Publications in Linguistics).
  1975 Memorial issue of *RomPh* 26.4.

Buyssens, Eric
  1970 *Linguistique contemporaine: Hommage à Eric Buyssens* (Bruxelles: U.P.).

Çabej, Eqrem
  1962a "Studime rreth etimologjisë se gjuhës shqipe" [Etymological studies in the Albanian language] *Buletin i Universitetit shterëror të Tiranës. Seria shkencat shoqërore* 1: 83-120; 2: 225-232; 3: 49-75.
  1962b "Zur Charakteristik der lateinischen Lehnwörter im Albanischen", *RRLing* 7: 161-199.
  1964 "Einige Grundprobleme der älteren albanischen Sprachgeschichte", *SAlb* 1: 68-89.
  1965 "Betrachtungen über die rumänisch-albanischen Sprachbeziehungen", *RRLing* 10: 101-115.
  1967 "Der Beitrag des Albanischen zum Balkansprachbund", *SAlb* 4: 47-58.

Cagnon, M.–S. Smith
  1971 "Le vocabulaire de l'architecture en France de 1500 à 1550", *CLex* 18: 89-108; 19: 94-108.

Câmara, J. Mattoso jr.
  1964 *Princípios de linguística geral* (4th edition) (Rio de Janeiro).

Campanile, Enrico
  1965 *Rapporti linguistici fra il mondo celtico e il mondo neolatine* (Napoli: Corvino).
  1967 *Appunti sul latino preromanzo* (Napoli).

1969 "Note sulle glosse e sui rapporti linguistici fra siculo e latino", *Studia classica et orientalia A. Pagliaro oblata* (Roma: Bardi), 293-322.
1971 "Due studi sul latino volgare", *ID* 34: 1-64.

Campbell, R. - M. G. Goldin - M. C. Wang
1974 *Linguistic studies in Romance languages* (Georgestown: U.P.).

Camporeale-Giacomelli, G.-G.
1959 "Problemi della stele di Novilara", *I Piceni e la civiltà etrusco-italica* (Firenze: Olschki), 95-104.

Camproux, Charles
1967 "Situation actuelle des lettres d'oc", *NPh* 51: 128-141.
1974 *Les langues romanes* (Paris: P.U.F.).

Candrea, I. A.
1932 *Elementele latine dispărute din limba române* (București).

Canfield, D. L. - J. Cary Davis
1975 *An introduction to Romance linguistics* (S. Illinois U.P.).

Capidan, T.
1940 "Le bilinguisme chez les roumains", *Langue et Littérature, Bulletin de la Section Littéraire de l'Académie Roumaine* 1: 73-94.

Carageani, Georghe
1978 "Dell'influsso italiano sul dialetto aromeno", in *Cong.* 14.2: 427-436.

Caravalheira, Maria dos Santos
1953 *Francesismos na terminologia da culinária portuguesa* (unpublished thesis, Coimbra).

Carlton, Charles Merrit
1973 *A linguistic analysis of a collection of Late Latin documents composed in Ravenna between A.D. 445-700: A quantitative approach* (The Hague: Mouton).

Carnoy, Albert J.
1906 *Le latin d'Espagne d'après les inscriptions* (Bruxelles: Misch & Thron).

Carrascal Sánches, Jésus
1963-1964 "La penetración de la lengua catalana en el dominio gascón", *Archivo de Filología Aragonesa* 14-15: 103-233.

Carroll, J. M. - M. K. Tanenhaus
1975 "Prolegomena to a functional theory of word formation". *Chicago Linguistic Society Parasession on Functionalism:* 47-62.

Carvalho = Herculano de Carvalho

Casagrande, J. - B. Saciuk
1972 *Generative studies in Romance languages* (Rowley, Mass.: Newbury House).

Cassano, P.-V.
1972 "The French influence on the Spanish of the River Plate", *Orbis* 21.1: 174-182.

Castellani, Arrigo
1952 *Nuovi testi fiorentini del Dugento con introduzione, trattazione linguistica e glossario*, 2 vols. (Firenze: Sansoni).
1961 "Precisazioni sulla gorgia toscana", in *Cong* 9.2: 241-262.
1962 "Quelques remarques à propos de la diphtongaison toscane. Réponse à M. Schürr", *ZRPh* 68: 482-502.
1965 "La diphtongaison des 'e' et 'o' ouverts en italien", in *Cong.* 10. 3: 951-964.
1970 "Ancora sul dittongamento italiano e romanzo, seconda risposta a Friedrich Schürr", *CultNeol* 30: 117-130.

Castello, M.
1954 "Gli italianismi della lingua spagnola", *Bollettino dell'Istituto di lingue estere* 3: 26-45.
Castro, A.
1924 "Los Galicismos", in *Lengua, enseñanza y literatura* (= *Biblioteca española de divulgación cientifica* 5) (Madrid: Suárez).
1948 *España en su historia: cristianos, moros y judíos* (Buenos Aires: Losada).
1950 "Antiguo español *fijodalgo – ibn-al-homs*", *RomPh* 4: 57-53.
Catalán, Diego
1954 "Resultados ápico-palatales y dorso-palatales de -LL- y -NN-", *RFE* 38: 1-44.
1957 "The end of the phoneme /z/ in Spanish", *Word* 13: 283-322.
1972 "Ibero-Romance", in *Current Trends* 9.2: 927-1127.
Catalán, Diego – Álvaro Galmés
1954 "La diptongación en leonés", *Archivum* 4: 87-147.
Cavaliere, Alfredo
1949-1950 *Introduzione allo studio della filologia romanza* (Milano: La Goliardica).
Chaurand, Jacques
1977 *Introduction à l'histoire du vocabulaire français* (Paris: Bordas).
Chaves, Luís
1944 "Apontamentos e notas de um português", *RP* 4 (No. 18, March 1944): 201-203.
Chelara, V. Gr. – Elisabeta Soşa
1970 "Eléments lexicaux de structure romane dans le premier document roumain original (1521)", in *Cong.* 12.1: 995-1010.
Chevalier, Jean-Claude
1968 *Histoire de la syntaxe. Naissance de la notion du complément* (= *Publications romanes et françaises* 100) (Genève: Droz).
Cigna, M.
1957 "I gallicismi nel *Raguet* di Scipione Maffei", *LN* 18: 63-68.
Ciureanu, P.
1951-1953 "Parole commerciali francesi di origine italiana. Note storico-linguistiche", *Bollettina dell'Istituto di lingue estere* 1: 25-48; 2: 89-92.
Claussen, Th.
1904 "Die griechischen Wörter im Französischen", *RF* 15: 774-883.
Clifford, Paula M.
1973 *Inversion of the subject in French narrative prose from 1500 to the present day* (= *Publications of the Philosophical Society* 24) (Oxford: Blackwell).
Close, Elizabeth
1974 *The development of Modern Rumanian. Linguistic theory and practice in Muntenia 1821-1838* (Oxford: U.P.).
Coelho, J. do Prado
1955 "Garrett prosador", *Revista da Faculdade de Letras de Lisboa* 21.1.
Cohen, Marcel
1943 "Langage et transfusions de civilisation", *Annales Sociologiques,* séries E, F 3: 1-15.
1947 *Histoire d'une langue: le français, des lointaines origines à nos jours* (Paris: Editions Hier et Aujourd'hui) (3rd edition 1967).
1970 *Mélanges Marcel Cohen: Etudes de linguistique, éthnographie et sciences connexes offertes par ses élèves à l'occasion de son 80ᵉ anniversaire. Avec des articles et études inédits de Marcel Cohen* (The Hague: Mouton).
1971 *Matériaux pour une sociologie du langage* (Paris: Albin Michel).

Colón, Germá
  1958   "Español antiguo *encobar, encobo, encobamiento*", in Wartburg 1958: 129-154.
  1962   "L'étymologie organique dans le cas du français *orin* et de l'espagnol *orinque*",
          RLR 26: 170-183.
  1966   "Un problema de préstamo: español *turrón*", *TLL* 4: 105-114.
  1967a "Catalanismos", *Enciclopedia lingüística hispánica* 2: 193-238.
  1967b "Occitanismos", *Enciclopedia lingüística hispánica* 2: 153-192.
  1957c Review of Buschmann 1965, *VR* 26: 376-378.
  1973a "Ein volkstümlicher Fortsetzer von *indagare*", *ASNS* 210: 279-294.
  1973b "Quelques considérations sur le lexique catalan", in *La linguistique catalane*
          edited by A. Badía Margarit and G. Straka (Paris: Klincksieck).
  1976   *El léxico catalán en la Romania* (Madrid: Gredos).
Cong. 7
  1955   *Actes et mémoires*, 2 vols. (Barcelona: San Cugat del Vallès).
Cong. 9
  1961-1962   *Actas do IX Congresso internacional de lingüística romanica (Lisboa 31 de
          Março - 4 de Abril de 1959)*, 3 vols. (Lisboa: Centro de estudos filológicos).
Cong. 10
  1965   *Actes du Xᵉ Congrès international de linguistique et philologie romane* (Stras-
          bourg, 1962), 3 vols. (Paris: Klincksieck).
Cong. 11
  1968   *Actas del XIº Congresso internacional de lingüística y filología románicas (Ma-
          drid 1965)*, 4 vols. (= *RFE* anejo 86) (Madrid: CSIC).
Cong. 12
  1970-1971   *Actele celui de al XII-lea Congres internaţional de linguistică şi filologie
          romanică (Bucureşti 1968)*, 2 vols. (Bucureşti: Ed. Acad.).
Cong. 13
  1976   *Actes du XIIIᵉ Congrès international de linguistique et philologie romanes tenu à
          l'Université Laval (Québec, Canada) du 29 août au 5 septembre 1971*, 2 vols.
          (Québec: Laval U.P.).
Cong. 14
  1976-1977   *Atti. XIV Congresso internazionale di linguistica e filologia romanza, Napo-
          li, 15-20 aprile, 1974*, 5 vols. (Napoli: G. Macchiaroli/Amsterdam: Benjamins).
Cong. RSc.
  1973   *Actes du 5ᵉ Congrès des romanistes scandinaves* (Turku: Annales Universitatis
          Turkuensis).
Contini, Gianfranco
  1961   "Per un'interpretazione strutturale della cosidetta 'gorgia' toscana", in *Cong.*
          9.2: 263-281.
  1970-1971   "Rapporti fra la filologia (come critica testuale) e la linguistica romanza",
          in *Cong.* 12.1: 47-65.
Contini, Michel
  1970a "Tendances phonétiques et phonologiques actuelles d'un parler logoudorien",
          in *Cong.* 12.1: 325–333.
  1970b "Résistance et passivité de sujets logoudoriens face à l'italianisation de leur
          langue", *RLR* 34: 366-376.
  1973   Review of Pellegrini 1972, *RLR* 37: 517-525.
Contreras, Heles
  1963   "Una clasificación morfo-sintáctica de las lenguas románicas", *RomPh* 16: 261-
          268.

Corbett, Noel
  1969   "The French verbal flexion -*ons* as a result of homonymy: A study in structure
          and analogy", *RomPh* 22: 421-431.
  1970   "Reconstructing the diachronic phonology of Romance", *RomPh* 24: 273-290.
Corominas, Joan [Juan]
  1936a "Mots catalans d'origin arâbic", *Butlletí de dialectologia catalana* 24: 1-81,
          286-8.
  1936b "Les relacions am Grècia reflectides en el nostre vocabulari", *Homenatge
          Rubió i Lluch* 3: 282-315 (Barcelona).
  1951   *Estudios sobre los gitanismos en español* (Madrid).
Corréard, G.
  1958   "Contributions à l'étymologie de *rêver* et *desver*", *TLL* 3: 95-135.
Correia, J. da Silva
  1936   "Algumas observações num domínio da história da língua portuguesa",
          Arquivo Histórico de Portugal: 2/1936.
Cortelazzo, Manlio
  1946   "L'italiano a Corfù: di alcuni scambi linguistici italo-corfioti", *LN* 7: 66-9.
  1947   "Vicende storiche della lingua italiana a Corfù", *LN* 8: 44-50.
  1948   "Caratteristiche dell'italiano parlato a Corfù", *LN* 9: 29-34.
  1957   "Arabismi di Pisa e arabismi di Venezia", *LN* 18: 95-97.
  1965a "Corrispondenze italo-balcaniche nei prestiti dal turco", *Omagiu lui Alexan-
          dru Rosetti la 70 de ani* (Bucureşti), 147-152.
  1965b "Che cosa s'intendesse per 'lingua franca'", *LN* 26: 108-110.
  1970   *L'influsso linguistico greco a Venezia* (= *Linguistica* 2) (Bologna: Patròn).
Corti, Maria
  1953   "Studi sulla sintassi della lingua poetica avanti lo Stilnovo", *AMAT,* n.s. 4: 263-
          365.
Coseriu, Eugenio
  1954   *El llamado latín vulgar y las primeras diferenciaciones. Breve introducción a la
          lingüística románica* (Montevideo: U.P.).
  1957   "Sobre el futuro romance", *Revista Brasiliera de Filologia* 3: 3-18.
  1961   "Arabismos o romanismos?", *NRFH* 15: 4-22.
  1964   "Pour une sémantique diachronique structurale", *TLL* 2.1: 139-186.
  1965   "Critique de la glottochronologie appliquée aux langues romanes", in *Cong.*
          10.1: 87-96.
  1968   "Les structures lexématiques", in Elwert 1968: 7-15.
  1971   "Das Problem des griechischen Einflusses auf das Vulgärlatein", in Meier
          1971: 135-147.
  1972   "Las etimologías de Giambullari", in Tovar 1972: 95-103.
  1975a "Andreas Müller und die Latinität des Rumänischen", *RRLing* 20: 327-332.
  1975b "Die rumänische Sprache bei Hieronymus Megiser (1603)", *SCL* 26: 473-480.
  1976a "Vers une typologie des champs lexicaux", *CLex* 27: 30-51.
  1976b "Zur Kenntnis der rumänischen Sprache in Westeuropa im 16. Jahrhundert
          (Genebrard und Andrés de Poza)", in Bonfante 1976.
Coseriu, Eugenio – Horst Geckeler
  1974   "Linguistics and semantics", in *Current Trends* 12: 103–172.
Cotarelo y Mori, E.
  1925   "Una nueva casta de galicismos", *BRAE* 12: 117-121.
Coteanu, I.
  1958   "Realitatea obiectivă a fondului principal lexical", *SCL* 9: 399-340.

Coterlan, L. D. C.
1965   *Dacoromania germanica* (Madrid).
Crabb, Daniel M.
1955   *A comparative study of word order in Old Spanish and Old French prose works*
        (= *The Catholic University of America Studies in Romance Languages and
        Literatures* 2) (Washington, D.C.: The Catholic University of America Press).
Craddock, Jerry R.
1965   "A critique of recent studies in Romance diminutives", *RomPh* 19: 286-325.
1967-1968   "Latin diminutive versus Latin-'Mediterranean' hybrid. On proparoxy-
        tonic derivatives of *GALLA* in Hispano-Romance and Sardinian", *RomPh* 21:
        436-449.
1969   *Latin legacy versus substratum residue: The unstressed "derivational" suffixes in
        the Romance vernaculars of the Western Mediterranean* (= *University of
        California Publications in Linguistics* 53) (Berkeley/Los Angeles: California
        U.P.).
1971-1972   Review of Höfler 1967, *RomPh* 25: 363-364.
1973a   "Spanish in North America", in *Current Trends* 10: 422-439.
1973b   Review of J. W. Harris 1969, *Linguistics* 109: 83-109.
1974   "Las categorías derivacionales de los sufijos átones: *pícaro, páparo* y afines", in
        Lapesa 1974. 3.
Cremona, Joseph
1973   "The Romance languages", in *The medieval world,* edited by D. Daiches and
        A. Thorlby, vol. 2.
Crews, Cynthia M.
1935   *Recherches sur le judéo-espagnol dans les pays balkaniques* (Paris: Droz).
Croce, Benedetto
1895   *La lingua spagnuola in Italia. Appunti, con un'appendice di Arturo Farinelli*
        (Roma).
1917   *La Spagna nella vita italiana durante la Rinascenza* (Bari: Laterza).
Csécsy, Madeleine
1971   "Les prépositions. Interférences franco-hongroises", *Le français dans le monde*
        81: 43-50.
Current Trends
1963-   *Current Trends in Linguistics* edited by T. A. Sebeok (The Hague: Mouton)
        1968 vol. 4 *Ibero-American and Caribbean linguistics*
        1972 vol. 9 *Linguistics in Western Europe,* 2 vols.
        1973 vol. 10 *Linguistics in North America,* 2 vols.
        1973 vol. 11 *Diachronic, areal and typological linguistics*
        1974 vol. 12 *Linguistics and adjacent arts and sciences,* 4 vols.
Dąbska-Prokop, Urszula
1965   *L'expression syntaxique des notions de cause et de conséquence dans les 'Chroni-
        ques' de Jean Molinet* (= *Acta scientiarum litterarumque* 107, *Schedae gram-
        maticae* 14) (Kraków: Sumptibus Universitatis Iagellonicae).
Dalgado, Sebastião R.
1919-1921   *Glossario luso-asiatico,* 2 vols. (Coimbra).
Damourette, Jacques – Edouard Pichon
1930-1956   *Des mots à la pensée. Essai de grammaire de la langue française,* 7 vols.
        (Paris: Collections de linguistes modernes).
Darbelnet, Jean
1971   "Sémantique et civilisation", *Le français dans le monde* 81: 15-19.

Dardano, Maurizio
 1969   *Lingue e tecnica narrativa nel duecento* (Roma: Bulzoni).
Dardel, Robert de
 1958   *Le parfait fort en roman commun* (Genève/Paris: Droz).
 1964   "Considérations sur la déclinaison romane à trois cas", *CFS* 21: 7-23.
Dauzat, Albert
 1930   *Histoire de la langue française* (Paris: Payot).
 1935   "Les pluriels italiens en français", *FM* 3: 148.
 1939   *Tableau de la langue française* (Paris: Payot).
 1943   "Mots français d'origine orientale, d'après les documents fournis par Jean Deny", *FM* 11: 241-251.
 1946   "Les mots d'emprunt dans l'argot français", in A. Dauzat, *Etudes de linguistique française* (2nd edition) (Paris).
 1950   *Phonétique et grammaire historique de la langue française* (Paris: Larousse).
 1951   *Mélanges de linguistique offerts à Albert Dauzat* (Paris: d'Artrey).
Davau, M.
 1950   "Adjectifs invariables, 4. Adjectifs formés de locution latines ou étrangères", *FM* 18: 45-53.
Deanović, Mirko
 1956   "Projet d'un atlas linguistique méditerranéen", *RLR* 20: 145-146.
 1968-1970   *Studi offerti a Mirko Deanović* (= *BALM* 10-12).
 1971   Issue dedicated to M. D., *SRAZ* 29-32 (1970-1971).
Delattre, Pierre
 1972   *Papers in linguistics and phonetics to the memory of Pierre Delattre* (The Hague: Mouton).
Delille, Karl Heinz
 1970   *Die geschichtliche Entwicklung des präpositionalen Akkusativs im Portugiesischen* (Diss., Bonn).
Dembowski, Peter F.
 1966   "Linguistic and stylistic approaches to Romance historical syntax", *RomPh* 20: 521-530.
Demetresco, A.
 1888   *L'influence de la langue et de la littérature française en Roumanie* (Lausanne).
Denison, N.
 1969   "Sociolinguistics and plurilingualism", *Actes du Xe Congrès International de Linguistes, Bucarest 28 août-2 septembre 1967* (Bucureşti: Ed. Ac.), 1: 551-559.
 1971   "Some observations on language variety and plurilingualism", in *Social anthropology and language,* edited by E. Ardener. [Excerpts in *Sociolinguistics,* edited by J. B. Pride and J. Holmes (Harmondsworth: Penguin, 1972), 65-77.]
Densusianu, O.
 1924   "Irano-romanica", *Grai şi suflet* 1: 235-250.
Deroy, Louis
 1956   *L'emprunt linguistique* (Paris: Les belles lettres).
Deschermeier, L.
 1923   *Zur Geschichte der italienischen Lehnwörter in der französischen Schriftsprache: Die Wörter des Militärgedankenkreises (bis ca. 1600)* (Thesis, München).
Detschew, D.
 1957   *Die thrakischen Sprachreste* (Wien: (Wien: Robrer).
Deutschmann, Olaf
 1947   "Französisch *aveugle.* Ein Beitrag zur Methodik und Problematik etymologischer Forschung", *RJb* 1: 87-153.

1959   *Zum Adverb im Romanischen. Anläßlich französisch: 'il est terriblement riche -- il a terriblement d'argent'* (Tübingen: Niemeyer).
1971   *Lateinisch und Romanisch: Versuch eines Überblicks* (München: Hueber).
Devoto, Giacomo
1930   "I fondamenti del sistema delle vocali romanze", *RIL* 63: 593-605.
1944   *Storia della lingua di Roma* (Bologna: Cappelli).
1948   *Le Tavole di Gubbio* (Firenze: Sansoni).
1962a   "Pour l'histoire de l'indo-européanisation de l'Italie septentrionale: quelques étymologies lépontiques", *RPh* 36: 197-208.
1962b   *Tabulae Iguvinae* (3rd edition) (Roma: Accademia dei Lincei).
1967a   *Scritti minori II* (Firenze: Le Monnier).
1967b   *Gli antichi Italici* (3rd edition) (Firenze: Vallecchi).
1970   "L'Italia dialettale", *Atti del quinto convegno di studi umbri (I dialetti dell'Italia mediana),* 93-127.
1972   "Studies of Latin and languages of Ancient Italy", *Current Trends* 9: 817-834.
1974a   *Il linguaggio d'Italia. Storia e strutture linguistiche dalla preistoria ai nostri giorni* (Milano: Rizzoli).
1974b   *Dialetti ligure* (Genova: SAGEP).
1975   "Dedicato alla memoria di G. Devoto", *AGI* 60.
Diaz Castañon, Carmen
1966   *El Bable de "el Cabo Peñas"* (Oviedo: Instituto de Estudios Asturianos).
Díaz y Díaz, Manuel
1960a   "El latín de la península ibérica: rasgos lingüísticos", in Alvar et al. 1960-1962, 1: 154-197.
1960b   "El latín de la península ibérica: dialectalismos", in Alvar et al. 1960-1962, 1: 237-250.
Dietrich, W.
1973   *Der periphrastische Verbalaspekt in den romanischen Sprachen* (= *ZRPh* Beiheft 140).
Diez, Friedrich
1836-1843   *Grammatik der romanischen Sprachen,* 3 vols. (Bonn: Eduard Weber).
1976   *In memoriam F. Diez. Akten des Kolloquiums zur Wissenschaftsgeschichte der Romanistik* (Amsterdam: Benjamins).
Dillon, M.
1945   "Linguistic borrowing and historical evidence", *Lg* 21: 12-17.
Dimitriu, Ion G.
1965   "Die deutsch-siebenbürgischen Elemente des rumänischen Wortschatzes", *Acts of 2nd International dialect congress, Sept. 1965.*
Doman, Mary Gray
1969   "H aspirada y F moderna", *Thesaurus* 24: 426-458.
Domaschke, W.
1919   "Der lateinische Wortschatz des Rumänischen", *Jahresbericht des Instituts für rumänische Sprache zu Leipzig* 21-25: 65-173.
Donghi de Holperin, R.
1925   "Contribución al estudio del italianismo en la Republica Argentina", *Cuadernos del Instituto de Filologia (Buenos Aires)* 1.
1958   "Los italianos y la lengua de los argentinos", *Quaderni Ibero-Americani* 3: 446-449.
Dorfman, Eugene
1968   "Correlation and core-relation in diachronic Romance phonology", *Word* 24: 81-98.

Dottin, G.
  1920 *La langue gauloise* (Paris).
Doussinet, R.
  1971 *Grammaire Saintongeaise. Etude des structures d'un parler régional* (La Rochelle: Rupella).
Drimba, V.
  1950 "Note di lexicologie aromână". Elemente turceşti", *SCL* 1: 290-296.
  1957 "Imprumuturi turceşti în dialectale româneşti suddunarene", *SCL* 8: 225-237.
  1960 "Materiale pentru studiul raporturilor lingvistice româno-maghiare", *CLing* 5: 115-130.
  1964 Review of Wendt 1960, *RRLing* 9: 99-109.
Dubois, Jean
  1963 "L'emprunt en français", *Informations Littéraires* 15.10-16.
  1965 "Essai de lexicostatistique du français contemporain (les mots commençant par h)", *Linguistique* 2: 103-15.
Dubois, Jean – Claude Dubois
  1971 *Introduction à la lexicographie: les dictionnaires* (Paris: Larousse).
Ducháček, Otto
  1960 *Le champ conceptuel de la beauté en français moderne* (Praha).
  1961 "Sur le problème de la migration des mots d'un champ conceptuel dans l'autre", *Lingua* 10: 57-78.
  1968a "Les lacunes dans la structure du lexique", in Gamillscheg 1968: 169-176.
  1968b "Déficiences du lexique", *ERB* 7: 7-21.
  1968c "Différents types de champs linguistiques et l'importance de leur exploration", in Elwert 1968: 26-36.
  1971 "Bibliographie", *ERB* 5: 9-10.
  1976 "Le rôle de la sémantique dans la structure du lexique", in *Cong.* 14.4: 319-326.
Dulong, G.
  1973 "Histoire du français en Amérique du Nord", in *Current Trends* 10: 407-421.
Dumistrăcel, Stelian
  1970 "L'influence de la langue littéraire sur les parlers populaires roumains. Prémisses", *RLR* 34: 349-365.
  1971 "Les conditions de l'influence de la langue littéraire sur les parlers populaires roumains", in *Cong.* 12.2: 421-427.
Dumonceau, P.
  1975 *Langue et sensibilité au 17ᵉ s. L'évolution du vocabulaire affectif* (Genève: Droz).
Durante, Marcello
  1961 "L'iscrizione di Centuripe", *Kokalos* 7: 91-108.
  1963 "Commento all'inscrizione di Novilara", *Ricerche linguistiche* 5: 65-86.
  1964-5 "Il siculo e la sua documentazione", *Kokalos* 10-11: 417-450.
Dworkin, S. N.
  1971-1972 "*Mester* and *menester:* An early Gallicism and a cognate Provençalism as rivals in older Hispano-Romance", *RomPh* 25: 373-389.
  1973-1974 "Latin *SARCĪRE, SERERE, SUERE, SURGERE* in Hispano-Romance: A study in homonymy, 'weak' sound change, lexical contamination", *RomPh* 27: 26-36.
  1974-1975 "Therapeutic reactions to excessive phonetic erosion: The descendants of *RIGIDU* in Hispano- and Luso-Romance", *RomPh* 28: 462-472.
  in Press Review of Burr 1975, *ZRPh*.

Dyen, Isidore
1975   *Linguistic subgrouping and lexicostatistics* (The Hague: Mouton).
Ebneter, Theodor
1973   *Das bündnerromanische Futur. Syntax der mit* vegnir *und* habere *gebildeten Futurtypen in Gegenwart und Vergangenheit* (= *Romanica Helvetica* 84) (Bern: Francke).
Ehrliholzer, Hans-Peter
1965   *Der sprachliche Ausdruck der Kausalität im Altitalienischen* (Winterthur: Keller).
Elcock, William D.
1938   *De quelques affinités phonétiques entre l'aragonais et le béarnais* (Paris: Droz).
1960   *The Romance languages* (London: Faber/New York: MacMillan). [2nd edition, revised, 1975.]
ELH
1960-1967   *Enciclopedia lingüística hispánica* (Madrid: CSIC).
Elwert, T.
1950   "Über das 'Nachleben' phanariotischer Gräzismen im Rumänischen", *ByzZ* 43: 272-300.
Elwert, W. T.
1965   "L'emploi des langues étrangères comme procédé stylistique", *Revue de Littérature Comparée* 29: 409-437.
1968   (ed.) *Probleme der Semantik* (= *ZFSL* Beiheft NF1) (Wiesbaden: Steiner).
1973   *Das zweisprachige Individuum und andere Aufsätze zur romanischen und allgemeinen Sprachwissenschaft* (Wiesbaden: Steiner).
Engels, J.
1970   "Latin vulgaire – roman commun – latin médiéval", *Cong.* 12.1: 120-124.
Entwistle, William J.
1936   *The Spanish language, together with Portuguese, Catalan and Basque* (London: Faber/New York: MacMillan). [2nd edition 1962.]
Epiphânio da Silva Dias, Augusto
1918 [1959]   *Syntaxe histórica portuguêsa* (Lisboa: Livreria Classica).
Ernout, A.
1956   *"Venus, venia, cūpīdo"*, RPh 30: 7-27.
Ernst, Gerhard
1970   *"Die Toskanisierung des römischen Dialekts im 15. und 16. Jahrhundert* (= *ZRPh* Beiheft 121).
Escarpit, R.
1953   "Du nahuatl au français", *Vie et Langage* 2: 249-250.
Esenkova, E.
1957   "Mots d'origine byzantine dans le roumain", *Actes du Xe Congrès International d'Etudes Byzantines (15-21 sept. 1955)* (Istambul: Publication du Comité d'organisation), 266-271.
Estienne, Henri
1578 [1885]   *Dialogues du nouveau langage français italianisé* (edited by Ristelhuber, Paris 1885).
Estrany Gendre, M.
1970a   "Calcos sintácticos del inglés", *FMod* 38: 199-203.
1970b   *El lenguaje de la sociedad de consumo. Neologismos* (unpublished doctoral thesis, Univ. Complutense de Madrid).

Etiemble, René
  1961 *Questions de poétique comparée. Le Babélien* (Paris: Les Cours de Sorbonne).
  1973 *Parlez-vous franglais?* (2nd edition, augmented) (Paris: Gallimard).
Ettinger, Stefan
  1974a *Form und Funktion in der Wortbildung: Die Diminutiv- und Augmentativ-modifikation im Lateinischen, Deutschen und Romanischen: Ein kritischer For-schungsbericht 1900-1970* (Tübingen: Niemeyer).
  1974b *Diminutiv- und Augmentativbildung: Regeln und Restriktionen: Mor-phologische und semantische Probleme der Distribution und der Restriktion bei der Substantivmodifikation im Italienischen, Portugiesischen, Spanischen und Rumänischen* (Tübingen: Niemeyer).
Ettmayer, Karl von
  1930-1936 *Analytische Syntax der französischen Sprache mit besonderer Berück-sichtigung des Altfranzösischen*, 2 vols. (Halle: Niemeyer).
Ewert, Alfred
  1933 *The French language* (London: Faber). [2nd edition 1943.]
Feijó, L. C. Saraiva
  1965 "Aspectos da gíria no futebol", *Miscelânea Clóvis Monteiro* (Rio de Janeiro).
Feldman, David M.
  1964 "Analytic versus synthetic: A problem in the Portuguese verbal system", *Lin-guistics* 10: 16-21.
Felice, Emidio de
  1962 "La romanizzazione dell'estremo sud d'Italia", *AMAT* 26: 231-282.
Ferguson, Charles A.
  1959 "Diglossia", *Word* 15: 325-340.
Ferguson, Thaddeus J.
  1976 *A history of the Romance vowel systems through paradigmatic reconstruction* (The Hague: Mouton).
Fernández García, Antonio
  1969 *Anglicismos en el español (1891-1936)* (Madrid).
Figge, Udo
  1966 *Die romanische Anlautsonorisation* (= *Romanistische Versuche und Vorar-beiten* 19) (Bonn: Rom. Sem.).
Figueiredo, Cândido de
  1938 *Estrangeirismos*, 2 vols. (Lisboa). [5th edition of 1st volume, 1938; 3rd edition of 2nd volume, 1928.]
Finoli, A. M.
  1947-1948 "Note sul lessico degli economisti del Settecento", *LN* 9: 67-71.
Fisher, J.
  1976 *The lexical affiliations of Vegliote* (Cranbury, N. J.: Fairleigh Dickinson U.P.).
Fishman, Joshua A.
  1967 "Bilingualism with and without diglossia: Diglossia with and without bilingual-ism", *Journal of Social Issues* 23.2: 29-38.
  1968 "Sociolinguistic perspective on the study of bilingualism", *Linguistics* 39: 21-49.
Flasche, Hans
  1969 "Die Bedeutung des Syntagmas *de*-Adjektiv (bzw. Partizip des Perfekts) im Portugiesischen. Zur syntaktischen Interpretation der *Lusiaden*", in Piel 1969: 62-77.
  1973 *Studia Iberica. Festschrift für Hans Flasche* (Bern: Franke).

Fleischmann, Suzanne
1973 "Collision of homophonous suffixes entailing transfer of semantic content. The Luso-Hispanic action nouns in *-ón* and *-dela/-dilla*", *RomPh* 26: 635-663.
1976 "The suffix *-age* in Modern French: Language change viewed in a historico-cultural perspective", *RomPh* 30: 42-58.
Fogarasi, Miklós
1969 "Alcuni termini nuovi del lessico italiano del primo Ottocento", *LN* 30: 43-49.
Folena, Gianfranco
1969-1970 "Introduzione al veneziano 'de là de mar'", *BALM* 10-12: 331-376.
Fonseca, Fernando Venâncio Peixoto da
1956 "A expansão da língua portuguesa e a sua influência no léxico francês", *RP* 21: 211-219.
1957-1969 "Vocábulos franceses de origem portuguesa vernácula", *RP* 22-34.
Forest, John B. de
1916 "Old French borrowed words in the Old Spanish of the twelfth and thirteenth centuries", *RR* 7: 369-413.
Fossat, J.-L.
1971 *La formation du vocabulaire gascon de la boucherie et de la charcuterie: Etude de lexicologie historique et descriptive* (Toulouse).
Foster, David W.
1968 "A survey of the development of Latin *e* and *o* in Italian in relation to consonantal gemination", *Orbis* 17: 399-407.
Fouché, Pierre
1924 *Phonétique historique du roussillonnais* (Toulouse: E. Privat).
1952-1961 *Phonétique historique du français*, 3 vols. (Paris: Klincksieck). [2nd edition 1966.]
1970 *Mélanges de linguistique et de philologie dédiés à la mémoire de Pierre Fouché* (Paris: Klincksieck).
Foulet, Lucien
1919 *La petite syntaxe de l'ancien français* (= *Classiques français du moyen age, 2e série: Manuels*) (Paris: Champion). [3rd edition 1930.]
1935 "L'extension de la forme oblique du pronom personnel en ancien français", *Romania* 61: 257-315, 401-463.
Fox, John H. – R. Wood
1968 *A concise history of the French language: Phonology and morphology* (Oxford: Blackwell).
Frago-García, Juan A.
1977 "Una perspectiva histórica sobre la relación entre el léxico navarroaragonés y el del área occitana", *RLR* 41: 302-332.
forthcoming "La lexicología aragonesa en sus aspectos diacrónico y sincrónico", *Archivo de Filología Aragonesa* 16.
Francescato, Giuseppe
1957 "Il bilinguismo friulano-veneto (indagine fonologica)", *Atti dell'Accademia di Udine* 14: 5-29.
François, Alexis
1959 *Histoire de la langue française cultivée des origines à nos jours*, 2 vols. (Genève: A. Jullien).
Franzén, Torsten
1939 *Etude sur la syntaxe des pronoms personnels sujets en ancien français* (unpublished thesis, Uppsala).

Frappier, Jean
1976 Memorial issue *RomPh* 30.1.
Freda, Rossana Melis
1968 "Alcuni aspetti linguistici della 'letteratura di consumo' nel Ottocento", *LN* 29: 4-13.
Fronzaroli, P.
1954 "Nota sulla formazione della lingua franca", *AMAT* n.s. 19: 213-252.
Gadzaru, D.
1969 *Ensayos de filología y lingüística románicas* (La Plata: Inst. de Fil.).
Gaeng, Paul A.
1968 *An inquiry into local variations in Vulgar Latin as reflected in the vocalism of Christian inscriptions* (= University of North Carolina Studies in Romance Languages and Literatures 77) (Chapel Hill: North Carolina U.P.).
Gáldi, L.
1939a *Les mots d'origine néo-grecque en roumain à l'époque des Phanariotes* (Budapest: Institut de Philologie Hellénique).
1939b "Contributo alla storia degli italianismi della lingua romana", *AGI* 31: 115-20.
1940a "Les premiers verbes d'origine française dans la langue romaine", *ZFSL* 63: 176-189.
1940b "Italianismi diretti e italianismi indiretti in rumeno", *LN* 2: 2-4.
1948 "Graeco-Valachica", *Etudes slaves et roumaines* 1: 42-47, 111-118, 177-186.
Galmés, A.
1956 *Influencias sintácticas y estilísticas del árabe en la prosa medieval castellana* (Madrid).
1962 *Las sibilantes en la Romania* (Madrid: Gredos).
Gamillscheg, Ernst
1913 *Studien zur Vorgeschichte einer romanischen Tempuslehre (Kaiserliche Akademie der Wissenschaften, Sitzungsberichte)* (Wien).
1919-1922 "Französische Etymologien", *ZRPh* 40: 129-190, 513-542; 41: 503-547, 631-647.
1923 Review of Wartburg 1922- , *ZRPh* 43: 513-577.
1927 "Zur Methodik der etymologischen Forschung", *ZFSL* 50: 216-298.
1934-1936 *Romania germanica*, 3 vols. (Leipzig/Berlin: de Gruyter). [2nd edition 1970. Especially "Die altgermanischen Bestandteile des Ostromanischen", 2: 231-266.]
1948 "Zur Entwicklungsgeschichte des Alpenromanischen", *RF* 61: 267-299.
1952 *Festgabe ... zu seinem 65. Geburtstag am 28. Oktober 1952 von Freunden und Schülern überreicht* (Tübingen: Niemeyer).
1957 *Syntactica und Stilistica. Festschrift für ... zum 70. Geburtstag, 28. Oktober 1957* (Tübingen: Niemeyer).
1957a *Historische französische Syntax* (Tübingen: Niemeyer).
1968 *Verba et vocabula. Ernst Gamillscheg zum 80. Geburtstag*, edited by H. Stimm and J. Wilhelm (München: Fink).
1968a "Zur Geschichte der Assibilierung und der Palatalisierung", *Festschrift Walther von Wartburg zum 80. Geburtstag*, edited by Kurt Baldinger (Tübingen: Niemeyer), 1: 445-450.
Gamulescu, Dorin
1967 "Etimologii româneşti: contribuţii la studiul unor cuvinte de origine slavă din limba română", *SCL* 18: 563-569.

García de Diego, Vicente
1920 "Cruces de sinónimos", *RR* 11: 65-69.
1922 "Cruces de sinónimos", *RFE* 9: 113-153.
1926 *Problemas etimológicos* (Ávila: Senén Martín).
1928 "Etimología idealista", *RFE* 15: 225-243.
1951 *Gramática histórica española* (Madrid: Gredos). [2nd edition 1961.]
1958 "Notas etimológicas", *Boletín de la Real Academia Española* 38: 7-54.
1964 *Etimologías españolas* (Madrid: Aguilar).
García Hernandez, B.
1977 "El campo semántico de 'oir' en la lengua latina. Estudio estructural", *REL* 7: 115-136.
Gardette, Pierre
1974 "Hommage à Monseigneur Pierre Gardette", *RLR* 38.
Gartner, Theodor
1883 *Raetoromanische Grammatik* (Heilbronn: Henniger).
1910 *Handbuch der rätoromanischen Sprache und Literatur* (Halle: Niemeyer).
Gauger, H. M.
1971 *Untersuchungen zur spanischen und französischen Wortbildung* (Heidelberg: Winter).
Gazdar, G. – E. Klein – G. K. Pullum
1978 *A bibliography of contemporary linguistic research* (New York/London: Garland).
Gazdaru, Demetrio
1949 "Español *no más* y rumano *númai* en su desarrollo paralelo", *Filología* (Buenos Aires) 1: 23-42.
Gebhardt, Karl
1974a *Das okzitanische Lehngut im Französischen* (= *Heidelberger Beiträge zur Romanistik* 3) (Bern/Frankfurt: Lang).
1947b "Les emprunts français à l'occitan", *RLaR* 80: 57-92.
1974c "Les francoprovençalismes de la langue française", *LRL* 38: 198-209.
1975 "Gallizismen im Englischen. Anglizismen im Französischen: ein statistischer Vergleich", *ZRPh* 91: 292-309.
1977 "A propos des occitanismes en français", in *Cong.* 14: 187-204.
forthcoming Review of Messner 1975, *ZRPh.*
Geckeler, Horst
1971a *Zur Wortfelddiskussion. Untersuchungen zur Gliederung des Wortfeldes alt-jung-neu im heutigen Französisch* (München: Fink).
1971b *Strukturelle Semantik und Wortfeldtheorie. Ein Überblick* (München: Fink).
1973 *Strukturelle Semantik des Französischen* (Tübingen: Niemeyer).
1974 "Le problème des lacunes linguistiques", *CLex* 25: 31-45.
1976 "Remarques sur quelques travaux de sémantique structurale", in *Cong.* 14.4: 335-342.
forthcoming *Strukturelle Bedeutungslehre* (Darmstadt: Wissenschaftliche Buchgesellschaft).
Geissendörfer, Dieter
1964 *Der Ursprung der 'gorgia toscana'* (Diss., Erlangen).
Gemmingen-Obstfelder, B.
1973 *Semantische Studien zum Wortfeld Arbeit im Französischen* (Tübingen: Niemeyer).

Genaust, H.
1972 Review of Grieve 1970, *VR* 31: 381-391.

Gendron, Jean-Denis
1974a "La définition d'une norme de langue parlée au Québec: une approche sociologique", *RLR* 38: 198-209.
1974b "Les francoprovençalismes de la langue française", *RLR* 38: 182-197.
1974c "La lingua quale polisistema socio-culturale", *Colloquio (1973) del Centro per lo studio dell'insegnamento all'estero dell'italiano* (Trieste).
1975 "Plaidoyer pour le plurilinguisme", *RLR* 39: 108-121.

Georges, Emanuel S.
1970 *Studies in Romance nouns extracted from past participles* (Berkeley: California U.P.).

Georgiev, V.
1961 *La toponymie ancienne de la Péninsule Balkanique et la thèse méditerranéenne* (= *Linguistique balkanique* 3.1) (Sofia: Acad. Bulgare des Sciences).

Giacalone Ramat, Anna
1967 "Colori germanici nel mondo romanzo", *AMAT* 32: 105-211.

Giacomelli, Gabriella
1962 *La lingua falisca* (Firenze: Olschki).

Gianelli, Luciano
1973 "*K, P* e *T* intervocaliche in Toscana", *AMAT* 38: 337-347.

Giese, Walter
1972 *Festschrift* (Hamburg: Helmut Buske).

Giese, Wilhelm
1952 "Balkansyntax oder thrakisches Substrat", *SNPh* 24: 46-54.

Gilliéron, Jules
1919 *Etude sur la défectivité des verbes. La faillite de l'étymologie phonétique* (Neuveville).

Giovanni, Marcello de
1970 "Le cacuminali abruzzesi", *Abruzzo* 8: 33-42.

Giuglea, G.
1909 *Cercetări lexicologice. Elemente latine în limba română*, 1 (Bucureşti: Göbl).
1944 *Uralte Schichten und Entwicklungen in der Struktur der dakoromanischen Sprache* (= *Bibliotheca Rerum Transylvaniae* 7) (Sibiu: Centrul de Studii şi Cercetări Privitoare la Transilvania).

Giurescu, Anca
1975 *Les mots composés dans les langues romanes* (= *Janua Linguarum, series practica* 228) (The Hague: Mouton).

Goddard, Keith Arthur
1966 *Spanish influence on French vocabulary (1500-1800)* (unpublished M.A. thesis, Univ. of Leeds).
1969 "Loan-words and lexical borrowing in Romance", *RLR* 33: 337-348.
1972 "Translation and bilingualism", *Babel* 18: 18-23.
1976 "Quelques tendances et perspectives de l'étude des mots d'emprunt dans les langues romanes", in *Cong.* 13.2: 425-431.
1978 "Le bilinguisme et la diglossie: leur importance pour l'étude des mots d'emprunt dans les langues romanes", in *Cong.* 14.2: 401-406.

Godel, R.
1974 *Studi Saussuriani per R. Godel* (Bologna: Il Mulino).

Goldiş-Poalelungi, Ana
1973   *L'influence du français sur le roumain (vocabulaire et syntaxe)* (= *Publications de l'Université de Dijon* 64) (Paris).
Gómez-Moreno, M.
1949   *Misceláneas, historia, arte, arqueología* (Madrid).
Goosse, A.
1973   "La date de décès des mots", *TLL* 11: 63-77.
Gorog, Ralph Paul de
1958   *The Scandinavian element in French and Norman* (New York).
1972   "The concept 'to destroy' in Old French and the question of synonymy", *Linguistics* 93: 27-43.
1977   "L'étymologie et la formation des mots désignant 'bruit' en français médiéval", *RLR* 41: 358-382.
Gougenheim, Georges
1948   "La fausse étymologie savante", *RomPh* 1: 277-286.
Grafschaft, W. K.
1974   *Die Onomasiologie von 'sterben' im Französischen* (Bonn: Rom. Sem.).
Grammont, Maurice
1936   *Traité de phonétique* (Paris: Delagrave). [7th edition 1963.]
Grana, Gianni
1965   "Lingua italiana e lingua francese nella polemica Galeani Napione – Cesarotti", in *Problemi de lingua e letteratura italiana del Settecento: Atti del Quarto Congresso dell'Assoc. internaz. per gli studi di lingua e letteratura italiana (Magenza e Colonia 1962)* (Wiesbaden: Steiner).
Granda, Germán de
1966a   "La estructura silábica y su influencia en la evolución fonética del dominio iberorrománico", *RFE* anejo 81.
1966b   "La velarización de RR en el español de Puerto Rico", *RFE* 49: 180-227.
1969   "La desfonologización de /R/ – /R̄/ en el dominio lingüístico hispánico", *Thesaurus* 24: 1-11.
Grand Combe, F. de
1954   "De l'anglomanie en français", *FM* 22: 187-200, 267-276.
Grandgent, Charles H.
1927   *From Latin to Italian. An historical outline of the phonology and morphology of the Italian language* (Cambridge, Mass.: Harvard U.P.). [3rd edition 1940.]
1962   *An introduction to Vulgar Latin* (New York: Hafner). [Reprint of 1934 edition. Spanish translation: *Introducción al latín vulgar* (Madrid: CSIC, 3rd edition 1963).]
Graur, Al
1929   "Les mots récents en roumain", *BSLP* 29: 122-131.
1934   "Mots 'reconstruits' et mots attestés", *BL* 2: 11-20.
1934-1936   "Les mots tsiganes en roumain", *BL* 2: 108-200; 3: 185-186; 4: 196-200.
1937a   "Sur le genre neutre en roumain", *BL* 5: 5-11.
1937b   "Neologismele", *Revista fundaţiilor regale* 8: 346-364.
1937c   "Autour de l'article postposé", *BL* 5: 204ff.
1950   "Etimologie multiplă", *SCL* 1: 22-34.
1954   *Incercare asupra fondului principal lexical al limbii române* (Bucureşti: Ed. Acad.).
1960a   *Omagiu lui Al. Graur cu prilejul împlinirii a 60 de ani* (= *SCL* 11).
1960b   *Studi di lingvistică generală* (Bucureşti).

324   Bibliography

1963   *Etimologii româneşti* (Bucureşti: Ed. Acad.).
1965   *La romanité du roumain* (Bucureşti).
1970   "Latin vulgaire?" in *Cong.* 12.1: 117-119.
1975   "Bibliographie", *RRLing* 20.4: 313.320.
Grayson, Cecil
1960   *A Renaissance controversy: Latin or Italian (An inaugural lecture)* (Oxford: U.P.).
Green, John N.
1971-1979   "Romance linguistics", *YWMLS* 31-39.
1972b   "Spanish conditionals: Systems or rules?" *ArchL* 3: 75-86.
Greenberg, Joseph
1954   "Concerning inferences from linguistic to non-linguistic data", in *Language and culture,* edited by H. Hoijer (Chicago: U.P.), 3-19.
Greimas, A.-J.
1966   *Sémantique structurale* (Paris: Larousse).
1970   *Du sens. Essais sémiotiques* (Paris: Larousse).
Greive, Artur
1968   "Phonologische Betrachtungen zur Entwicklung des westromanischen Wortauslautes", *Romanistisches Jahrbuch* 19: 48-52.
1970   *Etymologische Untersuchungen zum französischen h aspiré* (= *Romanische Etymologien* 3) (Heidelberg: Winter).
1976   "Contribution méthodologique à la lexicologie des mots savants", in *Cong.* 13.1: 615-625.
Griera i Gaja, Antoni
1965   *Gramática histórica catalana* (Barcelona: San Cugat del Vallés).
Gröber, Gustav (ed.)
1888   *Grundriß der romanischen Philologie,* vol. 1 (Straßburg: Trübner). [2nd edition 1904-1906.]
Grossmann, M.
1969   "La adaptación de los fonemas árabes al sistema fonológico del romance", *RRLing* 14: 51-64.
Grossmann, Maria – Bruno Mazzoni
1974   *Bibliographie de phonologie romane* (= *Janua Linguarum, series practica* 232) (The Hague: Mouton).
Grossmann, R.
1926   *Das ausländische Sprachgut im Spanischen des Rio de la Plata* (= *Mitteilungen und Abhandlungen aus dem Gebiet der romanischen Philologie veröffentlicht vom Seminar für romanische Sprachen und Kultur)* (Hamburg).
Guasch Leguizamon, J.
1951   *Galicismos aceptados, aceptables y vitandos* (Buenos Aires).
Guerra, Maria José Flor
1957   *Galicismos no português do século XVIII* (unpublished thesis, Coimbra).
Guilbert, Louis
1969   (ed.) *Le lexique* (= *Lfr* 2).
1975   *La créativité lexicale* (Paris: Larousse).
Guillaume, Gustave
1919   *Le problème de l'article et sa solution dans la langue française* (Paris: Hachette).
1929   *Temps et verbe. Théorie des aspects, des modes et des temps* (Paris: Champion). [2nd edition 1965.]

Guiraud, Pierre
1956 "Les champs morpho-sémantiques: critères externes et critères internes en étymologie", *BSLP* 52: 265-288.
1958 "Emprunts et équilibre phonologique", *ZRPh* 74: 78-88.
1960 "Le champ morpho-sémantique du verbe *chiquer*", *BSLP* 55: 135-154.
1964 *L'étymologie* (= *Que sais-je?* 1122) (Paris: P.U.F.).
1965 *Les mots étrangers* (= *Que sais-je?* 1166) (Paris: P.U.F.).
1967 *Les structures étymologiques du français* (Paris: Larousse).
1968 "Inventaire des mots français d'origine dialectale", *CLex* 12: 103-123.
Guitarte, Guillermo L.
1955 "El ensordecimento del žeísmo porteño", *RFE* 39: 260-283.
Guiter, Henri
1940-1945 "Etude sur la sonorisation du k initial dans les langues romanes", *RLR* 69:
66-79, 169-171.
1966 "Quelques paramètres caracteristiques des systèmes vocaliques", *RLR* 30:
39-56.
1969 "Corrélations de signifiants et de signifiés dans les langues romanes", *TLL* 8:
195-200.
Gutschmidt, Karl
1967 "Slavische Vermittlung bei deutschen Lehnwörtern im Aromänischen", *WZUB*
16: 731-732.
Gysling, F.
1959 "Italianismi negli *Abschiede* svizzeri", *LN* 20: 54-58.
Haadsma, R. A. – J. Nuchelmans
1963 *Précis de latin vulgaire* (Groningen: Wolters).
Haas, Otto
1962 *Messapische Studien* (Heidelberg: Winter).
Haden, Ernest F.
1973 "French dialect geography in North America", in *Current Trends* 10: 422-439.
Hadlich, Roger L.
1965 *The phonological history of Vegliote* (= *Studies in Romance Languages and
Literatures* 52) (Chapel Hill: North Carolina U.P.).
Hafner, Hans
1955 *Grundzüge einer Lautlehre des Altfrankoprovenzalischen* (= *Romanica Helvetica* 52) (Bern: Francke).
Hagiwara, M. P. (ed.)
1977 *Studies in Romance linguistics* (Rowley, Mass.: Newbury House).
Hall, Robert A. Jr.
1942 "Latin -ks- in Italian and its dialects", *Lg* 18: 117-124.
1949 "A note on 'gorgia toscana'", *Italica* 26: 65-71.
1950 "The reconstruction of Proto-Romance", *Lg* 36: 203-206. [Reprinted in Joos
1957: 303-314 (page references to this edition); and in Keiler 1972: 25-48.]
1950a "Nasal and homorganic plosive in Central and South Italian", *ArchL* 1: 151-
156.
1952 "Bilingualism and applied linguistics", *ZPhon* 6: 13-30.
1955 "The development of vowel pattern in Romance", *Lingua* 4: 394-406.
1962 "Latin -s (-ēs, -ās, -ōs) in Italian", *RomPh* 15: 234-244.
1963 *Idealism in Romance linguistics* (Ithaca: Cornell U.P.).
1964 "Initial consonants and syntactic doubling in West Romance", *Lg* 40: 551-556.
1964a *Introductory linguistics* (Philadelphia: Chilton).

1965 "Old Spanish stress-timed verse and Germanic substratum", *RomPh* 19: 227-234.
1965a "The neuter in Romance: A pseudo-problem", *Word* 21: 421-427.
1968 "Langue standard et dialectes en Italie", *Revue Tunisienne de Sciences Sociales* 5/13: 49-53, 54-62.
1968a "'Neuters', mass nouns, and the ablative in Romance", *Lg* 44: 480-486.
1973 *Bibliographia essenziale della linguistica italiana e romanza* (Firenze: Sansoni).
1974 *Comparative Romance grammar I. External history of the Romance languages* (New York: Elsevier).
1976 *Comparative Romance grammar II. Proto-Romance phonology* (New York: Elsevier).
1977 *Studia gratularia in honor of Robert A. Hall Jr.* (Madrid: Playor).

Hallig, R.
1970 *Spracherlebnis und Sprachforschung. Aufsätze zur romanischen Philologie* (Heidelberg: Winter).

Hallig, R. – W. von Wartburg
1952 *Begriffssystem als Grundlage für die Lexikographie. Versuch eines Ordnungsschemas* (= *Abhandlungen der Deutschen Akademie der Wissenschaften, Klasse für Sprachen, Literatur und Kunst* 1952.4) (Berlin).

Hamlin, F. R.
1970-1976 "Bibliographie des études romanes en Amérique du Nord", *RLaR* 78: 261-274; 79: 95-106; 80: 171-188; 81: 197-216– 82: 227-248.

Hanes, Petre V.
1927 *Desvoltare limbii literare române in prima jumătate a secolului al XIX* (București).

Hanssen, Friedrich
1913 *Gramática histórica de la lengua castellana* (Paris: Ediciones hispanoamericanas). [Facsimile 1966.]

Harmer, Lewis C.
1970 *The French language. Studies presented to L. C. Harmer* (London: Harrap).

Harris, James W.
1969 *Spanish phonology* (= *Research monograph* 54) (Cambridge, Mass./London: M.I.T.).
1975 "Morphological change and generative grammar", *RomPh* 27: 535-545.

Harris, Martin B.
1971 "The history of the conditional complex from Latin to Spanish: Some structural considerations", *ArchL* 2: 25-33.
1972 "Systems or rules: A false dichotomy", *ArchL* 3: 87-95.
1974 "The subjunctive mood as a changing category in Romance", in Anderson – Jones 1974.2: 169-188.
1976 (ed.) *Romance syntax: Synchronic and diachronic perspectives* (Salford U.P.).
1978 *The evolution of French syntax. A comparative approach* (London: Longman).

Harris, M. Roy
1969-1970 "Hispanic *barda* and Occitanian *barta,* a Romance word family of pre-Latin stock", *RomPh* 23: 529-548.
1971 "Spanish *barruntar,* an etymological study", *Kentucky Romance Quarterly* 18: 265-292.

Harris, Roy.
1967 "Piedmontese influence on Valdôtain syntax", *RLR* 31: 180-189.

Hart, Thomas R., Jr.
1955   "Notes on sixteenth-century Portuguese pronunciation" *Word* 11: 404-415.
Haşeganu, I.
1941   *Elemente francese, italiane şi germane în terminologia comercială românească* (Braşov).
Hasselrot, Bengt
1944-1945 "Ancien français *blou, bloi, pou, poi* et questions connexes", *SNPh* 17: 284-292.
1957   *Etudes sur la formation diminutive dans les langues romanes* (Uppsala/Wiesbaden).
1972   *Etude sur la vitalité de la formation diminutive française au XXe siècle (Studia Romanica Upsalensia)* (Uppsala).
Hatzfeld, Helmut A.
1953   *Critical bibliography of the new stylistics applied to Romance literatures (1900-1952) (= University of North Carolina Studies in Comparative Literature 5)* (Chapel Hill, N.C.).
1971   *Analisi e interpretazioni stilistiche* (Bari: Adriatica).
1975a   (ed.) *Romanistische Stilforschung* (Darmstadt: WBG).
1975b   *Estudios de estilistica* (Barcelona: Planeta).
Hatzfeld, Helmut A. – Yves Le Hir
1961   *Essai de bibliographie de stylistique française et romane (1955-1960) (= Publications de la Faculté de Lettres et des Sciences Humaines de l'Université de Grenoble)* (Paris: P.U.F.).
Haudricourt, André
1946   "Les systèmes vocaliques en gallo-roman du haut moyen-âge du point de vue de la phonologie diachronique", *BSLP* 43: xxx-xxxi.
1947a   *"En/an* en français", *Word* 3: 39-47.
1947b   "Problèmes de phonologie diachronique (français ei > oi)", *Lingua* 1: 209-215.
Haudricourt, André G. – Alphonse G. Juilland
1949   [1970] *Essai pour une histoire structurale du phonétisme français* (Paris: Klincksieck). [2nd edition 1970 (The Hague: Mouton).]
Haugen, Einar
1950a   "Problems of bilingualism", *Lingua* 2: 271-290.
1950b   "The analysis of linguistic borrowing", *Lg* 26: 210-231.
1953   *The Norwegian language in America. A study in bilingual behaviour*, 2 vols. (Philadelphia). [2nd edition 1969 (Bloomington: Indiana U.P.).]
1958   "Language contact", *8th Int. Cong. of Linguists (Oslo):* 771-785.
1973   "Bilingualism, language contact and immigrant languages in the United States: a research report, 1956-1970", in *Current Trends* 10: 505-591.
Heger, Klaus
1963   *Die Bezeichnung temporal-deiktischer Begriffskategorien im französischen und spanischen Konjugationssystem (= ZRPh* Beiheft 104) (Tübingen: Niemeyer).
1965   "Les bases méthodologiques de l'onomasiologie et du classement par concepts", *TLL* 3.1: 7-32.
1968   "Structures immanentes et structures conceptuelles", in Elwert 1968: 17-24.
Heilmann, Luigi
1955   *La parlata di Moena* (Bologna: Zanichelli).
Heinimann, Siegfried
1946   "Wort- und Bedeutungsentlehnung durch die italienische Tagespresse im ersten Weltkrieg (1914-1919)", *Romanica Helvetica* 25.

1948   "Tendenze recenti nell'evoluzione delle lingue italiana e francese", *LN* 9: 49-53.

1953   "Die heutigen Mundartgrenzen in Mittelitalien und das sogenannte Substrat", *Orbis* 2: 302-317.

1963   *Das Abstraktum in der französischen Literatursprache des Mittelalters* (= *Romanica Helvetica* 73) (Bern: Francke).

Henry, Albert

1968   *C'était il y a des lunes. Etudes de syntaxe française* (= *Bibliothèque française et romane. Série A: Manuels et études linguistiques*) (Paris: Klincksieck).

Herbillon, J.

1961   Eléments espagnols en Wallon et dans le français des anciens Pays-Bas (= *Mémoires de la Commission Royale de Toponymie et de la Dialectologie (section wallonne)* 10) (Liège: Michiels).

Herculano de Carvalho, José Gonçalo C.

1952   "O vocabulário exótico da *Histoire des Indes* (1553)", *Biblos* 27.

1956   "A evolução portuguesa dos grupos *-ky-* e *-ty-* intervocálicos", *VR* 15: 259-278.

1962   "Nota sobre o vocalismo antigo português: valor dos grafemas *e* e *o* em sílaba átona", *RPF* 12: 17-39.

Herman, Jozsef

1963   *La formation du système roman des conjonctions de subordination* (Berlin: Akademie).

1965   "Aspects de la différenciation territoriale du latin sous l'empire", *BSLP* 60.1: 53-70.

1970a   *Le latin vulgaire* (Paris: P.U.F.). [1st edition 1967.]

1970b   "Les particularités de l'évolution de latin provincial", in *Cong.* 12.1: 125-131.

1976   "La latinité dans les provinces de l'Empire romain: Problèmes de sociolinguistique", in *Cong.* 14.2: 7-15.

Hermann, Walter

1955   "Zur Entstehung der französischen Personalendung *-ons*", *ASNS* 191: 224.

Hillen, W.

1973   *Sainéans und Gilliérons Methode und die romanische Etymologie* (= *Romanische Versuche und Vorarbeiten* 45) (Bonn: Rom. Sem.).

Hilty, Gerold

1969   "Zur Diphtongierung im Galloromanischen und Iberoromanischen", in Piel 1969: 95-107.

Hjelmslev, Louis

1972   *Sprogsystem og sprogforandring* [Language system and language change] (København: Nordisk Sprog- og Kulturforlag).

Höfler, Manfred

1966a   Review of Vidos 1965, *ZRPh* 82: 458-466.

1966b   "Zum spanischen Lehngut im Französischen der Niederlande", *ZRPh* 82: 66-74.

1966c   "Eine fragwürdige Methode der Lehnwortforschung", *ZRPh* 82: 458-466.

1967a   "Zum französischen Wortschatz orientalischen Ursprungs", *ZRPh* 83: 43-66.

1967b   *Untersuchungen zur Tuch- und Stoffbenennung in der französischen Urkundensprache. Vom Ortsnamen zum Appellativum* (= *ZRPh* Beiheft 114) (Tübingen: Niemeyer).

1968   Review of Guiraud 1967, *ZRPh* 84: 489-492.

1969   "Zum Stand der französischen Datenforschung", *ZRPh* 85: 93-107.

Hollyman, K. J.
1957   *Le développement du vocabulaire féodal en France pendant le haut moyen-âge.*
       Mots témoins de l'histoire – structures sémantiques (Genève).
1968   *A short descriptive grammar of Old French (with texts)* (Auckland: U.P.).
Holmes, Urban T. – Alexander Schutz
1933   *A history of the French language* (Columbus, Ohio: Harold Hedrick).
Holtzmann, R.
in preparation *Gilles Ménage, étymologiste français* (Ph.D. dissertation, University of
       California) (Berkeley).
Hope, Thomas Edward
1960   "An analysis of semantic borrowing", *Essays presented to C. M. Girdlestone*
       (Newcastle upon Tyne: U.P.), 125-141.
1962-1963 "Loan-words as cultural and lexical systems", *ArchL* 14.2: 111-121; 15.1:
       29-42.
1964   "The process of neologism reconsidered with reference to lexical borrowings in
       Romance", *TPhS* 1964: 46-84.
1965   "L'interprétation des mots d'emprunt et la structure lexicale", in *Cong.* 10:
       149-155.
1971a *Lexical borrowing in the Romance languages: A critical study of Italianisms in
       French and Gallicisms in Italian from 1100 to 1900* (Oxford: Blackwell).
1971b "Language and stereotype: a Romance philologist's parable", *Univ. of Leeds
       Review* 14.2: 219-38. [Inaugural lecture.]
1973   "Gallicisms in Dante's *Divina Commedia*: a stylistic problem?", *Studies in
       memory of Frederick Whitehead* (Manchester: U.P.), 153-172.
Hottinger, A.
1958   *Kalila und Dimna. Ein Versuch zur Darstellung der arabisch-altspanischen
       Übersetzungskunst* (Bern).
Householder, Fred W. – Sol Saporta (eds.)
1962   *Problems in lexicography* (= *IJAL* 38.2). [2nd edition 1967.]
Høybe, Poul
1973   *Mélanges Poul Høybe* (= *RevR* 8).
Hriştea, Theodor
1967   "Le calque de structure dans la langue roumaine", *RRLing* 12: 297-288.
1968   *Probleme de etimologie* (Bucureşti: Ed. Ştiinţifică).
1971   "Etimologia multiplă internă", *LbR* 20: 479-488.
1972   "Împrumuturi şi creaţii lexicale neologice în limba română", *LbR* 21: 185-199.
1974   "Pseudoanglicisme de provenientă francesă în limba română", *LbR* 23.1: 185
1977   "Contribuţii la studiul etimologic al frazeologiei româneşti moderne", *LbR* 26:
       590-598.
Hübner, Aem
1893   *Monumenta linguae Ibericae* (Berlin).
Hubschmid, Johannes
1949   Praeromanica (Bern: Francke).
1950a "Ein etruskisch-iberischer Pflanzenname", *MH* 7: 221-226.
1950b "Vorindogermanische und jüngere Wortschichten in den romanischen Mun-
       darten der Ostalpen", *ZRPh* 66: 1-94.
1951   *Alpenwörter romanischen und vorromanischen Ursprungs* (Bern: Francke).
1953   *Sardische Studien* (Bern: Francke).
1954   *Pyrenäenwörter vorromanischen Ursprungs und vorromanische Substrata der
       Alpen* (= *Acta Salmanticensia* 7.2) (Salamanca).

1955 *Schläuche und Fässer* (= *Romanica Helvetica* 54) (Bern: Francke).
1959a "Lenguas preromanas indoeuropeas: testimonios románicos", in *Enciclopedia lingüística hispánica* 1: 127-149.
1959b "Lenguas preromanas no indoeuropeas: Testimonios románicos", in *Enciclopedia lingüística hispánica* 1: 27-66.
1960 "Substratprobleme. Eine neue iberoromanisch-alpin-lombardische Wortgleichung vorindogermanischen Ursprungs und die vorindogermanischen Suffixe *-ano-* und *-s(s)-*", *VR* 19: 124-179, 245-299.
1960a *Mediterrane Substrate mit besonderer Berücksichtigung des Baskischen und der westöstlichen Sprachbeziehung* (Bern: Francke).
1963-1965 *Thesaurus praeromanicus*, 2 vols. (Bern: Francke). [2: *Probleme der baskischen Lautlehre und baskisch-vorromanische Etymologien* (1965).]
1964 "Substrate in den Balkansprachen", in *Die Kultur Südosteuropas, ihre Geschichte und ihre Ausdrucksformen* (Balkanologen-Tagung der Südosteuropa-Gesellschaft, München, 7-10 Nov 1962) (= *Südosteuropa-Schriften* 6: 90-102).
1970 "Romanisch-germanische Wortprobleme", *VR* 29: 82-122, 283-302.

Huguet, Edmond
1965 *Mots disparus ou vieillis depuis le 16ᵉ siècle* (Genève: Droz). [2nd edition 1961.]

Humboldt, Wilhelm von
1821 *Prüfung der Untersuchungen über die Urbewohnern Hispaniens vermittelst der baskischen Sprache* (Berlin).

Iliescu, Maria
1959 "La productivité de la IVᵉ conjugaison latine dans les langues romanes", *Recueil d'études romanes, publié à l'occasion du IXᵉ Congrès de linguistique romane* (Bucureşti), 87-102.
1967 "Observaţii asupra limbii friulanilor din România", *SCL* 18: 159-168.
1968a "Graiurile Friulanor din România", *SCL* 19: 375-415.
1968b "Esquisse d'une phonologie frioulane I (des dialectes parlés en Roumanie)", *RRLing* 13: 277-285.
1969 "Ressemblances et dissemblances entre les langues romanes du point de vue de la morpho-syntaxe verbale", *RLR* 33: 113-132.
1972 *Le frioulan à partir des dialectes parlés en Roumanie* (= *Janua Linguarum, series practica* 184) (The Hague: Mouton).

Imbs, Paul
1956 *Les propositions temporelles en ancien français* (= *Publications de la Faculté des Lettres de l'Université de Strasbourg* 120) (Paris: Les Belles Lettres).
1961 (ed.) *Lexicologie et lexicographie françaises et romanes: orientations et exigences actuelles (Strasbourg, 12-16 novembre 1957)* (Paris: CNRS).
1973 *Mélanges de linguistique française et de philologie et littérature médiévales offerts à M. Paul Imbs, membre de l'Institut, par ses collègues, ses élèves, et ses amis* (= *TLL* 11.1).

Ineichen, Gustav
1972 *Romanische Bibliographie: 1965-1966; 1967-1968; 1969-1970* (= Supplement to *ZRPh* 81-86).

Iordan, Iorgu
1949 "Influenţe ruseşti asupra limbii romane", *Analele Academia RPR* seria C 1: 51-122.
1962 *Lingvistica romanică: Evoluţie, curente, metode* (Bucureşti: Ed. Acad.). [German translation: *Einführung in die Geschichte und Methoden der romanischen*

Sprachwissenschaft (Berlin: Akademie, 1962); Spanish translation: *Lingüística románica. Evolución-corrientes-métodos* (Madrid: Alcalá, 1967).]
1962-1974 (ed.) *Crestomaţie romanică* (Bucureşti: Ed. Acad.).
1972 "Ce este etimologia", *LbR* 21: 175-183.
1973 Issue dedicated to I.I., *SCL* 24-25.
1974 *Titluri şi Lucrari: 1911-1973* (Bucureşti: Ed. Acad.).
Iordan, Iorgu – Maria Manoliu Manea
1962-1965 *Introducere în lingvistica romanică* (Bucureşti: Ed. didactică şi pedagogică).
1972 *Manual de lingüística románica: revisión, reelaboración parcial y notas por Manuel Alvar*, 2 vols. (Madrid: Gredos).
1974 *Linguistica romanza, a cura de Alberto Limentani* (traduzione di Marinella Lörinczi Angioni) (Padova: Liviana).
Iordan, Iorgu – John Orr
1937 *An introduction to Romance linguistics, its schools and its scholars* (London: Methuen). [New edition 1970 (Oxford: Blackwell), cf. Posner 1970; Italian version *Introduzione alla linguistica romanza* (Torino: Einaudi, 1973).]
Isbăşescu, M.
1969 "Influenţa germanică", *Analele Academia RPR* 1965-1969. 2: 368-370.
Isopescu, C.
1935 "Sugli elementi italiani del romeno", in *Atti del III Congr. Int. dei Linguisti (Roma 1933)* (Firenze), 320.
Itkonen, E.
1969 "Un conflit entre facteurs phonétiques et facteurs fonctionnels dans un texte en latin mérovingien", *NphM* 70:471-484.
Ivănescu, G. - L. Leonte
1956 "Fonetica şi morfologia neologismelor române de origine romanică", *Studii şi cercetări stiinţifice* 7: 1-24.
Jaberg, Karl
1905 "Pejorative Bedeutungsentwicklung im Französischen", *ZRPh* 29: 57-71.
1925 "Französisch-italienische Kulturbeziehungen im Spiegel des Lehnwortes: zu Reto R. Bezzola, *Abozzo* ...", *Der Kleine Bund* 20: (17 May 1925): 157-159.
1940-1942 "Ancora esotismi, altri esotismi", etc., *LN* 2: 117-118; 3: 42-43, 92-93; 4: 42-45.
Jaberg, K. – J. Jud
1928-1940 *Sprach- und Sachatlas Italiens und der Südschweiz* (= *AIS*), 8 vols. (Zofingen: Ringier).
1960 *Index zum Sprach- und Sachatlas Italiens und der Südschweiz. Ein propädeutisches etymologisches Wörterbuch der italienischen Mundarten* (Bern: Stämpfli).
Jackson, Kenneth
1948 "On the Vulgar Latin of Roman Britain", *Medieval Studies in honor of Jeremiah Denis Matthias Ford,* edited by Urban T. Holmes and A. J. Denomy (Cambridge, Mass.: Harvard U.P.) 8: 3-103.
Janner, H.
1949 "Etimologías hispánicas", *Filología* 1: 151-164.
1977 Review of Joppich-Hagemann – Korth 1973, *RomPh* 30: 487-489.
Jasanoff, Jay H.
1975 "Nominal suffixation in Romance: two approaches", *RomPh* 28: 555-564.

Jeanjaquet, J.
1894 *Recherches sur l'origine de la conjonction* que *et des formes romanes équivalentes* (thesis: Neuchâtel).
Jochnowitz, G.
1973 *Dialect boundaries and the question of Franco-Provençal* (The Hague: Mouton).
Johnson, Phyllis
1973 "Dolor, dolent et soi doloir. Le vocabulaire de la douleur et la conception de l'amour selon Béroul et Thomas", *RomPh* 28: 546-554.
Jonas, Pol
1971 *Le système comparatif à deux termes en ancien français* (= *Travaux de la Faculté de Philosophie et Lettres, Université libre de Bruxelles*) (Bruxelles: P.U.).
Joos, Martin
1952 "The medieval sibilants", *Lg* 28: 222-231.
1957 *Readings in linguistics* (Washington: American Council of Learned Societies).
Joppich-Hagemann, U. – U. Korth
1973 *Untersuchungen zu Wortfamilien der Romania Germanica* (= *Romanische Versuche und Vorarbeiten* 46) (Bonn: Rom. Sem.).
Jorge, Ricardo
1936 "As desordens mentais de languagem", in *Diário de Notícias,* 25th and 28th April 1936.
Jud, Jakob
1907 *Recherches sur la genèse et la diffusion des accusatifs en* -ain *et en* -on (thesis: Halle).
1911 "Dalla storia delle parole lombardo-ladine", *BDR* 3: 1-18, 63-86.
1973 *Romanische Sprachgeschichte und Sprachgeographie* (Zurich: Atlantis).
Jungemann, Frederick H.
1953 *The substratum theory and the Hispano-Romance and Gascon dialects: a funcional-structural analysis of some phonological problems* (New York: University Microfilms/Ann Arbor: Michigan Publications 5193).
1955 *La teoría del sustrato y los dialectos hispano-romances y gascones* (Madrid: Gredos). [= Translation of Jungemann 1953, by Alarcos Llorach.]
Kahane, Henry
1951 "The sea as a medium of linguistic diffusion", *Italica* 28: 287-291.
1975 "The etymologist as transformationalist", in Saltarelli – Wanner 1975: 99-106.
Kahane, Henry – Renée Kahane
1965 "Four Graeco-Romance etymologies", *RomPh* 19: 261-267.
1966 "Les éléments byzantins dans les langues romanes", *CFS* 22: 67-73.
1966 "Greek in Southern Italy", *RomPh* 20: 404-438.
1968 "Risk", in Gamillscheg 1968: 275-283.
1973 *Issues in linguistics. Papers in honor of Henry and Renée Kahane,* edited by B. B. Kachru et al. (Urbana: Illinois U.P.)
1973-1974 Review of Cortelazzo 1970, *RomPh* 27: 356-357.
1977 Review of Joppich-Hagemann – Korth 1973, *RomPh* 30: 487-489.
Kahane, Henry – Renée Kahane – Andreas Tietze
1958 *The lingua franca in the Levant. Turkish nautical terms of Italian and Greek origin* (Urbana: Illinois U.P.).
Karlinger, F. (ed.)
1974 *Das romanische Volksbuch, Römische Tagung 17-25.9.1974* (Seekirchen).

Katagochtina, N.-A.
1976 "Etude phonologique comparée des langues étroitement apparentées (langues romanes modernes): Problèmes et méthodes", in *Cong.* 13.1: 1137-1145.
Kelemen, B.
1971 "Unele aspecte ale împrumuturilor maghiare în limba română", *CLing* 16: 17-27.
Keiler, Allan R. (ed.)
1972 *A reader in historical and comparative linguistics* (New York: Holt, Rinehart and Winston).
Kent, Roland G.
1932 *The sounds of Latin* (= *Language monographs* 12) (Baltimore: L.S.A.).
Kidman, J.
1969 *Les emprunts lexicologiques du français à l'espagnol des origines jusqu'à la fin du XVe s* (thesis: Paris).
Kiefer, Ferenc
1973 *Generative Morphologie des Neufranzösischen* (Tübingen: Niemeyer).
King, Robert D.
1969 *Historical linguistics and generative grammar* (Englewood Cliffs, N.J.: Prentice-Hall).
Kiparsky, V.
1959 "Über etymologische Wörterbücher", *NphM* 60: 209-230.
1966 "Etymologie gestern und heute", *Kratylos* 11: 68-78.
Király, F.
1964 "Precizări etimologice", *LbR* 13: 557-564.
1967 "Etimologia şi împrumuturile: despre unele împrumuturi maghiare", *LbR* 16: 407-411.
1972 "Accentul românesc şi împrumuturile (cu privire specială asupra împrumuturilor din limba maghiară)", in *Studii de limba şi stil* (Timişoara: Ed. Facla).
1973 "Formaţii interne considerate împrumuturi", *CLing* 18: 249-265.
Kiss, Sándor
1972 *Les transformations de la structure syllabique en latin tardif* (= *Studia romanica universitatis Debreceniensis de Ludovice Kossuth nominatae Series linguistica* 2) (Debrecen: Kussuth Lajos Tudományegytem).
Kjellmann, Hilding
1928 *Etude sur les termes démonstratifs en provençal* (Göteborg).
Klajn, Ivan
1972 *Influssi inglesi nella lingua italiana* (Firenze).
Klausenburger, Jürgen
1970 *French prosodies and phonotactics; an historical typology* (= *ZRPh*, Beiheft 124).
Klein, H.-W.
1961 "Contribution à la différentiation sémantique de la Romania", *Orbis* 10: 144-156.
Klein, H.-W. – A. Labhardt
1968 *Die Reichenauer Glossen* (München: *BRPhM* 1).
Klemperer, V.
1914 "Italienische Elemente im französischen Wortschatz zur Zeit der Renaissance", *GRM* 6: 664-677.

Klinck, R.
  1970 *Die lateinische Etymologie des Mittelalters* (= *Medium Aevum: Philologische Studien* 17) (München: Fink).
Kloss, H.
  1967 "Bilingualism and nationalism", in *Problems of bilingualism* (= *The Journal of Social Issues* 23.2), 39-47.
Klum, Arne
  1968 "Notional versus formal analysis applied to Romance conjugation", *RomPh* 22: 158-173.
Koenig, D.
  1973 *Sen/sens et savoir et leurs synonymes dans quelques romans courtois du 12e et du début du 13e s* (Bern: Lang).
Kohler, K.
  1970 "Etymologie und strukturelle Sprachbetrachtung", *IF* 75: 16-31.
Kohlmann, G.
  1901 *Die italienischen Lehnworte in der neufranzösischen Schriftsprache (seit dem 16. Jahrhundert)* (thesis: Kiel).
König, K.
  1940-1941
        "Premières traces en français de quelques mots orientaux", *FM* 9: 129-144.
Kontzi, Reinhold
  1957 "Die italienische Reflexivkonstruktion als Ausdruck für das Passiv und für *man*", in Gamillscheg 1957: 277-292.
  1970 "Ist die aragonesische Präposition *enta* ein Arabismus?" *ZRPh* 86: 372-381.
  1976 "Die Bedeutungen von altspan. *poridad,* neuspan. *puridad* als Ergebnis der arabisch-romanischen Zweisprachigkeit", *ZRPh* 92: 469-472.
  1978a (ed.) *Substrate und Superstrate in den romanischen Sprachen* (Darmstadt: Wissenschaftliche Buchgesellschaft).
  1978b (ed.) *Zur Entstehung der romanischen Sprachen* (Darmstadt: Wissenschaftliche Buchgesellschaft).
Körner, Karl-Hermann
  1968 *Die 'Aktionsgemeinschaft finites Verb–Infinitiv' im spanischen Formensystem. Vorstudie zu einer Untersuchung der Sprache Pedro Calderón de la Bercas* (diss., Hamburg) (Berlin: Walter de Gruyter).
Kovaček, August
  1963 "Notes sur la lexicologie istro-roumaine: sur la disparition des mots anciens et leur remplacement par des mots croates", *SRAZ* 15-16: 3-40.
Krahe, Hans
  1955 *Die Sprache der Illyrier I. Die Quellen* (Wiesbaden: Harrassowitz).
Kramer, J.
  1976 "Poziţia ladinei dolomitice în cadrul limbilor romanice", *SCL* 27: 601-607.
Krauss, Werner
  1967 "Sobre el destino español de la palabra francesa *civilisation* en el siglo XVIII", *BH* 69: 436-440.
Křepinský, M.
  1950 "Romanica I", *Královska česka společnost nauk. Věstník. Třida filosoficko-historicko-filologická* (Praha) 5: 1-49.
  1952 "L'élément slave dans le lexique roumain", *Mélanges Mario Roques* (Paris) 4: 158-161.

1958 *Romanica II: la naissance des langues romanes et l'existence d'une période de leur évolution commune (latin vulgaire, période romane)* (= *Rozpravy česko-slovenské akademie* ved 68) (Praha).

Kröll, Heinz
1952 "Sobre *nada* e algumas expressões equivalentes em portuês", *Boletim de Filologia* 13: 1-19.
1969 *Os estudos de lingüística románica na Europa e na America* (Coimbra: Casa do Costelo).

Kronasser, H.
1965 "Illyrier und Illyricum", *Sprache* 11: 155-183.

Kuen, Heinrich
1932-1934 "El dialecto de Alguer y su posición en la historia de la llengua catalana", *Anuari de l'Oficina Románica de Lingüística i Literatura* 5: 121-177; 7: 41-112.
1950 "Die sprachlichen Verhältnisse auf der Pyrenäenhalbinsel", *ZRPh* 66: 95-125.
1952 "Rückläufige Bewegungen in der Entwicklung der romanischen Sprachen zum analytischen Typus", in Gamillscheg 1952: 140-163.
1957 "Die Gewohnheit der mehrfachen Bezeichnung des Subjekts in der Romania und die Gründe ihres Aufkommens", in Gamillscheg 1957: 293-326.
1973 "Die Stellung des Katalanischen in der romanischen Sprachfamilie", in Flasche 1973: 331-351.

Kühn, Alwin
1939 "Das aragonesische Perfekt. Arag. -ll- > -tš-", *ZRPh* 59: 73-82.
1951 *Romanische Philologie. Erster Teil. Die romanischen Sprachen* (Bern: Francke).

Kukenheim, Louis
1967 *Grammaire historique de la langue française. Les parties du discours* (= *Publications romanes de l'Université de Leyde* 13) (Leiden: U.P.).
1968 *Grammaire historique de la langue française. Les syntagmes* (= *Publications romanes de l'Université de Leyde* 14) (Leiden: U.P.).

Kunitsch, P.
1973 Review of Pellegrini 1972, *ZRPh* 89: 535-541.

Kvavik, Karen H.
1975 "Patterns of derivational affixation in a Romance dialect", *RomPh* 29: 57-66.

Labov, William
1968 "The reflection of social processes in linguistic structures", in *Readings in the sociology of language,* edited by Joshua A. Fishman (The Hague: Mouton), 240-251.
1970 "The study of language in its social context", *Studium generale* 23: 50-87. [Partly reproduced in Pride – Holmes, *Sociolinguistics* (Harmondsworth: Penguin), 180-202.]
1972 "Some principles in linguistic methodology", *Language in society* 1: 97-120.

Lafon, René
1952 *Etudes basques et caucasiques* (= *Acta Salmanticensia* 5.2) (Salamanca).

Lafont, Robert
1964 "Remarques sur la situation du niçois écrit jusqu'au milieu du XVIe siècle", *RLaR* 76: 37-50.

Lahovary, N.
1954-1955 "Contribution à l'histoire linguistique ancienne de la région balkano-danubienne et à la constitution de la langue roumaine. Les éléments pré-indo-européens", *VR* 14: 109-136, 310-346.

336   Bibliography

Lakoff, Robin T.
1968   *Abstract syntax and Latin complementation* (= *Research Monograph Series* 49) (Cambridge, Mass.: M.I.T.).
1972   "Another look at drift", in Stockwell – Macaulay 1972: 172-198.
Lanusse, M.
1893   *De l'influence du dialecte gascon sur la langue française, de la fin du XVe à la 2e moitié du XVIIe s* (thesis, Paris) (Grenoble).
Lapa, M. Rodrigues
1959   "O estrangeirismo; os galicismos", in *Estilistica da lingua portuguesa:* 39-46 (3rd edition) (Rio de Janeiro).
Lapesa, Rafael
1942   *Historia de la lengua española* (Madrid: Escelicer). [5th edition 1962.]
1949   Review of Castro 1948, *NRFH* 3: 297-307.
1972   "Los provenzalismos del Fuero de Valfermoso de las Monjas", *PhQ* 51: 54-59.
1974   *Studia hispanica in honorem R. Lapesa* (Madrid: Gredos).
Latham, J. D.
1968   "*Infierno, mal lugar:* an Arabism", *BHS* 45: 177-180.
Lausberg, Heinrich
1939   *Die Mundarten Südlukaniens* (= *ZRPh* Beiheft 90).
1947a   "Zum romanischen Vokalismus", *RF* 60: 295-307.
1947b   "Vergleichende Charakteristik der italienischen und der spanischen Schriftsprache", *ZRPh* 64: 106-122.
1947c   "Zum französischen Vokalismus", *RF* 60: 308-315.
1948   "Beiträge zur italienischen Lautlehre", *RF* 61: 300-323.
1951   "Bemerkungen zur italienischen Lautlehre", *ZRPh* 67: 319-332.
1956-1962   *Romanische Sprachwissenschaft,* 4 vols. (Berlin: de Gruyter). [2nd edition 1967; Spanish translation: *Lingüística románica* (Madrid: Gredos, 1965); Italian translation: *Linguistica romanza* (Milano: Feltrenelli, 1971).]
1968   "Zur synchronischen Umstrukturierung diachronisch überlieferter Sprachzustände", in von Wartburg 1968.1: 106-128.
Leão, Ângela Vaz
1961a   "Em favor de um neologismo", in *Historia de palavras:* 45-52 (Belo Horizonte).
1961b   *O periodo hipotetico iniciado por 'se'* (Belo Horizonte: Univ. Minas Geras).
Le Bidois, Georges – Robert Le Bidois
1935-1938   *Syntaxe du français moderne, ses fondements historiques et psychiques,* 2 vols. (Paris: Picard). [2nd edition 1967.]
Lecointre, S. – J. Le Galliot
1971   "Le lexique dans l'histoire: problèmes et perspectives", *LFr* 10: 57-82.
Lecoy, F.
1953-1954   "A propos de l'espagnol *alrededor.* Essai d'étymologie", *RomPh* 7: 35-43.
Leech, Geoffrey
1974   *Semantics* (Harmondsworth: Penguin).
Lejeune, Michel
1955   *Celtiberica* (= *Acta Salmanticensia* 7.4) (Salamanca).
1968-1969   "Inscriptions lapidaires de la Narbonnaise", *EC* 12: 21-91.
1970   "Observations sur l'épigraphe élyme", *REL* 47: 133-185.
1971a   "Une *Antiquissima* vénète: Le bronze votif de Lozzo Atestino", *REL* 49: 78-102.

1971 b "Il santuario lucano di Macchia de Rossano di Vaglio", *MALinc* S. 8, 16:2: 47-83.
1971 c *Lepontica* (Paris: Les Belles Lettres).
1972 a "Inscriptions de Rossano di Vaglio 1971", *RALinc* 26: 663-684.
1972 b "Un problème de nomenclature: Lépontiens et Lépontique", *SE* 40: 259-270.
1974 "La grande inscription celtibère de Botorrita (Saragosse)", *Académie des Inscriptions et Belles-Lettres. Comptes rendus* (Paris: Klincksieck), 622-647.

Leonard, Clifford S. Jr
1964 "Proto-Rhaeto-Romance and French", *Lg* 40: 23-32.
1968 "Initial alternation in Proto-Romance", *Lg* 44: 267-273.
1969 "A reconstruction of Proto-Lucanian", *Orbis* 18: 439-484.
1970 "The Romance 'Stammbaum' in the West", *RomPh* 23: 261-276.
1972 "The vocalism of Proto-Rhaeto-Romance", *Orbis* 21: 61-100.
1977 "The taxonomy of Sicilian vocalism", in Hall 1977: 165-171.
1978 *Umlaut in Romance: An essay in linguistic archaeology* (Grossen-Linden: Hoffmann).

Lerch, Eugen
1925-1934 *Historische französische Syntax,* 3 vols. (Leipzig: Reisland).
1930 "Die spanische Kultur im Spiegel des spanischen Wortschatzes", *Neuphilologische Monatsschrift* 1: 525-540, 596-609.
1940 Review of Schürr 1938, *ZRPh* 60: 557-559.

Levi, A.
1930 "Gallicismi d'antica data", *Atti della Reale Acc. di Scienze di Torino* 65: 249-267.

Lévi, P.
1950-1952 *La langue allemande en France. Pénétration et diffusion des origines à nos jours,* 2 vols. (Lyon).

Levy, Anita Katz
1965-1967 "Contrastive development in Hispano-Romance of borrowed Gallo-Romance suffixes", *RomPh* 18: 399-429; 20: 296-320.

Levy, J. F.
1973-1974 "Tendential transfer of Old Spanish *hedo* < *FOEDU* to the family of *heder* < *FOETERE*", *RomPh* 27: 204-210.

Lewicka, H.
1968 "Pour une histoire structurale de la formation des mots en français", in *Cong.* 11.2: 649-659.

Littlefield, M. G.
1974 *Bibliographical index to Romance Philology* (Berkeley: California U.P.)

Livingston, C.
1957 *Skein-winding reels. Studies in word history and etymology* (= *University of Michigan Publications in Language and Literature* 30) (Ann Arbor: Michigan U.P.).

Llorente Maldonado y Guevara, Antonio
1955 *Morfología y sintaxis. El problema de la división de la gramática* (= *Colección filológica* 13) (Granada: U.P.).

Lloyd, James A.
1968 *Historical introduction to French phonetics* (London: Dawsons of Pall Mall).

Löfstedt, Einar
1911 *Philologischer Kommentar zur Peregrinatio Aetheriae* (Uppsala).

338   Bibliography

1933   "Zur Auflösung des Futurums und des Lokativs", *Syntactica* (Lund) 2: 63-78.
1959   *Late Latin* (Oslo: Aschehoug).
Löfstedt, Leena
1966   *Les expressions du commandement et de la défense en latin et leur survie dans les langues romanes* (= *Mémoires de la Société Néophilologique de Helsinki* 29) (Helsinki).
Lohmann, J.
1966   "Der Sinn der indogermanischen Etymologie", *Kratylos* 11: 79-98.
Lombard, Alf
1934   *Le groupement des pronoms personnels régimes atones en italien* (Uppsala).
1936   "Die Bedeutungsentwicklung zweier iberoromanischer Verba", *ZRPh* 56: 637-642.
1943   Review of *Le roman du Comte de Poitiers* by Bertil Malmberg, *ZRPh* 63: 542-545.
1954-1955 *Le verbe roumain. Etude morphologique*, I-II (Lund).
Lope Blanch, Juan M.
1956   "La expresión temporal en Berceo", *NRFH* 10: 36-41.
López-Morillas, Consuelo
1973-1974 "A midway report on an etymological crux: Sp. *roña*", *RomPh* 27: 488-496.
1975   "Aljamiado *akošegir* and its Old Provençal counterparts; Studies in the Romance transmission of Latin *CŌN-S*", *RomPh* 28: 445-461.
Lorenzo, E.
1966   *El español de hoy, lengua en ebullición* (Madrid).
Lorenzo, R.
1969   "Notas sobre léxico gallego-portugués y castellano", in Piel 1969: 136-139.
Lőrinczi, Marinella
1969   "Consideraciones semánticas de las palabras españolas de origen árabe", *RRLing* 14: 65-75.
Lovas, B.
1932   *Mots d'origine hongroise dans la langue et la littérature française* (Szeged: Institut Français).
Luchaire, Achille
1877   *Origines linguistiques de l'Aquitaine* (Paris).
Lüdtke, Helmut
1953   "Fonemática portuguesa. Il vocalismo", *Boletim de filologica* 14: 197-217.
1956   *Die strukturelle Entwicklung des romanischen Vokalismus* (Bonn: Rom. Sem.).
1956a "La etimología de burdégano", *RFE* 40: 237-238.
1961   "Attestazioni latine di innovazioni romanze", in *Cong.* 9.1: 5-10.
1965   "Die lateinischen Endungen *-um/-im/-unt* und ihre romanischen Ergebnisse", in *Omagiu lui Alexandru Rosetti* (Bucureşti: Ed. Ac.), 239-258.
1974   *Historia del léxico románico* (Madrid: Gredos). [= Spanish version of *Geschichte des romanischen Wortschatzes* (Freiburg, 1968).]
Lüdtke, Jens
1978   *Prädikative Nominalisierung mit Suffixen im Französischen, Katalanischen und Spanischen* (Tübingen: Niemeyer).
Luján, M. – F. G. Hensey (eds.)
1976   *Current studies in Romance linguistics* (Georgetown U.P.).
Lurati, O.
1972   "Per un diverso 'modo' lessicologico", *VR* 31: 55-75.

Maccarone, N.
1929 "Il concetto dei dialetti e l'"Italia dialettale" nel pensiero ascoliano", in Ascoli
1929: 302-332.
Mackel, E.
1887 *Die germanischen Elemente in der französischen und provenzalischen Sprache*
(Heilbronn).
Mackenzie, Frazer
1939 *Les relations de l'Angleterre et de la France d'après le vocabulaire*, 2 vols. (Paris).
Mackey, William F.
1976 *Bilinguisme et contact des langues* (Paris: Klincksieck).
Macpherson, I. R.
1967 "Past participle agreement in Old Spanish: Transitive verbs", *BHS* 44: 241-
254.
Macrea, Dumitru
1941-1943 "Fizionomia lexicală a limbii române", *Dacoromania* 10: 362-373.
1954 "Contribuţie la studiul fondului principal de cuvinte al limbii române", *SCL* 5:
7-18.
1961 *Probleme de lingvistică romana* (Bucureşti).
1965 "La tradition de la langue roumaine littéraire et le phénomène de la palatalisation des labiales", in *Cong.* 10.3: 1219-1231.
1966 "Terminologia ştiinţifică şi tecnică in limba româna contemporană", *SCL* 11.1:
17-23.
Màfera, Giovanni
1957 "Profilo fonetico-morfologico dei dialetti da Venezia a Belluno", *ID* 22: 131-
184.
Maher, J. Peter
1971 "Etymology and generative phonology in traditional lexicon: a study of Latin
aqua 'water', *aquila* 'eagle', *aquilus* 'dark', and *aquilo* 'northwind' ", *GL* 11: 71-
98.
Makarov, Vladimir V.
1971 "Différenciation lexicale des langues romanes (problèmes et méthodes)", in
Cong. 12.1: 841-846.
Malita, Tatiana – Solomon Vaimberg
1972 "Le calque linguistique dans la perspective du rapport entre l'immanent et le
transcendant dans la langue", *XI Inter. Cong. of Linguists (Bologna 1972)*
(Bologna). [Reprint of papers.]
Malkiel, Yakov
1945 *The development of the Latin suffixes -antia and -entia in the Romance languages* (= *University of California Publications in Linguistics* 14) (Berkeley:
California U.P.).
1946 "Castilian *albricias* and its Ibero-Romance congeners", *Studies in Philology* 43:
498-521.
1947 "The etymology of Hispanic *lo(u)çano* and congeners", in Yakov Malkiel,
Three Hispanic word studies (= *University of California Publications in Linguistics* 1.7), 227-296.
1950a "The etymology of Hispanic *destroçar* and *troço*", *PhQ* 29: 151-171.
1950b "The hypothetical base in Romance etymology", *Word* 6: 42-69.
1951 "Lexical polarization in Romance", *Lg* 27: 485-518.
1952a "Ancient Hispanic *vera(s)* and *mentira(s):* A study in lexical polarization",
RomPh 6: 121-172.

1952c "Studies in Hispano-Latin homonymics: *PESSULUS; PECTUS, DĒSPEC-TUS, SUSPECTUS, FISTULA* in Ibero-Romance", *Lg* 28: 299-338.

1953a *"Apretar, pr(i)eto, perto:* historia de un cruce hispanolatiano", *Boletín del Instituto Caro y Cuervo* 9: 1-139.

1953b "A cluster of four homophones in Ibero-Romance", *MR* 21: 20-36, 120-134.

1954   *Studies in the reconstruction of Hispano-Latin word families* (= *University of California Publications in Linguistics* 11) (Berkeley: California U.P.).

1954a "La *F* inicial adventicia en español", *RLR* 18: 160-191.

1955a "En torno a la evolución de *cansar, canso, cansa(n)cio*", *NRFH* 9: 225-276.

1955-1956 Review of Wagner 1953, *RomPh* 9: 50-68.

1956   "Linguistic problems in a new Hispanic etymological dictionary", *Word* 12: 35-50.

1957-1958 "Diachronic hypercharacterization in Romance", *ArchL* 9: 79-113; 10: 1-36.

1958   "Español antiguo *cuer* y *corazón*", *BH* 60: 180-207, 327-363.

1958-1959 "The skein-winding reel in Gallo-Romance. Studies in etymology, dialect geography, and material civilization", *RomPh* 12: 262-282.

1958-1960 "Distinctive features in lexicography: A typological approach to dictionaries exemplified in Spanish", *RomPh* 12: 366-399; 13: 111-155.

1961   "Etimología y cambio fonético débil: trayectoria iberorrománica de *MEDICUS, MEDICĀMEN, MEDICĪNA*", *Ibérida* 6: 127-171 (= *Homenaje a Marcel Bataillon*).

1961-1962 "Three definitions of Romance linguistics", *RomPh* 15: 1-7.

1962a Review of Hubschmid 1955 and 1961, *Lg* 38: 149-185.

1962b "A typological classification of dictionaries on the basis of distinctive features", in Householder – Saporta 1962: 3-24.

1962c "Weak phonetic change, spontaneous sound shift, lexical contamination", *Lingua* 11: 262-275.

1962d "Towards a unified system of classification of Latin-Spanish vowel correspondences", *RomPh* 16: 153-169.

1963-1964 "The interlocking of narrow sound change, broad phonological pattern, level of transmission, areal configuration, sound symbolism. Diachronic studies in the Hispano-Latin consonant clusters *cl-, fl-, pl-*", *ArchL* 15: 144-173; 16: 1-33.

1964   "Distinctive traits of Romance linguistics", in *Language in culture and society,* edited by Dell Hymes (New York: Harper & Row), 671-686. [Reprinted in Malkiel 1968a and in Anderson – Creore 1972.]

1966   "Diphthongization, monophthongization, metaphony: Studies in their interaction in the paradigm of the Old Spanish *-ir* verbs", *Lg* 42: 430-472.

1966a "Form versus meaning in etymological analysis: Old Spanish *auze* 'luck'", in *Estudios dedicados a James Homer Herriott* (Madison: Wisconsin U.P.).

1966b "Genetic analysis of word formation", in *Current Trends* 3: 305-364.

1967a "Linguistics as a genetic science", *Lg* 43: 223-245.

1967b "Multiple versus simple causation in linguistic change", in *To honor Roman Jakobson* (The Hague: Mouton) 2: 1228-1246.

1968a *Essays on linguistic themes* (Oxford: Blackwell).

1968b "Hispanic philology", in *Current Trends* 4: 158-228.

1968-1969 "Identification of origin and justification of spread in etymological analysis: Studies in Sp. *s(ol)ombra, en-sueño,* dial. *em-berano*", *RomPh* 22: 259-280.

1969   "The five sources of epenthetic j in Western Romance: A study in multiple causation", *HR* 37: 239-275.

1970   *Patterns of derivational affixation in the Cabraniego dialect of East-Central Asturian (= University of California Publications in Linguistics* 64) (Berkeley: California U.P.).

1970a *Linguistica generale, filologia romanza, etimologica* (Firenze: Sansoni).

1971   Review of Hubschmid 1963-1965, *Lg* 47: 465-487.

1971a "Derivational transparency as an occasional co-determinant of sound change: A new causal ingredient in the distribution of -ç- and -z- in ancient Hispano-Romance", *RomPh* 25: 1-52.

1972a "Comparative Romance linguistics", in *Current Trends* 9.2: 835-925.

1972b "The rise of nominal augments in Romance. Graeco-Latin and Tuscan clues to the prehistory of Hispano-Romance", *RomPh* 26: 306-334.

1972c "The Pan-European suffix *-esco, -esque* in stratigraphic projection", in *Papers in linguistics and phonetics to the memory of Pierre Delattre* (The Hague: Mouton), 357-387.

1972d "The first quarter century (and some antecedents)", *RomPh* 26: 3-15.

1973a "Phonological irregularity vs. lexical complexity in diachronic projection: The etymological substructure of Luso-Hispanic *abarcar* 'to clasp, embrace, contain'", in Kahane 1973: 605-635.

1973b "The double affixation in OFr. *gens-es-or, bel-ez-or,* OProv. *bel-az-or*", *SN* 45: 217-225.

1973c "Quelques avatars romans d'un zoonyme et d'un ornithonyme latins", in *Etudes de langue et de littérature du Moyen Age offertes à Félix Lecoy* (Paris: Champion), 377-384.

1973d "Two problems of Hispanic morpho-etymology", in *Studies in honor of Tatiana Fotitch* (Washington, D. C.: Catholic University of America Press), 261-270.

1973e "Deux frontières entre la phonologie et la morphologie en diachronie", *Langages* 32: 79-87.

1973-1974 Necrology of E. Gamillscheg, *RomPh* 27: 172-189.

1974   "Primary, secondary, and tertiary etymologies: The three lexical kernels of Hispanic *saña, ensañar, sañudo*", *HR* 42: 1-32.

1975a "Etymology and modern linguistics", *Lingua* 36: 101-120.

1975b "Deux catégories d'étymologies 'intéressantes'", *RLR* 39: 255-295.

1975c "Diachronic lexical polarization once more. The case of Sp. *primero* – OSp. *postrimero* – Class.Sp. *postrero*", *RRLing* 20: 523-533.

1975d Review of Hope 1971a, *Lg* 51: 962-976.

1976a *Etymological dictionaries: a tentative typology* (Chicago: U.P.).

1976b "Perspectives d'un renouvellement de l'étymologie romane", in *Cong.* 13.1: 967-984.

1976c "The interlocking of etymology and historical grammar (exemplified with the analysis of Spanish *desleír* ", in *Proceedings of the Second International Conference on Historical Linguistics,* edited by W. M. Christie, Jr. (Amsterdam: North Holland), 285-312.

1977   "The social matrix of Palaeo-Romance postverbal nouns", *RomPh* 31: 55-90.

1978   "The classification of Romance languages", *RomPh* 31: 467-500.

Malmberg, Bertil

1944   "Ancien français *blou, bloi, pou, poi* et questions connexes", *RF* 18: 8-17.

1947-1948 "L'espagnol dans le nouveau monde", *SL* 1: 79-116; 2: 20-26. [Reprinted in Malmberg 1973: 265-318.]

1950 *Etudes sur la phonétique de l'espagnol parlé en Argentine* (Lund: U.P.).
1958 "Le passage castillan f<h, perte d'un trait redondant", *CLing* 3: 337-343.
1959a Review of Martinet 1955, *SNPh* 31: 298-306.
1959b "L'extension du castillan et le problème des substrats"? *Actes du colloque international de civilisations, littératures et langues romanes* (Bucureşti: UNESCO), 249-260.
1961 "Linguistique ibérique et ibéro-romane, problèmes et méthodes", *SL* 15: 57-113.
1962 "Structure phonétique de quelques langues romanes", *Orbis* 11: 130-178. [Reprinted in Malmberg 1971.]
1963a "Tradición hispánica e influencia indígena en la fonética hispanoamericana", *Presente y futuro de la lengua española, Actas de la asamblea de filología del I Congreso de instituciones hispánicas (Madrid) 1963* (Madrid: Ed. Cultura hispánica, 1964). Reprinted in Malmberg 1971.
1963b "Encore une fois le substrat", *SL* 17: 40-46.
1971 *Phonétique générale et romane: Etudes en allemand, anglais, espagnol et français* (The Hague: Mouton).
1973 *Linguistique générale et romane. Etudes en allemand, anglais, espagnol et français* (The Hague: Mouton).

Mańczak, Witold
1959 "Le problème de la classification des langues romanes", *BF* 18: 81-90.
1962 *Phonétique et morphologie historiques du français* (Warszawa/Kraków). [New edition 1973.]
1965 "Développement phonétique irrégulier et fréquence d'emploi en français", in *Cong.* 10.3: 911-924.
1968 "Développement irrégulier dû à la fréquence d'emploi en français et en espagnol: Données numériques", in *Cong.* 11.1: 549-559.
1969 *Développment phonétique des langues romanes et la fréquence* (Kraków).
1970 "Evolution phonétique et rendement fonctionel", *RRLing* 15: 531-537.
1970-1971 "Développement de l'*ŏ* tonique libre devant nasale en français", in *Cong.* 12.1: 291-297.
1974 "La langue romane commune: latin vulgaire ou latin classique?", *RR* 9: 218-231.
1977 *Le latin classique: - langue romane commune* (Warszawa: Ossolineum).

Maneca, Constant
1966 "La struttura etimologica della lingua romena letteraria contemporanea dal punto di vista della frequenza dei vocaboli", *RRLing* 11: 219-238.
1967 "Fisionomia lessicale del romeno letterario contemporaneo", *RLR* 31: 190-204.
1968 "Saggio di periodizzazione della storia linguistica italiana", *RRLing* 13: 131-138.
1969 "Caratteri generali dell' evoluzione del' elemento originario del lessico rumeno ed italiano", *RRLing* 14: 549-567.
1971 "La fréquence des genres du substantif en roumain et en español", in *Cong.* 11.2: 1467-1471.
1972 "La fisionomia lessicale comparata del rumeno e dell' italiano", *RRLing* 17: 203-216.
1976 "Tipologia romanza quantitativa", in *Cong.* 14.2: 84-95.

Manoliu (-Manea), Maria
1963 "Note de fonologie romanică diacronică", *Revista de fonologie romanică şi germanică* 7: 9-15.

1965   "Innovations dans la structure du groupe nominal roman", *RRL* 10: 299-307.
1971   "Un peu de sémantique avant toute chose (sémantique paradigmatique et grammaire universelle)", *RRLing* 16: 241-249.
1971a *Gramatica comparată a limbilor romanice* (Bucureşti: Ed. didactică şi pedagogică).
1973   *Structuralismul lingvistic. Lecturi critice* (Bucureşti: Ed. didactică şi pedagogică).
Marcos Pérez, Pedro Jesús
1971   *Los anglicismos en el ámbito peroidístico* (Valladolid: U.P.).
Marre, A.
1910   "Petit vocabulaire des mots de la langue française d'importation hispano-portuguaise", *Revue de Linguistique et de Philologie Comparée* 42.
Martin, J. W.
1960   "Remarks on the origin of the Portuguese inflected infinitive", *Word* 16: 337-343.
Martin, Robert
1966   *Le mot 'rien' et ses concurrents en français du XIVe siècle à l'époque contemporaine* (= *Bibliothèque française et romane. Série A: Manuels et études linguistiques*) (Paris: Klincksieck).
1967   "Quelques réflexions sur le système relatif-interrogatif QUI/CUI//QUE-COI en ancien français", *TLL* 5: 97-122.
Martinet, André
1949   "Occlusives and affricates with reference to some problems of Romance phonology", *Word* 5: 116-122.
1950   "De la sonorisation des occlusives initiales en Basque", *Word* 6: 224-233.
1951   "The unvoicing of Old Spanish sibilants", *RomPh* 5: 133-156. [Expanded version in Martinet 1955: 257-296.]
1952   "Celtic lenition and Western Romance consonants", *Lg* 27: 192-217. [French version chapter 11 of Martinet 1955.]
1952-1953 "Diffusion of language and structural linguistics", *RomPh* 6: 5-13.
1955   *Economie des changements phonétiques* (Bern: Francke).
1956   *La description phonologique avec application au parler franco-provençal d'Hauteville (Savoie)* (Genève/Paris: Droz).
1960   *Eléments de linguistique générale* (Paris: Armand Colin).
1962   "R du latin au français d'aujourd'hui", *Phonetica* 8: 193-202.
Mastrelli, Carlo Alberto
1965   "L'origine germanica dell'italiano regionale 'stolzare', 'stolzo'", *AAAd* 69: 225-252.
1974   "I germanismi dell'italiano, problemi geo-sociolinguistici", Communication to *Cong.* 14.
Matei, Ion
1967   "Notes sur les 'turcismes' du dialecte roumain du Banat: un problème de méthode", *RESEE* 5: 567-571.
Matoré, Georges
1951   *Le vocabulaire et la société sous Louis-Philippe* (Genève/Lille: Droz).
1952   "Le néologisme, naissance et diffusion", *FM* 20: 87-92.
1953   *La méthode en lexicologie* (Paris: Didier).
1968   *Histoire des dictionnaires français* (Paris: Larousse).
Mattei, R. de
1942- "Ospizio di parole politiche perdute", *LN* 4 (1942) and subsequent volumes.

Maurer, Teodoro Henrique, Jr.
1951   *A unidade da Romania ocidental* (São Paulo: Univ. Fac. Filosofia, *Bol.* 126).
1959   *Gramática do latim vulgar* (Rio de Janeiro: *BBF* 16).
1962   *O problema do latim volgar* (Rio de Janeiro: *BBF* 17).
1966   *O infinito flexionado português. Estudo histórico-descriptivo* (= *Biblioteca Universitária, Serie 5, Letras e Linguística* 1) (São Paulo: Ed. Nacional).
Mauro, Tullio de
1963   *Storia linguistica dell'Italia unita* (Bari: Latzera). [2nd edition 1970.]
Mayer, Anton
1957-1959   *Die Sprache der alten Illyrier* (Wien: Robrer).
Mazzola, Michael L.
1967   *The place of Sicilian in the reconstruction of Proto-Romance* (Diss, Cornell Univ.) (Ann Arbor: University Microfilms).
1970-1971   "La position du sicilien dans la reconstruction du proto-roman", in *Cong.* 12.1:161-167.
1976   *Proto-Romance and Sicilian* (Lisse: de Ridder).
Mazzoni, G.
1939   "Strani francesismi del Machiavelli", *LN* 1: 12-13.
Meadows, Gail K.
1948   "The development of Latin hiatus groups in the Romance languages", *PMLA* 63: 765-784.
Meier, Harri
1941   *Die Entstehung der romanischen Sprachen und Nationen* (Frankfurt a.M.: Klostermann).
1950   "A gênese do infinito flexionado português", *BF* 11: 115-132.
1952   "Mirages prélatins. Kritische Betrachtungen zur romanischen Substratetymologie", *RF* 64: 1-62.
1958   "G. Rohlfs 1928 und 1958. Erläuterungen zum Substratproblem", *RJb* 9: 41-58.
1969   Review of Guiraud 1967, *RF* 81: 595-600.
1971   *Sprache und Geschichte. Festschrift für Harri Meier zum 65. Geburtstag,* edited by E. Coseriu and W.-D. Stempel (München: Fink).
1972   "¡ Estamos conchabados!", in *Homenaje a Casalduero: crítica y poesía,* edited by R. P. Sigele and G. Sobejano (Madrid: Gredos), 389-393.
1975a   *Neue Beiträge zur romanischen Etymologie* (Heidelberg: Winter).
1975b   *Primäre und sekundäre Onomatopöien und andere Untersuchungen zur romanischen Etymologie* (Heidelberg: Winter).
Meier, Harri – W. Roth (eds.)
. 1968   *Vermischte Beiträge* (= *Romanische Etymologien* 1) (Heidelberg: Winter).
Meillet, Antoine
1913   "De la différenciation de phonèmes", *MSLP* 12: 14-34.
1926   "Sur la disparition des formes simples du prétérit", *Linguistique historique et linguistique générale* (Paris).
1927-1929   Review of Gamillscheg 1926-1928, *BSLP* 27: 117-120; 28: 143-146; 29: 141-142.
1928   *Esquisse d'une histoire de la langue latine* (Paris: Hachette). [6th edition 1952.]
1931   "Sur une période de bilinguisme en France", *CRAI:* 29-38.
Meillet, Antoine – A. Sauvageot
1934   "Le bilinguisme des hommes cultivés", *Conférence de l'Institut de Linguistique* (Paris), 5-14.

Melander, Johan
  1925 "Le sort des prépositions *cum* et *apud* dans les langues romanes", *Mélanges Vising:* 359-374.
  1938 "La date du passage de *le me* à *me le* en français", *SNPh* 11: 101-114.
Ménardière, Christian de la
  1971 "Le français tel qu'on le parle", *FR* 44: 709-712.
Menarini, Alberto
  1947 *Ai margini della lingua* (Firenze).
  1951 *Profili di vita italiana nello parole nuove* (Firenze).
Mendeloff, Henry
  1969 *A manual of comparative Romance linguistics. Phonology and morphology* (Washington, D.C.: The Catholic University of America Press).
Menéndez Pidal, Ramón
  1904 *Manual elemental de gramática histórica española* (Madrid: Suárez). [6th edition 1941 (Madrid: Espasa Calpe).]
  1926 [1950] *Orígines del español; estado lingüístico de la Península Ibérica hasta el siglo XI* (= *RFE* anejo 1) (Madrid: Hernando). [3rd edition 1950 (Madrid: Espasa Calpe).]
Meo Zilio, G.
  1958 "Un morfema italiano con funzione stilistica nello spagnolo rioplatense", *LN* 19: 58-64.
  1960 "Sull'elemento italiano nello spagnolo rioplatense", *LN* 21: 97-103.
Meo Zilio, G. – Ettore Rossi
  1970 *El elemento italiano en el habla de Buenos Aires* (Firenze: Valmartina).
Merlo, Clemente
  1927 "Lazio sannita ed Etruria latina", *ID* 3: 84-92.
  1933 "Il sostrato ètnico e i dialetti italiani", *ID* 9: 1-24.
  1938 "Contributo alla conoscenza dei dialetti della Liguria odierna", *ID* 14: 23-58.
  1942 "Tracce de sostrato ligure in alcune parlate odierne dell'Italia settentrionale e della Francia meridionale", *Rend. Accad. d'Italia* S. 7.3: 1-17.
  1948 "Degli esiti toscani dei nessi g+j e d+j intervocalici", *LN* 9: 26-29.
  1954 "Del sostrato nelle parlate italiane", *Orbis* 3: 7-13.
  1957 "Chiara risposta a un ingrato", *ID* 21: 195-199.
Messner, Dietrich
  1973 "Der portugiesische Anteil am Dictionnaire chronologique" in *Portugiesische Forschungen der Goerres Gesellschaft* 11.
  1974-1975 *Dictionnaire chronologique des langues ibéroromanes*, 4 vols. (Heidelberg: Winter).
  1974 a *Chronologische und etymologische Studien zu den iberoromanischen Sprachen und zum Französischen* (Tübingen: Niemeyer).
  1974 b "Quelques regards sur la chronologie du lexique français", *CLex* 24: 107-114.
  1975 *Essai de lexicochronologie française* (Salzburg: Selbstverlag).
  forthcoming ,*Einführung in die Geschichte des französischen Wortschatzes* (Darmstadt: Wissenschaftliche Buchgesellschaft).
Meyer, Paul
  1904 *De l'expansion de la langue française en Italie pendant le moyen-âge (12e et 13e siècle)* (Roma).
Meyer-Lübke, Wilhelm
  1890-1902 *Grammatik der romanischen Sprachen*, 4 vols. (Leipzig: Reisland). [Vol. 3: *Romanische Syntax*, 1899.]

346   Bibliography

1900   *Grammaire des langues romanes,* traduite par Auguste et Georges Doutrepont, vol. 3: *Syntaxe* (Paris/Leipzig: Welter).
1913   "Zur u-ü Frage", *ZFSL* 41: 1-7.
1920   *Einführung in das Studium der romanischen Sprachwissenschaft* (3rd edition) (Heidelberg: Winter).
1925   "La sonorización de las sordas intervocálicas latinas en español", *RFE* 11: 1-32.
1935   *Romanisches etymologisches Wörterbuch* (Heidelberg: Winter).
1936   Review of Gamillscheg 1934-1936, *DLZ* 57: 2043-2047.

Michäelis de Vasconcelos, Carolina
1932   "Sources du lexique portugais; les éléments français", *Bulletin des Etudes Portugaises* 2.3: 137-153.

Michel, Louis
1949   "Le français à Carcassonne", *Annales de l'Institut d'Etudes Occitanes* (Toulouse), 196-208.
1953   *Etudes du son "S" en latin et en roman, des origines aux langues romanes, de la phonétique au style* (= *Univ. de Montpellier, Faculté de Lettres, Publications* 6) (Paris: P.U.F.).

Michelena, Luis
1964   "Románico y circunrománico", *Archivum* 14: 40-60.
1968   "Lat. S: El testimonio vasco", in *Cong.* 11.2: 473-489.

Migliorini, Bruno
1927   *Dal nome proprio al nome comune. Studi semantici sul mutamento dei nomi propri di persona in nomi comuni negl'idiomi romanzi* (= *Biblioteca dell'Archivum Romanicum,* serie II, *Linguistica* 13) (Genève: Olschki).
1941   "La sostituzione dei forestierismi: Improvvisa o graduale?", *LN* 3: 138-140.
1950   "Convergences linguistiques en Europe", *Synthèses* (Bruxelles) 4.47: 5-11.
1963 a *Parole nuove. Dodicimila voci a complemento del "Dizionario moderno" di A. Panzini* (Milano).
1963 b *Storia della lingua italiana* (4th edition) (Firenze).
1964   *Lingua contemporanea* (4th revised and augmented edition) (Firenze: Sansoni).
1967   *La lingua italiana d'oggi* (2nd edition) (Torino).
1968   *Profili di parole* (Firenze).
1971   "Parole 'più italiane' e 'meno italiane'", *LN* 32: 50-52.

Mihăescu, Haralambie
1960   *Limba latină în provinciile dunărene ale imperului român* (= *Comisia pentru studiul formarii limbii si poporului român* 3) (Bucureşti: Ed. Acad.).
1965   "E indreptăţita reconstituirea?", in *Omagiu lui Alexandru Rosetti la 70 de ani* (Bucureşti: Ed. Acad.). 567-571.
1966 a "Les éléments latins de la langue albanaise", *RESEE* 4: 5-33, 323-353.
1966 b *Influenţa greceasca asupra limbii române pina în secolul al XV-lea* (Bucureşti: Ed. Acad.).
1967   "L'influence byzantino-slave en roumain au XIIIe et XIVe siècle", *RRLing* 12(6): 489-505.
1971-1974 "La diffusion de la langue latine dans le Sud-Est de l'Europe", I-VIII, *RESEE* 9: 497-510 ... 12: 17-32.

Mihăilă, G.
1960   *Împrumuturi vechi sud-slave în limba română. Studiu lexico-semantic* (Bucureşti: Ed. Acad.).
1965   "Eléments slaves des parlers daco-romains", *RRLing* 10: 213-227.

Miklosich, Fr.
1862 "Die slavischen Elemente im Rumänischen", *Denkschriften der Wiener Akademie* (Phil.-Hist. Klasse) 12: 1-70.
Milan, W. G. – John J. Staczek – J. C. Zamora (eds.)
1975 *1974 Colloquium on Spanish and Portuguese linguistics* (Georgetown: U.P.).
Millardet, Georges
1923 *Linguistique et dialectologie romane. Problèmes et méthodes* (Montpellier/Paris: Société des langues romanes).
1933 "Sur un ancien substrat commun à la Sicilie, la Corse et la Sardaigne", *RLR* 9: 346-369.
Mohl, Friedrich G.
1899 *Introduction à la chronologie du latin vulgaire: Etude de philologie historique* (= *BEHE* 102) (Paris).
Mohrmann, Christine
1973 *Mélanges Christine Mohrmann* (Utrecht: Spectrum)
Moignet, Gérard
1958 "La forme en RE(T) dans le système verbal du plus ancien français", *RLaR* 73: 1-65.
1959 *Essai sur le mode subjonctif en latin postclassique et en ancien français*, 2 vols. (= *Publications de la Faculté de Lettres et Sciences Humaines d'Alger*) (Paris: P.U.F.)
1959a *Les signes de l'exception dans l'histoire du français* (= *Société de publications françaises et romanes* 65) 2nd edition 1972, 124) (Genève: Droz).
1965 *Le pronom personnel français. Essai de psycho-systématique historique* (= *Bibliothèque française et romane. Série A, Manuels et études linguistiques* 9) (Paris: Klincksieck).
1965a "L'opposition NON/NE en ancien français", *TLL* 3: 41-65.
1966 "Sur le système de la flexion à deux cas de l'ancien français", *TLL* 4: 339-356.
1967 "Le système du paradigme QUI-QUE-QUOI", *TLL* 5: 75-85.
1973 *Grammaire de l'ancien français* (= *Initiation à la linguistique, Série B, Problèmes et méthodes* 2) (Paris: Klincksieck).
Moldovanu, C.
1952 "Contributions à l'étude des mots roumains d'origine orientale", *Cahiers Sextil Puşcariu* 1: 421-428.
Moll (y Casasnovas), Francisco de B.
1952 *Gramática histórica catalana* (= *Biblioteca romanica hispanica* 3: *Manuales*) (Madrid: Gredos).
Møller, Christian
1933 *Zur Methodik der Fremdwortkunde* (= *Acta Jutlandica* 5) (Aarhus).
Moltoni, Vittoria
1954 "Gli influssi dell'Osco sulle iscrizione latine della Regio I". *RIL* 87: 193-232.
Mondéjar, José
1967 "Areas léxicas (sobre relaciones entre Hispania y la Italia meridional)", *RDyTP* 23: 181-200.
1970 "Préstamos hispánicos al sardo. Estudio de geografica", *ZRPh* 86: 128-167.
forthcoming "Un aragonesismo ornitológico en sardo: *cardelina (carduelis carduelis L.)*", *AFA*.
Monelli, Paolo
1943 *Barbaro dominio; cinquecento esotismi* (2nd edition) (Milano: Hoepli). [1st edition 1933.]

Monteverdi, Angelo
1952   *Manuale de avviamento agli studi romanzi I. Le lingue romanze* (Milano: Vallardi).
Montgomery, T.
1976   "Complementarity of stem-vowels in the Spanish second and third conjuga-. tions", *RomPh* 29: 281-296.
Moreno, Augusto
1943   "Estrangeirismos", *RP* (série A: *Lingua portuguesa)* 2.6: 25-28.
Mounin, Georges
1965a   "Essai sur la structuration du lexique de l'habitation", *CLex* 6: 9-24.
1965b   "Un champ sémantique : La dénomination des animaux domestiques", *Linguistique* 1: 31-54.
Mourin, Louis
1959   "Définition de l'imparfait et du plus-que-parfait de l'indicatif et du subjonctif et des deux formes du conditionnel en portugais moderne", *Romanica Gandensia* 7: 105-202.
Mourin, Louis – Jacques Pohl
1971   *Bibliographie de linguistique romane* (4th revised edition) (Bruxelles: U.P.).
Muljačić, Zarko
1965-1968   "Tipologiya jezičnoga kalka" [Typology of loan-translations], *Radovi Filozofski Fakultetu Zadru* 7: 5-19.
1967   "Die Klassifikation der romanischen Sprachen", *RJb* 18: 23-37.
1969   "Bibliographie de linguistique romane: Domaine dalmate et istriote avec les zones limitrophes (1906-1966)", *RLR* 33: 144-167, 356-391.
1971   *Introduzione allo studio della lingua italiana* (Torino: Einaudi).
1971a   "La posizione dell'occitano", *RLR* 35: 83-89.
Muller, Bodo
1971   "Das morphemmarkierte Satzobjekt der romanischen Sprachen (der sogenannte präpositionale Akkusativ)", *ZRPh* 87: 477-519.
1971a   "Die typologische Klassifikation der romanischen Sprachen. Methode und Entwurf", in Wandruszka 1971: 242-253.
1971b   "La bi-partition linguistique de la France", *RLR* 35: 17-30.
1974   "La structure linguistique de la France et la romanisation", *TLL* 12: 7-29.
Muller, H.-F.
1929   *Chronology of Vulgar Latin* (Halle).
1945   *L'époque mérovingienne. Essai de synthèse de philologie et d'histoire* (New York: Vanni).
Nagel, I.
1972   *Die Bezeichnung für "dumm" und "verrückt" im Spanischen unter Berücksichtigung ihrer Entsprechungen in anderen romanischen Sprachen insbesondere im Katalanischen und Portugiesischen* (= *ZRPh* Beiheft 126) (Tübingen: Niemeyer).
Nandriş, Grigore
1951   "The development and structure of Rumanian", *Slavonic Review* 30: 7-39.
Nandriş, Octave
1963a   "La langue roumaine dans la correspondance du XVIe siècle", *RLR* 27: 84-100.
1963b   *Phonétique historique du romain* (Paris: Klincksieck).
1965   "Le problème de l (ll) en latin et dans les langues romanes", in *Cong.* 10.3: 925-943.

1973   "Le mot français dans la langue roumaine", *TLL* 11: 105-116.

Nannucci, V.
1840   *Voci e locuzioni italiane derivate della lingua provenzale* (Firenze).

Naro, Anthony J.
1971a   "Resolution of vocalic hiatus in Portuguese: Diachronic evidence for binary features", *Lg* 47: 381-393.
1971b   "The history of *e* and *o* in Portuguese: A study in linguistic drift", *Lg* 47: 615-645.

Nedelcu, Monica
1976   "Observaciones sobre el léxico fundamental de dos lenguas romances: el romano y el francés", in *Cong.* 13.1: 745-752.

Neira Martínez, Jesus
1955   *El habla de Lena* (Oviedo: Instituto de Estudios Asturianos).

Nemésio, Vitorino
1936   *Relações françesas do Romantismo português* (Coimbra).

Neuenschwander, R.
1970   "Die rätoromanische Volksgruppe im Schweizer Kanton Graubünden", *Handbuch der europäischen Volksgruppen* (Wien), *Ethnos* 8: 180-192.

Neuhaus, H. J.
1971   "Towards a diachronic analysis of vocabulary", *CLex* 18: 29-42.

Neuvonen, Eero K.
1941   *Los arabismos en español en el siglo XIII* (Helsinki).

Niculescu, Alexandru
1965   *Individualitatea limbii române între limbile romanice. Contribuţii gramaticale* (Bucureşti).
1971   "Premesse sul problema dei rapporti cultural-linguistici italo-romeni", in *Cong.* 12.2: 839-904.
1976   "L'occidentalisation romane du romain moderne", in *Mélanges offerts à Carl Theodor Gossen*, edited by G. Colón and R. Kopp (Bern/Liège), 665-692.
1977   "Romanité roumaine – une analyse socio-culturelle", *VR* 36: 1-16.
1978   "Cultura di classe e cultura popolare nell'occidentalizzazione romanza del rumeno moderno. Premesse socioculturali", in *Cong.* 14.2: 283-290.

Niederehe, H.-J.
1968   "Wort- und Namenerklärung in Leomartes *Suma de historia troyana*", *RJb* 19: 223-251.
1969   "Boccaccio als Etymologe", in Piel 1969: 166-171.
1974   *Die Sprachauffassung Alfons des Weisen. Studien zur Sprach- und Wissenschaftsgeschichte* (= *ZRPh* Beiheft 144) (Tübingen: Niemeyer).

Niedermann, Max
1904 [1953]   *Spécimen d'un précis de phonétique du latin à l'usage des gymnases, lycées et athénées. Esquisse linguistique annexée au rapport du gymnase de La Chaux-de-Fonds sur l'exercice 1903/04* (La Chaux-de-Fonds). [3rd edition 1953: *Précis de phonétique hisotrique du latin* (Paris: Klincksieck); German translation by E. Hermann: *Historische Lautlehre des Lateinischen* (Heidelberg: Winter, 1907; 3rd edition 1953).]

Nissen, H.
1883   *Italienische Landeskunde* I (Berlin).

Nogueira, Rodrigo de Sá
1936   "Notas de divulgacão. Salvemos a nossa língua", *Lingua Portuguesa* 5: 49-62.

Nouvel, Alain
    1978 "Situation politico-culturelle de la langue d'oc", in *Cong.* 14.2: 335-338.
Nunes, Jose J.
    1919 *Compêndio de gramática histórica portuguesa, fonetica-morfologia* (Lisboa: Teixeira). [3rd edition 1945.]
Nyrop, Kristoff
    1899-1930 *Grammaire historique de la langue française*, 6 vols. (København: Gyldendal). [Revised by P. Laurent, 1930-1960.]
O'Hare, P. J
    1974 *The contemporary influence of foreign languages on Spanish in the field of popular culture, as illustrated in the Spanish press 1968-1974* (Ph. D. Diss, Univ. Manchester).
Öhmann, E.
    1968 *Genusbeeinflussung von Substantiven durch eine fremde Sprache* (Helsinki: Suomaleinen Tiedakademia).
Oksaar, Els
    1972 "Bilingualism", in *Current Trends* 9: 475-511.
Oliver Asín, Jaime
    1938 *Iniciación al estudio de la historia de la lengua española* (Pamplona). [6th edition 1941: *Historia de la lengua española* (Madrid: Diana).]
Oliver, T. Buesa
    1965 *Indoamericanismos léxicos en español* (Madrid: CSIC).
Önnersfors, Alf (ed.).
    1975 *Mittellateinische Philologie* (Darmstadt: Wissenschaftliche Buchgesellschaft).
Oostendorp, H. Th.
    1966 "La evolución semántica de las palabras españolas 'actor' a la luz de la estética medieval", *BH* 68: 338-352.
Orr, John
    1935 "Les anglicismes du vocabulaire sportif", *FM* 3: 293-311.
    1953 *Words and sounds in English and French* (Oxford: Blackwell).
    1954 "L'étymologie populaire", *RLR* 18: 129-142.
    1962 *Old French and Modern English idioms* (Oxford: Blackwell).
Osswald, P.
    1970 *Frz. 'campagne' und seine Nachbarwörter im Vergleich zum Deutschen, Englischen, Italienischen und Spanischen. Ein Beitrag zur Wortfeldtheorie* (Tübingen).
Ostrà, Ruzena
    1966 "Etude comparative des champs conceptuels dans les langues romanes", *ERB* 2: 23-33.
    1967 "Le champ conceptuel du travail dans les langues romanes", *ERB* 3: 7-84.
    1971 "Le champ conceptuel du travail en ancien français", *ERB* 5: 19-44.
Otero Álvarez, Aníbal
    1949-1971 "Hipótesis etimológicas referentes al gallego-português", *CEG* 4: 171-200; 6: 83-114 (1951); 8: 87-119 (1953); 9: 272-292 (1954); 10: 405-427 (1955); 11: 117-139, 245-269 (1956); 12: 107-126, 213-227 (1957); 13: 77-94 (1958); 14: 87-105, 331-348 (1959); 15: 89-104 (1960); 16: 159-175 (1961); 17: 329-347 (1962); 18: 16-34 (1963); 19: 143-160 (1964); 20: 12-30, 330-349 (1965); 21: 170-188 (1966); 22: 165-182 (1967); 23: 70-88 (1968); 25: 70-88 (1970); 26: 287-306 (1971).
    1967 *Contribución al diccionario gallego* (Vigo: Galaxia).

Otero, Carlos
1971 *Evolución y revolución en romance* (Barcelona: Seix Barral).
Pacquot, Annette
1976 "L'évolution d'un champ sémantique du latin à l'ancien français: essai de sémantique diachronique structurale", in *Cong.* 13.1: 797-807.
Pagliaro, Antonio
1934 "Aspetti della storia linguistica della Sicilia", *Archivum Romanicum* 18: 356-380.
Palmer, Leonard R.
1954 *The Latin language* (London: Faber & Faber).
1972 *Descriptive and comparative linguistics: A critical introduction* (London: Faber & Faber).
Pariente, A.
1970 "Sobre 'trasto' y 'traste'", *RFE* 53: 115-136.
Parlangèli, Oronzo.
1960 *Studi messapici Iscrizioni, lessico, glosse, indici* (Milano: Istitudo Lombardo).
1960a *Storia linguistica e storia politica nell'Italia meridionale* (Firenze: le Monnier).
1964-1965 "Il sostrato linguistico in Sicilia", *Kokalos* 10-11: 211-244.
1969 "Considerazioni sulla classificazione dei dialetti italiani", in Pisani 1969: 715-760.
1970 *Scritti in memoria de Oronzo Parlangèli* (Lecce).
Parrino, Flavio
1967 "Su alcune particolarità della coniugazione nel dialetto di Ripatransone", *ID* 30: 156-166.
Pătruţ, I.
1953 "Influenţe maghiare în română", *SCL* 4: 211-217.
1971a "Despre vechea influenţă slavă din limba română. Probleme de metodă şi terminologie", *CLing* 16: 241-246.
1971b "Latin et slave dans le lexique de roumain", *RRLing* 16: 299-309.
Patterson, William T.
1968 "On the genealogical structure of the Spanish vocabulary", *Word* 24: 321ff.
Patterson, William T. – Hector N. Urrutibéheity
1975 *The lexical structure of Spanish* (The Hague: Mouton).
Pattison, D. G.
1975 *Early Spanish suffixes. A functional study of the principal nominal suffixes of Spanish up to 1300* (Oxford: Blackwell).
Pei, Mario A.
1932 *The language of the eighth-century texts in Northern France* (New York: Carranza/Columbia U.P.).
1941 *The Italian language* (New York: Vanni).
1943 "Latin and Italian front vowels", *MLN* 58: 116-120.
1949 "A new methodology for Romance classification", *Word* 5: 135-146.
1973 *Studies in honor of Mario A. Pei* (North Carolina U.P.).
1976 *The story of Latin and the Romance languages* (New York: Harper & Row).
Pellegrini, Carlo
1948 *Relazioni tra la letteratura italiana e la letteratura francese,* in the series *Problemi ed orientamenti critici di lingua e di letteratura italiana* (Milano).
Pellegrini, Giovanni B.
1949 "Le interdentali nel Veneto", *Atti del Laboratorio di Fonetica dell'Università di Padova* 1: 25-38.

352   Bibliography

1954   "Noterelle epigrafico linguistiche", *AAAd* 48: 419-431.
1957   "MN > UN nel latino dalmatico", *PP* 52: 55-58.
1960   "Tra lingua e dialetto in Italia", *SMV* 8: 137-153.
1962-1963   "Appunti su alcuni italianismi delle biografie trobadoriche", *AIV* 121: 443-466.
1964   "Tra prelatino e latino nell'Italia superiore", *Arte e civiltà romana nell'Italia settentrionale* (Bologna: Alfa), 73-79.
1965   "Appunti etimologici arabo-siculi", *BCSS* 9: 63-73.
1966   *Grammatica storica spagnola* (= *Collana di grammatiche storiche neolatine* 2) (Bari: Leonardo da Vinci).
1969   "Postille venetiche", *Athenaeum* 47: 236-255.
1970   "La classificazione delle lingue romanze e i dialetti italiani", *FI* 4: 211-237.
1972   *Gli arabismi nelle lingue neolatine con speciale riguardo all'Italia*, 2 vols. (Brescia: Paideia).
1972a *Saggi sul ladino dolomitico e sul friulano* (Bari: L'Adriatica).
1973a "Popoli e lingue nell'Italia superiore prelatina", *Aquilaia e Milano. Antichità Altoadriatiche* 4: 11-34.
1973b "I cinque sistemi linguistici dell'italo-romanzo", *RRLing* 18: 105-129.
1974a *Saggi de storia linguistica italiana* (Torino: Boringhieri).
1974b "Il Cadore preromano e le nuove iscrizioni di Valle", *Archivio Veneto* 136: 5-34.
Pellegrini, G. B. – A. L. Prosdocimi
1967   *La lingua venetica*, 2 vols. (Padova/Firenze).
Pellegrini, Silvio
1971   *Studi di filologia romanza offerti a S. Pellegrini* (Padova).
Penny, Ralph J.
1970   *El habla pasiega: ensayo de dialectología montañesa* (London: Támesis).
1972   "Verb class as a determiner of stem-vowel in the historical phonology of Spanish verbs", *RLR* 36: 343-359.
Pensado Tomé, J. L.
1965   *Estudios etimológicos galaico-portugueses* (= *Acta Salmanticensia, Filosofía y Letras* 51) (Salamanca).
Pereira, Sara Sarmento
1949   *Subsídios para o estudo da linguagem dos jornais portugueses da actualidade* (unpublished diss., Univ. of Coimbra).
Peruzzi, Emilio
1948   Review of Heinimann 1946 with additional words relating to the Second World War, *Symposium* 2.1: 124-126.
1970-1973 *Origini di Roma* I, II (Bologna: Pàtron).
Peter, Herbert
1969   *Entstehung und Ausbildung der italienischen Eisenbahnterminologie* (= *Wiener Romanistische Arbeiten* 8) (Wien/Stuttgart: Braumüller).
1971   "Retrodatazione nella traduzione italiana del *Dictionnaire universel de commerce* dei fratelli Savary", *LN* 33: 80-82.
Petrovici, Emil
1938   "Les éléments slaves d'origine savante en roumain et les suffixes *-anie, -enie*", *Balcania* 1: 83-87.
1957a *Kann das Phonemsystem einer Sprache durch fremden Einfluß umgestaltet werden?* (The Hague: Mouton).
1957b "Fenomene de sinarmonism în fonetica istorică a limbii romîne", *CL* 2: 97-126.

1958 "Le roumain a-t-il hérité du roman commun la corrélation palatale des consonnes?", *RRLing* 3: 5-11.

1959 "Interpenetraţia unei fonologii slave şi a unei morfologii latine", *CL* 4: 31-41.

1960 "'Depalatizarea' consoanelor înainte de *e* in Muntenia, Sud-Estul Transilvaniei şi în dialectul istroromîn", *CL* 5: 9-22.

1963 "Raportul dintre izoglosele dialectale slave şi izoglosele elementelor slave ale limbii române", *Romanoslavica* 7: 11-22.

1964 "Résistance du système phonologique à une forte influence phonétique étrangère", *ZPhon* 17: 281-285.

1966 "Le latin oriental possédait-il des éléments slaves?", *RRLing* 11: 313-321.

1970-1971 "L'hiatus au cours de l'évolution phonétique du roumain", in *Cong.* 12.1: 377-380.

Pfister, Max

1960 *Die Entwicklung der inlautenden Konsonantengruppe -ps- in den romanischen Sprachen mit besonderer Berücksichtigung des Altprovenzalischen* (= *Romanica Helvetica* 69) (Bern: Francke).

Piccitto, Giorgio

1950 "La classificazione delle parlate siciliane e la metafonese in Sicilia", *Archivio Storico della Sicilia Orientale* 47: 1-34.

1959 "Il siciliano dialetto italiano", *Orbis* 8: 183-199.

1970 "La "propagginazione" dans les dialectes siciliens", *RRLing* 15: 135-145.

Pichon, E.

1935 "L'enrichissement lexical dans le français d'aujourd'hui", *FM* 3: 209-222.

Picoche, Jacqueline

1970 "Problèmes des dictionnaires étymologiques", *CLex* 16: 53-62.

1971 "Typologie de quelques dictionnaires étymologiques courants", *LFr* 10: 107-113.

1976 *Le vocabulaire psychologique dans les chroniques de Froissart* (Paris: Klincksieck).

1977 *Précis de lexicologie française* (Paris: Nathan).

Piel, J. M.

1953 *Miscelânea de etimologia portuguesa e galega (Primeira série)* (Coimbra: Acta Universitatis Conimbrigensis).

1958 "Gallicische Etymologien", in Lausberg 1958: 362-371.

1965 "Caractères généraux et sources du lexique galicien", in *Cong.* 10.3: 1261-1267.

1967 "Apontamentos de etimologia galega", in *Estudos filológicos. Homenagem a Serafim da Silva Neto* (= *Biblioteca de estudos literários* 6) (Rio de Janeiro: Ed. Tempo Brasiliero).

1968 "Amboss, Ziegenbock und betrogener Ehemann: Betrachtungen zu asturisch-galicisch *cabruñar* 'dengeln'", in Rohlfs 1968: 171-174.

1969 *Philologische Studien für Joseph M. Piel,* edited by W. D. Lange and H. J. Wolf (Heidelberg: Winter).

Pieri, Silvio

1898 "Toponomastica delle valli del Serchio e della Lima", *AGI* supplement 5: 1-242.

1919 *Toponomastica della Valle dell'Arno* (Roma: Lincei).

1928 "In cerca di nomi etruschi (noterella toponomastica)", *ID* 4: 186-211.

1969 *Toponomastica della Toscana meridionale e dell'archipelago toscano* (Siena: Ac. degli Intronati). [Posthumous edition].

Pietro, R. J. di
  1961   "Borrowing: its effect as a mechanism of linguistic change in American Sici-
          lian", *GL* 5: 30-36.
  1968   "Bilingualism", in *Current Trends* 4: 399-414.
Pirson, Jules
  1901   *La langue des inscriptions latines de la Gaule* (Bruxelles: Office de publicité).
Pisani, Vittore
  1954   "Palatalizzazioni osche e latine", *AGI* 39: 112-119.
  1959a *Saggi de linguistica storica* (Torino: Rosemberg & Sellier).
  1959b "Le iscrizione sudpicene", in *I Picene e la civiltà etrusco-italica,* Supplement to
          SE 26: 75-92.
  1967   *L'etimologia. Storia – questioni – metodo* (2nd edition) (= *Studi grammaticali e
          linguistici* 9) (Brescia: Paideia).
  1967a Review of Reichenkron 1966, *AGI* 52: 69-72.
  1969   *Studi linguistici in onore di V. Pisani* (Brescia: Paideia).
  1970   "Il sostrato osco-umbro", *Atti del quinto convegno di studi umbri (I dialetti
          dell'Italia mediana con particolare riguardo alla regione umbra)* (Perugia: Uni-
          versità di Perugia), 149-169.
Poalelungi, Ana Goldis
  1973   *L'influence du français sur le roumain (vocabulaire et syntaxe)* (Paris: Les Belles
          Lettres).
Poghirc, Cicerone
  1967   "Considérations sur les éléments autochtones de la langue roumaine", *RRLing*
          12: 19-36.
  1968a *Bogdan Petriceicu Hasdeu, lingvist și filolog* (București: Ed. științifica).
  1968b "Problèmes actuels de l'étymologie roumaine", *RRLing* 13: 199-214.
  1971   *Le roumain dans le contexte de la linguistique indo-européenne* (București).
  1972   "Irano-daco-romanica", *Studia et Acta Orientalia* 8: 25-28.
  1973   "Sur les éléments de substrat du roumain", *Dacoromania* 1: 197-209.
Polge, Henri
  1962   "En marge de l'Atlas linguistique de la Gascogne. L'innovation lexicale et son
          conditionnement", *Via Domitia* 17: 51-62.
Politzer, Frieda N. – Robert L. Politzer
  1955   *Romance trends in the 7th and 8th century Latin documents* (= *University of
          North Carolina Studies in the Romance Languages and Literatures* 21) Chapel
          Hill: North Carolina U.P.).
Politzer, Robert L.
  1947   "Final -*s* in the Romania", *RR* 38: 156-166.
  1949   *A study of the language of eighth century Lombardic documents: A statistical
          analysis of the Codice Paleografico Lombardo* (New York: Columbia U.P.).
  1951a "The phonemic interpretation of Late Latin orthography", *Lg* 27: 151-154.
  1951b "Vulgar Latin -*es* >Italian -*i*", *Italica* 28: 1-5.
  1951c "On the chronology of the simplification of geminates in Northern France",
          MLN 66: 527-532.
  1952   "On *b* and *v* in Latin and Romance", *Word* 8: 211-215.
  1953   "On the Rumanian and Sardinian treatment of Latin *qua* and *gua*", *MLN* 68:
          487-489.
  1954a "On the development of Latin -*ll*- to -*dd*- in Romance", *MLN* 69: 325-331.
  1954b "On the development of Latin stops in Aragonese", *Word* 10: 60-65.
  1955   "A note on North Italian voicing of intervocalic stops", *Word* 11: 416-419.

1967   *Beitrag zur Phonologie der Nonsberger Mundart* (= *Romanica Aenipontana* 6) (Innsbruck: Inst. rom. Phil. der Leopold-Franzens-Universität).

1968   "Causality and prediction in the diachronic phonemics of the Val di Non", *Word* 24.2: 371-379.

Pompiliu, Eliade

1898   *De l'influence française sur l'esprit public en Roumanie* (Paris).

Pop, Sever

1948   *Grammaire roumaine* (Bern: Francke).

Pope, Mildred K.

1934   *From Latin to Modern French with especial consideration of Anglo-Norman: Phonology and morphology* (Manchester: U.P.). [2nd edition 1952.]

Popović, Ivan

1960   "Balkanlateinisches Á im Südslavischen und Albanischen", *ZRPh* 76: 218-230.

Posner, Rebecca

1961 a   *Consonantal dissimilation in the Romance languages* (= *Philological Society, London, Publications* 19) (Oxford: Blackwell).

1961 b   "The imperfect endings in Romance", *TPhS* (1961): 17-55.

1963   "Phonology and analogy in the formation of the Romance perfect", *RomPh* 17: 419-431.

1965   "Romance imperfect and conditional endings", *SNPh* 37: 3-10.

1966   *The Romance languages: A linguistic introduction* (Garden City, N.Y.: Doubleday).

1967   "Positivism in historical linguistics", *RomPh* 20: 321-331.

1970   "Thirty years on", Supplement to 2nd edition of Iordan – Orr 1937: 399-579.

1971   "On synchronic and diachronic rules: French nasalization", *Lingua* 27: 184-197.

1973   "Homonymy, polysemy and semantic change", *Language Sciences* 27: 1-8.

1974   "The ordering of historical phonological rules in Romance", *TPhS* (1974): 98-127.

1975   "Semantic change or lexical change?", in Saltarelli – Wanner 1975: 177-182.

1976   "The relevance of comparative and historical data for the description and definition of a language", *York Papers in Linguistics* 6: 75-87.

1977   "Mentalist historical phonology - an infantile disorder", in Hall 1977: 229-236.

Pottier, Bernard

1954   "L'influence française sur le vocabulaire espagnol", *Vie et Langage* 3: 301-302.

1957   *Introduction à l'étude de la philologie hispanique* I (Paris: Payot). [2nd edition 1960.]

1958   *Introduction á l'étude de la philologie hispanique* II: *Morphosyntaxe espagnole – étude structurale* (Bordeaux). [2nd edition 1960 (Paris: Ed. Hispano-Americanas).]

1962   *Systématique des éléments de relation. Etude de morphosyntaxe romane* (= *Bibliothèque française et romane*, série A: *Manuels et études linguistiques* 2) (Paris: Klincksieck).

1967   "Galicismos", *ELH* 2: 127-151.

Poultney, J. W.

1959   *The bronze tablets of Iguvium* (= *Philological monograph* 18) (Baltimore: American Philological Association).

Prati, A.

1968   *Etimologie venete,* edited by G. Folena and G. Pellegrini (Venezia/Roma: Istituto per la Collaborazione Culturale).

Pratola, Daniel J.
1952 *Portuguese words of Italian origin* (unpublished PhD diss.) (University of California).

Pratt, Christopher J.
1976 *Anglicism in contemporary peninsular Castilian* (unpublished PhD diss.) (University of Oxford).

Price, Glanville
1964 "The problem of modern literary Occitan", *ArchL* 16: 34-53.
1967 "Influences espagnole, italienne et occitane sur la langue de Brantôme", *RLR* 31: 147-179.
1971 *The French language: Present and past* (London: Clowes).
1976 "Language standardisation in the Romance field. A survey of recent work", *Semasia* 3: 7-32.

Prosdocimi, Aldo L.
1967 "L'iscrizione di Prestino", *SE* 35: 199-222.
1969a "Una iscrizione inedita dal territorio atestino", *AIV* 127: 123-183.
1969b "Studi iguvini", *AMAT* 34: 3-124.
1969c "Note linguistiche italiche", *AMAP* 81: 263-296.
1971 "Note di epigrafia retica", *Studien zur Namenkunde und Sprachgeographie. Festschrift K. Finsterwalder* (= *Innsbrucker Beiträge zur Kulturwissenschaft* 16) (Innsbruck).
1972a "Una nuova iscrizione da Cartura (Padova)" *AGI* 57: 97-134.
1972b "Redazione e struttura testuale delle Tavole iguvine", in *Aufstieg und Niedergang der römischen Welt* (Berlin: de Gruyter) 2: 593-699.
1972c "Venetico", *SE* 40: 193-245.
1973 "Rivista de epigrafia italica", *SE* 41: 363-409.

Pulgram, Ernst
1958 *The tongues of Italy. Prehistory and history* (Cambridge, Mass.: Harvard U.P.).
1964 "Proto-languages as Proto-diasystems: Proto-Romance", *Word* 20: 373-383.
1967 "Trends and predictions", in *To honor Roman Jakobson* (= *Janua Linguarum, series maior* 32) (The Hague: Mouton), 1634-1649.
1975 *Latin-Romance phonology. Prosodics and metrics* (München: Fink).

Pullum, Geoffrey
1976 "Sequential and simultaneous rule application in Spanish phonology", *Lingua* 38: 221-262.

Purczinsky, Julius
1964 "Additional Frankish superstratum influence in Old French", *RomPh* 18: 27-31.
1970 "A Neo-Schuchardtian theory of general Romance diphthongization", *RomPh* 23: 492-528.

Puşcariu, Sextil I.
1940 *Limba română volumnul I: Privire generală* (Bucureşti: Fundaţia pentru literatură şi artă Regele Carol II). [German translation by Heinrich Kuen: *Die rumänische Sprache* (Leipzig: Harrassowitz, 1943).]

Quadri, B.
1952 *Aufgaben und Methoden der onomasiologischen Forschung. Eine entwicklungsgeschichtliche Darstellung* (Bern).

Quemada, Bernard
1955 *Introduction à l'étude du vocabulaire médical 1600-1710* (Paris).

1959   *Matériaux pour l'histoire du vocabulaire français. Datations et documents lex-icologiques* (Paris: Klincksieck).
1968   *Les dictionnaires du français moderne (1539-1863). Etude sur leur histoire, leurs types et leurs méthodes,* 2 vols. (Paris: Didier).
1972   "Lexicology and lexicography", in *Current Trends* 9: 395-475.

Radford, Andrew
1977   *Italian syntax: Transformational and relational grammar* (Cambridge: U.P.).
1978   "Agentive causatives in Romance: Accessibility versus passivation", *JL* 14: 35-58.

Ramalho, Maria A. da Costa
1951   *Os elementos franceses no vocabulário português: A costure* (unpublished diss.) (Coimbra).

Ramsden, Herbert
1963   *Weak pronoun position in the Early Romance languages* (= *Publications of the Faculty of Arts* 14) (Manchester: U.P.).

Rando, Gaetano
1967   "Alcuni anglicismi nel dialetto di Filicudi Pecorini", *LN* 28: 31-32.
1969   "Anglicismi nel *Dizionario Moderno* dalla quarto alla decima edizione", *LN* 30: 107-112.
1970   "The assimilation of English loan-words in Italian", *Italica* 47.2.
1973   "Influssi inglesi nel lessico italiano contemporaneo", *LN* 34: 111-120.

Rea, John A.
1958   "Concerning the validity of lexicostatics", *IJAL* 24: 145-150.
1973   "The Romance data of studies for glottochronology", in *Current Trends* 11: 359-367.

Redfern, James
1971   *A lexical study of Rhaeto-Romance and contiguous Italian dialect areas* (The Hague: Mouton).

Referovskaja, E. A.
1964   *Razvitie predložnyx konstrukcii v latinskom jazyke pozdnogo perioda* [The development of prepositional constructions in Late Latin] (Moskva/Leningrad: Nauka).

Regula, Moritz
1951   *Grundlegung und Grundprobleme der Syntax* (= *Bibliothek der allgemeinen Sprachwissenschaft,* Reihe 2: *Einzeluntersuchungen und Darstellungen*) (Heidelberg: Winter).
1955-1966 *Historische Grammatik des Französischen,* 3 vols. (Heidelberg: Winter).

Reichenkron, Günter
1951   "Das präpositionale Akkusativ-Objekt im ältesten Spanisch", *RF* 63: 342-397.
1952   "Einige grundsätzliche Bemerkungen zum Vigesimalsystem", in Gamillscheg 1952: 164-184.
1953   "Hungaro-Valachica", *Ural-altaische Jahrbücher* 25: 73-91.
1958   "Der lokativische Zähltypus für die Reihe 11 bis 19: ein auf zehn", *Südostfor-schungen* 17: 152-174.
1959   "Methodisches zu den ungarischen Lehnwörtern im Rumänsichen ", in *Gedenkschrift für Julius v. Farkas* (= *Ural-altaische Jahrbücher* 31), 328-335.
1965   *Historische latein-altromanische Grammatik* I (Wiesbaden: Harrassowitz).
1966   *Das Dakische (rekonstruiert aus dem Rumänischen)* (Heidelberg: Winter).

Reid, T. B. W.
1972   *History and structure of French. Essays in honour of Professor T. B. W. Reid* (Oxford: Blackwell).

358   Bibliography

Reiner, Erwin
  1968   *La place de l'adjectif épithète en français. Théories traditionnelles et essai de solution* (diss., Wien) (= *Wiener Romanistische Arbeiten* 7) (Wien/Stuttgart: Braumüller).
Reinheimer-Rîpeanu, Sanda
  1974   *Les dérives parasynthétiques dans les langues romanes: roumain, italien, français, espagnol* (The Hague: Mouton).
Rensch, Karl O.
  1968   "Zur Entwicklung der lat. Lateralkonsonanz in Kalabrien und der Basilikata. Ein Beitrag zur diachronischen Phonologie", *ZRPh* 84: 593-605.
Renzi, Lorenzo
  1973   "Il campo semantico di 'conoscere'", in *La traduzione: saggi e studi* (Trieste: LINT), 375-386.
  1977   *Introduzione alla filologia romanza* (Bologna: Il Mulino).
Révah, Israel S.
  1958   "L'évolution de la prononciation au Portugal et au Brésil du XVIe siècle à nos jours", *Anais do I Congresso brasiliero de língua falada no teatro (Salvador) 1956* (Rio de Janeiro: Ministério de educação e cultura), 387-399.
Rey, Alain
  1970   "Typologie génétique des dictionnaires", *Langages* 19: 48-68 [Reprinted in Rey 1977.]
  1977   *Le lexique: Images et modèles; du dictionnaire à la lexicologie* (Paris: Colin).
Rey-Debove, Josette
  1971   *Etude linguistique et sémiotique des dictionnaires français contemporains* (The Hague: Mouton).
  1973   "La sémiotique de l'emprunt lexical", *TLL* 11: 109-123.
Rheinfelder, H.
  1937   *Altfranzösische Grammatik*, 2 vols. (München: Hueber). [2nd edition 1953-1967.]
Ribezzo, Francesco
  1921   "L'originaria unità tirrenica dell'Italia nella toponomastica", *Rivista indo-greco-italica* 4: 220-226.
  1932   "Unità italica ed unità italo-celtica. Del rapporto originario e storico tra Laziali-ausonici e Umbro-sabellici", *Rivista indo-greco-italica* 16: 27-40.
  1938   "La stele di Novilara e l'etrusco-piceno", *Scritti in onore di A. Trombetti* (Milano: Hoepli), 53-65.
Richman, Stephen H.
  1967   "The relative conservation of Spanish and Portuguese", *Orbis* 16: 225-230.
Richter, Elise
  1919   *Fremdwortkunde* (Leipzig).
  1934   *Beiträge zur Geschichte der Romanismen* (= *ZRPh* Beiheft 82).
  1973   "A bibliography of the writings of Elise Richter", prepared by Benjamin M. Woodbridge Jr., *RomPh* 26: 342-360.
Riegler, R.
  1921   "Italienisch-spanische Sprachmischung", *NS* 29: 218-221.
Ries, John
  1894   *Was ist Syntax? Ein kritischer Versuch* (Praha: Taussig). [2nd edition 1927.]
Risk, Mirna O.
  1976   *La campagna per l'autarchia della lingua italiana, 1922-43* (unpublished thesis) (University of Leeds).

Rizescu, I.
1958 *Contribuţii la studiul calculului lingvistic* (Bucureşti).
Rohlfs, Gerhard
1924 *Griechen und Romanen in Unteritalien. Ein Beitrag zur Geschichte der unteritalienischen Gräzität* (Genève: Olschki).
1929 "Zu der Entwicklung von *-ll-* im Romanischen", in *Festschrift E. Wechssler* (*Berliner Beiträge zur Rom. Phil.*), 388-401.
1930a *Etymologisches Wörterbuch der unteritalienischen Gräzität* (Halle: Niemeyer).
1930b "Vorlateinische Einflüsse in den Mundarten des heutigen Italiens?", *GRM* 18: 37-56.
1933 *Scavi linguistici nella Magna Grecia. Con una cartina geografica* (Halle: Niemeyer).
1935 *Le gascon, études de philologie pyrénéenne* (= *ZRPh* Beiheft 85). [2nd edition 1970 (Tübingen: Niemeyer/Pau: Marrimpouey Jeune).]
1941 *L'italianità linguistica della Corsica.* [Translated in Rohlfs 1952.]
1943 "Die Zählung nach Zwanzigern im Romanischen", *ASNS* 183: 126-131.
1949-1954 *Historische Grammatik der italienischen Sprache und ihrer Mundarten*, 3 vols. (Bern: Francke). [Italian translation: *Grammatica storica della lingua italiana e dei suoi dialetti* (Torino: Einaudi, 1966-1969).]
1950 *Historische Grammatik der unteritalienischen Gräzität* (München: Bayerische Akademie der Wissenschaft).
1950-1952 *Romanische Philologie I. Allgemeine Romanistik: Französische und provenzalische Philologie, II. Italienische Philologie. Die sardische und rätoromanische Sprachen* (Heidelberg: Winter). [2nd edition of vol. 1 with supplement 1966, as *Einführung in das Studium der Romanistik.*]
1951 *Sermo vulgaris latinus: Vulgärlateinisches Lesebuch* (Halle: Niemeyer). [3rd edition 1976.]
1952 *Estudios sobre geografía lingüística de Italia* (Univ. Granada).
1954 *Die lexikalische Differenzierung der romanischen Sprachen, Versuch einer romanischen Wortgeographie* (München: Bayerische Akademie der Wissenschaft). [Spanish translation: *Diferenciación léxica de las lenguas románicas* (Madrid: CSIC, 1960).]
1957 "Zur Methodologie der romanischen Substratforschung (Substratomanie und Substratophobie)", in Gamillscheg 1957: 495-509.
1958 "Messapisches und Griechisches aus dem Salento", *Sybaris. Festschrift H. Krahe* (Wiesbaden: Harrassowitz), 121-128.
1958a "Das Wundersuffix *-ica* (**rupica, *rotica, *statica*)", *ZRPh* 75: 507-522.
1958b *Romanica. Festschrift für Gerhard Rohlfs,* edited by H. Lausberg (Halle: Niemeyer).
1958c "La perdita dell'infinito nelle lingue balcaniche e nell'Italia meridionale", *Omagiu lui I. Iordan* (Bucureşti), 733-744.
1959 "Influence des éléments autochtones sur les langues romanes", *Actes du Colloque international de civilisations, littératures et langues romanes* (Bucureşti), 240-249.
1964 *Lexicon graecanicum Italiae inferioris* (Tübingen: Niemeyer).
1968 *Serta Romanica. Festschrift für Gerhard Rohlfs,* edited by R. Baehr and K. Wais (Tübingen: Niemeyer).
1969 "Nomina tusca in Toscana?", in Pisani 1969: 857-861.
1971a *Italogriechische Sprichwörter in linguistischer Konfrontation mit neugriechischen Dialekten* (München: Bayerische Akad. der Wiss.).

1971b "Toskanische 'gorgia': ein etruskischer Mythos", *ZRPh* 87: 349-358.
1971c "Autour de l'accusatif prépositionnel dans les langues romanes", *RLR* 35: 312-334.
1971d "Les avatars du latin vulgaire: promenade de géographie linguistique à travers les langues romanes", in *Cong.* 12.1: 18-46.
1971e *Romanische Sprachgeographie. Geschichte und Grundlagen. Aspekte und Probleme mit dem Versuch eines Sprachatlas der romanischen Sprachen* (München: Beck).
1972   *Studi e ricerche su lingua e dialetti d'Italia* (Firenze: Sansoni).
Rohr, Rupprecht
1964   *Einführung in das Studium der Romanistik* (Berlin: Schmidt).
Romeo, Luigi
1963   "Structural pressure and paradigmatic diphthongization in East Romance", *Word* 19: 1-19.
1968   *The economy of diphthongization in Early Romance* (The Hague: Mouton).
Roncaglia, Aurelio
1950   Review of Hall 1950, *CultNeol* 10: 99-102.
1965   *La lingua dei trovatori* (Roma: Ateneo).
Ronjat, Jules
1930   *Grammaire historique des parlers provençaux modernes* (Montpellier).
Roques, Mario
1905   "Méthodes étymologiques", *JdS* n.s. 3: 419-433.
1948   "Sur l'incertitude sémantique des mots d'emprunt", *Miscellanea Gessler* (Deurne/Anvers: C. Govaerts) 2: 1066-1072.
Rosellini, Aldo
1967   "Quelques remarques sur l'italian du *Journal de voyage* de Michel de Montaigne", *ZRPh* 83: 381-408.
1969   *Trattato di fonetica storica dell'italiano* (Milano: La Goliardica).
Rosenkranz, Bernhard
1955   "Die Gliederung des Dalmatischen", *ZRPh* 71: 269-279.
Rosetti, Alexandru
1938-1946 *Istoria limbii române* (Bucureşti: Fondaţia pentru literatură şi artă Regele Carol II). [3rd edition 1966-1968 (Bucureşti: Ed. ştiinţifică).]
1945-1949 "Langage mixte et mélange des langues", *AL* 5: 73-79.
1947   *Mélanges de linguistique et de philologie* (= *Société Roumaine de Linguistique* 2.5) (København: Munksgaard/Bucureşti: Inst. de Ling. Română).
1955   *Studii lingvistice* (Bucureşti: Ed. Acad.).
1962   *Istoria limbii române II. Limbile balcanice* (3rd edition) (Bucureşti: Ed. Acad.).
1965   *Linguistica* (= *Janua Linguarum, series maiior* 16) (The Hague: Mouton).
1968   "Sur le roumain commun", in *Cong.* 11.3: 1139-1148.
1970   "Sur les frontières du latin balkanique", *RRLing* 15: 505-506.
1975   Issue to celebrate A.R.'s 80th birthday, *RRLing* 25.
Rösler, Margareta
1910   "Das Vigesimalsystem im Romanischen", *ZRPh* Beiheft 26: 187-203.
1929   "Das Vigesimalsystem im Romanischen", *ZRPh* 49: 274-286.
Ross, Alan S. C.
1958   *Etymology with especial reference to English* (Fair Lawn, N.J.: Essential Books). [2nd edition 1965: *Etymology* (= *University Paperbacks* 110) (London: Methuen).]

Rostaing, Charles
1942 "Le français de Marseille dans la 'Trilogie' de Marcel Pagnol", *FM* 10: 29-44, 117-131.
Rothe, Wolfgang
1957 *Einführung in die historische Laut- und Formenlehre des Rumänischen* (Halle: Niemeyer).
Rothenberg, J. G.
1969 "'Un hobby per i cocktails': an examination of Anglicisms in Italian", *Italica* 46.2: 146-165.
Rubio, A.
1937 *La crítica del galicismo en España (1726-1832)* (Mexico).
Ruffini, Mario
1952 "L'influsso italiano sull'arumeno", *Cahiers Sextil Pușcariu* 1: 91-110, 318-342.
Rundle, Stanley
1946 *Language as a social and political factor in Europe* (London).
Ruppert, R.
1915 *Die spanischen Lehn- und Fremdwörter in der französischen Schriftsprache aus Heereswesen und Politik* (Diss.) (München).
Russu, I. I.
1959 [1967] *Limba traco-dacilor* (București: Ed. tehnica). [2nd edition 1967.]
1962 "Die Beziehungen der rumänischen Sprache zum Albanischen und zum karpatisch-balkanischen Substrat", *CLing* 7: 107-127.
1970 *Elemente autohtone în limba română. Substratul comun româno-albanez* (București: Ed. Acad.).
Rychner, Jean
1970 *Formes et structures de la prose française médiévale: L'articulation des phrases dans la Mort Artu* (= *Recueil des travaux de la Faculté de Lettres, Univ. de Neuchâtel*) (Genève: Droz).
Sá, José de
1953-1954 "Evolucão semântica do pronome reflexivo", *RP* 18: 307-316; 19: 16-24, 45-57.
Saaraw, C.
1920 *Die Italianismen in der französischen Sprache des 16. Jahrhunderts* (Borna/ Leipzig).
Šabršula, Jan
1966 "A propos de la différenciation lexématique des langues romanes", *PhP* 9: 23-29.
1974 "L'état actuel des études occitanes et franco-provençales", *PhP* 56: 197-208.
Sădeanu, Florența
1971 "L'équilibre de la structure étymologique en roumain et en espagnol. Aperçu statistique", in *Cong.* 12.2: 883-889.
1972 "La estructura etimológica del vocabulario jurídico reflejo de la historia en rumano y español", *RRLing* 17: 289-294.
1973 "Premise pentru un studiu despre relatinizarea vocabularului în limba româna", *SCL* 24: 627-633.
Safarewicz, J.
1969 "A quelle époque commence le latin dit vulgaire?", in Pisani 1969: 863-872.
Șăineanu, Lazăr [= Lazare Sainéan]
1900 *Influența orientala asupra limbei și culturei romane*, 2 vols. (București: Socecu & Gutenberg).

1901-1902 "Les éléments orientaux en roumain", *Romania* 30: 539-566; 31: 82-99, 557-589.
1925-1930 *Les sources indigènes de l'étymologie française,* 3 vols. (Paris: Boccard).
1935   *Autour des sources indigènes: Etudes d'étymologie française et romane* (Firenze: Olschki).

Sala, Marius
1963   "La Romania occidentale et la Romania orientale: sur le traitement de sonantes", *SL* 17: 26-37.
1964   "Romania orientale et Romania occidentale. II. Sur la corrélation de quantité consonantique", *RRLing* 9: 445-459.
1968   "Fonologia iudeospaniolei din Bucureşti", *SCL* 19: 525-552.
1971   *Phonétique et phonologie du judéo-espagnol de Bucharest* (The Hague: Mouton).
1974-1975 "Aspecte ale contactului dintre limbi in domeniul romanic", *SCL* 25: 583-594; 26: 3-12, 107-117, 219-238.
1975   "Împrumut sau interferenţa?", *SCL* 26: 421-423.

Sala, Marius – Sanda Reinheimer
1967-1968 "Bibliographie franco-provençale", *RLR* 31: 383-429; 32: 199-234.

Saltarelli, Mario
1976   "Le regole fonologiche nella classificazione delle lingue neolatine", in *Cong.* 13.1: 1165-1173.

Saltarelli, Mario – Dieter Wanner (eds.)
1975   *Diachronic studies in Romance linguistics. Papers presented at the Conference on Diachronic Romance Linguistics, University of Illinois, April 1972* (The Hague: Mouton).

Salvador, G.
1967   "Lusismos", in *ELH* 2: 231-261.

Salverda de Grave, J. J.
1907   "Quelques observations sur les mots d'emprunt", *RF* 23: 145-153.

Samarin, William J.
1968   "Lingua francas of the world", in *Readings in the sociology of language,* edited by Joshua Fishman (The Hague: Mouton), 660-672.

Sánchez Regueira, M.
1971   "Un etimologista del s. XVI", *IbRom* 3: 131-141.

Sanchis Guarner, Manuel
1960   "El mozárabe peninsular", in *ELH* 1: 293-342.

Sanders, W.
1967   "Grundzüge und Wandlungen der Etymologie", *Wirkendes Wort* 17: 361-384.

Sandfeld, Kristian
1900   *Rumænske studier* (thesis, København). [Resumed in 1902: "Der Schwund des Infinitivs im Rumänischen und den Balkansprachen", *Jahresbericht des Inst. für rumänische Sprache* 9 (Leipzig), 75-131.]
1926   *Balkanfilologien* (København).
1930   *Linguistique balkanique. Problèmes et résultats* (Paris: Champion).

Sandmann, Manfred
1953   "Narrative tenses of the past in the *Cantar de mio Cid",* Studies in Romance philology and French presented to John Orr* (Manchester: U.P.), 258-282.
1973   *Expériences et critiques. Essais de linguistique générale et de philologie romane* (= *Bibliothèque française et romane,* série A 25) (Paris: Klincksieck).

Şandru (Olteanu), Tudora
1965   "Sobre la fisionomia léxica del español contemporáneo", *RRLing* 10: 401-410.
Şandru, Tudora – Constant Maneca
1973   "Tipología léxica románica a base de criterios cuantitativos", *RRLing* 18: 177-196.
Sanna, A.
1957   *Introduzione agli studi di linguistica sarda* (Regione Autonoma della Sardegna).
Sanzewitsch, C. von
1895   "Die russischen Elemente romanischen und germanischen Ursprungs im Rumänischen", *Jahresbericht des Instituts für rumänische Sprache zu Leipzig* 2: 193-214.
Sauro, Antonio
1952   *Storia della lingua francese* (Napoli: Majella). [Also in *Grammatica storica della lingua* (Bari: Adriatica, 1952).]
Saussure, Ferdinand de
1916   *Cours de linguistique générale* (Paris: Payot).
Saya, A.
1905   *Contribution de l'Italie à l'enrichissement du lexique français* (Messina).
Scaglione, Aldo D.
1967-1968 "Periodic syntax and flexible metre in the *Divina Commedia*", *RomPh* 21: 1-22.
Schane, Sanford A.
1971   "The phoneme revisited", *Lg* 47: 503-521.
Schellert, Dietrich
1958   *Syntax und Stilistik der Subjektstellung im Portugiesischen* (Bonn: Rom. Sem.).
Scheludko, D.
1927   "Über die arabischen Lehnwörter im Altprovenzalischen", *ZRPh* 47: 418ff.
Schiaffini, Alfredo
1937   "Aspetti della crisi linguistica italiana del Settecento", *ZRPh* 57: 275-295.
1953   *Momenti di storia della lingua italiana* (2nd edition) (Bari: Leonardo da Vinci).
Schlieben-Lange, Brigitte
1971   "La conscience linguistique des occitans", *RLR* 35: 298-303.
1971a   "Das sprachliche Selbstverständnis der Okzitanen im Vergleich mit der Situation des Katalanischen", in Wandruszka 1971: 174-190.
1971b   *Okzitanisch und Katalanisch: Ein Beitrag zur Soziolinguistik zwei romanischer Sprachen* (= *Tübinger Beiträge zur Linguistik* 20) (Tübingen: Narr).
Schmid, Heinrich
1949   *Zur Formenbildung von* dare *und* stare *im Romanischen* (Bern: Francke).
1951   "Zur Geschichte der rätoromanischen Deklination", *VR* 12: 21-81.
1956   "Über Randgebiete und Sprachgrenzen. III. Über die Palatalisierung von c, g, vor A im Romanischen", *VR* 15: 53-80.
Schmidt, Lothar (ed.).
1973   *Wortfeldforschung. Zur Geschichte und Theorie des sprachlichen Feldes* (Darmstadt: Wissenschaftliche Buchgesellschaft).
Schmidt, W. F.
1914   *Die spanischen Elemente im französischen Wortschatz* (= *ZRPh* Beiheft 54).
Schmitt, Christian
1974a   *Die Sprachlandschaften der Galloromania. Eine lexikalische Studie zum Problem der Entstehung und Charakterisierung* (= *Heidelberger Beiträge zur Romanistik* 2) (Bern/Frankfurt:Lang).

1974b "Genèse et typologie des domaines linguistiques de la Galloromania", *TLL* 12: 31-83.
1976   "La latinité du gascon", in *Cong.* 14.2: 31-49.
Schmoll, Ulrich
1958   *Die vorgriechischen Sprachen Siziliens* (Wiesbaden: Harrassowitz).
Schösler, Lene
1973   "Sur la disparition de la déclinaison casuelle de l'ancien français", *RRom* 8: 242-261.
Schogt, H. G.
1964   "L'aspect verbal en français et l'élimination du passé simple", *Word* 20: 1-17.
Schroeder, Klaus-Henning
1965   "Probleme der Wortzählung im Rumänischen", *Zeitschrift für Balkanologie* 3: 169-179.
1967   *Einführung in das Studium des Rumänischen. Sprachwissenschaft und Literaturgeschichte* (Berlin: de Gruyter).
Schuchard, Barbara
1970   *Valor: zu seiner Wortgeschichte im Lateinischen und Romanischen des Mittelalters* (Bonn: Rom. Sem.).
Schuchardt, Hugo
1866-1868
       Der Vokalismus des Vulgärlateins, 3 vols. (Leipzig: Teubner).
1900   *Über die Klassifikation der romanischen Mundarten,* Probevorlesung gehalten zu Leipzig am 30. April 1870 (Graz).
1918   *Die romanischen Lehnwörter im Berberischen* (= *Sitzungsberichte Wien* 188).
Schürr, Friedrich
1926   "Lautgesetz oder Lautnorm", *ZRPh* 46: 294-305.
1933   "La posizione del romagnolo fra i dialetti contermini", *RLR* 9: 203-228.
1936   "Umlaut und Diphthongierung", *RF* 50: 275-316.
1938   "Nochmals über Umlaut und Diphthongierung in der Romania", *RF* 52: 311-318.
1940   "Die nordfranzösische Diphthongierung", *RF* 54: 60-66.
1949   "Die rumänische Diphthongierung", *ASNS* 186: 146-154.
1951   "La diptongación ibero-románica", *RDyTP* 7: 379-390.
1952   Review of Kuhn 1951, *RJb* 5: 349-358.
1953a "Substrattheorie und Phonologie aus dem Blickwinkel des Rumänischen", *Cahiers Sextil Puşcariu* 2: 24-34.
1953b "La posición del catalán en el conjunto de la diptongación románica", in *Cong.* 7.2: 151-163.
1956   *La diphtongaison romane* (= *Tübinger Beiträge zur Linguistik* 5) (Tübingen: Niemeyer). [2nd edition 1970.]
1963   "Die Alpenromanen", *VR* 22: 100-126.
1964   "La inflexión y la diptongación del español en comparación con las otras lenguas románicas", *Presente y future de la lengua española, Actas de la Asamblea de filología del 1 Congreso de instituciones hispánicas (Madrid) 1963* (Madrid: Ed. cultura hispánica). 2: 135-150.
1965   "Grundsätzliches zu den Fragen der romanischen, insbesondere italienischen Diphthongierung", *ASNS* 201: 321-339.
1969   "Epilegomena à la diphtongaison romane en général et ibéroromane en particulier", *RLR* 33: 2-37.
1970   Review of Tagliavini 1948, *RJb* 21: 199-202.

1971   *Probleme und Prinzipien romanischer Sprachwissenschaft* (Halle: Niemeyer).
1972   "Epilogo alla discussione sulla dittongazione romanza. Risposta ad A. Castellani", *RLR* 36: 311-321.
Schwake, H. P.
1968   "Zur Frage der Chronologie französischer Wörter", in Wartburg 1968.2: 481-511.
Schwan, Eduard – Dietrich Behrens
1898   *Grammatik des Altfranzösischen. Laut und Formenlehre* (3rd edition) (Leipzig: Reisland).
1932   *Grammaire de l'ancien français. Première et deuxième parties: Phonétique et morphologie (d'après la douzième édition allemande).* (4th edition) (Leipzig: Reisland). [Translation by Oscar Bloch.]
Segre, Cesare
1952   "La sintassi del periodo nei primi prosatori italiani (Guittone, Brunetto, Dante)", *Atti dell'Accademia Nazionale dei Lincei. Scienze morali, storiche e filologiche* 4.2: 39-193. [Republished in: *Lingua stile e societa. Studi sulla storia della prosa italiana* (Milano: Feltrinelli, 1963), 81-270.]
Séguy, Jean
1950   *Le français parlé à Toulouse* (Toulouse: Privat).
1971   "La relation entre la distance spatiale et la distance lexicale" *RLR* 35: 335-357.
1973   "La dialectométrie dans l'ALG", *RLR* 37: 1-24.
1973 a "L'accusatif prépositionnel en gascon et dans le français du Sud-Ouest", in Imbs 1973: 429-434.
Sequeira, F. J. Martins
1952   *Rol de estrangierismos e respectivas correspondências em português de lei* (Lisboa).
Serbat, G.
1975   *Les structures du latin: Le système de la langue classique, son évolution jusqu'aux langues romanes* (Paris: Picard).
Sergijevskij, M. V.
1946   "Problema dialektal'nosti vul'garnoj latyni v svete dannyx romanskoge jazykoznanija" [The problem of the dialect of Vulgar latin in the light of Romance linguistics], *Vestnik Moskovskogo Universiteta* 1: 28 ff.
Serra, Giandomenico
1960   "L'action du substrat lybique sur la structure des mots de la langue sarde", *Orbis* 9: 404-418.
Serrano Martínez, Encarnación
1956   *"Honneur" y "Honor": su significación a través de las literaturas francesa y española (desde los orígenes hasta el siglo XVI)* (Univ. of Murcia).
Setti, M. V.
1953   "Francesismi trecenteschi nella lingua de F. Algarotti", *LN* 14: 8-13.
Şiadbei, I.
1957   "Arii lexicale în România orientale", *SCL* 8: 17-25.
Silva Neto, Serafim da
1952   *Historia da língua portuguesa* (Rio de Janeiro: Livros de Portugal). [2nd edition 1970.]
1957   *Historia do latim vulgar* (= *BBF* 13) (Rio de Janeiro).
Simone, Carlo de
1962   "Die messapische Sprache (seit 1939)", *Kratylos* 7: 113-135.
1964   *Die messapischen Inschriften* (Wiesbaden: Harrassowitz).

1968-1970 *Die griechischen Entlehnungen im Etruskischen* (Wiesbaden: Harrassowitz).
Skårup, Poul
   1969 "Sur la date de l'amuïssement de /d/ final en ancien français", *RRom* 4: 86-90.
   1970 "Les descendants romans du latin *ille*", *Problèmes de linguistique roumaine* (= Special issue of *RRom*): 54-73.
Skelton, R. B.
   1970a "Spanish *baldío* and the Settled Village Economy", *Forum Linguisticum* 4: 359-372.
   1970b "Spanish *baldosa:* A study in homonymy", *Linguistics* 58: 57-67.
   1971 "Spanish *baldar* and Islamic penology", *RomPh* 25: 173-182.
Skok, Peter
   1926 "Zur Chronologie der Palatalisierung von c g qu gu vor e i y im Balkanlatein", *ZRPh* 46: 385-410.
   1928 "Zum Balkanlatein", *ZRPh* 48: 398-413.
   1930 "Zum Balkanlatein III", *ZRPh* 50: 484-532.
   1934 "Zum Balkanlatein IV", *ZRPh* 54: 175-215, 424-499.
   1943 "Considerations générales sur le plus ancien istro-roman", *Sache, Ort und Wort* (= *Romanica Helvetica* 20) (Bern: Francke), 472-485.
Skousen, Royal
   1975 *Substantive evidence in phonology: The evidence from French and Finnish* (The Hague: Mouton).
Sletsjøe, Leif
   1959 *Le développement de l et n en ancien portugais* (Oslo: Gyldendal).
Sneyders de Vogel
   1919 *Syntaxe historique du français* (Groningen/The Hague: Wolters). [2nd edition 1927.]
Sofer, J.
   1963 *Zur Problematik des Vulgärlateins: Ergebnisse und Anregungen* (Wien: Gerold).
   1970 "Der Stand der Erforschungen des Vulgärlateins", *Forum Linguisticum* 4: 148-156.
Sofietti, J. P.
   1955 "Bilingualism and biculturalism", *Journal of Educational Psychology* 46: 222-227.
Solano, L. F.
   1947 "Diphthongization and metaphony in Rumanian", *Medieval Studies in honor of Jeremiah Denis Matthias Ford,* edited by Urban T. Holmes and A. J. Denomy (Cambridge, Mass.: Harvard U.P.), 291-298.
Soler Pastor, Teresa
   1957 *Las palabras "Gloria" y "Gloire": sus distinctos significados en las literaturas francesa y española (desde los orígenes hasta el siglo XVI)* (Univ. of Murcia).
Söll, L.
   1967 *Die Bezeichnungen für den Wald in den romanischen Sprachen* (= *Münchener Romanistische Arbeiten* 25) (München: Hueber).
Spaulding, Robert K.
   1943 *How Spanish grew* (Berkeley: California U.P.).
Spence, Nicol C. W.
   1961 "Linguistic fields, conceptual systems and the Weltbild", *TPhS* 1961: 87-106.
   1965 "Quantity and quality in the vowel system of Vulgar Latin", *Word* 11: 1-18.

1973   "The Old French pronoun subjects and the problem of stress", *RLR* 37: 377-386.

Spiess, Federico
1956   *Die Verwendung des Subjekts-Personalpronomens in den lombardischen Mundarten* (= *Romanica Helvetica* 59) (Bern: Francke).

Spitzer, Leo
1923   "Sprachmischung als Stilmittel und als Ausdruck der Klangphantasie", *GRM* 11: 193-217.
1925   "Aus der Werkstatt des Etymologen", *Jahrbuch für Philologie* 1: 129-159.
1943   "Why does language change?", *MLQ* 4: 413-431.
1949   *"Mesturar* y la semántica hispano-arabe", *NRFH:* 141-149.

Stampa, Renato Agostino
1937   *Contributo al lessico preromanzo dei dialetti lombardo-alpini e romanici* (Zürich/Leipzig: Niehans).

Stati, Sorin
1961   *Limba latină în inscripțiile din Dacia și Scythia Minor* (= *Comisia pentru studiul formării limbii și poporului român* 4) (București: Ed. Acad.).

Stefanini, Jean
1962   *La voix pronominale en ancien et en moyen français* (= *Publications des Annales de la Faculté des Lettres d'Aix-en-Provence,* n.s. 31) (Gap: Ophrys).
1970   "Notes sur les formes surcomposées", *TLL* 8: 287-296.

Stefenelli, Arnulf
1962   *Die Volkssprache im Werk des Petron, im Hinblick auf die romanischen Sprachen* (= *Wiener Romanistische Arbeiten* 1) (Wien).

Stefenelli-Fürst, Friederike
1966   *Die Tempora der Vergangenheit in der chanson de geste* (= *Wiener Romanistische Arbeiten* 5) (Wien/Stuttgart: Braumüller).

Steiger, Arnald
1943   "Zur Sprache der Mozaraber", in *Sache, Ort und Wort: Jakob Jud zum sechzigsten Geburtstag, 12 Januar 1942,* edited by A. Steiger (Genève: Droz/Zürich: Rentsch), 624-734.
1948-1949 "Aufmarschstraßen des morgenländischen Wortgutes", *VR* 10: 1-26.
1955   "La penetración del léxico arábico en el catalan y el provenzal", in *Cong.* 7: 555-570.
1960   "Voces de origen oriental contenidas en el *Tesoro lexicográfico* de Samuel Gili Gaya", *RFE* 43: 1-56.
1963   *The origin and spread of Oriental words in European languages* (New York).

Sten, Holger
1953   "Les temps de l'infinitif portugais", *Boletim de Filologia* 14: 96-127.

Stimm, Helmut
1968   "Fränkische Lehnprägungen im französischen Wortschatz", in Gamillscheg 1968: 593-617.

Stockwell, Robert P. – Ronald K. S. Macaulay (eds.)
1972   *Linguistic change and generative theory. Essays from the UCLA Conference on historical linguistics in the perspective of transformational theory, February 1968* (= *Indiana University Studies in the History and Theory of Linguistics*) (Bloomington, Ind./London: Indiana U.P.).

Straka, Georges
1953   "Observations sur la chronologie et les dates de quelques modifications phonétiques en roman et en français prélittéraire", *RLaR* 71: 247-307.

1955   "Remarques sur les voyelles nasales, leur origine et leur évolution en français", *RLR* 19: 245-275.
1956   "La dislocation linguistique de la Romania et la formation des langues romanes à la lumière de la chronologie des changements phonétiques", *RLR* 20: 249-267.
1959   "Durée et timbre vocaliques. Observations de phonétique générale, appliquées à la phonétique historique des langues romanes", *Zeitschrift für Phonetik und Allgemeine Sprachwissenschaft* 12: 276-300.
1964   "L'évolution phonétique du latin au français sous l'effet de l'énergie et de la faiblesse articulatoires", *TLL* 2: 16-97.
1966   "Sur la date de l'amuïssement du -t final non appuyé en ancien français", *TLL* 4.1: 449-468.
1968   "Contributions à la description et à l'histoire des consonnes L", *TLL* 6: 267-326.
1970   *Phonétique et linguistique romanes. Mélanges offerts à M. Georges Straka* (Lyon/Strasbourg).
1973   (ed.) *Les dialectes romans de France à la lumière des atlas régionaux (Colloque, Strasbourg, 24-28 mai 1971)* (Paris: CNRS).
Sturtevant, Edgar H.
1920   *The pronunciation of Greek and Latin* (Chicago: U.P.). [2nd edition 1940.]
Sykorra, Wolfgang
1973   *Friedrich Diez' Etymologisches Wörterbuch der romanischen Sprachen und seine Quellen* (Bonn: Rom. Sem.).
Szemerényi, Otto
1962   "Principles of etymological research in the Indo-European languages", *IBS* 15: 175-212.
Tabouret-Keller, Andrée
1964   "Contribution à l'étude sociologique des bilinguismes", *9th Int. Congress Linguists (Cambridge, Mass., 1962):* 612-621.
Tagliavini, Carlo
1949   *Le origini delle lingue neolatine. Introduzione alla filologia romanza* (Bologna: Pàtron). [Revised 5th edition 1969; 7th edition 1972; German translation: *Einführung in die romanische Philologie* (München: Beck, 1973).]
Tamás, L.
1959   "Zum ungarisch-slawisch-deutschen Wortgut des Rumänischen", *ALH* 9: 241-260.
Tătaru, Ana
1968   "Unusual mistakes in hearing and pronouncing foreign sound-sequences", *RRLing* 13: 139-141.
Taylor, Pauline
1932   *The Latinity of the Liber Historiae Francorum* (New York: Columbia U.P.).
Tekavčić, Pavao
1972   *Grammatica storica dell'italiano, 2. Morfosintassi* (Bologna: Il Mulino).
Teodorescu, S.
1946   *Din tezaurul latin al limbei române* (București).
Terlingen, Juan H.
1943   *Los italianismos en español desde la formación del idioma hasta principios del siglo XVII* (Amsterdam: North Holland).
1967   "Italianismos", *ELH* 2: 263-305.
Terracini, Benvenuto
1938   "Sostratto", *Scritti in onore de Alfredo Trombetti* (Milano: Hoepli), 321-364.

Thiele, J.
1975 "Zu Probleme und Methoden der romanistischen Wortbildungsforschung",
       BRPh 14: 151-161.
Thomas, Earl W.
1962 "The resurgence of Catalan", *Hispania* 45: 43-48.
Tibiletti Bruno, Maria Grazia
1966 "L'iscrizione di Prestino", *RIL* 100: 279-319.
1968 "Discussione su Prestino", *RIL* 102: 385-395.
Tilander, Gunnar
1946 "Provençal *eis* 'même', catalan *eix*, aragonais *exe, eixe* 'ce...là'", *SNPh* 19:
       294-296.
1955 *Maint. Origine et histoire d'un mot* (= *Filologiskt Arkiv* 1) (Lund: Kungl.
       Vetterhets- ock Antikvitetsakademien, Stockholm).
1958 "O uso de rapar a cabeça aos loucos e a etimologia do port. esp. it. *tonto,* rom.
       tint, tont ('louco')", *RP* 23: 223-232.
1973 *Publications 1918-1973. Bibliographie établie en l'honneur du 50ᵉ anniversaire
       de sa soutenance de thèse* (= *Acta Bibliothecae* 15) (Stockholm).
Timpanaro, Sebastiano
1969 *Classicismo e illuminismo nell'Ottocento italiano* (Pisa: Nistri-Lischi).
1972 "Graziado Ascoli", *Belfagor* 27: 149-176.
Titone, R.
1961 "Difficulties on the part of younger adolescents in the perception of some of the
       phonological features of the English and French languages", *Orientamenti
       Pedagogici* (Torino) 8: 684-716.
Todoran, R.
1965 "Despre influenţa maghiară in lexicul graiurilor românești din Transilvania",
       Omagiu lui Alexandru Rosetti (București), 921-927.
Togeby, Knud
1953 "Le neutre en roumain et en albanais", *Cahiers Sextil Pușcariu* 2: 121-131.
       [Republished 1968 in *Immanence et structure* (= *RRom,* numéro spécial 2),
       150-164.]
1955 "L'énigmatique infinitif personnel en portugais", *SNPh* 27: 211-218. [Repub-
       lished 1968 in *Immanence et structure* (= *RRom* numéro spécial 2), 131-138.]
1960 "Les explications phonologiques historiques sont-elles possibles?", *RomPh* 13:
       401-413.
1962 "L'infinitif dans les langues balkaniques", *RomPh* 15: 221-233.
1964 "Les désinences de l'imparfait (et du parfait) dans les langues romanes", *SNPh*
       36: 3-8.
1968 "*Suus* et *illorum* dans les langues romanes", *RRom* 3: 66-71.
1972 "L'apophonie des verbes espagnols et portugais en *-ir*", *RomPh* 26: 256-264.
1975 Memorial issue of *RRom* 10.1
Tovar, Antonio
1949 *Estudios sobre las primitivas lenguas hispánicas* (Buenos Aires: Coni).
1950 *La lengua vasca* (San Sebastián: Biblioteca Vascongada de los Amigos del País).
1951 "Léxico de las inscripciones ibéricas (celtibérico e ibérico)", *Estudios dedicados
       a Menéndez Pidal* 2: 273-323.
1951a "La sonorisation et la chute des intervocaliques, phénomène latin occidentale",
       REL 29: 102-120.
1952 "Sobre la cronología de la sonorización y caída de intervocálicas en la Romania
       occidental", *Homenaje a Fritz Krüger* (Mendoza: Cuyo U.P.), 9-15.

1955   "Latín vulgar, latín de Hispania", *Jornal de filología* 3: 81-89.
1958   "Das Keltiberische, ein neuer Zweig des Festlandkeltischen", *Kratylos* 3: 1-14.
1960   "Lenguas indoeuropeas: Testimonios antiguos", *ELH* 1: 101-126.
1961   *The ancient languages of Spain and Portugal* (New York: Vanni).
1964   "A research report on Vulgar Latin and its local variations", *Kratylos* 9: 113-134.
1972   *Homenaje a A. Tovar ofrecido por sus discípulos, colegas y amigos* (Madrid: Gredos).

Tracconaglia, G.
1917   *Contributo allo studio dell'italianismo in Francia, 1: Henri Estienne e gli italianismi* (Lodi).

Trend, J. B.
1953   *The languages and history of Spain* (London: Hutchinson).

Trier, J.
1952   *Holz: Etymologien aus dem Niederwald* (= *Münsterische Forschungen* 6) (Münster: Bohlau).

Trombetti, Alfredo
1925a "Saggio di antica onomastica mediterranea", *Archiv za arbanasku starinu jezik i etnologiju* 3: 1-116. [Republished 1942 (Firenze: Olschki).]
1925b *Le origini della lingua basca* (Bologna). [Reprinted 1966 (Bologna: Forni).]

Tropea, G.
1963a "Un dialetto moribundo. Il gallo-italico di Francavilla Sicilia", *BCSS* 9: 12-36.
1963b "Ancora sugli americanismi del siciliano (seconda serie)", *AGI* 48: 170-175.
1966   "Effetti di simbiosi linguistica nelle parlate gallo-italiche di Aidone, Nicosia e Novara di Sicilia", *BALI* 13-14: 3-50.

Trujillo, Ramón
1970   *El campo semántico de la valoración intelectual en español* (La Laguna: U.P.).

Tuaillon, G.
1968   "Aspects géographiques de la palatalisation u > ü en gallo-roman et notamment en franco-provençal", *RLR* 32: 100-125.

Tudose, Claudia
1965   "Lexicul de bază în secolul al XVI-lea", *SCL* 16: 619-653, 801-828.

Tuțescu, M.
1976   "Sur la créativité lexicale", *RRLing* 21: 23-25.

Tuttle, Edward
1975   *Studies in the derivational suffix-āculum: Its Latin origin and its Romance development* (= *ZRPh* Beiheft 146) (Tübingen: Niemeyer).

Uhler, V. – V. Vlasák
1959   "Contribution au problème de la répartition du lexique latin dans les langues romanes. Essai d'une statistique", *AUC-Phil* 3; *Romanistica Pragensia* 1: 85-97.

Ullmann, Stephen
1950   "The stylistic role of Anglicisms in Vigny", *FS* 4: 1-15.
1951   "Couleur locale anglaise et théâtre français", *Mélanges Dauzat:* 339-350.
1957a *Style in the French novel* (Oxford: Blackwell).
1957b *Principles of semantics* (Oxford: Blackwell). [2nd edition 1963.]
1958-1959 "Semantique et étymologie", *CAIEF* 10-11: 323-335.
1962   *Semantics, an introduction to the sciences of meaning* (Oxford: Blackwell).
1965   *Précis de sémantique française* (3rd edition) (Bern: Francke).
1966   *Language and style* (Oxford: Blackwell).

1967 "Où en sont les études de sémantique historique?", *Actes du Xe Congrès de la Fédération Internationale des Langues at Littératures Modernes* (Paris), 105-122.

1972 "Semantics", in *Current Trends* 9.1: 343-394.

1972a *Sprache und Stil* (Tübingen: Niemeyer). [Translation of Ullmann 1966.]

Undhagen, Lydia

1975 *Morale et les autres lexèmes formés sur le radical MORAL étudiés dans les dictionnaires et dans les textes littéraires français dans la seconde moitié du XVIIIe siècle. Etude de sémantique structurale* (Gleerup).

Untermann, Jürgen

1960 "Die iguvinischen Tafeln (seit 1940)", *Kratylos* 5.2: 113-125.

1961 *Sprachräume und Sprachbewegungen im vorrömischen Hispanien* (Wiesbaden: Harrassowitz).

Urciolo, Raphael G.

1965 *The intervocalic plosives in Tuscan (-p- -t- -c-)* (= *Romanica Helvetica* 74) (Bern: Francke).

Urrutibéheity, Hector N.

1972 "The statistical properties of the Spanish lexicon", *CLex* 20.1: 78-95.

Ursu, D.

1964 "Glosare de neologisme din perioada 1830-60", *LbR* 13: 250-260.

Ursu, D. – N. A. Ursu

1966 "Observaţii privitoare la adaptarea neologismelor în limba româna", *LbR* 15:3.

Ursu, N. A.

1962 *Formarea terminologiei ştiinţifice româneşti* (Bucureşti: Ed. Ştiinţifica).

1964 "Observaţii asupra adaptării adjectivelor neologice la sistemul morfologic al limbii române în jurul anului 1800", *LbR* 13: 413-422.

1965 "Le problème de l'étymologie des néologismes du roumain", *RRLing* 10: 53-59.

Väänänen, Veiko

1950 "A propos de l's final dans les langues romanes", *Miscelânia Adolfo Coelho* (Lisboa).

1951 '*Il est venu comme ambassadeur', 'il agit en soldat' et locutions analogues en latin, français, italien et espagnol. Essai de syntaxe historique et comparée* (= *Annales Academiae Scientiarum Fennicae*, series B 73.1) (Helsinki).

1958 "Le latin vulgaire des inscriptions pompéiennes", *ADAW* 1958.3. [3rd edition 1966.]

1963a *Introduction au latin vulgaire* (Paris: Klincksieck). [2nd edition 1969; Italian translation: *Introduzione al latino volgare* (Bologna: Pàtron, 1971); Spanish translation: *Introducción al latín vulgar* (Madrid, 1968).]

1963b "Unità de latino: realtà o illusione", *AION-L* 5: 63-65.

1966 *Le latin vulgaire des inscriptions pompéiennes* (3rd edition) (Berlin).

1969 "Trimalchion et ses convives parlaient-ils italien?", *NphM* 70: 604-611.

Valesio, P.

1968 "The Romance synthetic future pattern and its first attestations", *Lingua* 20: 113-161, 279-307.

1972 "The synthetic future again", *Lingua* 24: 181-193.

Valin, Roch

1964 *La méthode comparative en linguistique historique et en psychosystématique du langage* (= *Cahiers de psychomécanique du langage* 6) (Quebec: Laval U.P.).

Valkhoff, Marius
  1931   *Etude sur les mots français d'origine néerlandaise* (Amersfoort).
  1955   "Echanges néerlando-romans en France et dans la Péninsule Ibérique", *Revista da Facultade da Letras de Lisboa* 21.
  1967   "Préstamos de lenguas modernas", in *ELH* 2: 365-376.
Vallverdú, F. de
  1968   *L'escriptor català i el problema de la llengua* (Barcelona).
  1970   *Dues llengues: Dues fonctions?* (Barcelona: Edicions 62).
  1973   *El fet lingüístic com a fet social* (Barcelona: Edicions 62).
Vàrvaro, Alberto
  1968   *Storia, problemi e metodi della linguistica romanza* (Napoli: Liguori).
  1972-1973   "Storia della lingua: Passato e prospettive di categoria controversa", *RomPh* 26: 16-51, 509-531.
  1973   "Notizie sul lessico della Sicilia medievale: 1. Francesismi", *BCSS* 12: 2-37.
  1974   Review of Wartburg 1971, *Medioevo Romanzo* 1: 317-324.
  1974a "Prima ricognizione dei catalanismi nel dialetto siciliano", *Medioevo Romanzo* 1: 86-110.
Vasiliu, Emanuel
  1956   "On the history of central vowels in Daco-Romanian dialects", *RRLing* 1: 330-334.
  1966   "Towards a transformational phonology of Daco-Romanian dialects", *JL* 2.1: 79-98.
  1968a *Fonologia istorică a dialectilor dacoromâne* (Bucureşti: Ed. Acad.).
  1969   "Quelques remarques phonologiques sur l'évolution du lat. ī en roumain", *Bulletin de la Société roumaine de linguistique roumaine* 6: 89-90.
  1970-1971 "La chronologie de la diphtongaison des lat. Ĕ, E et quelques problèmes connexes", in *Cong.* 12.1: 391-392.
Vendryès, J.
  1953   "Pour une étymologie statique", *BSL* 49: 1-19.
Vetter, Emil
  1953   *Handbuch der italischen Dialekte I. Texte mit Erklärung* (Heidelberg: Winter).
Vianello, N.
  1955   "'Lingua franca' di Barberia e 'lingua franca' di Dalmazia", *LN* 16: 67.
Vidos, B. E.
  1932   *La forza di espansione della lingua italiana* (Nijmegen/Utrecht: Dekker-van de Vegt).
  1939   *Storia delle parole marinaresche passate in francese* (= *Bibl. ARom.*, series 2.24) (Firenze).
  1954   "Fr. 'gouffre', 'golfe'; note méthodologique", *RPF* 7: 1-15.
  1956   *Handboek tot de Romaanse taalkunde* ('s-Hertogenbosch: Malmberg). [Italian Translation: *Manuale di linguistica romanza* (Firenze: Olschki, 1959); Spanish translation: *Manual de lingüística románica* (Madrid: Aguilar, 1963); German translation: *Handbuch der romanischen Sprachwissenschaft* (München: Hueber, 1968).]
  1957   "Etymologie organique", *RLR* 21: 93-105.
  1959   "It. caravella", *BALM* 1: 179-183.
  1960   "Le bilinguisme et le mécanisme de l'emprunt", *RLR* 24: 19.
  1961   "Osservazioni methodologiche sui termini nautici turchi provenienti dall'Italia", *RF* 73: 85-131.

1962   "I problemi dell'espanzione della lingua nautica veneziana con particolare riguardo al oriente balcanica", *BALM* 4: 13-20.

1965a *Prestito, espanzione e migrazione di termini tecnici nelle lingue romanze e non romanze. Problemi, metodo e risultati* (= *Bibl. dell'Arch. Rom,* serie 2: 31) (Firenze: Olschki). [Orginally published in *RF* 73 (1961): 85-131.]

1965b "Italianismi francesi adattati diventati italianismi crudi", *Omagiu lui Alexandru Rosetti* (Bucureşti), 989-991.

1969a "Français *frise,* espagnol *frisa*", *ASNSL* 120: 376-378.

1969b "Italianismi in un trattato di nautica francese del Cinquecento", in Pisani 1969.2: 1033-1041.

1968-1970 "I problemi dei termini nautici turchi di origine italiana", *BALM* 11-12: 263-269.

1970   "Fr. *bonace, bonasse*", in Fouché 1970: 263-269.

1971-1973 "In margine al nuovo *Glossaire nautique* dello Jal", *BALM* 13-15: 665-672.

1972   "Relaciones antiguas entre España y los Países Bajos y problemas de los préstamos holandeses (flamencos) en castellano", *RFE* 55: 233-242.

1974-1975 "Sobre la penetración de hispanismos en napoletano e italiano", *RFE* 57: 65-78.

1977a "Contributo ai portoghesismi nel *Diario* de Cristoforo Colombo", *ArchSSL* 214: 49-60.

1977b "Saggio sugli iberismi in Pigafetta", *Actas del V Cong. Internat. de Estudios Ling. del Mediterraneo (Madrid 1977):* 57-67.

Vildomec, V.
1963   *Multilingualism. General linguistics and the psychology of speech* (Leyden).

Vilela, M.
1974   "Estudo semasiológico e onomasiológico (1850-1910)", *Sillages* 4: 7-42.

Vinay, Jean-Paul
1973   "Le français en Amérique du Nord: Problèmes et réalisations", in *Current Trends* 10: 323-406.

Vincent, Nigel
1974   "Analogy reconsidered", in Anderson – Jones (eds.) 1964.2: 427-441.

Vintilă-Rădulescu, Ioana
1974   "Statistica şi determinarea vocabularului de baza", *SCL* 25: 243-263.

Viscardi, A.
1970   *Ricerche e interpretazioni mediolatine e romanze* (Milano/Varese: Cisalpino).

Vossler, Karl
1904   *Positivismus und Idealismus in der Sprachwissenschaft* (Heidelberg).
1913   *Frankreichs Kultur im Spiegel seiner Sprachentwicklung* (Heidelberg: Winter).
1925   *Geist und Kultur in der Sprache (Heidelberg: Winter).*
1926   *Italienisch, Spanisch, ihre literarischen und sprachlichen Physiognomien",* *ZMaF* 2: 136-163.
1953   *Langue et culture de la France* (Paris). [Translation of Vossler 1913.]
1954   *Einführung ins Vulgärlatein* (München: Hueber).

Voyles, Joseph B.
1973   "Accounting for semantic change", *Lingua* 31: 95-124.

Vraciu, A.
1963-1964 "Aktual'nye voprosy izučenija substratnyx elementov rumynskogo jazyka" [Current questions in the study of substratum elements in Rumanian], *Linguistique balkanique* 6: 119-132; 8: 15-45.

Vrbková, V.
1971 "Quelques problèmes de délimitation des champs conceptuels", *ERB* 5: 45-50.
Wagner, Max Leopold
1928 Review of Donghi de Holperin 1925, *RFE* 15: 191-196.
1938-1939 "La flessione nominale e verbale del sardo antico e moderne", *ID* 14-15.
1941 "Sobre algunas palabras gitano-españolas y otras jergales", *RFE* 25: 161-181.
1941a *Historische Lautlehre des Sardischen* (= *ZRPh* Beiheft 93).
1943 "Betrachtungen über die Methodenfragen der Etymologie", *CultNeol* 3: 5-26.
1948 "Sobre os nomes da *moega* nas línguas ibero-romanicas", *Biblos* 24: 247-265.
1950 "Ojos de agua", *NRFH* 4: 40-43.
1951 *La lingua sarda: Storia, spirito e forma* (Bern: Francke).
1952 "Anotaciones etimológicas sobre algunas palabras iberoromanicas", *AIL* 5: 139-154.
1957 "Die Punier und ihre Sprache in Sardinien", *Die Sprache* 3: 27-43, 78-109.
1970 *Bibliografia degli scritti di Max Leopold Wagner,* by G. Manuppella (Coimbra: U.P.).
Wagner, Robert-Léon
1939 *Les phrases hypothétiques commençant par 'si' dans la langue française, des origines à la fin du XVIe siècle* (Paris: Droz).
1967-1970 *Les vocabulaires français,* 2 vols. (Paris: Didier).
Walsh, John K.
1967 "Supervivencia del árabe *š-r-q* y *g-r-b* en el léxico peninsular", *Al-Andalus* 32: 261-275.
1968 "The loss of Arabisms in the Spanish lexicon", *Dissertation Abstracts* (*PMLA Bibliog.*) 28: 2670A.
Wandruszka, Mario
1958 "Neubelebung des Partizipiums auf *-ante, -ente, -iente*", in Rohlfs 1958b: 478-484.
1971 *Interlinguistica. Sprachvergleich und Übersetzung. Festschrift zum 60. Geburtstag von Mario Wandruszka* (Tübingen: Niemeyer).
1974 "La lingua quale polisistema socioculturale", *Colloquio (1973) del Centro per lo Studio dell'insegnamento all'estero dell'italiano* (Trieste).
1975 "Plaidoyer pour le plurilinguisme", *RLR* 39: 108-121.
Wanner, Dietrich
1975 "Die historische Motivierung der Endung *-iamo* im Italienischen", *ZRPh* 91: 153-173.
Warnant, Léon
1974 "Le subjonctif imparfait en français et en wallon", *FM* 42: 42-69.
Wartburg, Walter von
1931 "Grundfragen der etymologischen Forschung", *Neue Jahrbücher für Wissenschaft und Jugendbildung* 7: 222-235.
1934 *Evolution et structure de la langue française* (Bern: Francke). [8th edition 1967.]
1936-1950 "Die Ausgliederung der romanischen Sprachräume", *ZRPh* 56: 1-48. [2nd edition 1950 (Bern: Francke). Spanish translation: *La fragmentación lingüística de la Romania* (Madrid: Gredos, 1952); French translation: *La fragmentation de la Romania* (Paris: Klincksieck, 1967).]
1938a *Die Entstehung der romanischen Völker* (Tübingen: Niemeyer). [2nd edition 1951. French translation: *Les origines des peuples romanes* (Paris: P.U.F., 1941).]
1938b Review of Schürr 1936, *ZRPh* 58: 378-382.

1941   "Los pronoms sujets en français", *RFE* 25: 465-477.
1943   *Einführung in die Problematik und Methodik der Sprachwissenschaft* (Halle: Niemeyer) [2nd edition 1962 (Tübingen: Niemeyer). French translation by P. Maillard: *Problèmes et méthodes de la linguistique* (Paris: P.U.F., 1946; 2nd edition P. Maillard and S. Ullmann, 1963); English translation by J.M.H. Veid, revised W. von Wartburg and Stephen Ullmann: *Problems and methods in linguistics* (Oxford: Blackwell, 1969).]
1949   "Los nombres de los días de la semana", *RFE* 33: 1-14.
1950   *Die Ausgliederung der romanischen Sprachräume* (Bern: Francke). [= Wartburg 1936, 2nd edition).]
1952a   "La délimitation des familles de mots voisines de sens et de forme", *RFE* 36: 308-310.
1952b   "Die griechische Kolonisation in Südgallien und ihre sprachlichen Zeugen im Westromanischen", *ZRPh* 68: 1-148.
1958   *Etymologica. Walter von Wartburg zum 70. Geburtstag 18. Mai 1958,* edited by H.-E. Keller (Tübingen: Niemeyer).
1964   "Les origines des mots à radical *chic-*", in *Mélanges de linguistique romane et de philologie médiévale offerts à M. Maurice Delbouille* (Gembloux: Duculot), 1: 675-699.
1968   *Festschrift Walter von Wartburg zum 80. Geburtstag 18. Mai 1968,* 2 vols., edited by K. Baldinger (Tübingen: Niemeyer).
1970   *Einführung in Problematik und Methodik der Sprachwissenschaft* (3rd edition) (Tübingen: Niemeyer).
1971   *Walter von Wartburg (1888-1971). Beiträge zu Leben und Werk nebst einem vollständigen Schriftenverzeichnis* (= *ZRPh* 87), Sonderheft) (Tübingen: Niemeyer).
1974   "Walter von Wartburg", *Sonderdruck aus Jahrbuch (1971-2), Sächsische Akademie der Wissenschaft zu Leipzig:* 371-417.

Weigand, H.
1924   *Ethnographie von Makedonien* (Leipzig).

Weinreich, Uriel
1953   *Languages in contact. Findings and problems* (New York: Linguistic Circle of New York).
1963   "Lexicology", in *Current Trends* 1: 60-93.

Weinrich, Harald
1958   *Phonologische Studien zur romanischen Sprachgeschichte* (= *Forschungen zur romanischen Philologie* 6) (Münster: Aschendorff).

Weinsberg, Adam
1967   "Le français et les 'néologismes' roumains", *KNf* 14: 25-33.

Wendt, H. F.
1960   *Die türkischen Elemente im Rumänischen* (= *Berliner Byzantinische Arbeiten* 12) (Berlin: Akademie).

Werth, Paul
1974   "Accounting for semantic change in current linguistic theory", in Anderson – Jones 1974. 1: 377-419.

Wexler, Peter
1955   *La formation du vocabulaire des chemins de fer en France, 1778-1842* (Genève).
1969   "Towards a structural definition of 'Internationalisms'", *Linguistics* 48: 77-92.

Whatmough, Joshua
1970 *The dialects of ancient Gaul. Prolegomena and records of the dialects* (Cambridge, Mass.: Harvard U.P.).
Widmer, A.
1966 "Der Stand der bündnerromanischen Linguistik", *Orbis* 15: 560-574.
Wilkinson, Hugh E.
1967 "The Latinity of Ibero-Romance", *Aoyama Gakuin* (Tokyo: University Ronshu) 8: 1-34.
Williams, Edwin B.
1938 *From Latin to Portuguese: Historical phonology and morphology of the Portuguese language* (Philadelphia: Pennsylvania U.P.). [3rd edition 1968.]
Wilmet, Marc
1970 *Le système de l'indicatif en moyen français* (Genève: Droz).
1971 "Notes sur l'évolution sémantique et syntaxique de *il y a*", *TLL* 8: 283-307.
Wind, Bartina H.
1928 *Les mots italiens introduits en français au XVIe siècle* (thesis, Amsterdam) (Deventer: Kluwer).
Windisch, R.
1973 *Das Neutrum in Romanischen: Spanish, Italienisch, Rumänisch* (Bern: Francke).
Wright, R.
1976 "Semicultismo", *ArchL* 7: 13-28.
Wunderli, Peter
1966 "Zur Regression des Bündnerromanischen", *VR* 25: 56-81.
1976 *Modus und Tempus: Beiträge zur synchronischen und diachronischen Morphosyntax der romanischen Sprachen* (Tübingen: Niemeyer).
Yvon, Henri
1960 "Emploi dans la Vie de Saint Alexis (XIe siècle) de l'imparfait, du passé simple et du passé composé de l'indicatif", *Romania* 81: 244-250.
Zaccaria, E.
1905 *Contributo allo studio degl'iberismi in Italia e della* Wechselbeziehung *fra le lingue romanze* (Torino).
1927 *L'elemento iberico nella lingua italiana* (Bologna).
Zangger, Kurt
1945 *Contribution à la terminologie des tissus en ancien français attestée dans les textes français, provençaux, italiens, espagnols, allemands et latins* (Bienne).
Zavatti, Silvio
1959, 1963, 1965 "Terminologia polare", *LN* 20: 79-84; 24: 20-22; 26: 122-123.
Zdrenghea, Maria
1967 "Elemente slavone în limba română", *CLing* 12: 313-317.
Zolli, Paolo
1965 "Francesismi nel linguaggio politico italiano alla fine del Settecento", *LN* 26: 16-19.
1971 *L'influsso francese sul veneziano del XVIII secolo* (= *Mem. dell'istituto Veneto di Scienze, Lettere ad Arte* 35.2).
1971-1972 "Note storiche e bibliografiche sui dizionari di neologismi e barbarismi del XIX secolo", *AIV* 1971/1972: 161-208.

Index of Names